Integrated Marketing Communications
The holistic approach

The Chartered Institute of Marketing/Butterworth-Heinemann Marketing Series is the most comprehensive, widely used and important collection of books in marketing and sales currently available worldwide.

As the CIM's official publisher, Butterworth-Heinemann develops, produces and publishes the complete series in association with the CIM. We aim to provide definitive marketing books for students and practitioners that promote excellence in marketing education and practice.

The series titles are written by CIM senior examiners and leading marketing educators for professionals, students and those studying the CIM's Certificate, Advanced Certificate and Postgraduate Diploma courses. Now firmly established, these titles provide practical study support to CIM and other marketing students and to practitioners at all levels.

The Chartered
Institute of Marketing

Formed in 1911, The Chartered Institute of Marketing is now the largest professional marketing management body in the world with over 60,000 members located worldwide. Its primary objectives are focused on the development of awareness and understanding of marketing throughout UK industry and commerce and in the raising of standards of professionalism in the education, training and practice of this key business discipline.

Books in the series

Below-the-line Promotion, John Wilmshurst

The CIM Handbook of Export Marketing, Chris Noonan

The CIM Handbook of Selling and Sales Strategy, David Jobber

The CIM Handbook of Strategic Marketing, Colin Egan and Michael J. Thomas

CIM Marketing Dictionary (fifth edition), Norman A. Hart

Copywriting, Moi Ali

Creating Powerful Brands (second edition), Leslie de Chernatony and Malcolm McDonald

The Creative Marketer, Simon Majaro

The Customer Service Planner, Martin Christopher

Cybermarketing, Pauline Bickerton, Matthew Bickerton and Upkar Pardesi

The Effective Advertiser, Tom Brannan

Integrated Marketing Communications, Ian Linton and Kevin Morley

Key Account Management, Malcolm McDonald and Beth Rogers

Market-led Strategic Change (second edition), Nigel Piercy

The Marketing Book (third edition), Michael J. Baker

Marketing Logistics, Martin Christopher

The Marketing Manual, Michael J. Baker

The Marketing Planner, Malcolm McDonald

Marketing Planning for Services, Malcolm McDonald and Adrian Payne

Marketing Plans (third edition), Malcolm McDonald

Marketing Research for Managers (second edition), Sunny Crouch and Matthew Housden

Marketing Strategy (second edition), Paul Fifield

Practice of Advertising (fourth edition), Norman A. Hart

Practice of Public Relations (fourth edition), Sam Black

Profitable Product Management, Richard Collier

Relationship Marketing, Martin Christopher, Adrian Payne and David Ballantyne

Relationship Marketing for Competitive Advantage, Adrian Payne, Martin Christopher, Moira Clark and Helen Peck

Retail Marketing Plans, Malcolm McDonald and Christopher Tideman

Royal Mail Guide to Direct Mail for Small Businesses, Brian Thomas

Sales Management, Chris Noonan

Trade Marketing Strategies, Geoffrey Randall

Forthcoming

Relationship Marketing: Strategy and Implementation, Helen Peck, Adrian Payne, Martin Christopher and Moira Clark

Services Marketing, Colin Egan

Integrated Marketing Communications

The holistic approach

Tony Yeshin BSc(Econ), MCIM

Published in association with The Chartered Institute of Marketing

OXFORD AUCKLAND BOSTON JOHANNESBURG MELBOURNE NEW DELHI

To my family for all their support during the preparation and development of this textbook, and to the memory of my parents.

Butterworth-Heinemann
Linacre House, Jordan Hill, Oxford OX2 8DP
225 Wildwood Avenue, Woburn, MA 01801–2041
A division of Reed Educational and Professional Publishing Ltd

A member of the Reed Elsevier plc group

First published 1998

British Library Cataloguing in Publication Data
A catalogue record for this book is available from the British Library

ISBN 0 7506 1923 6

Composition by Genesis Typesetting, Rochester, Kent
Printed and bound in Great Britain

FOR EVERY TITLE THAT WE PUBLISH, BUTTERWORTH-HEINEMANN
WILL PAY FOR BTCV TO PLANT AND CARE FOR A TREE.

Contents

Preface   xiii
Acknowledgements   xv

Part One

1 Marketing communications – an overview   3
Aims and objectives   3
The changing nature and role of marketing communications   3
A brief historical perspective   3
The background to marketing communications   4
The growth of marketing communications   6
Blurring of the edges of the tools of marketing communications   8
The strategic challenges facing organizations   9
Strategic marketing communications   11
The expanded marketing communications mix   11
The communications process   12
Achieving integration within the communications mix   14
The philosophy and structure of the book   15
References   15
Additional reading   15

2 Understanding the marketplace   16
Aims and objectives   16
The dimensions of consumer and organizational buying behaviour   16
The consumer market   16
The changing consumer   19
Targeting   20
Positioning   21
Understanding consumer behaviour   21
Organizational buying behaviour   25
The contribution of market research   27
References   34
Additional reading   34

3 **Product and service strategies**   **36**
   Aims and objectives   36
   Managing products and services over the life cycle   36
   Branding definitions   37
   Strategic importance of branding   38
   Strategic brand building   39
   The dimensions of branding   39
   Branding strategy   44
   Brands and consumer perceptions   46
   Identifying and building brand values   49
   Altering brand imagery   51
   The strategic value of brand extensions and brand stretch   53
   The roles of marketing communications in branding   55
   The challenges facing brands   58
   Service brands   64
   References   65
   Additional reading   66

4 **The integration of marketing communications**   **67**
   Aims and objectives   67
   The impact of external factors on marketing communications   69
   The driving forces behind the growth of IMC   73
   The impact on marketing communications   74
   Relationship marketing   74
   The benefits of IMC   75
   The process of achieving integration   76
   Organizational approaches to integration   79
   The barriers to integration   80
   References   81
   Additional reading   82

5 **Managing the marketing communications mix**   **83**
   Aims and objectives   83
   Organizing for marketing communications   83
   The strategic dimension of human resources   84
   The brand manager   84
   Category management   85
   The category manager   85
   The use of agencies   86
   Establishing the budget   87
   Budgeting for integrated marketing communications   93
   References   96
   Additional reading   96

6 **Choosing and using marketing communications agencies**   **97**
   Aims and objectives   97
   The structure and roles of marketing communications agencies   97
   The UK agency scene   97

Agency structures 98
The advertising agency 99
Other services to the agency team 106
Other agency/consultancy structures 106
Regional agencies 107
The changing role of marketing communications 107
The agency/client relationship 109
Agency remuneration 110
The criteria for agency selection 113
References 115
Additional reading 115

Part Two

7 Advertising **119**
Aims and objectives 119
The diverse nature of advertising 119
The functions of advertising 120
The advantages and limitations of advertising 122
Types of advertising 123
The advertising process 124
Understanding the advertising process 126
The strategic aspects of advertising planning 130
Brand positioning 132
Implications for strategy development 134
Advertising strategy and the product life cycle 135
Determining the advertising objective 138
Developing the advertising plan 139
Business-to-business advertising 142
References 142
Additional reading 143

8 The development of advertising **144**
Aims and objectives 144
The creative brief 144
Creative strategies and tactics 149
The creative challenge 150
Advertising appeals 152
Styles of advertising 153
Using celebrities 156
Music in advertising 157
Non-verbal communications 158
Creativity in advertising 158
Advertising and the brand personality 161
Guidelines for evaluating creative output 161

Measuring advertising effectiveness and campaign evaluation   161
References   166
Additional reading   166

9 Media and media planning   **168**
Aims and objectives   168
The role of media planning   168
The changing face of the media   169
Access to media and their characteristics   171
The new media   174
The media plan   176
The importance of media strategy   178
Media information sources   179
Identifying target audiences   181
Strategic options   181
Media scheduling issues   182
Alternative approaches to media scheduling   185
Implementing the media plan   187
Other media considerations   188
Contingency planning   189
Evaluation of the media plan   189
The changing face of media implementation   190
References   191
Additional reading   191

10 Sales promotion   **192**
Aims and objectives   192
The growing role of sales promotion   192
The benefits of sales promotion   194
The limitations of sales promotion   195
The determination of objectives   196
Sales promotion objectives   197
Sales promotion strategy   199
Sales promotion techniques   200
Promoting to consumers   205
Brand franchise   206
Point of purchase communications   207
Strategic dimensions of sales promotion   207
Joint promotions (or cross promotions)   209
The evaluation of sales promotion   210
Research into sales promotion   213
The legal framework for sales promotion   215
The use of sales promotion agencies   216
Selecting promotional agencies   216
The integration of sales promotion activities   218
International sales promotion activity   218
References   218
Additional reading   219

11   Direct marketing   **220**
Aims and objectives   220
The growth of direct marketing   220
The impact of direct marketing   222
The factors contributing to the growth of direct marketing   222
The advantages of direct marketing techniques   224
The limitations of direct marketing   226
The importance of the database   227
The use of the database   230
The strategic approach to direct marketing   231
The objectives of direct marketing   231
Building relationships   233
The management of direct marketing   235
The planning process   235
Using direct marketing consultancies   237
The use of media   238
The use of market research in direct marketing   239
The use of testing in direct marketing   242
The application of direct marketing   243
Analysing direct marketing results   244
Business-to-business activity   245
Non-profit organizations   246
Relationship marketing   246
Integrating direct marketing   247
International direct marketing activity   248
References   248
Additional reading   249

12   Public relations   **250**
Aims and objectives   250
A comparison between public relations and advertising   251
Other benefits of public relations   252
The functions of public relations   254
The 'publics' of public relations   256
The management of public relations   259
Using PR consultancies   260
In-house versus consultancy   261
PR campaign development   261
The identification of public relations problems and opportunities   262
Programme planning   263
Evaluation of public relations   264
The tools of public relations   264
Corporate public relations objectives   265
Financial public relations   266
Charity PR   267
Integration of PR activities   268
International aspects of public relations   268
References   268
Additional reading   269

13   Sponsorship and product placement   **270**
Aims and objectives   270
Event management and business sponsorship   270
Product placement   278
References   280
Additional reading   280

14   Corporate communications   **281**
Aims and objectives   281
The growth of corporate activity   281
The growing importance of corporate communications   282
Corporate image and identity   283
The objectives of corporate communications   283
The communication of company image   286
The management of corporate communications   287
Audiences for corporate communications   289
The process of establishing a corporate identity   290
Types of corporate identity   291
Corporate communications   292
Measuring corporate communications   293
Key aspects of corporate communications   294
Crisis management: an important dimension of corporate communications   294
Key dimensions of crisis management   297
Handling a crisis   297
References   298
Additional reading   298

15   International marketing communications   **299**
Aims and objectives   299
The growth of international marketing   299
Multinational versus global marketing   299
The development of global brands   301
Global branding   301
Understanding the international consumer   305
Legal and regulatory requirements   310
Media availability and usage   311
The competitive environment   311
The move to global marketing communications   311
Central or local control of marketing communications   312
The merits and demerits of standardized communications   314
The development of multinational communications agencies   315
The selection of an agency for international business   318
International marketing and marketing communications strategy   320
The development of international advertising   320
The development of international sales promotion   322
The development of international public relations   323
The development of international direct marketing   323
The development of other international communications activities   325
International market research   325

References   326
Additional reading   327

16 Future developments in marketing communications   328
Aims and objectives   328
Changes in the broad environment   328
The impact on the marketing function   331
The changing face of the communications industry   332
References   335
Additional reading   335

Glossary of terms   337

Index   345

Preface

This text has its origins in the workbook which I prepared for the Chartered Institute of Marketing for the Diploma paper Marketing Communications Strategy. Due to the inevitable constraints imposed on that work, I wanted to develop a specific and comprehensive textbook examining the nature of marketing communications. This is the result.

In a field as fast-moving as this, I have tried to reflect contemporary views as to the way in which the process works and the benefits of developing an understanding of integration. Whilst, I hope, soundly based upon academic theory, it also examines the real world applications within the broad field of marketing communications. The focus remains the values of the brand and the contribution which marketing communications can make towards their development. To achieve that end, we need to develop an enduring understanding of consumer behaviour, increasingly on an international basis, as brands expand their horizons far beyond national borders.

The book is divided into two parts. The first section is designed to provide an overview of the important dynamics of marketing communications, an understanding of the consumer, an examination of the role of the brand and the process of developing, managing and integrating marketing communications. The second section provides an in-depth examination of the specific areas of the profession and the tools which are available to the marketer.

I hope that this book will be of interest to a variety of audiences, both those who are studying the subject as part of an academic programme, both at undergraduate and postgraduate level, as well as those who are embarking upon a career within the profession. Whilst the debate surrounding integrated marketing communications continues, the imperative is the development of a real understanding of all of the tools which are available to the professional. Only with that understanding will the true potential of integration begin to be realized.

Acknowledgements

Along the way I have been helped by many people who gave up both valuable time and the result of their long years of practical experience to help ensure that this work is true to the profession which it serves. I would like to thank especially the following who read through the various chapters or otherwise provided me with valuable input (I should add that these are in no particular order): Tim Armes, Media Group Director of MediaVest, for his help and assistance on the media chapter and for ensuring that the media cost information is up-to-date; Nina Mink, Planning Director of IMP, for her comments and suggestions on the sales promotion chapter, and especially for providing the guidelines on international sales promotion; Mike Dickson, Director of DMB&B, for reading through the international chapter; Debi Hayes, a colleague at the University of Greenwich, for suggestions on direct marketing; Jez Frampton at Saatchi & Saatchi for his help with the creative brief; and Sally Ford-Hutchinson, Global Planning Director at DMB&B (and also my wife) for painstakingly reading through everything I have written to ease out the bugs. I would also like to thank the people at Butterworth-Heinemann, and especially Tim Goodfellow and Diane Scarlett, for making this book happen.

To all of those I have mentioned, and those other colleagues past and present who have in some way contributed to this work, I am extremely grateful. However, such errors as remain are entirely down to me.

Tony Yeshin

Part One

Marketing communications – an overview

- To provide a historical perspective of marketing communications;
- To introduce the study of marketing communications and the reasons for its growing importance;
- To consider the impact of the overlap of the tools of marketing communications;
- To identify the strategic dimensions of marketing communications;
- To explain the communications process;
- To define the structure and philosophy of the book.

The changing nature and role of marketing communications

Even to the most casual observer of the marketing environment, it will be appreciated that recent years have witnessed an almost unprecedented series of changes. Competition between companies has increased dramatically, both domestically and internationally; mergers and acquisitions to confront the future needs of organizations are commonplace, yet at the same time, companies are divesting themselves of non-essential business, concentrating instead on core areas to ensure their ability to meet the challenges of the future. The nature of the retail environment continues to change with the simultaneous emergence of ever larger stores and the growth of speciality providers; the proliferation of brand choice renders the consumer simultaneously able to satisfy individual needs and confused at the array of choice; the pace of technological change is almost difficult to comprehend, with its twin impacts both on the nature of products and services which are provided to the consumer, and the means of communicating with them; the diversity of media channels available to companies brings both an increase in their ability to reach their targets, yet at a progressively increased cost.

Yet, within this array of confusion, marketing communications increasingly represents the single most important opportunity for companies to convince potential consumers of the superiority of their products and services.

A brief historical perspective

From the beginnings of time, man has sought to communicate. At its basic level, communications are the most important element of the social interchange between individuals. As time progressed and, importantly, with the development of even rudimentary printing processes, it became possible to expand communications to reach a wider audience. Early printed material provides examples of the emergence of a new form of communications designed to convey information about the availability of products and services to a broader public. The era of marketing communications had begun.

In their earliest form, these communications predominantly took the form of the printed word and, with the advent of newspapers, this style continued. With the development of industrialization, companies emerged to meet the expanding demand for consumer goods, and the growth of transportation meant that these companies could serve a wider market. Moving from a local to a regional or even national basis of sales introduced a new element to the process – companies needed to differentiate their products from those of their competitors – and even by the eighteenth century, we begin to see the rudimentary emergence of branding. Mostly, this was quite simplistic, consisting only of an association of the proprietor's name with the products he produced.

The background to marketing communications

Today, consumers are exposed to a vast amount of information on a daily basis – everything from news reports on television, radio and in the press, weather forecasts, traffic information, store signs, product packaging, in-store point of sale material, and so on. Advertising is just one of the elements with which the consumer must deal every day.

Recent years have seen an explosion in all forms of media. Apart from the land-based television channels – BBC1, BBC2, ITV, Channel 4 and Channel 5 – we have an increasing number of satellite and cable stations, and the number will continue to grow as the technology improves. We have radio on FM, medium wave and long wave and, apart from the BBC stations both national and local, we have three national commercial stations (Classic FM, Virgin 1215 on MW, and Atlantic on long wave) and some 180+ regional and local commercial radio stations. There are newspapers, national and regional, morning and evening, daily, weekly and Sunday. There are magazines, over 3500 of them, covering every form of interest area imaginable. There is a wide range of outdoor media, not just fixed poster sites, but posters on the sides of buses and taxi cabs, on the Underground and at railway stations. And many of us have become walking advertisements for the brands we wear, with our clothes bearing logos for all to see.

The dramatic explosion in the range of media outlets, and the complications that this has introduced to the task of media planning, can be seen visibly in Figure 1.1, contrasting the situation which obtained in 1975 with that of 1996.

In 1996, according to the Advertising Association (1997) (Advertising Statistics Yearbook, The Advertising Association/NTC Publications Ltd, 1997) some £11.9 billion was spent on advertising in the UK, representing some 1.89 per cent of our gross domestic product. This figure has fluctuated somewhat over recent years and currently stands at its highest level since 1989 (Table 1.1).

Of this total, 30 per cent was in the form of press display advertising (£3,645 million), representing a further decline. In fact, from a high point of 36 per cent in 1987, display advertising has fallen progressively over recent years – 36 per cent in 1987, 35 per cent in 1989, 33 per cent in 1992 and 1993 and 32 per cent in 1994 and 1995. A further 23 per cent was in the form of classified advertisements (£2,768 million). It is interesting to examine the pattern of press expenditure amongst the various outlets (Table 1.2).

28 per cent of total expenditure was on television (£3,333 million), which has

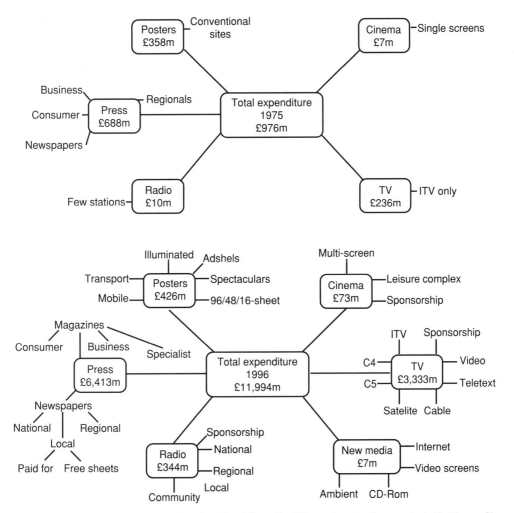

Figure 1.1 The media explosion. Adapted and updated from D. O'Donoghue in Cooper, A. (ed.), *How to Plan Advertising*, 1997. Statistics from AA Statistics Yearbook, Advertising Association/NTC Publications, 1997

remained at this level for the past five years. Of this total, some £418 million represented production costs, at their highest level since 1985. Direct mail represents 12 per cent of the total expenditure (£1,404 million), up from the level of 10 per cent which it has held over the previous three years; whilst the 'all other' category accounts for a further £843 million or 7 per cent. Other media represented much lower levels of expenditure. Some £426 million was spent on outdoor poster and transport advertising, £344 million on radio and £73 million in the cinema.

It is possible to compare the levels of advertising across a wide variety of countries. Table 1.3 depicts the advertising expenditure as a percentage of the gross domestic product for 1995, the latest year for which comparable figures are available:

It is in the context of these very considerable expenditure levels that marketing communications is considered a vital part of the marketing function. However, every aspect of the marketing communications mix is being re-examined to determine whether it makes an effective contribution to the continual

Table 1.1   UK advertising expenditure

	Total £ billion at current prices	% GDP
1985	5.05	1.64
1990	8.93	1.86
1991	8.53	1.72
1993	9.14	1.67
1995	10.98	1.82
1996	11.99	1.89

Source: AA Statistics Yearbook, 1997

The growth of marketing communications

The latter part of this century has seen considerable growth in the use of marketing communications driven by a wide variety of factors.

The growth of manufacturing and services

There has been a consistent level of growth in manufacturing output throughout the period. Increasingly, companies have joined together as a result of mergers and acquisitions which have further increased their potential levels of production and, in turn, the desire to increase the scale of markets, both domestically and internationally.

well-being of the brand. And it is increasingly being recognized that marketing communications is not merely a set of important tools, but rather fulfils a vital and strategic role for the organization.

Table 1.2

Total	National newspapers	Regional newspapers	Consumer magazines	Business & professional publications	Directories	Production costs
£6,413 m	£1,510 m	£2,061 m	£583 m	£1,018 m	£692 m	£550 m

Table 1.3   Advertising as a percentage of GDP, 1995

Austria	Belgium	Denmark	Finland	France	Germany	Greece	Ireland	Italy
0.84	0.74	0.85	0.89	0.65	0.91	1.82	0.99	0.5

Japan	Netherlands	Norway	Portugal	Spain	Sweden	Switzerland	UK	USA
0.84	0.9	0.73	1.19	0.85	0.81	0.96	1.16	1.27

Source: Advertising Statistics Yearbook, 1997

Improvements in transportation

Hitherto, many manufacturers, particularly those associated with the manufacture of products with comparatively short shelf lives, could only service consumers within easy reach of the manufacturing base. Increasingly, the development of refrigeration and other transportation components has meant that products can be rapidly and conveniently transported to distant geographic regions without fear of a deterioration in the quality of the products.

The proliferation of brands

As manufacturers recognize the potential for market segmentation – satisfying the distinct needs of different groups of consumers – with products more closely tailored to meet their particular needs, the consequence has been a proliferation of separate brands, each with a distinct positioning within the market category. Importantly, the tools of marketing communications have provided the means of communicating with these disparate groups.

The increasing separation of the manufacturer from the consumer

Under this heading we can consider several different but consistent factors. On the one hand, manufacturers have become increasingly distant from potential consumers as the chain of distribution has enlarged. Dependent upon the nature of these channels, the manufacturer may come to depend on wholesalers and retailers, franchising operations and other devices between himself and the ultimate consumer of his goods or services. At the same time, there has been an increased use of direct marketing techniques in which the manufacturer eliminates the use of intermediaries but, instead, establishes a direct line of communications between himself and potential consumers. In both cases, the need for extensive use of marketing communications is of paramount importance. It represents the sole means by which the manufacturer can achieve a dialogue with his potential markets.

The relative decline in personal selling

Where, previously, sales could be achieved through the efforts of the sales force, the progressive increase in costs associated with this approach to achieving sales has placed more emphasis on the use of more cost-effective methods. The need to communicate to substantial numbers of potential consumers has encouraged the growth and re-examination of the tools of communication.

The changing face of distribution

Increasingly, the process of distribution has been concentrated into comparatively few hands. In many markets a small number of companies dominate the retail scene. In the UK, for example, five companies control 50 per cent of the grocery trade; similarly, five companies represent around 25 per cent of the chemist trade. This factor is replicated worldwide, certainly in the more developed nations.

The growth in technology

Technological improvements have had wide-reaching consequences for the marketer. Progressive advances have ensured the achievement of mass production capabilities for almost all consumer goods. Recent years have seen the dramatic increase in media channels, and with them the progressive fragmentation of audiences. Simultaneously, technology has provided the means for the establishment of sophisticated databases, enabling the manufacturer to achieve a greater understanding of the needs and wants of potential consumers.

The increased use and sophistication of market research

The techniques of market research have dramatically improved, in parallel with the advances in technology which have provided the means for far more sophisticated analyses of consumers than has ever existed previously. Today's marketers have access to a variety of inputs from media research, lifestyle and attitude studies, purchasing profiles, to name but a few. Each of these components can be cross-tabulated with any other to achieve a more enduring understanding of the underlying nature of consumer purchases.

Increasing improvements in living standards

Today's consumer is significantly better educated and more prosperous than previous generations. Progressive increases in income have ensured that a smaller percentage is devoted to acquiring the necessities of life and more is available to improve the quality of life. People are living longer, opening up the opportunity for the introduction of new products and services specifically designed to meet the needs of an older population with a differing lifestyle.

Use of credit facilities

The dramatic increase in the percentage of the population who have access to credit facilities, and specifically credit cards, has opened up the opportunity for the growth of direct marketing. Such facilities provide the source of a 'charging platform' – the means by which consumers can agree to pay for goods and services ordered over the phone or by other means.

The wider reach of the media

Today's consumers have ready access to a wide range of media channels – TV, radio, print media. As we have seen, not only does the increase in the number of media channels mean that more consumers can be reached cost-effectively, they can be targeted with a much higher degree of precision.

A growing understanding of the use of marketing communications

Our understanding of the various tools of marketing communications has increased progressively, with the consequence that they can be employed with a far greater degree of confidence. Equally important, improved familiarity means that marketers can develop campaigns with a reasonable assurance of being able to predict the outcomes of their actions.

Access to specialist companies in the field of marketing communications

Along with the development of the tools of marketing communications, specialist companies have emerged to provide companies with dedicated inputs in the areas of strategic planning and implementation. These services augment the particular skills of the individuals and further enhance their confidence to employ the various techniques.

Blurring of the edges of the tools of marketing communications

Recent years have seen significant changes in the way that marketing communications campaigns have been developed and

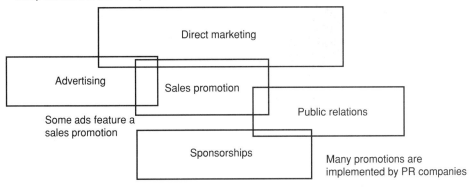

Figure 1.2

implemented. In the 1960s the primary source for the development of all forms of marketing communications campaigns was the advertising agency. At the time, separate departments provided their clients with advice in all of the appropriate areas.

Since then, two strands of change have taken place. On the one hand, the wider appreciation of the techniques, and the need for specialist personnel, have both resulted in the creation of specialist companies which deal with specific areas. The consequence has been a fragmentation of the provisions within the area, with the growth of sales promotion, public relations, direct marketing agencies and others, often separate and distinct from the advertising function. In turn, these too have fragmented further, with companies emerging to provide inputs and implementation in the areas of point of sale, incentive, sponsorship, product placement, and a myriad of other areas.

On the other, there has been a tendency for this variety of 'specialists' to provide inputs across a wide range of areas, with the consequence that several different companies will have the ability to develop campaigns utilizing the different tools of marketing communications. No longer do campaigns feature a single component or element; rather, they may employ several different devices which previously were the domain of dedicated and

specialist companies. This 'blurring' can be seen in Figure 1.2.

'Discipline overlap is blurring long standing distinctions. It's increasingly difficult to categorise work as sales promotion or direct marketing, for example. Most direct marketing offers contain some form of sales promotion and vice versa. And with the growth of direct response press and TV advertising, direct marketing is moving closer to conventional advertising.' (Cook, 1994)

The strategic challenges facing organizations

Marketing and, for that matter, marketing communications, are being readdressed by major corporations to determine the values which they derive from the adoption of their principles. Indeed, the very nature of these principles is being evaluated to determine their relevance in the context of the challenges being faced by companies in the late 1990s.

The evolution of the marketing concept is well documented, and will not be revisited here. However, many are now challenging the precepts which have become the basis of marketing planning. Nilson (1992), in his book *Value Added Marketing*, suggests that marketing has 'lost its way'. Despite employing high-quality management major organizations have, in many instances, seemed unable to face the challenges which they face in the broader environment. Growth has come more from acquisition than from brand development. The consequence of the inexorable process of chasing niche markets has been the continued and growing failure of new products to attract substantial and profitable audiences. The continued growth of private label products in a wide variety of market sectors evidences the fact that retailers are often more successful in the identification and satisfaction of consumer needs. New and innovative competitors have stolen share from the large multinational FMCG companies despite their comparative smaller scale, which should have precluded their entry into the market.

Nilson argues that the inability of marketing to achieve significant results stems from four key factors:

- It tends to be reactive rather than pro-active.
- It is often slow to respond to changes, rather than fast.

- It encourages creativity at the expense of business sense and experience.
- It is based on market growth rather than defending brand share in a stagnating market.

Several of these principles are reflected in Frederick Webster's 1996 paper on the new marketing concept. He suggests that companies need to adopt a value-delivery strategy in order to ensure success in the future. The implication is that marketing will no longer be the province of the marketing department. Indeed, he contends that 'a large marketing department will be seen as the antithesis of a market driven organisation, especially if it is part of a hierarchical, bureaucratic structure dominated by rules, policies and procedures'. The imperative will be a commitment to continuous improvement and development throughout the organization, designed to achieve customer focus.

This same view is expressed somewhat differently by Hugh Davidson (1997): 'Integrated marketing means that every part of the business combines to deliver superior

Table 1.4

The departmental approach	Integrated approach
Set overall five-year sales and profit targets	Review future markets, needs, technologies and competences
Develop individual supporting strategies and plans by department	Establish vision, priorities, competences, needed to win tomorrow
Combine departmental plans	Develop key strategies for value, innovation, competences, attitudes
Adjust five-year sales and profit targets	Convert into sales, profit and investment targets, and individual department strategy and plans
Characteristics of approach: Financially driven	Market and competence-driven
Department-based	Cross-departmental

Source: Davidson, H., *Even More Offensive Marketing*, 1997

customer value at minimum cost.' Davidson contrasts the different approaches reflecting the past (departmental approach) with the future (integrated marketing) in Table 1.4.

The essential requirement of the 'new marketing' approach is the development of a close customer focus throughout the organization which, in turn, demands an understanding of customers as individuals in order to appreciate their perceptions, expectations, needs and wants. In this context, an important role of marketing is the provision of information, in order that decisions are based on contemporary, relevant and accurate information about the marketplace, considering both competitors and customers. This implies, in many instances, the establishment of an effective database system which, if properly developed, becomes a key strategic resource of the organization. The information provided will enable far more sophisticated market segmentation, targeting and positioning, all of which are essential ingredients of the development of effective marketing communications.

Strategic marketing communications

Shultz, Tannenbaum and Lauterborn (1992) argue that marketing communications often presents the only real differentiating feature that can be offered to potential consumers. By recognizing the fact that everything a company does consists, in some form, as part of the communication which takes place between itself and its customers, it becomes aware of the increasingly important role of marketing communications as a strategic tool.

Just as the premise of the 'new marketing' places the consumer at the centre of all activity, so too marketing communications must be considered from the essential perspective of understanding consumer behaviour. This implies a consideration of more

than just the content of the message itself. Close attention needs to be paid to the context of the message (the vehicle used to communicate with the target audience) as well as the timing and tone of that message. An imperative is the identification of clear, concise and measurable communications objectives which will enable the selection of the appropriate communications tools to achieve the goals set.

By developing an understanding of the identity of the consumer and their particular needs and wants, we can determine the nature of the behaviour which the communications programme will seek to reinforce or change – and, in turn, the specific nature of the message which will affect that behaviour, and the means by which we can reach them.

The strategic role that marketing communications can play is increasingly evidenced by the impact of specific campaigns. These not only affect the way in which consumers think about the particular products and services which are offered to them, but the very way in which they consider the categories in which those products and services exist. The Virgin Airline campaign has resulted in businesspeople re-evaluating the in-flight experience; First Direct have made consumers consider the fundamental requirement of being able to access their bank account at times which suit them; the AA has moved people's thinking from the need to make a broken-down car go again towards the company's ability to resolve personal emergencies, and so on.

The expanded marketing communications mix

As we have already seen, the expanded marketing communications mix has moved our thinking way beyond the simple distinctions between advertising, public relations, sales promotions and similar categorizations of the various tools available to us. Not only are the tools themselves significantly enhanced with the availability of new and emergent forms of media, associating devices such as product placement and sponsorship, but their application has changed with the development of the Internet, electronic point of sale, virtual advertising and ambient media.

We have at our disposal an ever increasing array of means of reaching our target consumers in a cost-effective manner, but this demands an increasing understanding of the relevance and application of these tools and their individual contribution to the communications process.

The communications process

Understanding the basic process of communications is fundamental to the development of an appreciation of how marketing communications might function. It is important to identify how people extract information from the environment in which they live and, importantly, how they interpret this information to assist them in their daily lives. A great deal of work has been conducted in the field of psychology and the social sciences to gain knowledge of the processes involved, and some readers might wish to read a dedicated text in the area to assist them in their understanding.

According to Foxall and Goldsmith (1994) some 90 per cent of the stimuli that individuals perceive comes to them as a result of sight. Much of the remaining 10 per cent results from hearing. It should come as no surprise, therefore, that advertising relies heavily on these stimuli. However, because of possible distortions in the perception of a given message, what the consumer receives may not be what the advertiser intended.

The task of communication is to exchange information and convey meaning to others. However, it is apparent that conveying even

a simple idea is rarely easy. It is important, therefore, that communicators gain a detailed understanding of the way in which meaning is transmitted in order to be able to develop effective communications strategies. The process of communications is explained visually using the model developed by Wilbur Schramm in 1955. Although somewhat simplistic, it depicts the basic components essential to any form of communication (see Figure 1.3).

Figure 1.3

The process reflects the need of the sender, who might be an individual or company, wishing to communicate with some third party, the receiver, by sending a message. However, the model fails to acknowledge several other important elements upon which the communications process is dependent and which, more importantly, may affect the receiver's interpretation of that message.

Subsequent work by Schramm and Roberts (1971) and Dominick (1990) and others provides us with models which are somewhat more realistic and depicts some of the additional complexities of the process (Figure 1.4).

As in the simple model, the process commences with the sender, sometimes referred to as the source or communicator. However, these models recognize that the message itself is often sent in an 'encoded' form. This is a reflection of the fact that, in many instances, the message is of an abbreviated nature, as in the case of a 30-second commercial, in which the sender uses a variety of verbal and visual devices to communicate with the intended audience. The encoding process may assume prior knowledge on the part of the receiver, or use different mechanisms which assist the receiver to recall other relevant information.

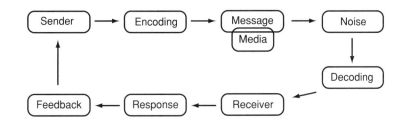

Figure 1.4

Once the message has been created, the sender will use one or more of a variety of channels of communication. These may be commercial channels such as television, radio, print media or posters, or the communication may consist of a letter, mailing or phone call. An important consideration here is the way in which the chosen medium may impact on the message itself. Since some channels of communication have a high level of credibility, the messages they carry will be enhanced. Conversely, some channels may have a negative impact on the message. In this context, it is worth remembering the words of Marshall McLuhan when he said, 'The medium is the message'.

A critical aspect of the communications process is the intervention of what is commonly known as 'noise' or 'interference'. The individual is bombarded with information on a daily basis – news and weather broadcasts, a wide variety of advertising messages, apart from interpersonal communications, to name but a few – and all of which may interfere with the ability to hear clearly the message sent by the particular advertiser. The inevitable consequence is that the decoding process, in which the receiver of the message interprets its meaning, can often become confused. The intended recipient may only see part of a commercial, or mishear some of the spoken words. He or she will bring their own views and beliefs to the interpretation process, which may also affect the way in which the message is understood.

The response which the receiver makes will vary according to the nature of the message and the impact of these and other extraneous factors. In some instances, the intention of the message may be to convey information. At other times, there may be a specific injunction to make a purchase. Needless to say, the sender of the message will be keen to understand the way in which the receiver has responded to it.

Some communications will have feedback mechanisms built in from the outset. This may consist of a telephone number which the receiver is invited to call, or a coupon to be returned. In other cases, the various tools of market research will be utilized to gain an understanding of how the consumer interprets the message and responds to it. It should be clear that the nature of the message itself is only one of the key components. If the medium selected to convey the message is poorly targeted; if the impact of the surrounding noise causes distractions; or if the intended receiver's prior experience distorts the meaning of the message, then the communications process has failed.

Communication may be considered to be a hierarchical process in which potential consumers are taken through a sequence of stages in order, hopefully, to convince them to purchase a product or service. Various models, of which the best known are AIDA, DAGMAR (Colley, 1961), Lavidge and Steiner (1961) and Ray (1973), depict the stages through which the consumer passes en route to purchase. The important stages are shown in Figure 1.5.

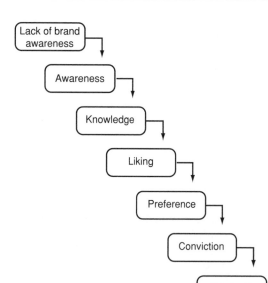

Figure 1.5

At the outset, potential consumers may be completely unaware of the product or service, and the role of marketing communications will be to provide them with relevant knowledge to transfer them to the next stage of awareness. Having achieved that goal, the objective will be to provide them with appropriate knowledge and understanding of the product or service in order that they can make an informed comparison with the offerings of competitors. Following this, the intention will be to create favourable impressions and, subsequently, to create a preference for the product versus other alternatives. The penultimate stage is the establishment of beliefs that the product is one that is appropriate for purchase. It is the final stage of the model which translates the previous activity into an actual purchase.

The importance of gaining an understanding of the way in which potential consumers interpret communications messages is vital to the development of effective communications strategies. All of these considerations will be explored in the chapters which follow.

Achieving integration within the communications mix

The thinking initiated by Shultz, Tannenbaum and Lauterborn (1992), referred to above, has brought about a sea change in the business of marketing communications. Witnessed by the plethora of journal articles on the topic, 'integration' has become the buzz word of the 1990s. Moreover, it has been reflected in the increasing number of marketing communications companies attempting to achieve integration within their own organizations.

For many years, the various tools of marketing communications have been considered as, essentially, separate elements planned and implemented individually, often without consideration for the impact of one tool on the workings of another. The underlying requirement of integrated marketing communications (IMC) is to force all aspects of the communication programme to deliver a single-minded and unified message to the target consumer. The imperative has become one of ensuring that each and every communications tactic serves to reinforce the work of the other parts of the communications programme.

This new thinking, of course, has a series of important impacts both on the planning and implementation process. To begin with, it demands that the planning of campaigns is considered holistically rather than, as in the past, as a series of individual components. Moreover, it requires a series of new skills, both on the part of those determining the strategy and tactics, as well as those responsible for the implementation of the resulting campaign. In order to achieve effective integration, there must be a comprehensive understanding of the contribution that can be made by each of the elements – and, further, an understanding of the way in which those elements may affect the overall communications process.

The philosophy and structure of the book

The premise of this text is to recognize and reflect the new thinking in the field of marketing communications. It is no longer sufficient to be an expert in a single area of communications, such as advertising or public relations. For the future, those charged with the responsibility for the development and implementation of marketing communications campaigns will need to achieve a comprehensive understanding of each of the component parts. This text has been designed to provide that level of understanding.

The book is divided into two parts. The first considers the broader issues which impact on the planning process. As such, there is an examination of aspects of both consumer and organizational buying behaviour; the contribution of market research; issues surrounding the development of brands and market segmentation; a detailed consideration of integration; the framework for the management of marketing communications; and the process of selecting partners in the communications process.

In the second part of the book, individual chapters deal with each of the separate tools of communications. The intention is to provide an in-depth understanding of both the theory and practice of developing those devices. These cover advertising and its development; media and media planning; sales promotion; direct marketing; public relations; sponsorship and product placement; and corporate communications. Reflecting the increasing move towards the creation of campaigns for international, rather than simply domestic, implementation, Chapter 15 deals specifically with the associated issues. The text concludes with a brief 'future-gazing' exercise in which the author attempts to anticipate some of the important factors likely to affect the field of communications.

References

Colley, R., *Defining Advertising Goals for Measured Advertising Effects*, Association of National Advertisers, 1961

Cook, 'The End of the Line', *Marketing*, Vol. 24, February, 1994

Davidson, H., *Even More Offensive Marketing*, Penguin Books, 1997

Dominick, J. R., *The Dynamics of Mass Communications*, Random House, 1990

Foxall, G. R. and Goldsmith, R. E., *Consumer Psychology for Marketing*, Routledge, 1994

Lavidge, R. J. and Steiner, G. A., 'A Model for the Predictive Measurements of Advertising Effectiveness', *Journal of Marketing*, October 1961

Nilson, T. S., *Value Added Marketing*, McGraw-Hill, 1992

Ray, M., Marketing Communication and the Hierarchy of Effects, in Clark, P. (ed.), *New Models for Communications Research*, Sage Publications, 1973

Schramm, W. (ed.), *The Process and Effects of Mass Communication*, University of Illinois Press, 1955

Schramm, W. and Roberts, D., *The Process and Effects of Mass Communications*, University of Illinois Press, 1971

Shultz, D., Tannenbaum, S. I. and Lauterborn, R. F., *Integrated Marketing Communications*, NTC Business Books, 1992

Webster, F. E., 'Executing the New Marketing Concept', *Marketing Management*, Vol. 3, No. 1, 1996

Additional reading

The following texts will help develop an understanding of the topics considered in this chapter:

Fill, Chris, *Marketing Communications: Frameworks, Theories and Applications*, 1995, Prentice Hall

Rossiter, John R. and Percy, Larry, *Advertising, Communications and Promotion Management*, 2nd international edition, 1997, McGraw-Hill

CHAPTER 2

Understanding the marketplace

Aims and objectives

- To introduce the concepts of consumer and industrial buying behaviour;
- To consider the variables for segmentation;
- To help understand the changing nature of the consumer;
- To appreciate the importance of targeting and positioning;
- To gain insight into the nature of the decision-making process and problem solving;
- To consider the influences affecting consumer behaviour;
- To explore the nature of organizational buying behaviour;
- To define the contribution of marketing research;
- To become aware of the dimensions of marketing communications research.

The dimensions of consumer and organizational buying behaviour

Gaining an understanding of the ways in which people set about making their purchase decisions is an essential part of determining effective communications strategies. In simple terms, potential customers can be divided into two broad groups. For most products and services, the largest group is represented by the consumer market, comprising large numbers of both individuals and households who purchase products and services for their own use. For others, their potential purchasers are made up of companies, both those who operate for profit together with non-profit organizations who buy goods and services for their own use.

The topic of consumer behaviour is an extensive one. It has been defined as:

'The study of the processes involved when individuals or groups select, purchase, use or dispose of products, services, ideas or experiences to satisfy needs and desires.' (Solomon, 1996)

This chapter will explore each of those aspects.

The consumer market

Certainly, the vast majority of products and services, particularly those with large marketing communications budgets, appeal to consumers. However, it would be naive in the extreme to assume that these products have an appeal to *all* consumers. Even the most popular products and services fail to appeal to all consumers. Take, for example, the ubiquitous Coca Cola. Whilst undeniably one of the world's largest brands, even within its own sector, not all consumers drink the product. Some prefer Pepsi, others Virgin cola or one of the myriad private label competitors. Some consumers reject cola beverages entirely, preferring instead other carbonated soft drinks or water; yet others consume hot beverages such as tea or coffee and so on. The range of drinks which can satisfy the basic need to quench a thirst is almost endless. It follows that, for products to succeed, they must identify the critical consumer dimensions which will ensure that their product or service achieves appeal to some or other segment of the overall population.

Market segmentation

Consumers can be differentiated against a wide range of variables, both demographic and psychographic, which are substantially self-explanatory.

Demographic variables

Age
Sex
Race
Religion
Income
Occupation
Social class
Education
Geographic location
Family life cycle
Life stage

Whilst these dimensions provide us with information about the consumer, it is important to remember that they often lack the ability to discriminate sufficiently. Simply because two consumers are of a similar age and gender, for example, does not indicate that their tastes and preferences for the products they desire will be similar.

Psychographic variables

Identifying the underlying psychological characteristics provides a much richer texture from which to develop an understanding of the important consumer variables. Psychographics is the understanding of the psychological basis of opinions and attitudes. Often, the term is used interchangeably with that of 'lifestyle' and, whilst there is some overlap, it is possible to distinguish between the two. The former term relates to the types of opinions which people hold, whereas lifestyle more appropriately describes the way that people live, and considers their personal values and actions in a social context.

Several factors can be considered in order to provide an understanding of the way people act in the way that they do – and, importantly, this can help us determine the reasons for the purchase of the products and services that they buy.

- *Attitudes*. It is clear that the attitudes people hold will impact on products and services.
- *Motivation*. Here we are considering the reasons which lay behind the particular purchase decision.
- *Desired benefits*. This involves segmenting the market on the basis of the benefits which purchasers seek from the product in question.
- *Lifestyle*. This considers a variety of important factors, such as activities, interests and opinions (AIO), and is based on a paper presented by Dr Joseph Plummer in 1974. The important lifestyle dimensions can be seen from Table 2.1.

One of the best known applications of this principle is VALS2 – a values and lifestyles model developed by SRI International (Figure 2.1). The model groups individuals into three broad categories based on their 'self-orientation' and considers their motivations against the characteristics of 'principles' (those who hold strong personal beliefs about what is or is not appropriate in given circumstances);

Table 2.1

Activities	Interests	Opinions
Work	Family	Themselves
Hobbies	Home	Social issues
Social events	Job	Politics
Vacation	Community	Business
Entertainment	Recreation	Economics
Club membership	Fashion	Education
Community	Mood	Products
Shopping	Media	Future
Sports	Achievements	Culture

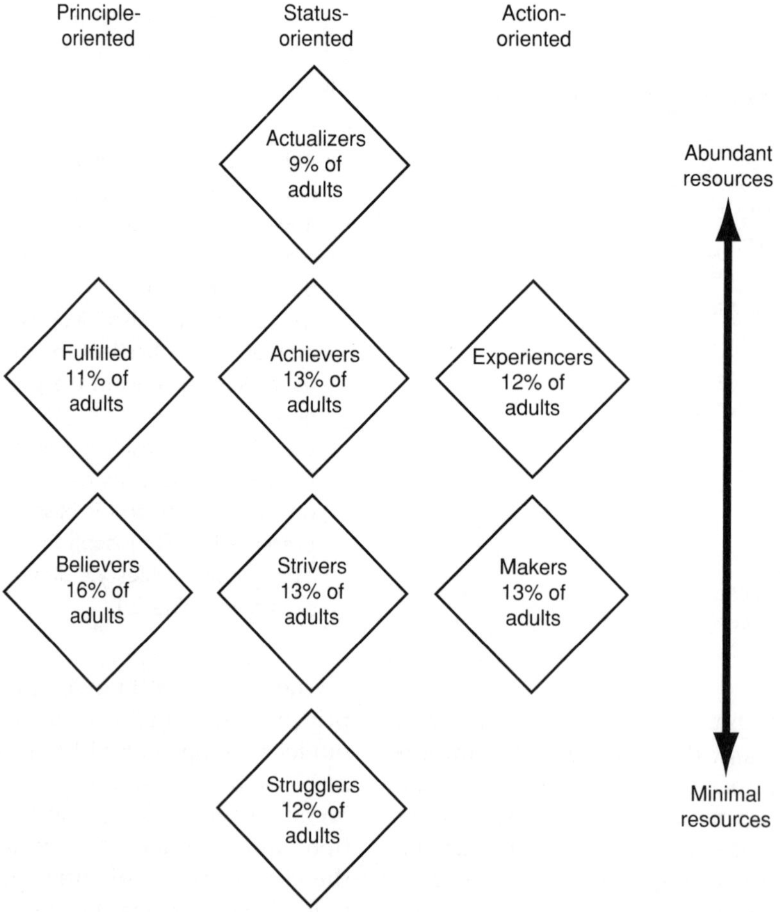

Figure 2.1   The VALS2 typology

'status' (those who are influenced by the approval of others within their social environment); or 'action' (individuals who are motivated by activity, variety and risk). These categories can be further examined on the basis of the financial resources which the individuals possess. The VALS typology adds two further categories: 'strugglers' (whose financial situation is so restricted that their psychological characteristics are unimportant); and 'actualisers' (individuals who possess sufficient financial resources that they can display all of the psychological orientations).

The changing consumer

Recent years have witnessed fundamental changes in the values and lifestyles of consumers as the view of the world around us changes dramatically. A few facts will illustrate.

- We have seen the progressive shift of the woman out of the home and into the domestic economy.
- Family roles are changing. In many instances, women are the main family income earners, whilst some men remain at home and fulfil the traditional parent role.
- Job security, the underpinning of society for many decades, is breaking down. Comparatively short tenure is much more the norm, and people are being hired on relatively short-term contracts.
- Expectation of the annual salary increase or bonus is rapidly diminishing and, even where it exists, it is constrained by economic circumstances.
- Continuing threats on personal safety are omnipresent.
- Public respect for the 'institutions of life' are diminishing.
- Personal values are changing. Things that were once the preserve of the 'middle classes' are now available to all.

- The office environment is losing its role. Already significant numbers of workers conduct their businesses from home, rather than from within a structured organization.
- Companies are no longer local or even national. In many cases, people are employed by organizations whose head offices are thousands of miles away.
- Environmental considerations apply to all aspects of daily life.

The data from the Social Trends and General Household survey, available from the Office for National Statistics, provides us with an interesting picture of both contemporary and future society. The overall picture indicates that population growth will be comparatively slow. The figure presently stands at 59 million, with the projection for 2031 being only 61 million. Despite this, there are fundamental changes in the underlying composition of society – all of which have an important bearing on marketing futures.

Age

The number of people over retirement age will increase progressively. The consequence of past fluctuations in fertility rates, together with increasing longevity, will result in an ageing population. Similarly, the number of children under 16 is projected to fall after the year 2000. The number of those of working age will continue to increase to around 2011 and then decline. These facts have important consequences for the consideration of both savings and pensions. There are some 18 million people in Britain aged over 50, who have a higher life expectancy than ever before (74 for men and 80 for women, compared to 45 and 49 in 1901). Whereas total consumer spending in the UK in 1991 was £335.5 billion, people over 40 spend £148.5 billion of this.

The changing roles and perceptions of differing age groups are clearly seen from a recent article which appeared in *The Times* (27 September, 1997) under the heading of 'Grandpa, What do you get up to all day?'.

What made the article so interesting was the fact that in many instances the grandparents depicted in the article were role models or icons for the youth generation. They included Linford Christie (a grandfather at 37), Mick Jagger and Nanette Newman.

Households

The number of households has increased dramatically, from 18 million in 1971 to 24 million currently. This number is projected to rise by another 4.4 million in England alone by 2016. Inevitably, this will have a significant impact on the demand for mortgages and other household services. In 1971, single-person households represented around 18 per cent of the total. By 2016, they will represent 36 per cent.

Targeting

The task of targeting is an essential part of the process of developing effective marketing communications campaigns. As with other aspects of marketing and marketing communications, the same word can be used in different contexts. This is the case with the use of the word 'targeting'. There are two important dimensions to this task which affect aspects of campaign development.

The targeting of markets

When used in the broader context of marketing, the task of targeting implies the appropriate evaluation and identification of one or more market segments in which it is desired to operate. This is a fundamental strategic decision which will help define the subsequent development of both marketing and marketing communications programmes.

There are four distinct strategic approaches, any one of which may be appropriate to the task in hand:

1 *Undifferentiated marketing* – sometimes referred to as mass marketing – in which the company offers the product to the entire marketplace. The company will ignore the differences which may exist between separate market segments and offer a single product designed to appeal to all consumers.

2 *Differentiated marketing* – in which the company develops different combinations of the marketing mix, each of which is designed to appeal individually to the separate identified segments of the market.

3 *Concentrated* or *targeted marketing* – in which the company identifies one or more target segments and develops different marketing mixes for each of those segments. In effect, rather than trying to obtain a share of the overall market, the company identifies one or more market segments where its reputation or experience enables it to provide a closer match between what it provides and the segment requirements.

4 *Custom marketing* – in which the company develops campaigns to respond to meet the needs of individual consumers. Most commonly applied through the techniques of direct marketing, this is the ultimate in differentiation.

The targeting of consumers

The same word is used somewhat differently in the context of marketing communications although, inevitably, there is some degree of overlap. Here we are concerned with the aspect of achieving coverage of a defined target audience through the use of appropriate media. We have already seen that we can apply many different consumer characteristics, either singly or in combination, to define the nature of one or more target audiences. This information will be used both in the development of the communications message and, particularly, in terms of the selection of the media vehicles which will be used to convey that message to the desired audience.

The process of targeting consumers has become significantly more sophisticated in recent years. Commonly, devices such as geodemographics have been used to classify people by where they live. Using this data to classify neighbourhoods is simple to effect and comparatively easy to use. Companies can access a variety of systems, such as ACORN, PiN, MOSAIC and DEFINE, all of which apply segmentation characteristics to regional neighbourhoods. To these has been added the establishment and growth of life-style databases, such as NDL, CMT and ICD. The retailing sector provided the initial impetus for the growth of the sector, although the subsequent growth of the financial services sector has continued to fuel that growth and enable the sophisticated application of direct marketing techniques.

These, and related issues, will be considered in greater depth in subsequent chapters of the book, but especially in Chapter 9 on media and media planning and Chapter 11 on direct marketing.

Positioning

Positioning involves the creation of an image for the product or service in order that consumers can clearly understand what the company provides relative to its competitors. A critical dimension of positioning is the gaining of an understanding of the needs and wants of consumers.

There are a variety of positioning characteristics which can be adopted by an organization, but the single-minded requirement is to identify a long-term proposition which positions the brand in the minds of consumers. For many years, Mars was the confectionery bar which 'helps you work, rest and play', whilst Gillette remains 'the best a man can get'.

Upshaw (1995) identifies several different types of positioning prompts:

1 Feature-driven prompts, which is the use of specific features of the product to differentiate the brand. Dyson has done precisely this by focusing attention on its 'bagless' vacuum cleaner.
2 Problem – solution prompts, in which the product is seen to be the 'unique' solution to a particular problem.
3 Target-driven positioning uses the nature of the consumer to identify a place in the market. In essence, the message is that 'people like you use this brand'.
4 Competitive-driven positioning, where the product adopts an overt stance relative to an identified competitor. This is the approach taken by Avis versus Hertz.
5 Emotional or psychological positioning.
6 Benefit-driven positioning.
7 Aspirational positioning. Successful people use this brand. Rolex is an example of this stance.
8 Value positioning, such as that adopted by McDonald's Value Meals.

Understanding consumer behaviour

A considerable body of work exists in the attempt to understand the important dynamics of consumer behaviour. Early theoretical studies tended to concentrate on the economic variables to explain the differences which existed among consumers. However, these provided only a limited understanding of the process, since they ignored the important psychological factors. George Katona introduced a new approach in 1963, known as behavioural economics, which sought to add these dimensions to the economic factors. The turning point for a proper appreciation of the complex nature of consumer behaviour was provided by Francesco Nicosia (1966), who was among the first to recognize the important role of marketing communications in determining the nature of consumer purchases.

Two further studies provide the basis for our contemporary understanding of the process of consumer behaviour. In 1968 the Engel, Kollat and Blackwell model first introduced the concept that the consumer passes through a series of separate stages during the decision-making process, whilst in 1969 John Howard and Jagdish Sheth developed their important model (known generally as the Howard–Sheth model) which introduced the notion that there are different levels of decision making dependent on the nature of the purchase being undertaken.

The decision-making process

The decision-making process consists, theoretically, of a number of separate and distinct stages (Figure 2.2). In practice, not all of the stages are necessarily followed in each purchasing decision, nor are they necessarily followed in the order shown below. However, the model provides a useful basis from which to examine the separate dimensions of decision making and to explore the potential impact of marketing communications upon them.

Problem recognition
At the outset, the consumer experiences a need or problem situation which, in simple terms, is the appreciation of some difference between his or her existing state and the desired state. This might be the experiencing of thirst or hunger, or some more complicated problem, such as a dissatisfaction with a domestic sound system.

Information gathering
Whereas the solution to the first problem is fairly straightforward – obtain a drink – in the second case, the individual will rarely possess sufficient knowledge on which to base a purchasing decision. It is likely, therefore, that he will set about obtaining relevant information from a variety of sources. These might include specialist publications, for example, *What Hi Fi?* and *Which?* magazines, together with the opinions of friends, relatives and others who might recently have gone through a similar process. Equally, he might visit a series of specialist outlets to gather leaflets, literature and the opinions of the dealers who stock the range of relevant products.

Evaluation
Once sufficient information has been gathered, the potential purchaser can consider the various alternatives on offer, and make an evaluation based on both objective and subjective criteria. An important consideration might be the amount of money available for the purchase, or the looks and styling of the different products. Familiarity with the various manufacturers' names might be a further basis of evaluation; similarly, the reputation of the retailer, and so on.

Purchase
Once the evaluation stage has been completed, the individual may decide to make the purchase. However, it is important to recognize that in some situations the decision may be deferred. Perhaps the available models fail to meet the criteria applied, or the individual does not possess sufficient money at that time to enable the desired purchase to be made.

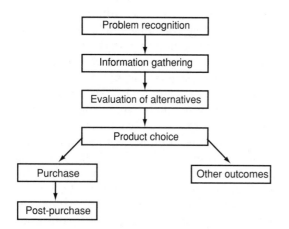

Figure 2.2   Stages in the decision-making process

Post-purchase

Even when the purchase has been made, the process does not cease. The purchaser will often seek justification for the purchase – which can be obtained from a number of sources. Advertising may serve to congratulate the purchaser on the wisdom of his or her choice; the comments of friends and others may similarly reinforce the purchase decision. However, in some instances, the consumer will fail to be satisfied with the product. Some consumers will complain directly to the outlet from which it was purchased, others will complain to the manufacturer, yet more will simply tell their acquaintances that the product failed to live up to expectations.

This notion of post-purchase dissatisfaction is important in the communications context since, if it is sufficiently widespread, it may undermine all of the efforts that the organization puts into marketing communications.

The nature of problem solving

We can distinguish between three types of purchase:

Routine problem solving

Often associated with frequent or regular purchases. Here, the consumer already possesses sufficient information upon which to base the purchase decision. Choices between competing brands are often made routinely, with minimal effort on the part of the consumer.

Limited problem solving

In those situations where a decision is required, such as a consideration of a new product or brand, some thought will be given to the nature of the purchase decision. In practical terms, this may simply consist of a comparison being made between a familiar brand and the new one on the basis of the ingredients, price or some other dimension. For the most part, the consumer follows a series of simple decision rules rather than

becoming involved in a rigorous evaluation of the various alternatives.

Extended problem solving

Purchasing decisions which are complex or involve the expenditure of considerable sums of money are, by their very nature, more extended. Since there is a level of risk associated with the decision, the consumer may well follow several or all of the stages outlined in the decision-making process described earlier.

Siamack Salari, head of behavioural research at J. Walter Thompson, has developed a model of the decision-making process within the shopping environment. It follows four stages. First, the consumer looks for a reference point, usually the benchmark brand. Then he or she compares other brands against the benchmark. The third stage is making a selection, followed by making a final check. 'It is a model and not everybody goes by it – people sometimes jump stages. We have timed how long people spend in stores. In some product categories, they find the reference point in two seconds, in others it is longer. Where that happens, there is confusion and it is an indication that the brand mix is not helping people get into selection' (reported in *Marketing Week*, 17 April, 1997).

Factors influencing buying behaviour

The consumer does not live in isolation of the environment which surrounds him. All of the factors shown in Figure 2.3 may play a part in influencing the decisions taken on a daily basis. Such things as psychological influences, needs and motives, attitudes and lifestyle, personality and self-concept, culture, social status, reference groups, word of mouth communication, household and situational influences, will often have a direct bearing on the nature of the decision taken.

To these, we can add other important variables:

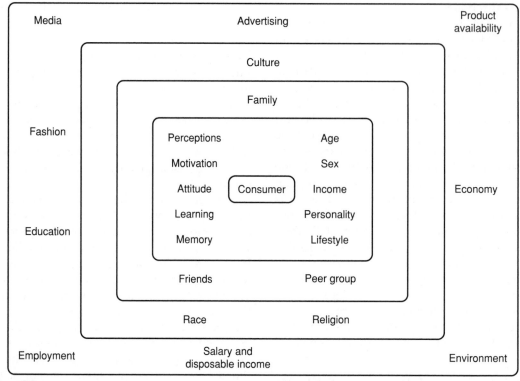

Figure 2.3

Perception

This is the process by which stimuli such as sight, sound, colour, touch, taste and others are selected, organized and interpreted (Figure 2.4).

External stimuli or sensory inputs

These represent a major part of the marketing communications process. Advertising, in particular, makes great use of these stimuli to communicate a message about a brand or service. The use of music in commercials is designed to evoke a series of memories or to create positive associations between the brand and the consumer.

- *Sight.* The visual components of marketing communications are especially important. The shape, size and, particularly, the colour of an item of packaging conveys specific meaning to the consumer regarding the identity of the brand. Given the speed with which the selection of products from crowded

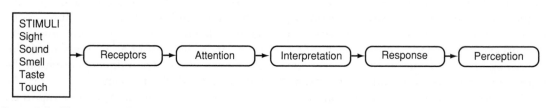

Figure 2.4   The perceptual process

supermarket shelves takes place, these visual cues are vitally important to the ability to convey specific brand information – so important, in fact, that recently British law has been altered to enable companies to protect the specific colours they use to identify their products and services. First among those to register for protection were BP (the specific colour green used on their forecourts) and Kodak (their shade of yellow used on packaging and other materials).

- *Sound.* The use of music in television commercials has already been mentioned. Often, the sound track selected is used to create associations with a particular product or service. Allied Dunbar Insurance, for example, uses 'Grey Skies' in each of its commercials, the result of which is to create an immediate identification of the brand. BA has used the same sound track for many years, whilst the process has been taken to the extreme point of identification by Intel, who use an audio link in the same way as a logo is used by other companies. Intel insist that every computer advertiser uses the mnemonic to identify the presence of the Intel chip inside the computer.
- *Smell.* The use of fragrance, especially within the retail environment, is designed to induce specific perceptions in the minds of shoppers. The smell of fresh bread, or freshly roasted ground coffee, is likely to create positive images regarding the outlet and induce sales not only of the specific product categories, but also of others where the positive association of fresh produce induces a favourable response.
- *Taste.* Many product categories are differentiated on the basis of taste, either real or perceived. Indeed, the process of taste differentiation is used by several companies, the most notable of which is Pepsi, to identify the difference between the brand and its competitors.
- *Touch.* The feel of a product, or the benefits associated with the use of a particular brand, are another dimension of differentiation. Lenor, Unilever's washing product, has long

used the benefit of softness to create a positive association with the brand.

Perceptual selection

Today's consumer is bombarded with information. Information is available at every moment in the day – from news and weather broadcasts, to roadside posters, point of sale material in shop windows and, of course, advertising messages. The fact is that there is simply too much information available to be processed simply. Consumers adopt a defence mechanism to limit the amount of information they absorb, known as perceptual selection. In effect, they subconsciously choose to accept or ignore information available to them.

Attention

A consequence of perceptual selection is the fact that many consumers either actively ignore advertising messages or find that their attention is directed elsewhere during an advertising break. It is for this reason that the creation of advertising uses specific devices to attract the consumer's attention at the beginning of a television or radio commercial, for example.

Organisational buying behaviour

In this section, we are dealing with the buying decisions taken by organizations as opposed to individuals, as in the consumer market. In many respects, there is a considerable overlap between the two. Indeed, an increasing number of writers in the area are applying directly, or with only slight modifications, the models developed for consumer behaviour to the organizational context. Although there are significant differences between the purchasing patterns of consumers and businesses, there is also an important similarity (Table 2.2).

Table 2.2	
The differences	
Consumer	Business
Uses own money	Uses company money
Large numbers of buyers	Small numbers of buyers
Individual (or family) decision	Group buying decision
Often short time scales	Extended buying time scales
The similarity	
All buying decisions are taken by people	

Source: Yeshin, T. (ed.), *Inside Advertising*, IPA, 1993

The buying centre

A major difference between consumer and organizational buying behaviour may be expressed in terms of the people who make the buying decision, and the nature of that decision. In the majority of instances, the organizational buyer is not the end-user of the product, since the purchase is a part of the overall manufacturing process. He may be buying ingredients, raw materials or manufacturing plant, all of which will be used in different ways to produce the products for which the company is responsible.

In many cases, the responsibility for buying involves a number of different individuals who, together, comprise the decision-making unit (DMU). Frederick Webster and Yoram Wind (1973), in their paper on organizational buying behaviour, identify several different roles undertaken within the DMU:

*   *Initiators* – these are the people within a company who first identify the particular need for a product or service;
*   *Influencers* – members of the organization who can, directly or indirectly, affect a purchasing decision;
*   *Decision makers* – those who have the ultimate responsibility for deciding which

supplier will be the source of the products or services required;

*   *Gatekeepers* – people who control the flow of information within the company, and whose responsibility it is to maintain information for the DMU;
*   *Purchasers* – the individual(s) who actually make the purchase;
*   *Users* – those who will use the product or service purchased.

Whether all of these functions are maintained separately within an organization will, to a large degree, depend both on its size and its operating culture. However, it is common for at least some of these functions to be maintained independently of the others. This, in turn, represents a level of complication in the communications process. It requires that the supplier will need to contact several different individuals in order to achieve a positive buying decision.

The organizational purchasing process

Although described differently, the nature of the organizational buying process has close parallels with purchases on the part of the consumer. In the same way that we distinguished between three types of buying decision among consumers, so too there are three types of organizational decision.

In many instances, the company will simply renew or repeat an order for products or services that have been purchased previously. Sometimes referred to as the 'straight rebuy', it reflects commonly purchased items which have been bought previously. Since substantial knowledge already exists concerning the quality of the items and of their supplier, the purchase is substantially similar to that of the 'routine' purchases made by consumers. The 'modified rebuy' is one in which the company purchases items similar to before, although against a somewhat different specification. In this instance, some information may be sought about the nature and facilities offered by alternative suppliers, although the purchase decision involves only limited problem solving. The final type of organizational purchase is that known as the 'new buy'. As with the extended problem-solving scenario on the part of the consumer, this purchase may well involve a more complex analysis, since the need for relevant information will be at a higher level. Potential suppliers will always need to be evaluated and the specifications of the purchase will need to be researched and prepared to meet the company requirements.

Derived demand

A further factor which needs to be considered in the context of organizational buying is that known as derived demand. The need for the products or services from a particular supplier will often be directly dependent on external considerations. If demand for the company's products increases, this will automatically increase its demand for raw materials. The converse is equally true. In the former context, it is difficult for a supplier to persuade the company to increase the level of purchases, since the obvious consequence will be the stockpiling of supplies rather than immediate consumption.

In order to understand both consumer and business markets, a series of questions must be answered:

1 Who is important in the buying decision?
2 How do they buy?
3 When do they buy?
4 Where do they buy?
5 What influences their choice decision?
6 How are choice criteria determined?

This information is an essential prerequisite to the planning of marketing communications strategies. The nature of the answers will have a substantial influence on the framing of the communications programme, its timing and targeting.

The contribution of market research

The means by which these issues can be resolved rests substantially in the use of the tools of market research, which is at the heart of planning effective marketing communications strategy. In a dynamic marketplace, the gathering and assessment of information is a vital precursor to the determination of strategy. Clearly, much information will already have been gathered to form the basis of marketing planning, and this will have equal relevance to the marketing communications process. Importantly, however, there are a number of specific aspects of market research which will have a more direct bearing on the planning of marketing communications.

The Market Research Society (MRS) defines research as:

The collection and analysis of data from a sample of individuals or organisations relating to their characteristics, behaviour, attitudes or possessions. It includes all forms of marketing and social research such as consumer and industrial surveys, psychological investigations, observations and panel studies.

The market research process

The process of market research is relatively straightforward and consists of a series of separate stages of data collection, organization and interpretation. The fundamental objectives of the process are twofold.

Firstly, there is the need to reduce or eliminate uncertainty in the various steps of the planning process. Although there will be a number of factors which are outside the direct control of the company, it is vitally important that the company is aware of those factors which may impact on the development and implementation of the strategic and marketing communications plan. By the same token, the company will need to be aware of fundamental movements in such areas as competitive activity, consumer purchasing patterns, attitudes and so on.

Secondly, there is the need to monitor the performance of the developed plan. We have already seen that marketing is not an exact science. The more rapid the feedback of response to the plan, the more likely it is that the company can make the necessary changes to ensure its effectiveness. And, of course, the information gained will make a substantial contribution to the long-term strategic planning process.

The stages of market research

The market research process consists of a series of interlinked stages (Figure 2.5). It is important to remember that, although the stages are linked, work can be conducted in several areas concurrently, and in many instances not all of the stages will be required.

Market planning

It is to be assumed that, in the development of the marketing strategy, considerable amounts

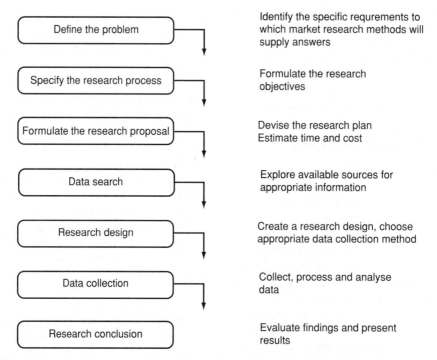

Figure 2.5 The market research process. Adapted from Crimp, M. and Wright, L. T., *The Marketing Research Process*, 4th edition, 1995, Prentice Hall

of information will already have been gathered. Both from internal sources and published data (secondary research) and from the commissioning of specific research programmes (primary research), a picture will have been built up of the general environment in which the brand competes, the nature of the competition, growth rates and potential, as well as information regarding the consumer. It is this latter area which has most bearing on marketing communications. The value of desk research should not be underestimated. Much valuable information can be derived from available and published data, with the advantage that it will be significantly cheaper than commissioning dedicated research studies. Moreover, since in many cases much of the important work of interpretation will have been carried out by others, the information will be easier to assimilate.

There are many important sources of information which should be examined at this stage.

Internal sources

These include the frequent and currently available information sourced from inside the organization, such as production information, sales statistics, field sales reports, together with any previous research which has been conducted. The latter will provide an important base of benchmarking, which will be referred to at several stages later in the book.

External sources

The company will be able to access considerable amounts of information from published sources. Important among these are the wide range of publications available from the Central Statistical Office (CSO). Although the list of publications is extensive, certain titles should be referred to on a regular basis. These include the *Annual Abstract of Statistics*, the *Monthly* and *Quarterly Digests of Statistics*, *Social Trends* – which is an invaluable source of

information for uncovering the underlying trends among the population – and special surveys, such as the *National Food Survey*, the *Family Expenditure Survey* and the *General Household Survey*. A comprehensive guide to government data is the *Guide to Official Statistics*, which is published by HMSO.

A second, but equally important, source of market information is provided by a number of titles, including The Economist Intelligence Unit's *Retail Business, Mintel*, and *Euromonitor*. All of these, and similar publications, provide frequent 'overviews' of specific markets which aggregate much of the information available and present it in a comprehensive form.

Thirdly, there are a number of published surveys available which will provide valuable information on different aspects of brand and consumer behaviour. These include the AGB Home Audits and Consumer Panels; Nielsen; British Audience Research Board (BARB) (which provides television viewing data); the JICNARS readership survey; and the Target Group Index (TGI), which relates the purchasing of products to media habits.

The fourth important source is the plethora of trade and specialist publications which, similarly, provide important information on issues relating to their own market areas.

It should be noted that this is but a small selection of the wide variety of published sources. For a more comprehensive listing, the reader is recommended to consult a specialist text in the field – *Marketing Research for Managers*, Crouch, S. and Housden, M., 2nd edition, Butterworth-Heinemann, 1996. Whilst the examples given above relate to the UK market, comparable sources from government and other agencies are available in most countries, and represent an important contribution to the planning process in the international context.

Understanding the market

A key area of understanding will be derived from *Usage and Attitude* (U&A) *Studies*, since these provide a consumer perspective of the brand and the market in which it exists. Whilst it is difficult to be prescriptive in this area – as with other forms of market research – there will generally be a number of specific areas which will need to be covered.

Awareness

U&A studies can indicate levels of awareness for own and competitors' products, as well as providing an indication of advertising awareness.

Usage

There are a number of dimensions of usage which it will be important to understand. On a general level, information will be required on the levels of loyalty and the propensity to trial other products on the part of the consumer. Since few consumers remain exclusively loyal to any one product – rather, they tend to build up a portfolio or repertoire of brands which they are prepared to consider as viable alternatives – it is important to understand the make up of the portfolio. On a more specific level, information will be needed on patterns of usage, in terms of frequency of purchase, source of purchase, how the product is used, on what occasions the product is used, and so on.

Attitudes

As the name suggests, a U&A study is the primary source of attitudinal information. And since marketing communications is concerned, in part, with the creation or reinforcement of attitudes, the study will provide important clues as to what potential consumers think about the brands available and their relative positionings and offerings.

Needs

Although the product purchased may be identical, the consumer needs which it fulfils may be very different. The U&A study will provide guidance as to the extent to which existing brands fulfil consumer needs and expectations and will also help in the identi-fication of potential gaps in the market. It goes without saying that it will be necessary to collect the information across a wide sample in order to enable a statistical analysis in terms of the demographic breakdown of the existing or potential market which it is desired to penetrate. U&A studies will often be supplemented with other forms of qualitative research.

For the most part, qualitative research is conducted either with small groups of individuals, or on a one-to-one basis. The specific purpose of such research is of an exploratory or investigative nature, although no attempt is made to draw definitive conclusions from the information gained. Its most important contribution is the ability to provide depth and texture to consumer information, which would not be available from quantitative studies. In some cases, the two forms of study are used in tandem. Qualitative studies are capable of making a valuable contribution to the strategic planning process because they are more flexible than the standardized form of research based on interviewing against a predetermined questionnaire. There are a number of specific areas where a qualitative approach will be favoured over a quantified one:

- to identify potential problem areas more fully, and in greater depth;
- to enable the formulation of hypotheses which can be the subject of further research study;
- to explore patterns of consumer behaviour, beliefs, attitudes and opinions;
- as a precursor to a quantitative study, where it is important to pilot questionnaires for comprehension. This is especially true within the field of marketing communications, where it is possible to explore concepts prior to further development;
- to establish the comprehension of communications campaigns both prior to and after they have been exposed to a mass audience, perhaps to assist in the identification of deficiencies in the communications process.

Qualitative research is a methodology which uniquely allows for the exploration of 'sensitive' or 'embarrassing' issues, since questions can be set in an oblique form for subsequent interpretation. Often, a one-to-one approach will enable the access to consumer information which would not be available in a group context.

Although not an ideal situation there are instances, resulting from the constraints of time or cost, where qualitative data is the only basis on which subsequent decisions are taken. This is particularly true, for example, in the development of communications concepts. It is clear that, on these occasions, there is a greater need for caution and care in interpretation than where a quantified study is used. Often, decisions will be based on the comments of a relatively small number of respondents. The importance, however, is not the *number* of respondents but the commonality of the *directions* of their responses. If a series of group discussions, say, are similarly negative in their views of an advertising proposition, then, in most cases, it is reasonable to consider dropping the particular approach in favour of some alternatives which are more positively received.

The main contribution of such studies is in terms of the group dynamics which the techniques allow for. Unlike conventional questionnaires, where the respondent is interviewed against a pre-set format, and where the aggregation of 'open-ended' comments may be difficult to interpret, group discussions enable the skilled interviewer to facilitate the interaction between respondents, and to explore their responses in far greater depth. This is of vital importance in the identification of appropriate communications dimensions.

A communications proposition may be rejected for a number of reasons. It may, for example, have the wrong tone of voice; there may be an inconsistency between the visual and verbal dimensions of the message; it may depict the wrong sort of people or environment. All of these, and other facets of the message, can be amended with relative ease in order to overcome the objections and enable the proper communication of the message which is desired. By the same token, such feedback can be instrumental in the determination of the most effective communications strategy and of defining the most appropriate positioning for the product or service in the marketplace. We will explore each of these dimensions in the sections which follow.

We have already seen that the potential consumers for a product or service can be subdivided in a variety of different ways in order to target a proposition more effectively. The socio-economic groupings, together with the important social, environmental and attitudinal factors which we have already considered, may be the basis for ensuring the differentiation of a product's positioning from that of its competitors. A great number of the initial directional indicators will derive from quantified studies, since these will enable us to dimensionalize the numbers of consumers who make up certain categories. We can, for example, separate out the number of young versus old, male versus female, high income versus middle income, and similar dimensions.

However, the point has already been made that these are relatively crude measures. It is far more important to consider the attitudinal and other dimensions which are likely to have a far greater bearing on the potential consumer's propensity to buy a particular product or service. It is clear that relatively few products are capable of satisfying all of the consumers' needs simultaneously. If we take a market such as that for instant coffee, we can see that some consumers prefer their beverage strong, while others like to drink it weak. Indeed, given the state of development of this market in most countries, it is immediately apparent that, on this one dimension alone, there are several distinct groups of consumers whose needs will require a somewhat different product delivery. The process of identifying these differing needs and requirements is of vital importance in the process of product positioning and the determination of the appropriate marketing communications strategy. By using the appropriate market research techniques we can develop market 'maps', which enable us to see the relative positions of the various brands available in the market.

We can approach this process from two different perspectives. On the one hand, we can identify factors which relate to product differentiation, such as those just described. Here we are concerned to identify the various product attributes which are considered desirable by differing groups of consumers. Alternatively, we can examine the market from the standpoint of the consumers' attitudes and behavioural patterns. We have already seen that, in many markets, product differentiation alone between competing brands is insufficient to achieve the differentiation of competing brands in the eyes of the consumer. The inevitable consequence of converging technology is the fact that competing products rapidly become almost indistinguishable from each other. Yet it remains true that consumers adopt very different attitudes towards those same brands based on key dimensions of image. Market research will enable us to identify the image dimensions and to scale them according to the importance which is attached to them by the consumer.

There are two strategic options at this stage.

The first is to seek to reinforce consumer perceptions if the brand's position is similar to that desired by consumers. The alternative is to seek to alter brand perceptions if it is found that the brand position differs. An excellent example of perceptual mapping is demonstrated in a recent paper outlining the contribution of advertising to the Levi Strauss Jeans brand in Europe (Baker, 1993).

In 1990, the agency Bogle, Bartle, Hegarty and its client undertook a major qualitative research study among young European males to identify the attitudes and behaviour with regard to the Levi brand. Some fifty group discussions were held throughout seven separate countries. The primary purpose of the study was to identify the role played by the

advertising in the creation of a consistent brand image across the variety of local markets. What emerged presented a fascinating picture both of the particular market and, more importantly, the relevance of the technique.

Marketing communications research

Any product or service is an amalgam of values which are presented to the consumer and reinterpreted by him or her into some form of whole. Inevitably, therefore, there are many factors beyond those of the product ingredients which influence the consumer to purchase or to refrain from purchasing a particular item.

However, the brand comprises a series of dimensions which are mostly perceptual and intangible. These include the brand name, the reputation of the parent company, quality and value perceptions, and the influences of external forces, such as the recommendations of others. Marketing communications plays a vital role in establishing these dimensions and reinforcing them in the minds of the potential consumer. And, here again, market research can make an important contribution both to the understanding of the important dimensions and in minimizing the potential problems resulting from poorly constructed communications messages.

Brand positioning and personality

Segmentation analysis and perceptual mapping techniques enable the creation of a detailed picture in which the brand exists, embracing both consumer typology and product differentiation. By identifying where the brand sits in relation to its competitors, marketing communications can then seek to reinforce the position or to change it. Similarly, we can identify the factors which serve to differentiate the brand from its competitors and provide it with a unique personality in the marketplace.

Brand promise

Marketing communications needs to provide 'evidence' for the consumer to accept the promise of the brand. This may involve the depiction of a tangible benefit resulting from some emotional value – for example, testimonial advertising showing 'people like me' who are satisfied with the performance of a brand.

Effective reach of target consumers

Specific research into patterns of television viewing, newspaper readership and so on is used to assist in the determination of both media strategy and execution. However, there is an increasingly important dimension of research – to identify the appropriateness of the media environment. If we accept Marshall McCluhan's statement that 'the medium is the message', then it follows that the environment in which the advertising is seen will have an important bearing on image dimensions.

Häagen Dazs determined that, in order to achieve a high-quality positioning in the minds of its consumers, and to differentiate itself from other, 'run of the mill', ice-creams, it would only use quality titles in which to place its advertising. The synergy between the medium and the message was apparent. In this instance, the surrounding 'noise' has a 'halo effect' on the advertising, and the same principle applies equally to the placement of an advertising message within specific television programmes.

The contribution to strategic direction

Market research has an important role to play in this context. Before we can determine the nature of the communications message itself, we must first identify the appropriate direction for the communications strategy. This, in turn, is dependent on the corporate direction and marketing strategy identified for the company. Several distinct communications strategies can be identified, and their appropriateness needs to be considered in the context of any marketing communications campaign.

Pioneer strategy

When a company creates a completely new product and, in the process, establishes a new market category, the purpose of the communications message is to ensure that potential consumers are told of the product's existence, its functions, its usage and the location of purchase. When, for example, Sony first introduced the Walkman, the support activity designed for the brand took on these characteristics. Similarly, when Swatch was introduced, it was important that it was not simply seen as just another watch. The marketing communications programme sought to position the product in the vein of a fashion accessory which offered other dimensions than simply telling the time. Inevitably, the thrust of pioneer activity is to develop a market category, rather than simply emphasizing the benefits of the brand.

Competitive strategy

Once a category has been established, it is likely that new entrants will begin to compete with the original brand. Accordingly, the owners of that brand must enter a phase of *competitive* communications. The imperative is to differentiate the brand from its competitors, and to isolate those features and benefits – real or perceived – which will induce potential purchasers to select that brand rather than others.

Defensive strategy

A third strategy will be that of *defensive* marketing communications, designed to offset the impact of competitive pressures. A good example of this can be seen in the current UK newspaper market, where each move taken by one title is immediately matched by a comparable move by one or more of its competitors.

In their book, *Integrated Marketing Communications* (1992), Shultz, Tannenbaum and Lauterborn identify eight key facets of the marketing communications strategy:

1 The need to pinpoint customer segments.
2 To identify a competitive benefit.
3 To understand how the consumer positions the brand.
4 To establish a unique, unified brand personality which differentiates the brand from its competitors.
5 To establish real and perceived reasons why the consumer should believe the promise of the brand.
6 To identify the means by which consumers can be reached effectively.
7 To establish the criteria for monitoring success or failure.
8 To determine the need for additional research which would further help refine the strategy.

In each of these areas of strategy determination, research techniques are available to assist the process.

Undeniably, market research has a vital role to play in all aspects of marketing and marketing communications. The techniques available are continuously being explored and developed to ensure that we gain a great facility in understanding the key consumer processes and the ways in which decisions are made as to which brand (if any) should be purchased. As Alan Hedges (1998) described it, 'Research can heighten the understanding of the market and of the consumer so that we can better understand the job that advertising has to do and the climate in which it has to operate'.

References

Baker, C. (ed), 'Jeans Sans Frontières', *Advertising Works 7*, Institute of Practitioners in Advertising/NTC, 1993

Engel, J. F., Kollat, D. T. and Blackwell, R. D., *Consumer Behaviour*, Holt, Rinehart and Winston, 1968

Hedges, A., *Testing to Destruction*, 2nd edition, revised by Ford-Hutchinson, S. and Hunter-Stewart, M., IPA), 1998

Howard, J. A. and Sheth, J. N., *The Theory of Buyer Behaviour*, Wiley, 1969

Katona, G. in Koch, S. (ed.), *Psychology: A Study of a Science*, McGraw-Hill, 1963

Nicosia, F., *Consumer Decision Processes: Marketing and Advertising Implications*, Prentice Hall, 1966

Plummer, J., 'The Concept and Application of Lifestyle Segmentation', *Journal of Marketing*, January 1974

Shultz, D., Tannenbaum, S. I. and Lauterborn, R. F., *Integrated Marketing Communications*, NTC Business Books, 1992

Solomon, M. R., *Consumer Behaviour*, 3rd edition, Prentice Hall International, 1996

Upshaw, L. B., *Building Brand Identity – A Strategy for Success in a Hostile Marketplace*, John Wiley & Sons, 1995

Webster, F. and Wind, Y., 'A General Model for Understanding Organisational Buying Behaviour', *Journal of Marketing*, No. 2, 1973

Additional reading

To gain a deeper understanding of issues relating to consumer and organizational behaviour, students may wish to consider the following texts:

Evans, Martin J., Moutinho, Luiz and Van Raaij, W. Fred, *Applied Consumer Behaviour*, 1996, Addison-Wesley

Chisnall, Peter M., *Consumer Behaviour*, 3rd edition, 1994, McGraw-Hill

Engel, James F., Blackwell, Roger D. and Miniard, Paul W., *Consumer Behaviour*, 8th international edition, 1995, The Dryden Press

Solomon, Michael R., *Consumer Behaviour*, 3rd edition, 1996, Prentice Hall

To provide knowledge in the fields of segmentation and the marketing environment, two texts will assist:

McDonald, Malcolm and Dunbar, Ian, *Market Segmentation*, 1995, Macmillan Press
Palmer, Adrian and Hartley, Bob, *The Business and Marketing Environment*, 2nd edition, 1996, McGraw-Hill

In the field of marketing research, the following will add to an understanding of the key issues:

Crouch, Sunny and Housden, Matthew, *Marketing Research for Managers*, 2nd edition, 1996, Butterworth-Heinemann

Crimp, Margaret and Wright, Len Tiu, *The Marketing Research Process*, 4th edition, 1995, Prentice Hall

More specific texts in the field of marketing communications research include:

Fletcher, Alan D. and Bowers, Thomas A., *Fundamentals of Advertising Research*, 4th edition, 1991, John Wiley and Sons
Haskins, Jack and Kendrick, Alice, *Successful Advertising Research Methods*, 1993, NTC Business Books

CHAPTER 3

Product and service strategies

- To appreciate the importance of managing products during the life cycle;
- To consider the nature and advantages of branding;
- To gain insight into the branding process;
- To examine the strategic dimensions of branding;
- To consider the relationship between branding and consumer perceptions;
- To explain the roles of marketing communications in the branding process;
- To become familiar with the challenges facing brands;
- To examine the dimensions of service brands.

Managing products and services over the life cycle

In many ways, an understanding of brands underpins much of what we attempt to achieve within the field of marketing communications, since, of course, the brand is at the centre of all such activity. Ultimately, the key responsibility of brand management is to sustain and develop the product or service for which they are responsible in such a way that it can respond positively to all eventualities.

The stewardship of the brand remains the singular goal of management, since it is the profitability of those brands which will determine the eventual survival of the companies which own them.

Major brands represent significant commercial value to their owners. Table 3.1, representing the twenty largest UK brands, reveals that even the twentieth is worth over £100 million.

The importance of brands (and their sustenance) is exemplified by the fact that many of the brands which occupy positions of leadership today were introduced as long as 100 or more years ago. Coca Cola, Anchor Butter and Heinz were all first launched in the 1880s, whilst Mars is a product of the 1920s. Only nine of the top fifty UK brands were launched since 1975. The significance of developing a strong brand is underpinned by a study conducted by Buzzell and Gale (1987), which indicated that strong brands achieve significantly more profit than their weaker counterparts. Their research of some 2600 businesses revealed that products with a market share of 40 per cent are capable of generating a return on investment three times greater than those with a share of 10 per cent. Moreover, according to the *Financial Times* (23 June 1997), 'Companies which base their businesses on brands have outperformed the stockmarket in the past 15 years'.

Table 3.1 UK's top twenty brands 1997

Brand	Owner	Estimated sales value (£ million)
Coca Cola	Coca Cola	>£542
Walkers	PepsiCo	£385–390
Nescafé	Nestlé	£245–250
Ariel	Procter & Gamble	£220–225
Andrex Toilet Tissues	Kimberley-Clark	£185–190
Pampers Nappies	Procter & Gamble	£185–190
Persil	Lever Bros.	£180–185
Pepsi	PepsiCo	£180–185
Robinsons	Britvic	£160–165
Whiskas	Pedigree Petfoods	£140–145
Kit Kat	Nestlé Rowntree	£140–145
Muller Yoghurt	Muller	£135–140
Ribena	SmithKline Beecham	£130–135
Bells Whisky	United Distillers	£120–125
Flora	Van Den Bergh	£125–130
Mars Bar	Mars	£120–125
Tetley Tea	Tetley	£115–120
Heinz Soup	H. J. Heinz	£115–120
Anchor	Anchor Foods	£115–120
Felix	Spillers Foods	£115–120

Source: Marketing/A. C. Nielsen, *Marketing*, 3 July, 1997

Branding itself is a comparatively recent process, evolving from the essential need for manufacturers to distinguish their products and services from the commodity sectors within which they operate. There is considerable debate as to when the process of branding began. It has been argued (Griffiths, 1992) that Sunlight Soap was one of the first true brands. William Lever recognized that consumers were dissatisfied with the characteristics of unbranded soap products then available. They were inconsistent in quality, smelt unpleasant, offered no consistency in weight and no packaging. Products were produced by a crude process of mixing tallow and the remnants of raw alkali in large cauldrons into large bars which were to be sliced into lengths by the grocer. The Sunlight brand remedied these defects. In February 1884 Lever registered the brand name and in 1885 created a formula comprising a mix of coconut and cottonseed oil, resin and tallow. The formula remained unchanged for many years. By the 1890s, the company was producing nearly 40 000 tons of soap. The process followed by Lever encapsulates some of the roles of branding.

Branding definitions

'A brand is defined as a name, term, design, symbol, or any other feature that identifies one seller's good or service as distinct from those of other sellers. A brand name may identify one item, a family of items, or all items of that seller.' (Bennett, 1988)

'A successful brand is an identifiable product, service, person or place, augmented in such a way that the buyer or user perceives relevant unique added values which match their needs most closely. Furthermore, its success results from being able to sustain these added values in the face of competition.' (de Chernatony and McDonald, 1992)

We will see below how the process of branding creates a unique identity for a product or service in the mind of the consumer and, with it, a level of distinctiveness which sets it apart from all its competitors. Reassurance derives from the fact that the consumer can readily identify the maker of the product and consider the company reputation and, importantly in the context of marketing communications activity, it provides the sense of focus for the promotion of the brand.

Strategic importance of branding

Branding offers important advantages to the manufacturer and consumer alike. By branding a product, the manufacturer can obtain legal protection for its composition and other features in order to avoid the problems of being copied by competitors. It creates a unique identity in the marketplace which assists in the process of attracting consumers who, over time, will establish patterns of loyalty to the product and, in turn, will enable the company to enhance its profitability. In many instances, branding enables manufacturers to charge a premium price for their products by associating a desirable image with it for which consumers may be encouraged to pay a higher price. It assists the manufacturer to plan his inventory more efficiently and to ensure the rapid processing of orders. Finally, it helps in the process of segmenting markets by providing distinctive product offerings designed to

satisfy the needs of smaller groups of consumers.

A critical element of the debate is an understanding of the fact that, for the most part, consumers are unable to differentiate between competing products. 'Most markets have a convergence of brands. They look alike, taste the same and have the same formulation. Brand choice is no longer about the rational product attributes. It is, and increasingly will be, all about brand personality' (Sampson, 1993). In most instances, the core product offered by a manufacturer may be indistinguishable from that of his competitors. Indeed, given the nature of technology, the specific product advantages which one manufacturer has over his competitors will often be readily and rapidly duplicated by them.

In countless 'blind taste' tests, consumers are unable to identify the identity of the brands and often select as 'the best' a product which they decry once the brand names are revealed. The perennial example of Coca Cola versus Pepsi serves to illustrate. In a direct comparison of the brands with the identities concealed, the preferences expressed were:

Prefer Pepsi	51%
Prefer Coke	44%
Equal/Can't say	5%

Once the brand identities were revealed, the following preferences were expressed:

Prefer Pepsi	23%
Prefer Coke	65%
Equal/Can't say	12%

(*Source*: de Chernatony and McDonald, 1992)

During the 1980s, the Stella Artois 'Reassuringly Expensive' campaign captured the spirit of the times and resulted in the brand becoming number one in the premium lager market. Interestingly, the brand comes last in blind taste tests! Add the brand name and it becomes first choice – a clear demonstration of the power of brand potency overcoming the limitations of product reality (Duckworth, 1996).

The consumer also benefits. Branding provides the potential buyer with a reassurance of quality. Consumers can reasonably expect that a branded product will, other things being equal, offer a consistency over time. Brands enhance the process of shopping, since consumers can rapidly identify products and services with which they are familiar. Finally, they enable consumers to identify new products in which they might be interested.

Strategic brand building

'Most people in marketing would agree that success will depend on developing skills in brand building. That is, using all the company's particular assets to create unique entities that certain customers really want; entities which have a lasting personality, based on a special combination of physical, functional and psychological values; and which have a competitive advantage in at least one area of marketing.' (King, 1991)

Peter Doyle, writing in *Excellence in Advertising* (1997), suggests that to succeed, a brand must have sustainable differential advantage. He argues that 'differential advantage' is the reason why consumers prefer the brand to those provided by competitors. 'Sustainable' is the provision of an advantage that is not easily copied by competitors. He further asserts that brands only become assets to the company if they possess both of these attributes. Brands which are negative (Lada, Hoover) achieve their profits as a result of property or distribution arrangements rather than as a result of differential advantage. Importantly, brands depreciate if they do not receive constant investment (Yardley's is a good example). However strong a brand may be, unless it continues to receive investment in the form of quality enhancement, service dimensions and brand image, then the brand will, inevitably, decline.

Successful brands are those which create a distinctive image or personality. By associating particular attributes with a brand, the product is differentiated in the minds of the consumers. Attributes may be real and tangible, such as product performance, value for money, or other aspects of quality, or emotional and intangible, providing status or being associated with trendiness.

A slightly different perspective is offered by Southgate (1994), who identifies branding as initially being purely a defensive device – to make it harder for the competition to steal one's products. In fact, branding is both defensive and aggressive. A strong brand will actively communicate with potential customers on a variety of levels, providing them with all manner of reasons to buy a product or service.

The dimensions of branding

The dimensions of a brand are visually depicted in Figure 3.1, taken from *Creating Powerful Brands* by Leslie de Chernatony and Malcolm McDonald (1992).

At the centre of the branding task is the core product. This may or may not be different from the products of competitive manufacturers. Indeed, increasingly, it is unlikely that there will be any significant difference at a level which the consumer can discriminate. What makes it different are the perceptual and tangible values which are associated with the core product and which are depicted above. Any or each of these important dimensions can be used by a company to distinguish its product or service from those of its competitors.

'A product is something that is made in a factory; a brand is something that is bought by a consumer. A product can be copied by a competitor; a brand is unique. A product can be quickly outdated; a successful brand, properly managed, can be timeless.' (King, 1996)

To the consumer, a product is something that satisfies needs or provides a solution to a particular problem. It is important to recognize that these needs are just as likely to be emotional as they are to be functional and

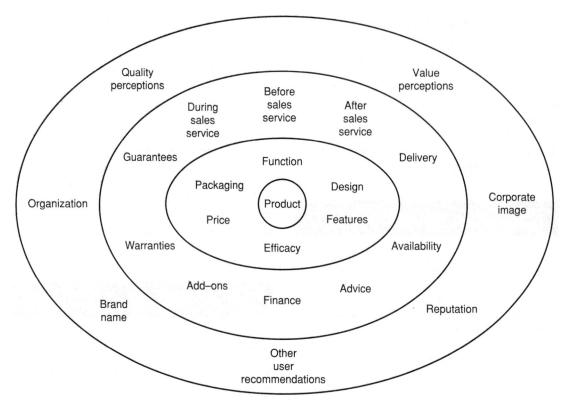

Figure 3.1

economic. The capacity of a product to fulfil the consumer's needs and desires are what, over time, builds its value.

It must be remembered, of course, that not all of the listed dimensions apply to all products and services. In some instances, the tangible aspects of the proposition will be more important; in others, differentiation may be achieved as a result of the quality of the services – before, during and after sales, guarantees, etc. – which are provided; in yet other instances, it will be the brand image and identity which will assume the greatest level of importance.

The brand name

Branding and packaging are the overt and tangible aspects of a product, and serve to distinguish a manufacturer's product from that of his competitors. In the crowded retail environment, it is these aspects of the product which assist the brand in standing out from the crowd.

Most brand names are made up of letters and numbers, and in some instances may also include an additional graphic design which is unique to that product. In most instances, manufacturers will register these logo designs to ensure legal protection of their mark, and to avoid the risks of 'passing off'. Bass Beer, with its red triangle logo, became the first registered trademark in the UK.

The source of brand names is interesting. BMW, for example, derives from Bayerische Motorenwerke; Aktien Gesellschaft für Anilinfabrikation becomes AGFA, whilst the first two letters from Durability and Reliability and one from Excellence spell out Durex. Joel Cheek named his instant coffee after the first hotel that agreed to try the product – Maxwell House; Adi Dassler created Adidas from his own name, as did the founder of IKEA, Ingvar Kampryd, who combined his initials with those of his home town and the farm where he was born. Nivea is taken from the Latin for snow white – *nivis*; and Hovis derives from *hominis vis* (the strength of man). Other names derive from 'functional' aspects of the product. The detergent, Daz, gets its name from a derivation of the product benefit – 'Dazzle'.

It is important to remember that in most cases a brand name will only be protected within the specific category of trading and thus other manufacturers will, potentially, be free to use the same name in another category. In the 1960s Granada, which had registered the name in the context of television production, TV rental and associated areas, attempted to preclude its use by Ford in the automotive industry. The legal case was decided in favour of Ford, and they were able to retain the use of the name for a range of cars.

Brand image

If, for one moment, we strip away the brand marks of Levi, Kellogg's, Cadbury's, Mercedes, and Johnson and Johnson, to name but a few, we are left with commodity products shorn of all of the brand values which are associated with those names. All the investment made by those companies over many years into the creation of image values through the use of marketing communications is lost. It is the function of marketing communications to establish a series of defined images and values in the minds of consumers which are instantly recalled on exposure to the brand name. Consumers buy brands. Thus, the loyalty which the brand identity can create in the marketplace is fundamental to the ability of a company to offset competitive activities.

The brand values are equally important to the company in terms of its longer-term extension of activities. Many brand names

have positive values associated with them which extend beyond the particular product with which the name is identified. These intangible values can be used by the company to extend its portfolio into other areas. Within the soap and detergent markets, two brands stand out as examples of the positive values of branding. 'Fairy' and 'Persil' have both been used as brands which have taken their owners into extended categories by the association of related new products with the positive values built up around those names.

'It is not sufficient to measure the rational attributes of a brand alone. That gives only a partial picture. The emotional attributes must also be measured to obtain the complete picture. And it is the emotional benefits that usually account for brand choice, to a larger degree than rational ones.' (Sampson, 1993)

The brand personality

One of the key issues in contemporary marketing communications is that of the brand personality, described by the advertising agency, J. Walter Thompson, in their *Directory of Market Research Terminology*, as 'The total impression created in the consumer's mind by a brand and all its associations, functional and non-functional'.

Since, as we have seen, few consumers can differentiate between products on purely functional grounds, other dimensions become important to their task of product selection. Over time, brands – substantially as a result of the investment made through marketing communications – develop a 'personality' of their own. They are seen by consumers to be 'young' or 'old', 'fashionable and trendy' or 'boring and out of date'. Inevitably, this is a major reflection of the contribution made by the tools of advertising and promotion, which serve to invest brands with a particular image.

'Consumers should feel that by buying a particular brand they are buying into their desired way of life or derived personality, that the brand is a symbol of external gratification.' (Sampson, 1993)

Brand protection

If the positive values associated with a brand are sufficiently strong, it will enable the owner to overcome major problems with product quality. Both in the UK and elsewhere, major brands have suffered from such things as contaminants, which have required the company to withdraw temporarily from the market. Early in 1990, some bottles of Perrier were found to contain benzene. Despite its dominant presence, and the obvious implications of its decision, the company determined to remove all stocks of its products from the shelves of supermarkets and other outlets. Advertising and public relations were used to inform the public of the action the company had taken and, following exhaustive research to eliminate the problem, the brand was relaunched. The fact that Perrier was able to regain much of its market share is a testament both to the strength of the brand name and to the positive approach taken by the company in dealing with the issue.

In the United States, Tylenol suffered similar problems when a dangerous chemical was introduced into a few containers on retailers' shelves. A similar response in dealing with the problem enabled the brand to return to the market with many of the values associated with the name intact.

The issue is one which, unfortunately (in the context of what it says about society), requires to be addressed by marketers. In the very recent past, several products have been removed from supermarket shelves following the disclosure of tampering with the product contents, sometimes with disastrous consequences for the purchaser. The issue of brand protection is an important one, both in a domestic and an international context, and we will return to the topic throughout this chapter.

Other uses of the brand

Brand names and identities may be used in a variety of other ways. Once a brand has built up a high level of recognition among consumers, it may be sold or leased to other manufacturers to provide them with an immediate entry into another sector of the market.

Mars demonstrated the power of their brands with their move into the ice-cream market. Despite the fact that the company had no prior representation within the sector, the values associated with the names of Mars, Bounty and others gave an immediate identity to the ice-cream products which bore these logos. This issue will be considered in more detail in the section on brand stretch.

Brand valuation

Although the value of branding has been long understood, it was brought into sharp focus with the valuation of the brand name of Guinness on the balance sheet during the Distillers' take-over battle. The practice has been followed by others, ensuring that the valuation of brands is given close consideration, since the value placed upon them may exceed the value of the tangible assets of a company. The brand has increasingly come to represent an important financial asset to the company which owns it. Rupert Murdoch capitalized the value of some of his newspaper titles. In 1985, Reckitt and Colman capitalized Airwick, followed two years later by GrandMet, who capitalized Pillsbury following its acquisition. In 1988 the real debate commenced when Rank Hovis McDougall identified more than fifty *existing* brands on its balance sheet with a combined value of £678 million. Thus, the goodwill represented by these brands was worth almost 60 per cent of the total value of the company.

In 1988, Philip Morris, the American food and tobacco company, bought Kraft for $12.9 billion, approximately four times the worth of the company's tangible assets. In the same year, Nestlé bought Rowntree for $4.5 billion – more than five times Rowntree's book value.

Table 3.2 Monetary value of strong brands	
Rank	*Return on investment %*
Market leaders	
Dominator	34
Marginal leader	26
Competitors	
No 2	21
No 3	16
Followers	12

Source: PIMS data

Aside from the financial implications of brand valuation, the topic is an important one in marketing terms for other reasons.

Philip Barnard (1993) of the Research International Group identified the monetary value of strong brands (Table 3.2).

Brand equity

There are two contrasting views of brand equity. On the one hand, there is the financial perspective. Here, the brand is viewed as an asset which can be used to deliver incremental cash flows. Thus, brands with greater brand equity can be expected to result in greater market shares, opportunities for premium pricing, reduced promotional costs, and increased trade leverage. The alternative is the marketing view of brand equity. In essence, this views the situation from the perspective of the consumer. Those brands which have achieved substantial equity are those which can sustain a platform of premium quality, differentiated clear imagery, and a uniqueness of proposition.

O'Shaughnessy (1995) defines brand equity as 'the set of assets such as name awareness,

loyal customers, perceived quality and other associations that are linked to a brand'.

Brand equity needs to be defined with some degree of precision. Uncles (1995) suggests that Interbrand's checklist of characteristics is a good starting point – market leadership, market growth, advertising and promotional support, internationality, technological stability, brand trend and brand protection. The company has developed a specific approach to brand valuation which consists of both objective and subjective evaluations of the brand performance and, currently, is one of the most widely used devices for assessment of a brand's strengths and weaknesses.

There are a series of important components of brand equity:

- *Perceived quality* is a measure of brand equity which, in research, has been shown to correlate closely to sales performance, price sensitivity and company value;
- *Salience* indicates the proportion of people who have sufficient knowledge of a brand to rate its equity;
- *Association* of a brand with positive images – the strength of the linkage of positive and relevant images to a brand;
- *Customer satisfaction*;
- *Customer loyalty* is an indicator of market success and of the strength of a brand;
- *Likelihood* to purchase on next occasion;
- *Willingness to recommend* – reflects level of regard for a brand;
- *Price premium potential* – the extent to which a brand is able to command a premium over the price of other products in its category.

In a recent paper, Alan Cooper and Paul Simmons (1997) have added an important new dimension to the consideration of brand equity. They suggest that brand equity consists of three elements:

1 *Brand description* – the image and associations that a brand has. This includes its distinctiveness, its quality, and the esteem in which it is held.

2 *Brand strength* is the prominence and relative dominance of that brand, which is based on levels of awareness, penetration, loyalty and personal involvement on the part of consumers.

3 *Brand future* is the additional new dimension proposed by the authors of this paper. This not only reflects the brand's ability to thrive despite future changes in legislation, technology, retail structure and consumer patterns, but it also indicates its growth potential.

Despite this ongoing debate, comparatively few companies use a brand valuation approach. A survey conducted by a specialist business research agency, Business Marketing Services, on behalf of Public Dialogue, among 120 senior marketing decision makers identified that only 23 per cent of the sample used brand valuations as a measure of marketing performance, and only 12 per cent included brand valuations in their balance sheets. Despite this, some 67 per cent of respondents believed that brand valuations would become more important over the next few years (High, 1994).

In *The Economist* of 14 November 1996, the value of the physical components of McDonald's – which Interbrand named as the world's leading brand, overtaking Coca Cola for the first time – was calculated as being worth $17 billion. At that time, the value of the company on the New York Stock Exchange stood at $33 billion. The difference of $16 billion can be attributed to the brand value. Paul Polman, of Procter & Gamble, asserted that the difference between his company's market value – around £37 billion – and the accountants' estimate of its asset value – around £8 billion – is largely made up by the value of the brands. Similarly, Grand Metropolitan's brands are worth £2.8 billion – 70 per cent of total shareholder funds.

Strong brand equity can be a powerful defence against competitive incursions and new product launches. It provides the brand owner with a springboard for brand extension, not just brand growth.

Branding strategy

We can discriminate between a series of very different branding strategies adopted by companies:

- Manufacturer branding
    Multi-product branding
    Multi-branding
    Combination branding
- Mixed branding
- Private branding
- Generic branding

Manufacturer branding

A key decision to be taken by all manufacturers is the branding policy towards the products which they introduce to the market.

In some instances, the manufacturer will choose to adopt a *multi-product* branding strategy. Here, the manufacturer uses the strength of the parent name to communicate a series of common values which 'endorse' all of the products which bear that name. Undeniably, there has been a gradual shift from product branding to umbrella branding (3M, Heinz); or dual branding (Nestlé and Kit Kat); or co-branding arrangements with complementary businesses (IBM Personal Computers and Intel chips, Diet Coke and NutraSweet).

Sony and JVC, for example, have both established strong reputations within various sectors of the consumer electronics market. Whether the consumer is intending to purchase a television, a CD player or a video recorder, the endorsement and reputation of the parent company singles out the appropriate product as being worthy of consideration. The name of Kellogg's is synonymous with breakfast cereals and that of Colgate with dental care. The same principle is equally true within the service sector. Products such as 'Liquid Gold' benefit from the endorsement of the parent company – the Leeds Building Society. Similarly, the standing of the

Automobile Association lends credibility to its offering of car and other insurance facilities.

Usually, although not always, manufacturers restrict such activity to directly related markets, since it can be reasonably expected that the products all have common values and attributes. If, for example, the consumer perceives the names of Black & Decker or Bosch as being those of manufacturers of quality power tools, those names can reasonably be expected to carry a similar weight within the broader do-it-yourself markets. Both of those companies have moved into gardening tools, for example.

In many instances, manufacturers maintain several brand names which are used to endorse separate market categories, but the names are kept distinct from each other to avoid the creation of confusion in the mind of the consumer. For example, Gillette maintains its name for the personal care market, but uses the Braun brand for the related electrical appliances market, embracing dry shaving, electric hair dryers and toothbrushes, and, so on.

Multi-branding is a strategy adopted by those manufacturers who choose to keep the parent name subservient to the end-user. For example, the name of Procter & Gamble is little known by consumers, although the brands they produce are all major players in their respective markets. P&G is the manufacturer of a variety of brands including, among many others, Ariel and Daz in the detergents market, Oil of Ulay (Olay), Vicks, Pampers and Pantène.

In some instances, the benefit of a multi-branding approach is that it enables the parent manufacturer to have competing products within the same sector of the market. This principle can be seen from the example of Procter & Gamble above, as well as Kraft, Jacobs, Suchard (itself a subsidiary of Philip Morris) which maintains several brands of coffee, including Maxwell House, Kenco and Mellow Birds, and Gevalia which variously compete with each other in different sectors of the market. This same principle is adopted in

the retail environment where, for example, Dixons has the same parent as Curry's, as does The Link and PC World. Each chain presents a different image and identity to the potential consumer, allowing for more appropriate targeting of differing consumer needs.

An important dimension of multiple branding which deserves mention is the use of third party endorsement. Increasingly, manufacturers are recognizing the importance of names which may be only distantly related to the product category as underpins to the product message. When P&G acquired the name of Vidal Sassoon, it was used to establish major credibility in the hair care sector. By the same token, the addition of names like Chanel and other couture houses has added a believable dimension to products which might otherwise not be distinguishable from their competitors.

In certain instances, typified by the approach of Nestlé, a *combination* approach is taken, where the parent name is used to endorse some products – directly or indirectly – but where others are left to stand alone. In the instant coffee market, for example, the brand name for their main product is a derivation of that of the parent company – Nescafé; Gold Blend, their premium quality product, is endorsed with the Nescafé logo; in the cereals, confectionery and other markets, the Nestlé symbol is used alongside that of brand names such as Cheerios and Kit Kat; whilst in the bottled water market, the name of Perrier is left to stand alone.

Mixed branding

Several manufacturers adopt a mixed branding approach to distinguish between products which they manufacture under their own brand names and identities and those which are supplied to retailers and packaged with their retail identities. Although several manufacturers have refused to supply product to private label – including Kellogg's – and, indeed, have used advertising to communicate that fact, others, such as Allied

Bakeries, United Biscuits, Dalgety and Britvic, to name just a few, simultaneously sell products under their own brand names to compete on-shelf with retail competitors which they have supplied.

Private branding

Within the retail sector, operators are becoming increasingly concerned with issues relating to branding. For many years they were content to use their operating name on the products which were manufactured on their behalf and sold by them. Consumers derived their perceptions from the support activity which surrounded the store identity. Retailers such as Sainsbury's, Safeway and others developed distinctive positionings within the marketplace in relation to quality, value for money and other dimensions, and the products which bore their logos reflected those values.

In recent years, however, the retailers have seen the need to elevate their own (private label) products to brand status. Sainsbury's introduced Novon – a range of washing powder and liquid products – and Gio – a competitor in the soft drinks market – with a distinctive identity. More recently, Tesco have announced a brand called 'Unbelievable' to compete with Unilever's 'I Can't Believe It's Not Butter'. Safeway maintains a comprehensive range of products with distinctive packaging and identities to compete with manufacturers' brands. We will consider other aspects of 'look-alike' brands later in this chapter.

Generic branding

In some instances, manufacturers or retailers have been content to sell their products under generic or 'no brand' identities. Often, this stance is taken to emphasize dimensions such as value for money. The notion of the 'white pack' originated in France to provide consumers with a range of 'no frills' products at considerable discounts against conventional

brands. The approach has met with mixed success, although there is little doubt that many of those consumers who purchased products packaged in this way expressed satisfaction and rated them highly in terms of value for money.

Onkvisit and Shaw (1989) provide an overview of the possible branding scenarios in their paper (Table 3.3).

Brands and consumer perceptions

Brands continue to maintain a considerable price premium, despite expressions to the contrary. It was anticipated that pressure on disposable income during the recession would force consumers progressively towards cheaper products. A sample pricing comparison between major brands and those bearing the Tesco name was carried out by Leo Burnett and reported in *Marketing* magazine (7 April, 1994). It revealed a differential of some 87 per cent in favour of branded goods. The same study, using Infoscan NMRA data, across market categories, revealed that the brand leader average price was some 45 per cent above that of private label products. Significantly, they also enjoyed a premium of around 10 per cent against secondary brands.

A contemporary study (Buck and Passingham, 1997) reinforces these findings. From an analysis of the AGB Superpanel data, involving over 10 000 respondents, the study found that consumers were continuing to pay a significant premium for branded products, as Table 3.4 shows:

Both studies support the belief that, although many consumers suggest that there is little to choose between branded and private label products, the perceptual values continue to be vitally important. The consequence is that major brands continue to hold significant shares of their market sectors.

Table 3.3 Advantages and disadvantages of branding

	Advantages	Disadvantages
No brand	Lower production cost Lower marketing cost Lower legal cost Flexible quality and quantity control	Severe price competition Lack of market identity
Branding	Better identification and awareness Better chance for product differentiation Possible brand loyalty Possible premium pricing	Higher production costs Higher marketing costs Higher legal costs
Private brand	Better margins for dealers Possibility for larger market share No promotional problems	Severe price competition Lack of market identity

Manufacturer's brand	Better price due to more price
	  inelasticity
	Retention of brand loyalty
	Better bargaining power
	Better control of distribution
		Difficulties for small manufacturers with
		  unknown brand or identity
		Brand promotion required

Single brand (in one market)	Marketing efficiency
	More focused marketing permitted
	Brand confusion eliminated
	Advantage for product with good
	  reputation
		Market homogeneity assumed
		Existing brand image damaged when
		  trading up or down
		Limited shelf space

Multiple brands (in one market)	Market segmented for varying needs Competitive spirit created Negative connotation of existing brand avoided More retail shelf space gained Existing brand image not damaged Possible halo effect	Higher marketing costs Higher inventory costs Loss of economies of scale

Local brands	Meaningful names
	Local identification
	Avoidance of taxation on international
	  brand
	Quick market penetration as a result of
	  acquiring local brand
	Variations of quality and quantity across
	  markets allowed
		Higher marketing costs
		Higher inventory costs
		Loss of economies of scale
		Diffused image

Worldwide brands	Maximum marketing efficiency
	Reduction of advertising costs
	Elimination of brand confusion
	Advantage of culture-free product
	Advantage of prestigious product
	Easy identification and recognition for
	  international travellers
	Uniform world-wide image
		Market homogeneity assumed
		Problems with grey and black market
		Possibility of negative associations
		Quality and quantity consistency
		  required
		Local opposition and resentment
		Legal complications

Table 3.4   Average prices in Tesco stores

Category	Premium brand	Tesco own label	Tesco 'Value' label
Instant coffee	185 p	139 p	57 p
Baked beans	33 p	23 p	10 p
Cola	65 p	30 p	13 p
Washing up liquid	136 p	82 p	20 p
Muesli	202 p	156 p	132 p
Yoghurt	184 p	161 p	95 p
Average index	100	69	35

Source: AGB Superpanel, 1997

We have already seen that consumer perceptions are influenced by a variety of internal and external factors. However, we have also seen that marketing communications plays an important role in influencing those perceptions and the creation of images which go far beyond the normal functional factors which may affect the choice of a brand. There are, of course, some areas where these added values may indeed be real and tangible. Virgin Airlines are currently stressing several key dimensions of their service delivery in their business class advertising – additional seating room; provision of in-air 'lounge facilities'; choice of movies; car pick-up at destination; and so on. In most cases, however, especially with low-involvement products – which include the vast majority of fast-moving consumer goods – it is the combination of the physical attributes of a brand, together with the values created by marketing communications, which are important to the creation of perceptual values.

In an article in *Campaign* magazine (5 August, 1994), Max Burt, then at Abbott Mead Vickers BBDO, argued that it is the brand personality which is the key to sparking consumer desire. We need to consider the impressions of the brand that are left, beyond the actual message being communicated. He cites, among others, Tango, John Smith's, Courage Best and Foster's as examples where the personality created by advertising is a major contributor to the consumer's propensity to purchase the brand. In many instances, the consumer may be more concerned with the intangible benefits delivered by the brand than the physical performance of the product itself. The reputation and lifestyle factors involved in, say, owning a Rolex watch, or wearing a Pierre Cardin suit have little to do with direct performance comparisons with other watch brands or other clothing manufacturers.

A study conducted in the United States by Doyle Dane Bernbach throws light on the nature of brand leadership. The study asked a large sample of people to identify the brand leader in a number of product categories. In most instances, the consumer's view of the brand leader coincided with the facts, but in some, it didn't. What consumers were talking about is 'leader brands', not so much of size but of leadership characteristics. Similar conclusions derive from a study conducted by DMB&B. In a comprehensive survey conducted in some sixteen different countries, consumers were asked to identify which brand or company was the leader in one of fifty-six different markets.

Table 3.5 Examples of strength of overall leadership in different categories

1st leader	(%)	2nd leader	(%)
Kodak	78	Fuji	6
AA	58	RAC	17
Heinz	51	Batchelors	13
Whiskas	44	Kit-e-Kat	25
Nescafé	42	Kenco	12
Tetley	40	PG Tips	22
Michelin	28	Dunlop	17
IBM	24	Apple	12
Carlsberg	19	Heineken	17

Source: DMB&B data 1992–95, Ford-Hutchinson, S. *Understanding Brand Leadership*, MRS, 1996

In categories as diverse as cereals, instant coffee, teabags, toothpaste and lager, the majority of consumers were able to clearly identify a 'leader'. In some markets, the dominant brand was clearly identified; elsewhere, the position, even for the most significant brand, is less clear-cut, as Table 3.5 shows.

Qualitative work associated with this study indicates that most consumers prefer to purchase a product which they consider to be the brand leader, even if they do not always do so.

Identifying and building brand values

The process of identifying and building brand values is interactive with that of marketing communications. As we have already seen, the environment of the message which is communicated to the potential consumer is as equally important as the nature of the message itself.

Tony O'Reilly, Chairman and CEO of Heinz, commenting on brand values in the BBC programme 'Branded' (transmitted on BBC2, 22 February 1996), said, 'The process of creating a popular brand is a long, slow process and trying to take brand share away from a dominant brand is a very long and expensive process. In modern retailing, not to be attempted ... that's why brands are so valuable'.

What values and expectations consumers have of a brand must be clearly identified *before* work on marketing communications can commence. The whole issue of positioning is one of great significance, but it starts with the consumer, rather than ending with him or her. The key to a proper understanding of the brand in the context of consumer expectations is market research. However, it is not possible to simply ask consumers what they think about a brand, or at least, not if the purpose is to identify the *underlying* characteristics which make up a brand image. In response to the question 'What do you think xxx product is like?', answers are likely to be physical and tangible, for example, it tastes good, it lasts a long time, and so on.

One approach to the problem is to use a series of *projective techniques*, which enable the respondent to use a series of other stimuli in order to make some form of meaningful response. The simplest technique is to ask consumers (and potential consumers) to identify the sorts of people that they think use the product. This will allow us to access the important dimension of user image. If consumers identify brand users as being substantially different from themselves, it is apparent that there is some form of dissonance between them and the offering. Where consumers identify more closely with the product being investigated, they will tend to describe users as 'people like me'. Identifying such dissonance may be a key dimension in rectifying an image problem, especially if the 'real' product delivery is felt to be appropriate to users who perceive themselves in a different light. An example will illustrate the point.

In the UK, users of cruises tend to be identified by non-users as being older (perhaps retired); fairly sedentary (what is there to do on board a ship?); wealthy (cruising is expensive) and so on. However, if exposed to the product, many non-users tend to find it attractive and rapidly become converts. Accordingly, companies like Royal Caribbean and P&O have sought to associate other values with their proposition to make it more appropriate to a younger audience.

An alternative research approach is to ask respondents to imagine what sort of personality the product would have if it were human. Some interesting results emerge, which are directly applicable to the identification of brand personality. A product might be seen as young or old, male or female, passive or aggressive, wealthy or impoverished. All of these, and many other dimensions, will provide important clues as to how the individual perceives a product or service. Other techniques involve getting the consumers, often in a group discussion format, to use visual elements – providing them with illustrations taken from newspapers and magazines – and

inviting them to prepare a collage of their impressions of a product or service. The key factor is that we identify what it is that makes a product 'behave' in the way that it does, in order that we can then determine whether the image is close to the one desired, or whether we will have to take action to change it.

An important way of depicting brand positionings is with the use of a *perceptual map*. Using the techniques outlined above, it is possible to build up a typology for all of the brands which compete in a market category. By identifying the key considerations in the mind of the consumer (to isolate the important dimensions of a desired brand) and placing them on a matrix, we can illustrate the relative positions of the competing brands within a market. The resultant 'map' relates all brands to each other, and allows for exploration of their relationship to an idealized position to occupy. Sometimes it will be necessary to build up multiple maps, where the market is segmented and where the desired values of each segment differ from those of the others.

The following example of consumer perceptions of the Levi's brand (Figure 3.2) is taken from the BBH paper entitled 'Jeans Sans Frontières' (Baker, 1993). It depicts a variety of brand attributes, derived from research, and the closer an attribute appears to correlate to a brand, the greater the degree of association with that brand.

Simon Clemmow (1997) has developed a framework to assist in identifying the status of the brand (Figure 3.3). The model stresses the importance of considering both the market and the consumer context in which the brand is seen.

The task of enhancing brand equity is a long-term consideration and, importantly, should be a primary responsibility of the chief executive of the company. In many cases, the management and development of the brand has traditionally fallen to the marketing director, who apportions the annual marketing budget. Often, this is a reflection of a short-term orientation designed to achieve immediate

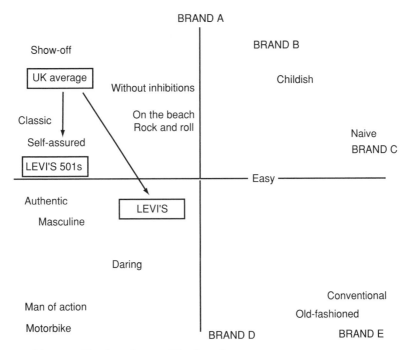

Figure 3.2 Perceptual images of Levi's and competitive brands

sales goals. Moreover, the tenure of the marketing director may, of itself, militate against taking a longer-term perspective. A survey conducted by Data Management Services in 1996 indicated that some 53 per cent of top marketing personnel in the leading 3000 advertisers have changed their job within an eighteen-month period. In contrast, the average tenure of CEOs in leading PLCs is eight years, whilst the average length of service with the company is twenty-five years. Clearly, it is the CEO who is best placed to take on the custodianship of the brand and its equity.

Altering brand imagery

It is important to understand that brand images are not fixed. They can be amended or changed completely by the appropriate use of marketing communications tools. Lucozade, historically, was a product associated with recovery from illness; today, marketing communications has transformed it into a product which is seen by its young audience as a trendy and refreshing beverage. Tango has been converted from a brand that was, at best, a conventional carbonated soft drink into something uniquely associated with 'orangeness' and an 'icon' brand to its target consumers. Hellmann's have transformed salad dressing from an old-fashioned to a modern and desirable accompaniment to food.

In the 1980s, the Levi's brand had become associated with a corporation rather than an aspiration. The ads were highly product oriented and featured middle-aged men engaged in middle-aged pursuits. They were perceived as being 'uncool' and communicated none of the values that the desired target market desired. The 'Laundrette' commercial changed all of that. Today, the brand is cool, gives street cred, and is an aspirational brand. It is now the dominant brand, with a significant share of the overall jeans market.

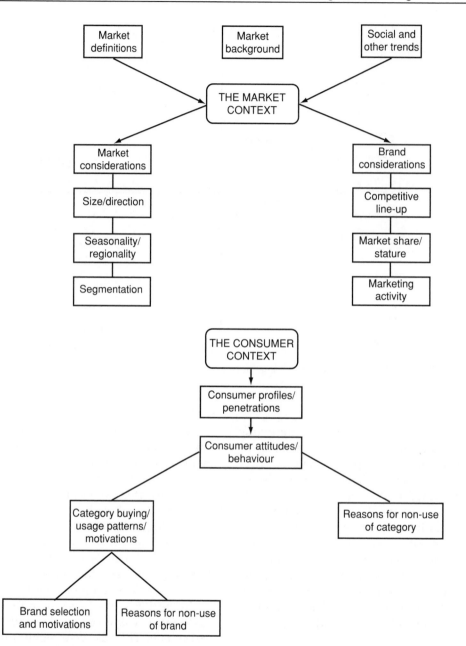

Figure 3.3   A framework to help establish the status of the brand

Cooper and Simmons (1997) have suggested that there is a new dimension in marketing based on the altering of values. They identify a series of companies as 'entrepreneurial revolutionaries'. These are companies and brands which set out to take risks in order to take control of a market by changing the equilibrium of values which, hitherto, have been regarded as important. They create fresh motivations in the consumer

Table 3.6 The re-framing of sector values

Sector	Brand	Sector value shift
Airlines	Virgin Atlantic	Re-framing business flight values from status to enjoyment of the experience
Banking	First Direct	The raising of importance of practical accessibility over (hollow) 'friendly' approachability
Breakdown services	AA	Breakdown services solve personal emergencies, not just make your car go again
Cars	Daewoo	Shifting the debate from product benefit or driver experience to the practicalities of purchase and ownership
Credit cards	Goldfish	Fun and emotional response is a discriminator, not simply functional performance
Personal computing	Microsoft	Shifting the debate from hardware to software – from 'What can you do with it?' to 'What can it do for you?'

Source: Palmer, A. and Simmons, P., *Brand Equity Lifestage, An Entrepreneurial Revolution*, TBWA Simmons Palmer, September 1997

agenda based on the premise that consumers have, or can be, changed. Their objective is to change the 'rules of the game'. By the actions they take, they are able to reposition the current sector leaders and undermine their brand equities. Such brands would include Virgin, First Direct, Daewoo, Microsoft and PlayStation. They contrast the performance of First Direct which, despite its comparatively short existence, has not only had a dramatic impact within the consumer banking sector, but has altered the choice criteria by which consumers assess competitive offerings, with successful growing brands such as Chicken Tonight, which take share from competitors but do not alter their fundamental perceptions. It is the former which fulfils their definition of 'revolutionaries'.

Palmer and Simmons (1997) identify a series of companies – and the communications programmes – which have served to re-frame the values of the sector in which they operate and change the choice criteria upon which consumers select competing brands (Table 3.6).

The strategic value of brand extensions and brand stretch

The area of brand extension – also referred to as 'brand stretch' – has been the subject of considerable debate in recent years. In essence, the process is one of transference, in which the name of an existing successful brand is attached to additional products.

The process provides the company with a series of potential benefits:

1 The existing awareness of the brand name tends to encourage consumer confidence in a new brand.

2 The same impact may be apparent within the retail environment, providing the opportunity to secure rapid distribution for a new product.

3 It may offer economies of scale in marketing communications, since several related brands can be grouped under a single umbrella campaign.

Brand elasticity is a concept that is undeniably gaining in importance. According to David Howard (1997), there are two key reasons for this phenomenon. First, the existence of brand elasticity is beginning to upset accepted areas of influence in terms of the demarcation of the particular market sectors in which a brand can operate. Second, the potential for brand extensions and new brand opportunities has focused corporate minds on the company brand as a new type of financial asset.

Doyle (1997) identifies three areas in which brand extension may be considered:

1 If the brands appeal to the same target market segment and have the same differential advantage.

2 If the differential advantage is the same, but the target market is different.

3 If a company has different differential advantages, it may find synergy of the brand's appeal to the same target market.

Brand elasticity is a measure of the ability of the individual brand to establish itself in new areas. To achieve this, the brand has to be able to exploit its values and reputation so as to create market confidence in a product or service new to the brand.

Sergeant (1997) argues that it is tempting to think that a basis for measuring brand stretch is to determine how close a potential new product is to the established core competences. Over time, elasticity would be generated by the accumulation of brand extensions, each one related to the previous one. However, this notion of 'proximity' does little to explain the failure on the part of the financial sector, especially the banks, to develop into other financial services. More-

over, it does equally little to explain the success of brands that cover a divergent range of sectors. Virgin appears to have developed brand credibility across a range of apparently unrelated products and services. Similarly, retailers have encompassed not only a wide variety of product offerings, but are increasingly moving into other areas, such as credit cards, holidays, insurance, petrol and banking services.

However, it is argued by many, among others Trout and Rivkin (1996), that brand extensions represent a dangerous trap for unwary companies. The existing awareness of the brand name may create an unrealistic confidence in the new product, with the result that the research process is either compressed or ignored. And, of course, if the new product fails, it may have a detrimental impact on the reputation of the original brand.

It is interesting to compare the Levi Strauss extension into Levi's tailored classic suits, which failed because the brand held the wrong connotations. Despite this failure, Levi's have more recently achieved success with Dockers – possibly because of its disassociation from the Levi's name.

Anheuser Busch is launching its own jeans and clothing range under the Budweiser label. The range is targeted at the core market for Bud drinkers, 18–24 year olds, and with jeans priced at around £60 they will be at a premium compared with Levi's. It will join brands such as Marlboro and Camel. According to Peter Jackson, Sales and Marketing Vice President, 'Brewing will always be our core activity but this is a natural brand extension and endorses our premium positioning. The range will be reflecting our heritage as well as supporting our future'. It will be interesting to see whether the brand extension delivers over time.

Many other companies are considering the potential value of brand extensions. BUPA has announced the extension of its brand into a series of high street health shops. The company, with a claimed 45 per cent of the private healthcare market, will provide a range of preventative healthcare products and services (*Marketing Week*, 31 January, 1997). P&G's leading skincare brand Oil of Ulay is moving into the cosmetics market (*Marketing Week*, 26 June, 1997), with the make-up range being priced to match mid-market brands such as Boots No 7 and Revlon.

Virgin has broken all the rules of branding. Instead of asking the question 'What business are we in?', Virgin has pursued a policy of which business can the brand go for? Will Whitehorn, Corporate Affairs Director for the Virgin Group, supports the diversity of Virgin branding: 'The UK's definition of a brand has remained far too narrow, too closely associated with a product rather than a set of corporate values.' (*Campaign*, 26 April, 1996).

The Virgin brand does not represent a faceless company. It embodies the positive aspirational associations and charisma derived from Richard Branson, according to Phillippe Mihailovic (1995). He argues that the order of brand extensions made by the Virgin company has been significant to its overall success. Importantly, the brand symbolized music first, then entertainment megastores, then an airline, a publishing business, a radio station and so on. The consumer accepted each of these extensions and, far from diluting its core properties or weakening its existing associations, the Virgin brand appears to be adding core properties with each new launch. The brand conveys fun, excitement, quality, value for money, innovation and more. Virgin is no longer considered a market-specific brand – Virgin has become the *people's* brand.

Mihailovic suggests that a house brand can stretch across various product markets and categories, although some house brands have fewer limitations than others. Coca Cola, for example, has the problem of a house brand name derived from a specific product such that other products carrying the name would be unlikely to benefit from it. Neither Fanta nor Sprite was launched as Coca Cola brand extensions as a result of the corporate decision not to jeopardize the core brand. Most house

brands have a much broader positioning (Revlon, Sony, Yves St Laurent, etc.). Colin Macrae (1995) argues that the Japanese have shown the business world that perceived quality is highest when the brand carries a corporate guarantee.

However, brand extensions are no panacea. The *Journal of Consumer Marketing* reported that Nielsen conducted a large-scale study of 115 new products launched in the UK and USA with market share measured two years after launch. Brand extensions performed significantly less well overall than those product launches with new brand names. In general, the most positive brand extensions have occurred when there is a high brand concept consistency together with high product feature similarity.

The roles of marketing communications in branding

David Ogilvy (1995), in his book *Ogilvy on Advertising*, says, 'Every advertisement should be thought of as a contribution to the brand image. It follows that your advertising should project the same image, year after year'. In the context of current thinking, the analogy should be taken to include more than just advertising. It is vitally important that all communications messages on behalf of the brand communicate a singular and consistent image.

We have seen that the consumer may be unaware of the source of the message, in specific terms. Often, he or she will be unable to determine whether the impressions were created by advertising, public relations, packaging or any other dimension of the brand activity. Nor, for that matter, does it really matter, provided that the impression the consumer receives is a favourable and positive one. But it does demand that the marketer examine all aspects of the communications message to ensure that the elements are consistent with one another, and that the consumer does not receive contradictory impressions of the brand. There are a number of important facets to consider.

Is the advertising proposition consistently applied?

Some of the most effective advertising campaigns, in terms of brand development, are those which have developed an enduring message. PG Tips, in the UK tea market, have used the same executional treatment since the 1960s – the chimps are synonymous with the brand; Cadbury's Flake advertising has conveyed the same message with essentially the same storyline in its commercials over much of the same time scale; the mnemonics employed by Procter & Gamble continue several decades after they were first used. The values contained in the Levi's jeans commercials have been constant over the past decade.

These, and many other examples, illustrate the importance of consistency in advertising. The specific treatment and the executional content may change, be refreshed and updated, but the underlying proposition about the brand remains the same – with the benefit that each advertising message delivered serves to reinforce all of those which have been received in the past.

This should not be taken to imply, however, that advertising, like all the other aspects of marketing communications, should not be subject to frequent review. Even long-running advertising campaigns may reach a point where the message needs to change. Both British Telecom and Perrier are examples of long-running and successful advertising campaigns, both of which won numerous awards, where the advertising strategies have been changed in response to underlying changes in the competitive environment. The advertising strategy should be re-examined and the executions monitored to ensure that the approach continues to be appropriate.

Does sales promotion underpin the brand image?

Here, we are not talking about the short-term use of sales promotion techniques designed to achieve specific objectives. Rather, we must consider the longer-term sales promotion strategy. If certain techniques are used frequently, then they will combine to build up an image of the brand. If, for example, a sequence of reduced price offers and money-off discounts are used to achieve short-term offtake, the likelihood is that consumers will build up an expectation of the reduced price as being the norm. This may be in direct conflict with the positioning of the brand as a high-quality, premium-priced, brand. By the same token, the offering of inferior quality free gifts and other merchandise, or the inconsistent presentation of the brand at the point of purchase, may, similarly, undermine the imagery of the brand which advertising and other activity has sought to build.

Are sponsorships and other involvements relevant and consistent?

As, increasingly, manufacturers become involved with other organizations to promote their brands, the question must be asked as to whether the visibility gained reflects favourably on the brand. Provided that an appropriate synergy exists between the brand and the sponsored activity, it is likely that favourable impressions will be created for both parties to the sponsorship. Stone's Bitter sponsors football programmes in the Midlands; The Prudential has long been involved with sponsorship of various of the arts, and so on. Guinness claim that their recent sponsorship of the Irish football team in the 1994 World Cup helped to boost the company's profits.

The converse, however, may equally be true. The choice of the wrong party, or the sponsorship of activity with the wrong image and franchise, may act detrimentally to the brand.

Do spokespersons for the brand reflect similar values?

In some instances, the brand uses a 'personality', either to endorse the product or to act as its spokesperson. This may have a positive impact on consumer perceptions of the brand if the image associated with the personality is a positive one. Nike have consistently used personalities with 'exceptional' sporting prowess to endorse their brand. The result has been to establish an enviable reputation in the marketplace. However, the adoption of Steffi Graf by BMW was, at best, a neutral benefit, whilst Pepsi were forced to terminate their use of Michael Jackson when scandals in his private life were alleged.

Do public relations activities reinforce the brand message?

Whilst the intention of public relations is to promote the values of the brand, it is important to ensure that the messages are consistent with those of other areas of marketing communications. Provided that a common communications strategy is adopted, PR will support the other aspects of the brand effort, but it has to be remembered that PR is the least controllable of the communications tools and, on some occasions, the intended message will be revised by the recipients before being passed on to the intended audience.

Is packaging reassessed to ensure consistency with the desired image?

Packaging is the consummate form of branding. It is the tangible representation of all dimensions of the brand to the consumer. When used well, the dimensions of packaging – the nature of the container, the colour of the label, the typeface, and other elements – can project and reinforce a desired image for the brand. However, it has to be remembered that image dimensions may change and, more importantly, so will consumer expectations of the brand. Whether the desire is to project traditional values, or stress modernity, packaging makes a vital contribution. If the nature of the pack proposition is not considered on a regular basis, a danger exists that this final presentation to the consumer may lag behind other communications dimensions.

The importance of packaging and pack design should not be underestimated. Although some products and services are supported by considerable marketing communications budgets, the vast majority receive minimal expenditure, and many receive none at all. In these circumstances, the weight of communicating the values of the brand rests entirely with their presentation to the consumer. Not only must the packaging provide a positive guide to the contents and their uses, it must also identify the benefits of the product. And, in the absence of media or other support, the packaging must also supply the emotional values which contribute to the brand's value.

A good example of the way in which packaging can contribute in this way is provided by several competitors within the bottled water market. The on-shelf aspirational values which high-quality packaging provides contributes to the various brands' ability to secure a considerable price premium over many of their competitors. Several packs are archetypical examples of the positive contribution that pack design makes to consumer recognition and differentiation – the box and jar (now plastic) that instantly communicate Vick's Vapour Rub; the immediately recognizable Heinz Tomato Ketchup and HP Sauce bottles; the gold packaging for Benson & Hedges cigarettes, for example.

And it should be remembered that the principles of 'packaging' apply equally to the retail environment. Few could fail to recognize a McDonald's outlet the world over. The selection of the style and colours of the decor, for these and other fast-food outlets, assists the consumer to identify 'freshness' and 'modernity' among other values.

Brand relationships

According to Max Blackston (1993), the concept of brand relations has, substantially, been applied to the development of advertising. It has proved invaluable in identifying the 'problem' that advertising is required to address and in providing specific direction for the attitude the brand should adopt in the advertising. However, as he points out, advertising is but one of the ways in which a brand communicates with its consumers via attitudes and behaviours. Consequently, brand relationships have a broad relevance for all areas of marketing communications.

This has been the greatest spur to the development of 'relationship' marketing, with its objective of marketing to consumers 'one at a time'. Similarly, brands' attitudes and behaviours, expressed through packaging, sales promotion and public relations, should all be consistent with their relationships. Tango, for example, have developed a positive relationship with their customers. Substantial numbers of their target audience – teenagers – have answered the invitations in advertising to call special Tango lines. According to Tango, over 2.5 million called the Apple Tango helpline and the Orange Tango Genetics 'demand' line.

The challenges facing brands

The weakening of brands

Recent years have seen a progressive weakening of the position of brands in the marketplace which, in turn, has given rise to the overall debate as to whether the 'era of brands' is drawing to a close. Undeniably, brand owners face increasing pressures from a variety of fronts. These pressures include a broader choice of products, each of which can satisfy differing consumer requirements; the lessening of product differentiation, as technology enables rival manufacturers to achieve the same, or very similar, product performance; and the increasing sophistication of consumers, which results in a greater degree of scepticism surrounding manufacturers' claims.

Scott Davis (1994), in 'Securing the Future of Your Brand', identifies several reasons for the erosion of brand strengths:

1 Private label intrusion.
2 Price discount back breaking.
3 Image devaluation.
4 New entrant encroachment.
5 Investment level withdrawal.

Where once the supermarket shelves were stocked with a wide variety of brands, and offered extensive choice to the consumer, the progressive erosion of retail margins has resulted in a concentration on comparatively few brands. In many cases, the consumer is offered the choice between the brand leader, the second brand and a private label alternative. Inevitably, the consequence, particularly for smaller brands, has been their removal from the shelves of the major retailers, whilst in some sectors the impact of price pressures is squeezing out even well-established brands.

The changes in retailing

Recent years have seen fundamental changes on the retail scene. Most significant among these has been the growing power of the major retailers. The progressive number of mergers and take-overs has resulted in a comparatively small number of substantial retailers dominating their market sectors. In turn, this consolidation of retailing is shifting the centre of power away from brand owners. The level of concentrated buying power has given the advantage to many large operators

Table 3.7 Leading advertisers

1968		1995	
Advertiser	Expenditure (£ million)	Advertiser	Expenditure (£ million)
Lever Brothers	5.87	Sainsbury's	40.48
Procter & Gamble	5.4	Curry's	38.5
Mars	3.96	Safeway	34.3
Cadbury's	3.86	McDonald's	34.21
Pedigree Petfoods	3.84	Boots	31.82
Gallagher	3.76	BT Call Stimulation	30.62
Van Den Bergh's	3.45	Tesco	23.71
W. D. & H. O. Wills	3.27	B&Q	22.16
Rowntree	2.94	Dixons Store Group	21.04
Kellogg	2.62	MFI	20.94

in mass-market retailing – Boots, Toys 'R' Us, Tesco, Sainsbury's. And, as a consequence, manufacturers must submit to the demands of these powerful retailers, or risk the consequence of being de-listed from their shelves. At the same time, these leading retailers have consolidated their hold on key consumer markets by becoming more efficient.

In 1994, the top six retailers accounted for 73 per cent of the total grocery trade (up from 67 per cent in 1991). During the same period, private label share increased from 35 per cent to 38 per cent. Retailer strategy has created very positive images for the corporate brand, which has translated itself into a brand equity for individual product lines. One only has to look closely at the strength of the corporate brands of such companies as Tesco and Marks & Spencer to see how retailers have wrested the initiative from manufacturers. Using all of the tools of marketing communications, retailers have created their own brand personalities which automatically invest their own label products with the same image. Their brand power is combined with heavyweight activity of both advertising and in-store support.

The dramatic transition can be seen from Table 3.7, contrasting the leading advertisers in 1968 with those in 1995.

The growth of private label

There are four key reasons why retailers are motivated to develop own label sales:

- to increase margin;
- to build store loyalty;
- to mask price comparisons;
- to generate greater supply chain efficiency.

The erosion of the branded share over recent years can be seen in Table 3.8, whilst the success of the major retailers in developing their private label business can be seen from Table 3.9, indicating the shares of the major grocery retailers.

In the three-month run-up to Christmas 1996, over 90 per cent of the population bought an own label product. Sixty-four per cent of the population spent more on own label grocery products than they did on brands. A recent A. C. Nielsen survey of some

Table 3.8 Percentage of value share – brand versus own label

	1994 (%)	1995 (%)	1996 (%)
Brands	56.7	53.6	49.5
Own label (economy)	8.6	10.8	9.9
Own label (standard)	34.7	35.6	40.6

Table 3.9 Private label shares

Retailer	Share 1996
Sainsbury	60.8
Safeway	53.4
Tesco	52.5
Asda	55.4
Kwik Save	20.9
Somerfield	37.5

Source: Sargeant, J., 'Own Label: Taking Stock in 1997', *Admap*, March 1997

10 000 homes revealed that only 18 per cent of respondents disagreed with the statement 'My own store's brands are of the same quality as the well-known brands'.

De Chernatony and McDonald (1992) have identified the following characteristics in markets where own label products are particularly strong:

1 Excess manufacturing capacity.
2 Products are perceived by consumers as commodities.
3 Low levels of manufacturers' investment are common.
4 The production process employs low technology.

5 Brand advertising is not that significant.

However, in some respects, events have overtaken these conclusions:

1 Private label brands are no longer dependent on major manufacturers to supply their products. New manufacturing facilities have been specifically built to produce own label products. Cott's, the supplier of Virgin Cola, together with many supermarket brands, is a prime example of this development.
2 In an increasing number of sectors, whilst the products are not perceived as commodities, there has been a failure on the part of the major manufacturers to differentiate their products sufficiently to prevent a switch to private label.
3 The growth of the international own label market allows the manufacturers to achieve considerable economies of scale.
4 As technology becomes cheaper and more accessible, manufacturers of private label products can invest in higher technology production facilities.
5 Many brands with high levels of advertising investment have been subjected to considerable private label attack, both in generic form and from look alikes. It would appear that the scale of the advertising spend is no longer seen as a deterrent to private label attack – examples are Coca Cola and Procter & Gamble.
6 There has been a fundamental shift in consumer attitudes towards private label products. Henley Centre research for the CIM (Miles, 1993) indicated that whilst 50 per cent of consumers perceived own label products to be the best value for money in 1981, this number had risen to 56 per cent by 1993.

The consequence of manufacturer failure

Three major manufacturer-led factors have contributed to the weakening of brand positions.

Firstly, many manufacturers have increasingly sought to compete on price, both with each other and with retailers' own products. This has served to erode the distinctive characteristics which, historically, set brands apart from their private label equivalents. The over-use of price-based promotional techniques has resulted in a focus on price as a purchase discriminator.

Secondly, partly to fund promotional activity and partly to improve overall short-term profitability, some manufacturers have withdrawn other forms of marketing communications support. It is clear that if manufacturers fail to reinforce brand images, particularly with advertising, consumers will rapidly forget the underlying reasons why they chose the brands in the first place. The only factor which remains is the comparative price of the products on the shelves. In this circumstance, the private label products will always win!

'The barrage of coupons and price specials has trained a generation of consumers to buy on price. Product proliferation and the seemingly endless stream of brand extensions and line extensions have blurred brand identity. As store brands improve in quality and as consumers gain confidence in their store chains, store brands are posing a strong challenge to manufacturers' brands.' (Kotler and Armstrong, 1996)

The third factor has been the move by manufacturers into the supply of private label products. Today, five of the world's top twelve food and drinks producers now produce own label products for retailers. Companies include Philip Morris, Nestlé, Campbell's Soups, Heinz and Sara Lee.

Both Unilever and Procter & Gamble avoid producing products for private label, whilst Kellogg's have used the fact in their advertising. However, Heinz, which previously adopted the same stance, now produces products for retailers, although it claims that the 'B brands' are sufficiently differentiated from their brand leader to avoid confusion. Their approach is to sell these products on the open market rather than link with individual retail chains.

A major study conducted by *Marketing* magazine (1997) reveals the extent to which major brands are now involved with the supply of products for private label sale. The article identified several manufacturers who also produce own label products:

- Cereals: Weetabix, Cereal Partners (Nestlé)
- Biscuits: McVities, Burton's
- Crisps: KP, Golden Wonder
- Chilled: Dairy Crest, St Ivel
- Bread: British Bakeries, Allied Bakeries
- Hot beverages: Premier Beverages, Kraft Jacob Suchard

This serves to confuse the issue relating to copycat brands. Asda used the fact that their Wheat Bisks product bore a striking resemblance to the Weetabix brand to defend their position in the claimed confusion between their Puffin brand and the McVities Penguin brand. However, the reason that Weetabix had not complained was due to the fact that they manufactured the product for Asda.

Many consumers are now aware that major brand manufacturers also make retailers' own label products. Given the increasing tendency for retailers to adopt the visual cues associated with major brand packaging identities, many consumers believe that the product is the same as the manufacturer's own.

Brand look-alikes

The role played by packaging in communicating brand values is receiving considerable attention in the context of brand look-alikes. The increasing number of retail products which take on the visual appearance of the brand leader is causing great concern for the manufacturers of branded products.

Increasingly, own brands are now being introduced into sectors with very strong brands and, moreover, in very similar packaging: same size, same type and shape of container and very similar graphics. The main reason for the growth of own label and, increasingly, look-alikes is the fact that

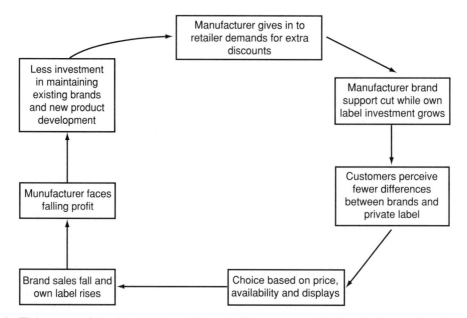

Figure 3.4 The pressures facing brands. Adapted from de Chernatony and McDonald, *Creating Powerful Brands*, Butterworth-Heinemann, 1992

supermarkets have become brands in their own right, with added values which appeal to their customers. They have achieved this using classic marketing techniques, including marketing communications. Retailers are now among the biggest advertisers.

A survey conducted for *Marketing* by National Opinion Poll (NOP) in March 1997 indicated that 41 per cent of shoppers believe that manufacturers make a supermarket's own label product if its pack design is similar to the branded version. Significantly, nearly one in five shoppers (17 per cent) have mistakenly bought own label brands because they confused their design with premium brand labels.

Recent years have seen a progressive quality improvement for private label products – a far cry from the days when their success was dependent entirely on their price position – and, with it, the packaging brief. Today's private label products look as good as their branded counterparts. However, at the same time there has been a tendency to 'borrow' the packaging cues.

In April 1994 Sainsbury launched its Classic Cola, with packaging strikingly similar to that of the brand leader Coca Cola. Ivor Hunt, the Marketing Director of Sainsbury's, defended the design, stating, 'The design identifies the product as being a Sainsbury's product. ... When you follow an established market, in order to compete you have to follow the same signposts and the same visual clues in order not to confuse the customer'. Tesco launched a low-fat spread called 'Unbelievable', corresponding to Unilever's 'I Can't Believe It's Not Butter'; Asda launched 'Puffin' against 'Penguin'.

The response from the brands has been understandable, typified by the statement of Sir Michael Perry, Chairman of Unilever: 'We understand that there are traditional packaging cues for certain product groups, such as a blue container for bleach. But look-alikes which set out to mislead are a parasitic form of competition, feeding on the investment in research, innovation and marketing expense of others.'

As we have seen, in many instances, particularly in a crowded retail environment, the consumer devotes little time to brand selection. The decision to purchase is made on the basis of a series of visual clues as to the identity of the brand. Until comparatively recently, such clues as the pack shape, its colour, the style of the typeface, and similar visual hints were a ready guide to the brand identity of the product purchased. Today, however, the situation is far less clear. Consumers could be forgiven for mistaking the identity of a product, given the number of packs which have been specifically designed to emulate the appearance of another. Retailers have, similarly, recognized the importance of packaging design and the contribution that it can make, not only to their profits but, importantly, to their overall images.

It is important to recognize that the issue of look-alikes is not limited to the fmcg sector, although most of the media attention has been devoted to that area. In fact, many other product categories are facing the same problem, sometimes at the hands of retailers, in other instances from rival manufacturers. Rolex look-alikes, for example, are produced by Seiko; the designs of personal computers are similar because there are only a few mass-produced components available; in the case of many small cars, the designs converge because the leading companies all use similar design techniques and submit their designs to the same wind tunnel assessments; whilst in the field of telephony, the services are substantially interchangeable with each other and represent no discernible differences, e.g. BT and Mercury, AT&T and MCI, etc. Similarly, rival service providers may utilize the same creative devices to communicate their propositions to potential consumers. For example, Insurance Direct offer a similar service to Direct Line, whilst Lloyds Bank Insurance Direct use a house/telephone device similar to Direct Lines car/telephone.

A quite separate problem, although no less concerning for the original manufacturers, is the dramatically increased numbers of fraudulent product copies. Many major brands face the problems of exact copies of the branded packaging, and bearing the same name – for example, pirate CDs and perfumes sold in many retail outlets.

The brand response

The central issue for manufacturers is to create a brand with a sustainable differential advantage and provide it with a distinctive personality which customers can relate to. The concern is no longer brand versus own label, but brand versus brand. Manufacturers must constantly improve their brands to stay ahead of the competition. In this context, the role of marketing communications is to communicate the added value of the brand versus any other, including retailer own label and look-alikes.

A response to the weakening position of brands could be found in the following process.

Companies must recognize the increasing importance of brands to their future survival. According to Chris Macrae 1991, whilst many brands have moved into the boardroom, as a result of the growing acceptance of the role of corporate branding, the role of the brand manager has either been downgraded or converted into a general management position. Often, the management of brands is devolved to promotions managers and service delivery managers. For brands to regain the initiative, there has to be a recognition of the important role of management of the branding process.

Manufacturers must ensure the continued investment in current brands and new product development. The withdrawal of brand support can only contribute to their further demise. At the same time, there is a need for improvements in both consumer and retailer communications programmes. This would encourage an increased recognition of the brand values, resulting in the securing of a wider distribution base. The success of retailers is, ironically, dependent upon having strong brands. Ultimately, they can only improve their profitability – even in the context of their private label products – if they have the major manufacturers' brands alongside them. The change of direction indicated by Sainsbury's – from a concentration on private label to an increased depiction of branded goods in their advertising – is a reflection of the fact that, ultimately, many consumers wish to purchase brands, even from their own preferred retailer.

The investment in research to identify the added values which are required by consumers is an important element within the process. In addition, there is a requirement for a continual investment in the new product development process. A similar investment will be required in terms of the communications programmes designed to associate the product benefits and justify the premium prices charged.

The move to get closer to the customer applies equally to the trade, inspiring increased co-operation between manufacturers and major retailers. The growth of category management is an important aspect of this co-operation. The retailer is less concerned with selling more of an individual brand than maximizing the overall profitability of the sector. This was summarized by Sir Michael Perry, Chairman of Unilever: 'It is utterly clear that there is no interest to the retailer whatsoever whether he sells more of brand A or brand B. All he is interested in is maximizing the profits from that shelf.'

By working together on ensuring greater efficiency in space planning and other joint initiatives in the areas of promotion and merchandising, manufacturers and retailers can co-operate to ensure increased sales and profits from each square foot of shelf space. For the manufacturer, this co-operation can bring about preferred supplier status and ensure that brand and private label strategies are implemented in a more harmonious manner.

Service brands

Although much of the chapter has referred to branding in the context of consumer goods, in reality much of the economy is devoted to service companies. According to Bateson (1995), the contribution of the service sector is significantly greater than that of manufacturing. Moreover, more people are employed within the services sector than in production. Dibb and Simkin (1993) suggest that some two-thirds of the British workforce is employed within service companies.

Most authors accept the premise that services possess four unique features:

1 Intangibility.
2 Inseparability of production and consumption.
3 Heterogeneity.
4 Perishability.

De Chernatony and Riley (1997) identify several different service branding strategies. Among these, there is considerable empirical evidence to support the notion that the size and reputation of the firm is often used by the consumer as an indication of the quality of the service provision. In the absence of the normal branding devices, service providers must take alternative routes to ensuring that there are tangible clues as to the identity of the provider. In the financial sector, for example, it is commonplace to create a visual device which can be used to identify the service brand. Direct Line Insurance has, for many years, used a mnemonic of a red telephone; Lloyd's Bank has used the Black Horse.

In many instances, the tangible evidence of service quality is provided by the staff of the company who interface directly with the consumer. Considerable efforts must, therefore, be devoted to providing adequate training to ensure that the appropriate standards are maintained. Some companies go somewhat further. Avis staff are easily identified by their red uniforms, as are the staff of such diverse organizations as WH Smith, PC World and Eddie Stobart.

As noted earlier, a key role is played by the ability of the consumer to identify the company providing the service. To this end, several corporate campaigns have been specifically designed to establish the identity of the company in the mind of the consumer. Few people could have failed to see the blitz campaign mounted by Cable and Wireless, for example. However, this is potentially limiting in the sense that, if different services are associated with the same company, consumers may have difficulty in differentiating between them. To this end, some organizations maintain the identities of several different brands to ensure clear separation for the consumers. First Direct has been given a distinctive identity which separates it from the Midland Bank, both of which are subsidiaries of the Hong Kong and Shanghai Bank.

Although it is reasonable to assume that many of the dimensions of services branding are similar to those for fmcg products, in fact, few service providers go sufficiently far to develop clear and distinctive brand identities. Importantly, comparatively few of them associate clear emotional values with their branding devices to achieve differentiation. De Chernatony and Riley (1997) suggest that 'Service organisations, in particular, financial services, have not given sufficient attention to developing their brands as effective shorthand devices to simplify the complexity consumers perceive when choosing between competing services brands'.

In the field of retail, these factors are extremely important. Substantially, competitors in the same area of retail provision offer a very similar range of products to their customers. Their point of difference depends on the extent to which they are able to create a clear identity based on both physical and emotional differences between themselves and their competitors. Tesco, Safeway and Asda have all done supremely well in providing consumers with discriminatory identities which enable them to occupy distinctive positions in the marketplace.

References

Baker, C. (ed.), *Advertising Works 7*, IPA/NTC, 1993

Barnard, P., 'Brandscapes', *Admap*, March 1993

Bateson, J. E. G., *Managing Services Marketing*, The Dryden Press, 1995

Bennett, P. D. (ed.), *Dictionary of Marketing Terms*, American Marketing Association, 1988

Blackston, M., 'The Levers of Brand Power', *Admap*, March 1993

Buck, S. and Passingham, J., *Brands vs. Private Label*, TN AGB, 1997

Buzzell, R. D. and Gale, B. T., *The PIMS Principles: Linking Strategy to Performance*, Collier Macmillan, 1987

Clemmow, S., The Role for Advertising, in Cooper, A. (ed.), *How to Plan Advertising*, Cassell, 1997

Cooper, A. and Simmons, P., *Brand Equity Lifestage, An Entrepreneurial Revolution*, TBWA Simmons Palmer, September 1997

Davis, S., 'Securing the Future of Your Brand', *Journal of Product and Brand Management*, Vol. 3, No. 2, 1994

de Chernatony, L. and McDonald, M., *Creating Powerful Brands*, Butterworth-Heinemann, 1992

de Chernatony, L. and Riley, F. Dall'Olmo, *Expert Views about Defining Services Brands and the Principles of Services Branding*, Open University Working Paper Series, 1997

Dibb, S. and Simkin, L., 'The Strength of Branding and Positioning in Services', *International Journal of Service Industries Management*, 1993

Doyle, P., Building Successful Brands, in *Excellence in Advertising*, Butterfield, L. (ed.), Butterworth-Heinemann, 1997

Duckworth, G., *Advertising Works 9*, IPA/NTC, 1996

Griffiths, C., 'Brand as Verb', *Admap*, July/August 1992

High, D., 'Taking Brands Offshore', *Admap*, November 1994

Howard D., 'Stretching a Point', *Admap*, March 1997

King, S., 'Brand Building in the 1990s', *Journal of Marketing Management*, Vol. 7, 1991

King, S., in Haigh, D., 'Brands', *Marketing Business*, March 1996

Kotler, P. and Armstrong, G., *The Principles of Marketing*, 7th edition, 1996, Prentice Hall

Macrae, C., 'Branding – A Core Business Process', *Journal of Brand Management*, April 1995

Macrae, C., World Class Brands, 1991, Addison-Wesley

Marketing magazine, 'Sleeping with the Enemy, 5 June 1977

Mihailovic, P., 'Time to Scrap the Rules', *Journal of Brand Management*, August, 1995

Miles, L., 'Metamorphosis in Marketing', *Marketing* magazine, July/August 1993

Ogilvy, D., *Ogilvy on Advertising*, 1995, Prion

Onkvisit. S. and Shaw, J. J., 'The International Dimension of Branding', *International Marketing Review*, No. 6, 1989

O'Shaughnessy, J., *Competitive Marketing – A Strategic Approach*, 3rd edition, Routledge, 1995

Sampson, P., 'Better Way to Measure Brand Image', *Admap*, July/August 1993

Sergeant, J., 'Own Label: Taking Stock in 1997', *Admap*, March 1997

Southgate, P., *Total Branding by Design*, Kogan Page, 1994

Trout, J. and Rivkin, S., *The New Positioning*, McGraw-Hill, 1996

Uncles, M., 'Branding – The Marketing Advantage', *Journal of Brand Management*, August 1995

Additional reading

There are several excellent books on branding and related issues, including:

de Chernatony, Leslie and McDonald, Malcolm, *Creating Powerful Brands*, 2nd edition (1998) Butterworth Heinemann

Aaker, David A., *Building Strong Brands*, 1996, The Free Press

Hankinson, Graham and Cowking, Philippa, *Branding in Action*, 1993, McGraw-Hill

Gilmore, Fiona (ed.), *Brand Warriors, Corporate Leaders Share their Winning Strategies*, 1997, HarperCollins Business

CHAPTER 4

The integration of marketing communications

Aims and objectives

- To grasp the importance of integration of marketing communications;
- To examine the external factors impacting on marketing communications;
- To understand the factors encouraging the adoption of integration;
- To discuss the benefits of integration;
- To consider the process of achieving integration;
- To outline organizational approaches towards integration;
- To examine the barriers to integration.

A major contemporary issue in the field of marketing communications is the drive towards integrated activity. There are a number of reasons for this fundamental change in thinking which need to be examined.

The marketing methods businesses used in the 1980s are no longer working and have lost their value as competitive weapons, such as the constant focus on new products, generic competitive strategies, promotional pricing tactics, and so on. Today's marketing environment has been described as an age of 'hyper-competition' in which there exists a vast array of products and services, both new and variations on existing themes. A casual look in the supermarket will confirm this view. Take, for example, the 'cook-in sauce' sector. The variety available to the consumer is little short of mind-blowing – whole fitments devoted to ethnic and other varieties, with each product replicated by several different brands.

Many of the fastest growing markets are rapidly becoming saturated with large numbers of competitors. And each competitor has similar technology. The consequence is that, as Schultz, Tannenbaum and Lauterborn (1992) put it, sustainable competitive advantage has been eroded away. In many categories, new products and services are copied in days or weeks rather than years. And, significantly, anything a company can do, someone else can do it cheaper.

Consumers are searching for more than a single element in any transaction. Instead, they seek to buy into the array of relevant experiences which surround the brand. Successful marketing in the 1990s will require total consumer orientation. It means communication with the individual, creating long-term relationships, quality-driven, and the aim is customer satisfaction, not just volume and share.

Integration, however, is not a new phenomenon, as the following quote from J. Walter Thompson in 1899 illustrates:

'We make it our business as advertising agents to advise on the best methods of advertising, in whatever form . . . as the best combination of work, such as we give, is the cheapest, as it brings the best results.'

A definition

The clearest definition of integrated marketing communications (IMC) is that of the American Association of Advertising Agencies:

'A concept of marketing communications planning that recognises the added value of a comprehensive plan that evaluates the strategic roles of a variety of communications disciplines and combines them to provide clarity, consistency and maximum communications impact through the seamless integration of discrete messages.'

The important dimension of this definition is the recognition of the need for a *comprehensive* plan that considers the strategic aspects of each of the tools of marketing communications in a holistic manner, rather than the development of them as separate elements. This approach represents a substantial shift in the underlying planning process, since it aims to ensure cohesion and the delivery of a single-minded message to the target audience.

Paul Smith (1996), writing in a recent *Admap* article, states, 'Integrated marketing communications is a simple concept. It brings together all forms of communication into a seamless solution. At its most basic level, IMC integrates all promotional tools so that they work together in harmony'.

Key to the issue is the fact that the consumer does not see advertising, public relations, sales promotion and other marketing communications techniques as separate and divisible components. As the receivers of a variety of messages from an equally wide range of sources they build up an image of a company, its brands and its services – both favourable and unfavourable. As far as they are concerned, the source of the message is unimportant. What they will be concerned with is the content of the message.

'A surge of interest by marketers in integrated communications strategies, where promotional messages are co-ordinated among advertising, public relations and sales promotion efforts, brings with it the implicit acknowledgement that consumers assimilate data about popular culture from many sources.' (*Journal of Advertising Research*, January/February, 1994)

Consumers receive impressions of brands from a whole range of sources – first-hand experience, impressions of where it can be bought, of people who use it or people who do not, from its role in cultural mores or rituals, from movies, literature, television, editorial, news, fashion, from its connections with events and activities, and finally from paid advertising media (Lannon, 1994).

A parallel consideration is the fact that the communicator desires to achieve a sense of cohesion in the messages which he communicates. If, for example, advertising is saying one thing about a brand and sales promotion something different, a sense of dissonance may be created, with the consumer left in some confusion as to what the brand is really trying to say. There is little doubt that marketing communications funds spent on a single communications message will achieve a far greater impact than when a series of different or contradictory messages are being sent out by the brand. And, with the pressure on funds, marketers desire to ensure that they are presenting a clear and precise picture of their products and services to the end-consumer.

Few companies are specifically concerned with issues of whether to spend their money on advertising, sales promotion, public relations or elsewhere. They are concerned with ensuring that they develop a cohesive marketing communications programme which most effectively communicates their proposition to the end consumer. The particular route of communication is far less important than the impact of the message. And, in budgetary terms, companies need to consider where their expenditure will best achieve their defined objectives. The previous notions of separate and distinct advertising, sales promotion, public relations and other budgets fails to appreciate that the considerations of the overall marketing communications budget needs to be addressed as a matter of priority.

But at the heart of the debate is the recognition that the consumer must be the focus of all marketing communications activity. If we return to the Chartered Institute of Marketing's definition of marketing, we can see that the primary need is the anticipation and satisfaction of consumer wants and needs. It is the development of an understanding of the consumer and his or her wants and needs that will ensure that marketing communications works effectively to achieve the objectives defined for it. This represents a fundamental change of focus: a shift from the functional activity of creating marketing communications campaigns to an attitudinal focus in which the consumer's needs are at the heart of all marketing communications planning – and, with it, a change from a focus on the product itself to the ultimate satisfaction of the end-consumer. Of course, there are functional implications.

Above all else, there is an increasing recognition that companies need to identify what position their product or service occupies in the mind of the consumer relative to that of other products or services. Only when they have gained that knowledge can they begin the process of planning marketing communications either to alter or enhance that position.

'As choice becomes an ever greater factor for consumers, both in the products they use and the way they learn about those products, it is increasingly clear that no marketer can rely on advertising alone to deliver its message. Integration permits us to focus the power of all messages. It holds the greatest, most exciting promise for the future.' (George Schweitzer, Senior Vice President, Marketing and Communications, CBE's Broadcast Group)

The impact of external factors on marketing communications

External and environmental factors have forced marketers to undertake a fundamental re-think both of marketing strategies and the positioning of products, and this, in turn, must impact on the process of marketing communications.

Information overload

As we noted earlier, the consumer is continuously bombarded with vast quantities of information. According to Dan O'Donoghue (1997), whereas the average consumer was subjected to about 300 commercial messages a day in 1995, today that figure has risen to around 3000. Whether the information is orchestrated by the marketer or the media in general is less relevant than the fact that there is simply too much information for the average consumer to process effectively. The inevitable consequence is that much of the material is simply screened out and discarded. The result is that the consumer may make purchasing decisions based on limited knowledge, or even a misunderstanding of the real facts. The individual is far less concerned with the average advertising message, which makes the task of ensuring appropriate communications with the target audience an even more daunting prospect.

An important dimension of the screening process is what I have described elsewhere as the 'submarine mentality'. In essence, since none of us can absorb all of the information around us, we establish personal defence mechanisms to screen out unwanted or irrelevant information. The analogy would be that of a submarine which goes underwater and, hence, avoids the surface bombardment. At periodic intervals, the submarine raises its periscope to examine particular aspects of the world around it. And when it has finished gathering the new information, it descends again – oblivious to any changes which might be taking place.

As consumers, our awareness of specific advertising messages is treated in a similar way. Some form of trigger mechanism is usually required to encourage us to pay attention to the variety of marketing communications messages. Usually, this is an internal recognition of an unfulfilled need which heightens the levels of awareness of pertinent advertising and other information. The principle can be commonly observed. If, for example, you have recently purchased a new car, your awareness of the marque will be enhanced and you will immediately become aware of similar vehicles all around you.

However, in the process of attempting to find better and more effective ways of communicating, we have also gained a greater appreciation of the nature of marketing communications itself. Much work has been done in the area of model construction and theoretical examination which has helped us to enhance areas of implementation.

The discerning consumer

The 1990s have seen the progressive improvement in levels of education which, in turn, has made consumers both more demanding concerning the information they receive and more discerning in their acceptance of it. Marketing communications propositions developed in the 1950s and 1960s would be treated with disdain by today's more aware consumers. Specious technical claims and pseudo-scientific jargon which were at the heart of many product claims are no longer given quite the same credence.

Consumers have changed from being deferential and generalised to personal and selective (Lannon, 1994).

A contradiction

The inability to store and process new information, coupled with the demand for a greater focus in marketing communications messages, has resulted in the consumer relying more on perceptual values than on factual information. All consumers build up a set of 'values' which they associate with a company or a brand. Some of these values will be based on personal experience, or the experience of others. Much of it will be based, however, on a set of 'shorthanded conclusions' based on overheard opinions, the evaluation of third party organizations, even the misinterpretation of information. These two factors combine to create a new dynamic for marketing communications.

However these thought processes are developed, and however the information is received is less important than the fact that, for the individual, their views represent the truth. A product which is perceived to be inferior (even though there is factual evidence to contradict this view) is unlikely to be chosen in a normal competitive environment. The imperative, therefore, is to understand the process of perceptual encoding and relate it to the task of marketing communications. A simple example will suffice.

Most consumers are responsive to a 'bargain' proposition. And certain assumptions are made, particularly in relation to well-known and familiar brands. If a potential consumer sees a product on sale in a market environment, there is some expectation that the price will be lower than, say, in the normal retail environment. If the brand name is well established, then it is likely that consumers will be able to draw from it the confidence and reassurance which will be necessary to the making of a purchase decision. Indeed, there is considerable evidence that these perceptual factors, influenced by the environment, will, for some consumers, induce them to make a purchase even though they might have been able to purchase the same product at a lower price elsewhere.

Many retailers have recognized this situation and have adopted a positioning of low price relative to their competitors. By marking down the prices of a narrow range of products, they encourage the consumer to believe that all products are similarly discounted. The result is that the consumer will decide to make all of his or her purchases at that outlet based on the perceptions derived from a limited comparison of those brands upon which the retailer has focused marketing communications activity. Since few consumers are in a position to make objective comparisons across a wide range of comparable outlets, these perceptions are accepted and become the reality.

The situation is compounded by the fact that price is only one consideration in a purchase decision. Most people have an ideal view of a price and quality combination. Needless to say, such a view is highly personal and subjective but becomes the basis of making subsequent purchase decisions for that individual. Thus reputation, both for retailers and brands, will be an important consideration in the purchase selection.

Changes in family composition

Long gone is the notion of the family comprising two adults and 2.4 children.

In all countries, the notion of family itself has different meanings. Some communities perceive the family as a small, integrated unit; others adopt a model of the extended family, with the elder children having responsibility for ageing members of the family, either parents or grandparents. The increasing levels of divorce, and the growing acceptance by some that marriage is not a norm with which they wish to comply, have resulted in growing numbers of single-parent families. In all these situations, their needs and expectations will be substantially different from each other, and effective marketing communications needs to recognize and respond to these underlying changes in society.

The ageing population

In many countries, the improved standards of living and better healthcare have resulted in two parallel changes. On the one hand, in order to sustain living standards, people are deferring having children or are having fewer of them. On the other, life expectancy is improving as medical care is enhanced. These forces have resulted in a progressively ageing population in most developed markets – and with it, a change in the values, needs and wants which consumers exhibit about products and services.

The green imperative

Increasing numbers of consumers are concerned with the environmental impact of the products and services they consume. The abandonment of CFCs, the reduction in the volume of packaging waste, the consumption of scarce and irreplaceable resources and similar factors, have all impacted on consumers' perceptions of desirable products and services. No longer is the single focus of their attention the efficacy or otherwise of the products they might buy. They require reassurance that not only do the products perform in the way that they expect, but that they also contribute to a better environment.

The growth of narrow casting

The advent of an increased number of media channels – land-based, cable and satellite television, an increasing number of radio networks, and a mammoth explosion in the number of 'specialist' magazine titles – has resulted in a fundamental shift in terms of media planning. Where once the advertiser had to recognize that the use of a chosen medium might, whilst providing excellent coverage of the desired target audience, carry with it a substantial wastage factor, the situation has now changed somewhat. Consumer groups can be targeted with a far higher level of precision. A specific message can be developed to appeal to a sub-group of users accessed by the nature of the television programmes they watch or the magazines they read. And the increasing use of direct marketing techniques has resulted in the possibility of one-to-one marketing – where the proposition can be tailored specifically to respond to the individual needs of the single consumer.

'Mass media advertising dominated marketing communications for decades, however, the nineties have seen companies place a greater emphasis on alternative communications mediums.' (Lannon, 1996)

The growth of global marketing

The changes brought about, substantially, by mass communications have, to some degree, encouraged the movement towards global marketing. With the recognition that national and cultural differences are growing ever fewer, major manufacturers have seized upon the opportunity to 'standardize' their marketing across different markets.

It is now possible to purchase an ostensibly similar product with the same name, same identity and similar product ingredients in many different markets. From the ubiquitous Coca Cola, now available in almost every country, to products like the Mars Bar, manufacturers are seizing the opportunity to ensure a parity of branding throughout all of the markets they serve, and to extend the territories in which they operate.

There are few markets (although the product contents may well be different) which would not recognize the Nescafé coffee label or what it stands for. The big M means McDonald's in any language, and Gillette runs the same copy platform for its Series range of male shaving preparations in many different countries.

We will examine the international dimensions of marketing communications in more detail in Chapter 15.

Non-verbal communications

We have already seen that the emergence of new media has enabled a more precise focus on target groups of consumers. But it has also demanded a new approach to the execution of marketing communications propositions, particularly on television.

Increasingly, satellite channels are becoming unrestricted in their availability. The same programmes can be watched simultaneously in France and Finland, Germany and Greece. And, if that is true of the programming, it is equally true of the advertising contained within it. However, whilst programmers have

the opportunity to overcome language and other barriers to communication within their formats, the same is not so readily true for the advertiser.

The response has been a growth in the recognition that visual communication has a vital role to play in the overall process. Increasing numbers of television commercials are being made with a pan-European or global audience in mind. The emphasis is less on the words being used than on the impact of the visual treatments employed.

Currently, a constant visual treatment is being utilized by Gillette to support their Series range of products across diverse markets. Here, the voiceover is modified to verbalize the proposition in each marketplace. In fact, the company has adopted an integrated approach for their six-year-old campaign embracing everything the company does. It is a much more single-minded strategic platform for the brand, according to Bruce Cleverly, General Manager for Gillette Northern Europe, 'It is the strategic premise of the entire Gillette grooming business'.

Other companies have gone considerably further. The verbal component of the proposition has been minimized, with the storyline being developed entirely, or almost so, in visual form. Current television commercials for Dunlop, Levi's and Pirelli are examples of this approach.

Speed of information access

Not only has the growth of information technology meant that information can be processed more rapidly, it has also meant that access to that information can be made far more speedily than at any time in the past. This has significant import for the marketer.

Census information, which was previously tabulated by hand, or on comparatively slow computers – and which was substantially out of date by the time it was made available – is now available within a relatively short period of time. Marketers can determine with far greater precision than at any time in the past the likely audience for their propositions, and can more readily segment markets into groups of users, rather than communicating with them as an aggregation.

At the same time, of course, this improved level of communication has a direct impact on the consumer. An increased level of media coverage of consumer-related issues means that any problem with a product or service is almost bound to receive media exposure. News stories about product withdrawals, the focus on product deficiencies in programmes like 'Watchdog', all ensure that large groups of consumers become aware of these issues within days, or even hours, of the occurrence.

The driving forces behind the growth of IMC

Value for money

The recession of recent years and increasing global competition have brought about substantial changes in the way that client companies are managed. On the one hand, there has been the impact of shrinking marketing departments, in which fewer people are allocated to the management of the products and services which the company produces. On the other, the pressure on margins has encouraged clients to become tougher negotiators. Companies are keen to gain the maximum value for money and the maximum impact from all relevant disciplines.

Increasing client sophistication

This is particularly true of areas such as an understanding of retailers, customers and consumers. There has been an increasing confidence in the use of other marketing communication disciplines, especially sales promotion, and the greater ability to take the lead in terms of their strategic direction.

A disillusionment with advertising

This has resulted in clients turning to other disciplines in the search to improve customer relationships and achieve more sales.

A disillusionment with agencies

Advertising agencies, in particular, which were often the primary source of strategic input for the clients with whom they worked, have lost significant ground in this respect. Specialist consultancies and other agencies are now being retained by client companies to advise them of the strategic directions they should be taking, with the agency role becoming progressively smaller in many instances.

Power shift towards retailers

In most consumer markets, comparatively small numbers of retailers have come to dominate their respective categories. In the grocery field, for example, the major supermarket chains – Tesco, Sainsbury, Asda and Safeway – account for a substantial part of the retail business. Together, these four companies account for around 40 per cent of retail sales. Inevitably, this has resulted in their taking the initiative in terms of marketing to consumers. To a large degree, even major manufacturers have to bow to the demands of the retailers or face the prospect of their products being delisted from the shelves.

Environmental factors

Consumers are becoming increasingly concerned with the way in which products impact on the general environment. In turn, companies have been forced to adopt a more environmentally friendly approach or risk consumers rejecting their products in favour of those which they consider to be more responsive to these broader concerns.

The impact on marketing communications

We have already seen that marketing communications needs to focus on the end user rather than on the nature of the product or service provided. But, it is suggested, marketing communications needs to respond more rapidly to these underlying changes in the social and environmental framework.

In their important work on integrated marketing communications, Shultz, Tannenbaum and Lauterborn (1992) propose that it is time to abandon the principles of the 4 Ps for the four Cs:

'Forget Product. Study Consumer wants and needs. You can no longer sell whatever you make. You can only sell something that someone specifically wants to buy.

Forget Price. Understand the consumer's Cost to satisfy that want or need.

Forget Place. Think Convenience to buy.

Forget Promotions. The word in the '90s is Communications'.

If marketing communications is to be effective, it is vitally important that we move from a situation of specialisation – in which marketers are experts in one area of marketing communications – to people who are trained in all marketing communications disciplines.

At the same time, as we have already seen, the process of change requires us to look at focused marketing approaches rather than adopt the litany of the 1960s – that of mass marketing. With the recognition that all consumers are different and, hence, have different needs and wants – even of the same product or service – there is the need to ensure that we are able to communicate with them as individuals rather than as a homogeneous unit. The increasing concern is the desire to communicate with ever smaller segments of the global market and, in an ideal world, reach a position where we can communicate with

them individually. This desire manifests itself in the increasing drive towards direct marketing techniques, the most rapidly growing sector of the marketing communications industry.

Relationship marketing

A development of the marketing communications process, as it moves through the 1990s, is the area known as relationship marketing. With the ability to reach consumers on a highly segmented or even one-to-one basis, so too has come the recognition that the process itself can become two-way. Hitherto, marketing communications primarily concerned itself with the process of communicating *to* the end-consumer. By encouraging the process of feedback, we can now communicate *with* the consumer.

Increasingly, companies such as Nestlé and Heinz have announced moves into club formats which enable the establishment of a direct relationship between the manufacturer and the consumer. Many loyalty programmes, such as the Frequent Flyer and Frequent Stayer programmes now run by most international airlines and hotel groups, have a similar objective of establishing a relationship with the consumer, to their mutual benefit. The increasing use of customer loyalty programmes within the major retail chains is further evidence of the desire to establish direct contact with the customer base – for long-term advantage. The encouragement of a 'feedback loop' is a facet of marketing communications which is destined to grow apace over the next few years and, as companies perceive the benefits of encouraging a positive relationship with their customers, their consumers, their suppliers and others, so we will witness the growth of developed two-way marketing communications programmes.

It has to be recognized that contemporary marketing is more complex than ever before. No longer is it sufficient to rely on the traditional marketing mix variables to achieve differentiation between manufacturers. Areas such as product design and development, pricing policies, distribution, in themselves, are no longer capable of delivering the long-term differentiation required. With an increasing level of convergent technologies, product innovation may be going on in parallel between rival manufacturers even without their knowing what the other is doing – and, even where this is not the case, any new feature can rapidly be copied by the competition. Where once a new feature, ingredient, or other product attribute would enable a manufacturer to achieve a unique stance for an extended period, today this is no longer the case. One has only to look at the area of the rapid innovation within the soap powder and detergent markets to see just how speedily rival manufacturers catch up with each other.

With the concentration of distribution into relatively few hands, the opportunities for achieving solus distribution of brands is minimized. Indeed, the retailers themselves represent an increasing threat to the manufacturers' brands as their packaging moves ever closer to that of the manufacturers' own.

Pricing, once a major area of differentiation, similarly provides less scope. The pressure on margins, brought about by the increasingly competitive nature of retailers' own products, has restricted the scope to use price to differentiate effectively. Clearly, this is particularly true of fast-moving consumer goods, where price dissimilarity can only operate over a very narrow range. Other products, such as perfumes and toiletries, and luxury goods, ranging from hi-fis to cars, still have more flexibility in the area of price.

We are left, therefore, with only one of the four marketing mix variables which can be utilized to achieve effective brand discrimination – marketing communications. Shultz, Tannenbaum and Lauterborn (1992) argue that the area of marketing communications will, through the 1990s and beyond, be the only opportunity of achieving sustainable competitive advantage.

If all other things are equal – or, at least, more or less so – then it is what people think, feel and believe about a product and its competitors which will be important. Since products in many areas will achieve parity or comparability in purely functional terms, it will be the perceptual differences which consumers will use to discriminate between rival brands. Only through the used of sustained and integrated marketing communications campaigns will manufacturers be able to achieve the differentiation they require.

To appreciate the impact of this statement, it is worth looking at a market which replicates many of the features described above. In the bottled water market, several brands coexist, each with unique positioning in the mind of the consumer. Yet, in repeated blind tastings, few consumers can identify any functional characteristics which could be used as the basis for brand discrimination.

The benefits of IMC

Undeniably, the process of integration affords a great number of benefits to the companies which adopt it.

Consistency of message delivery

By approaching the planning process in a holistic manner, companies can ensure that all components of the communications programme deliver the same message to the target audience. Importantly, this demands the adoption of an overall strategy for the brand, rather than developing individual strategies for the separate tools of marketing communications. The avoidance of potential confusion in the minds of consumers is a paramount consideration in the development of effective communications programmes.

Corporate cohesion

For the company, IMC can be used as a strategic tool in communicating its corporate image and product/service benefits. This has important consequences both on an internal and an external level. As consumers increasingly gravitate towards companies with whom they feel comfortable, it becomes important to ensure that the overall image projected by the organization is favourably received. This demands, in turn, the development of a cohesive communications programme within the organization – to ensure that all people working for the company fully understand the organization's goals and ambitions – and externally – to present the company in the most favourable light.

Client relationships

For the agency, it provides the opportunity to play a significantly more important role in the development of the communications programme, and to become a more effective partner in the relationship. By participating in the totality of the communications requirements, rather than having responsibility for one or more components, the agency can adopt a more strategic stance. This, in turn, yields significant power and provides important advantages over competitors.

Interaction

IMC ensures better communication between agencies and creates a stronger bond between them and the client company. By providing a more open flow of information it enables the participants in the communications programme to concentrate on the key areas of strategic development, rather than pursue individual and separate agendas.

Motivation

IMC offers the opportunity to motivate agencies. The combined thinking of a team is better than the sum of the parts (and unleashes everyone's creative potential).

Participation

Everyone owns the final plan, having worked together on the brainstorming and implementation, avoiding any internal politics. Potentially, this can overcome the divisive nature of individual departments 'fighting their own corner'.

Perhaps the most important benefit is the delivery of better measurability of response and accountability for the communications programme.

The process of achieving integration

The task of developing and implementing marketing communications campaigns is becoming increasingly divergent. No longer is the task in one pair of hands. As the specialist functions develop further, the marketer must seek and co-ordinate the input from a number of different sources. Many organizations will retain an advertising agency, a public relations consultancy, a sales promotion company and, perhaps, even a media specialist. Ensuring that all of these contributors work to the same set of objectives and deliver a cohesive message to the consumer is a task which is an increasingly challenging one.

Chris Fill (1995), in his book *Marketing Communications*, proposes a specific model for the achievement of campaign integration (Figure 4.1). The key facet is the establishment of a feedback mechanism between all elements of the strategic development process and, importantly, the consideration of all of the tools of marketing communications designed to fulfil the promotional objectives established for the campaign. It is the adoption of a holistic approach to campaign development which is at the heart of integration – a fundamental shift from the practice of

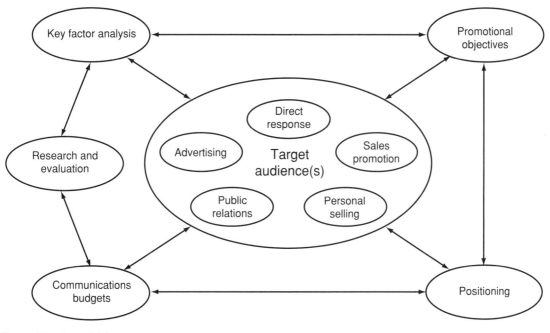

Figure 4.1 A model for campaign integration

developing each of the elements on a piece-meal basis.

'Integrated marketing communications offers strategic and creative integrity across all media' (Linton, 1995). This ensures that the company maintains a constant theme and style of communication which can be followed across all applications. In turn, this provides for a strong and unified visual identity in all areas of communication.

This does not imply that all material should have the same copy and visual execution. However, all items used must serve to tell the same story and to reinforce the overall message to the consumer. This enables each element of a campaign to reinforce the others and to achieve the maximum level of impact on the target audience. The best platforms for integrated campaigns are ideas that can be spread across the whole marketing communications mix: for example, American Express 'Membership Has Its Privileges' and Gillette's 'The Best A Man Can Get' will work in any discipline.

Andrex has for many years used the image of a Labrador puppy in its advertising to symbolize softness. More recently, however, the device has been extended into other promotional areas. Its 'Puppy Tales' campaign offered a series of books about the adventures of a puppy, which was featured on-pack and in television advertising. The promotion gained editorial coverage both for the promotion itself and by way of reviews of the author, Gerald Durrell. All of these devices reinforced the brand message.

Some companies go further. They produce a visual identity manual to which all items produced on behalf of the company must comply. This lays down a series of specific requirements – which may cover the typefaces used, the positioning of the logo and other important visual elements – which provides a high level of commonality in all materials produced. Often, this is associated with a re-design of the corporate image. When the author was working with the Prudential Corporation, Woolf Olins were engaged to re-design the company look and, as part of the package, created a corporate ID manual which covered all of the above areas, and with which all agencies were required to comply.

An essential part of IMC is the process of ensuring that the message conveyed is consistent. Whereas this is achievable in the context of a single agency which produces all of the materials required by its client, in the vast majority of cases, companies will employ several different agencies, often independent of each other. Indeed, some of the material will be produced by the company in-house. In this instance, someone must take overall responsibility for monitoring the consistency of the various items to ensure that there is an overall coherence in what is produced. This means that the person or department must consider not only the obvious items, such as advertising, point of sale and direct mail pieces, but everything else which is prepared to support the brand. This may include product leaflets and other literature, presentations and audio-visual material, sales training items, exhibition stands, and so on.

A key area within the requirement of IMC is the need for recommendations which are without structural bias. Historically (and still to a large degree) it was inevitable that agencies promoted their own particular corners. Advertising agencies would often present advertising solutions, promotions companies would offer sales promotion responses, and so on.

The move towards IMC has been hastened by the desire for agencies to become more accountable for their recommendations. Inherently, agencies have to be confident, as far as it is possible to be so, that the recommendations they make are those most likely to achieve the outcome desired by the client company.

To many writers on the topic, such as Schultz, Tannenbaum and Lauterborn, the central part of the IMC process is the maintenance of an effective database. Not only does this provide the opportunity to gain a greater understanding of existing customers,

but from an examination of their profiles (and using those profiles to identify similar target groups) it is possible to achieve a greater degree of precision in all subsequent communications activity.

At the conceptual level, integration is about capturing a single thought which expresses what we wish the brand to stand for and of ensuring that this thought is expressed, whatever the medium. At the process level, it is about ensuring that the development and implementation of communications lives up to that brand thought, and drives forward the relationship between the brand and the consumer.

As John Farrell, then Chief Executive of DMB&B, said: 'Unless there is close involvement of senior client personnel who truly have a full communications perspective, it's simply unfair on the agencies involved to expect them to drive the integration process from the outside.' Clients do not need specialist implementation functions within their businesses; rather, at a conceptual stage there has to be a structure and attitude which actively encourages the agency to recommend the most appropriate media solution to solve the particular problem.

Integration is not just about execution. It is about the single brand thought that expresses the essence of the brand personality and then interpreting that thought for the appropriate audience without changing or denigrating it. Integration extends to the point where the client and agency work together as a single team. The total team across all communications requirements is fully integrated with the customer and brand requirements, and that is what drives the focus of the team.

The position is summarized by the approaches adopted by two different companies. After Bisto's annual marketing communications plan has been developed, it is presented at a meeting with all of the Bisto agencies represented. Paula Ross, a group product manager at RHM, says, 'this creates a more open flow of information with all of the agencies focusing on the key objectives, not just their ideas. It motivates all who take part, everybody has ownership in the brand plan. And, most important, the combined thinking of the team is better than the parts'. Similarly, Tetley implements the IMC process by holding quarterly meetings when marketing staff meet with the agency, DMB&B, PR consultancy, Biss Lancaster, and sales promotion consultancy, Geoff Howe and Associates.

Organizational approaches to integration

Some writers suggest that the most efficient means of achieving integration is to appoint a single agency which is responsible for all aspects of the campaign, contracting out certain areas. The reality, except for a relatively small number of companies, is that such an approach is generally not possible. The need for specialist services in the wide variety of areas which make up the tools of marketing communications requires staff who are skilled in those specialisms.

Gronstedt and Thorson (1996) suggest five possible models for an integrated organizational structure.

The consortium

Here, one agency performs the role of main contractor to a consortium of specialist agencies. The main agency helps its client to develop a strategy and decides which persuasive tools to use. It typically executes traditional advertising but sub-contracts other tools. The account team at the main agency co-ordinates the specialist agencies to ensure that messages and timing are integrated.

Consortium with a dominant agency

These are agencies that have the capacity to plan an integrated campaign and execute

traditional advertising as well as some other communications tools. The main agency has various combinations of in-house services and outside suppliers.

Corporation with autonomous units

Here, all the specialists are brought in-house as separate and autonomous units. The specialist units are separate profit centres, sometimes with separate names and in separate buildings.

The matrix organization

These are agencies that not only have specialists in-house but they are integrated in a matrix structure. The matrix design combines functional division and cross-functional task force teams. The matrix structure requires that professionals work across functions whilst maintaining the functional division.

The integrated organization

In this, disciplines are incorporated into the advertising agency structure rather than forming separate units for each persuasive tool. The agency is no longer structured by functional departments but by accounts. Each person works for a particular client, not for a direct marketing or sales promotion department. Each account group comprises personnel who are capable of handling all communications disciplines.

Duncan and Everett (1993) suggest four agency–client relationships which could foster integration:

- The client and its agencies collectively establish strategies, then each communications function is executed by a different agency.
- The client and its agency establish the strategies, then the 'integrated' agency is responsible for the execution of all or most of the communications functions.

- The client determines overall strategies and assigns individual functions to individual agencies, but requires that all of these suppliers stay in touch with each other.
- The client alone determines overall strategies, then each communications function is executed by a different agency.

The barriers to integration

Despite the undeniable advantages afforded by integration, the situation suggests that comparatively few companies have yet reached the stage of integrating their communications campaigns.

Two recent studies provide an overview of the state of play in the UK market. The first, conducted by Helen Mitchell at the Cranfield University School of Management in 1996, consisted of a series of self-completion questionnaires sent to 540 leading marketing personnel in major UK organizations to which 231 replies were received; the second consisted of a series of in-depth interviews in selected market categories conducted by the author (1996) on behalf of DMB&B. Both studies indicate that, whilst much has been written on the topic, the subject remains largely misunderstood by many of those responsible for its implementation. This is clearly seen by the diversity of 'definitions' provided for IMC by the respondents:

'Co-ordinating all of the tools of promotion to ensure a consistent message.'

'Rolling out a single creative theme across all executions.'

'Using a single agency to deliver all requirements.'

Clearly, there is considerable confusion as to the nature of IMC, with some respondents regarding it as a process, others perceiving it as a facility for 'one-stop' shopping, whilst for others it was a means whereby cohesion might be achieved between creative executions and strategies, even if provided by a multiplicity of suppliers.

Several factors can be identified as presenting barriers to the integration process, both of an internal and an external nature. Internally, the lack of management understanding of the benefits of IMC; the short-term outlook adopted towards much of the planning process; the inherent nature of the 'political' battles between departments battling for supremacy; the fear of departmental budget reductions with the consequence of staff reductions; together with the turnover of staff and the fear of losing expertise in specialist areas, were all identified as contributing to the general lack of adoption of IMC within companies. Externally, issues such as agency egos; the agency's fear of losing control; the lack of expertise in the individual areas of communications; the concern over reductions in the scale of the communications budget; and the problems of the system of remuneration, were further restrictions on the progress of integration.

Structurally, few companies are in a position to ensure integration. Often, various functions compete with each other for the responsibility of briefing and implementation of the tools of marketing communications. These include the brand manager, the marketing manager, the marketing director, in a few instances, a communications director, together with a variety of 'specialist' heads of departments covering public relations, sales promotion and so on. Often, these individuals represent 'vested' interests and are protective of their own sectors to the preclusion of an integrated approach. Most importantly, few companies have truly recognized the issue of responsibility for the custodianship of the brand and the negative implications of divisive communications messages:

'...In practice, the situation is even worse. Company structures perpetuate this division, giving each "speciality" a different owner, based on technical skills required to execute, rather than conceptual skills required to plan' (Lannon, 1994).

Undeniably, there are significant problems for the client in terms of commissioning and managing several different agencies, especially in the context of the reduction in the size of marketing departments. The temptation for many of the integrated one-shop concept is overwhelmingly appealing. The attraction of using several different agencies is the possibility of selecting the best people in each field.

Moreover, there is a general lack of experienced people within the field of marketing communications who exhibit expertise in the variety of fields which make up the total communications process. The need for individuals with a 'broad perspective' and an understanding of the contribution which each of the marketing communications disciplines can provide is underlined by a study by Cleland (1995).

Lannon (1996) asserts that most company communications policies are rooted in an outmoded past, when competition was less intense and the retailer wasn't anything like the powerful force it is today:

- The discontinuities of the 1980s and into the 1990s have fractured and fragmented not only the conventional media scene, but also the corporate structures and cultures of a more stable past.
- Differing agendas of clients and agencies have eroded productive and trusting relationships between clients and their agencies.

Perhaps the most significant barrier to integration is the approach to communications budgeting. In most cases, budgets are substantially determined on a 'historic' basis – considering what has been spent in the past – rather than against an evaluation of specific objectives. Often, individual departments are required to argue for budget tenure, or an increase if the situation demands it. In the majority of cases, budgets are considered on a line-by-line basis, rather than holistically.

Despite this, some market sectors are more advanced than others in the adoption of an integrated approach. Two, in particular, stand out as having made significant progress in the integration of their campaigns – the financial sector and retailers. In both cases, there has been a more widespread recognition of the benefits of integration. Campaigns by many of the commercial banks together with high street retailers such as Safeway underpin the advantages of integration. Certainly, most companies agree that the process of integration will increase apace, as much because of the need to deal with substantial communications budgets in a more positive manner as from the drive towards global considerations, where the desire for a common communications policy and the obvious financial benefits are of major importance.

References

Cleland, K., 'A Lot of Talk, Little Action on IMC', *Business Marketing*, March 1995

Duncan, T. R. and Everett, S. E., 'Client Perceptions of Integrated Marketing Communications', *Journal of Advertising Research*, May/June 1993

Fill, C., *Marketing Communications*, Prentice Hall, 1995

Gronstedt, A. and Thorson, E., 'Five Approaches to Organise an Integrated Marketing Communications Agency', *Journal of Advertising Research*, March/April 1996

Lannon, J., 'What Brands Need Now', *Admap*, September 1994

Lannon, J., 'Integrated Communications from the Consumer End', *Admap*, February 1996

Linton, I., *Integrated Marketing Communications*, Butterworth-Heinemann, 1995

Mitchell, H., *Client Perceptions of Integrated Marketing Communications in the UK*, Cranfield University, 1996

O'Donoghue, D., Account Planning and Media Planning, in Cooper, A. (ed.), *How to Plan Advertising*, Cassell, 1997

Shultz, D., Tannenbaum, S. and Lauterborn, R., *Integrated Marketing Communications*, NTC Business Books, 1992

Shultz, D., Tannenbaum, S. and Lauterborn, R., *The Marketing Paradigm – Integrated Marketing Communications*, NTC Business Books, 1995

Smith, P., 'Benefits and Barriers to Integrated Communications', *Admap*, February 1996

Yeshin, T., *The Development and Implications of Integrated Marketing Communications*, Private Study, DMB&B, 1996

Additional reading

Undoubtedly, the foremost book in the field is:

Schultz, Don E., Tannenbaum, Stanley, I. and Lauterborn, Robert F., *Integrated Marketing Communications: Putting It Together and Making It Work*, 1992, NTC Business Books

For a contemporary view of integration, students are recommended to consult the various academic journals referenced in this chapter.

CHAPTER 5

Managing the marketing communications mix

Aims and objectives

- To consider the process of organizing for marketing communications;
- To appreciate the importance of human resources on the marketing communications process;
- To learn about the use of agencies;
- To understand the importance of establishing the marketing communications budget;
- To become familiar with the techniques of budgeting;
- To demonstrate an understanding of the task of budgeting for integration.

Organizing for marketing communications

Company structures

Companies organize themselves in somewhat different ways in order to ensure the appropriate management of their brand portfolios. Most companies are structured on functional bases, with separate departments responsible for production, research and development, sales, finance and brand management. Larger companies may have specific departments which control the various dimensions of marketing communications. These might include separate divisions for advertising, public relations, sales promotion, media and research. Again, some organizations bring these departments together under the function of the corporate communications manager.

What is certainly true is that no two companies adopt the same structure. Much will depend on the scale of the activity in which they are involved, the size of the budgets which will be deployed against the various categories, and the overall role of marketing communications within the organization.

The consequence is that several different individuals may play an important role in the determination of the marketing communications objectives, and will oversee their implementation, both directly and in conjunction with the appointed agency or agencies which will be responsible for the account. It is equally important to recognize that the hierarchy of approvals which will need to be sought prior to implementation will differ, depending on the importance which is attached to the proposed activity. In most instances, an advertising campaign will be presented to progressively more senior members of the company, often culminating in a formal presentation to the managing director or chief executive. However, in other areas, approval may be given at a significantly lower level of the company, perhaps at marketing or sales director level.

If one thing is clear about the internal structure of the many organizations involved with marketing communications, it is immediately apparent that there is no single framework which is universally adopted. In many organizations, the responsibility for the direct control of marketing communications is vested in the marketing director; in others, control is in the hands of the sales director; for a few, the whole area of communications remains with the managing director or chief executive.

At a lower level – often reflecting the size of the organization – there will be a pyramidal structure of marketing management, with marketing group managers, product group managers, product managers and so on. Elsewhere, individuals will be specifically charged with responsibilities in identified areas, possessing titles such as advertising manager, sales promotion manager, and so on. To confuse the situation yet further, some companies retain a corporate communications director or manager, whose responsibilities may embrace the totality of the organization's communications with its various publics.

Clearly, there can be no definitive prescription for the successful management of marketing communications tasks. Each company has identified its own approach, and employs the method which best suits its operational culture. However, whatever the titles and reporting structure, certain key elements remain important. Indeed, given much of what has been said earlier, they will become increasingly more important as the need to fuse the elements of marketing communications becomes more widely recognized.

The strategic dimension of human resources

It should be clear that the nature of the experience possessed by the staff within an organization will have an important bearing on the company's ability to deal effectively with the wide variety of issues and challenges that it faces. In both the overall strategic context and in the specific area of marketing communications, it is vitally important that the company conducts some form of 'people' or human resource audit to determine the ability of the individuals charged with specific responsibilities to deal with the tasks for which they are responsible.

Apart from identifying the nature of the structure of the organization, the level of skills required, the nature of selection, training and remuneration, an organization must also identify the specific dimensions of human resources which are essential for success within the category. This will often involve some form of comparison with leading competitors, a consideration of factors such as the quality of service delivery, an important aspect of marketing communications, and, in some instances, the international dimensions of the business operation.

The brand manager

Pivotal to the sustenance of the brand are the responsibilities of the brand or product manager. Their primary function is to manage the various resources of the company and to achieve their thorough integration for both the short and long term. Although brand managers can come from a variety of backgrounds, it is essential that they develop a sound understanding of the principles of marketing.

David Arnold (1992) describes brand management as being something of a balancing act:

'Balances have to be struck between the external market and the internal capabilities of the company; between the company's inputs into the product and the influences on consumer perception; between the short-term need to maximise profit and the long-term need to invest and develop.'

Category management

Several companies have made fundamental changes to their structures to reflect the underlying changes within the marketplace. On the one hand, the process has been driven by the desire to more closely reflect the underlying needs of their consumers. On the other, it is a reflection of the changing role and power of retailers.

The category manager

The creation of a new role – the category manager – is a response to the recognition of the limitations of the brand management system. Companies with extensive product portfolios, particularly those with several products competing for share within the same sector of the market, have come to realize that the traditional process of brand development is, potentially, divisive. Brand managers compete for the limited resources of the organization to achieve the betterment of the brand for which they are responsible – often without regard to the impact that such resource allocation may have on other products within the portfolio. The category manager, however, seeks to maximize the company's return on its investment from the category as a whole. Importantly, the category manager works closely with the retailer to develop merchandising strategies which are beneficial to both parties.

Nielsen (1992), the world-wide market research organization, has suggested that category management involves five distinct stages (Figure 5.1):

The first stage is the overall review of the product category. Manufacturers, particularly those with several product lines within a market category, obtain information regarding the roles that each of these products play, gather data on sales volume, share, line profitability, patterns of distribution, competitive analyses and so on. This information is used to gain a deeper understanding of the marketplace and to develop appropriate strategies to take advantage of the opportunities.

Nestlé, for example, has several different brands competing in the instant coffee market (Nescafé, Gold Blend and Blend 37 among others); Pedigree Petfoods has a number of different petfood products (Pedigree Chum, Whiskas, Pal, Kit-e-Kat, Cesar); Procter & Gamble maintains different brands within the detergents sector (Daz, Ariel, Bold, Fairy, Dreft and so on). In order for each of these companies to maximize their overall profitability, it is essential that each of the individual brands contributes effectively to the company performance within the sector.

At the second stage, it is essential for the company to gain a deep and thorough understanding of the potential consumers for its products and their particular needs – what differentiates them in terms of where they shop, for example, when and how often they make their purchases, what usage occasions are appropriate for different products in the category. Comprehensive profiles will need to be developed using all of the socio-economic and demographic information, together with an attitudinal understanding of the various consumer groups.

The third stage is the development of comprehensive strategies for all the products within the category portfolio – what is their relationship to each other, should they enjoy the same or different distribution patterns,

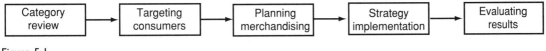

Figure 5.1

what mix of products and shelf space allocation will ensure that both the manufacturer
and the retailer achieve the maximum volume
and profit from the sector.

Once the previous stages have been completed, the manufacturer can embark upon the
implementation of the strategies. Associated
with this will be not only the development of
a close working relationship at the retail level,
but also the creation of appropriate advertising, sales promotion and other communications plans. These latter are of particular
importance in the context of the selling
process.

The final stage is the evaluation of the
results achieved to determine whether the
strategies fulfilled their objectives. This is a
critical element of the category management
process, as it enables manufacturers to revise
and enhance their strategies to achieve the
maximum impact.

The use of agencies

Most organizations employ a number of external agencies on a semi-permanent or ad hoc
basis to supplement their own communications skills. What particular skills they will
require will largely be dependent on the
nature of their business and the markets
within which they operate.

Procter & Gamble in the UK employs at
least four international advertising agencies to
handle its brands, a media specialist together
with other agencies in the areas of public
relations and sales promotion. H. J. Heinz
similarly uses separate mainstream advertising agencies, direct marketing agencies, sales
promotions companies, public relations specialists and so on. Even far smaller organizations call on the services of several different
communications companies to supply their
needs. The task of appointing and co-ordinating these activities is a considerable one, to
say the least.

1 It is vitally important that there are nominated
individuals in place to consider *all* aspects of
the marketing communications plan to ensure
their smooth integration. It remains true in
many organizations that specific individuals will
have control over the determination of the
individual communications elements, often
without regard to the longer-term issues
involved. In many companies, for example, the
brand manager is charged with the
responsibility of achieving sales targets. These
may be readily facilitated by means of, for
example, price cutting or other sales
promotional devices. The fact that these may,
potentially, undermine the longer-term impact
of, say, image advertising is outside his or her
remit and may be given scant consideration.
2 As such, companies must increasingly accept
that the responsibility for the adoption of a
long-term competitive positioning strategy
must be more important than the short-term
achievement of sales targets. Indeed, if the
internal approach is fully adopted, such
conflicts will be eliminated, with the long-term
strategic goals providing the framework for
the short-term determination of tactics.
3 One or more individuals must be responsible
for the smooth implementation of the
marketing communications campaign. As we
have already seen – and the point will be
developed further throughout this text –
implementing a campaign is, potentially, a
logistical nightmare. Even a simple
communications campaign will involve the
co-ordination of the efforts of a large number
of people and external organizations –
planners, copywriters, art directors,
typesetters, printers, media buyers, and so on.
The more complex the campaign, the greater
the need for effective control.
4 Few organizations possess the appropriate
management and creative skills to be able to
develop and manage campaigns activities in
isolation of external expertise.

However, this expertise may itself compli-
cate the issue as a result of its inherent
fragmented nature. Recent years have seen

the explosion in the numbers of specialist companies which offer individual input in areas such as advertising, sales promotion, public relations, direct marketing and so on. The onus for fusing and integrating the inputs provided, more often than not, remains within the company. Not only must this responsibility be recognized, specific policies must be established to ensure that it happens.

The determination of corporate objectives, and their dissemination throughout the organization, is a vital aspect of strategic management. Those charged with the responsibility of developing and implementing specific aspects of, say, a marketing communications campaign must be made fully aware of the corporate objectives against which these campaigns must be set. Only in this way can there be confidence that the two will be in harmony.

Campaign planning is a complex and multifaceted activity. At the minimum, it requires a thorough understanding of the different contributions that can be made by the variety of tools of marketing communications. These skills, and the appropriate knowledge base, must either be encompassed within the organization or the responsibilities must be devolved to partners in the marketing communications process. It is this factor, arguably, more than any other which either enhances or inhibits the organization's ability to develop integrated marketing communications campaigns.

Associated with this is the need to identify the fundamental differences between tactical and strategic communications objectives. Whilst the former may be essential for the short-term delivery of brand volumes, it is vital that these are consistent with the overall strategic and corporate objectives to ensure the long-term sustenance of the brand.

Establishing the budget

A key task within the framework of marketing communications is the appropriate determi-

nation of the levels of expenditure required to fulfil the task established. The amount of money spent on marketing communications differs widely among companies, even within the same industry.

The annual brand survey published by *Marketing* magazine in conjunction with Nielsen, which is the source of the following figures, provides a comprehensive analysis of many consumer goods markets (*Marketing Week*, 3 July 1997). For example:

In 1996, in the confectionery market, Nestlé Rowntree spent £4.7 million against sales in excess of £141 million for Kit Kat; however, Mars, with only slightly smaller sales – between 120 and 125 million – spent only £1.4 million. Cadbury spent £2.2 million defending Roses' sales of some £70–75 million, whilst Nestlé Rowntree spent £2.6 million on Quality Street, with sales estimated at between £60 million and £65 million.

In the butter and spreads sector, Van Den Bergh spent almost £5.2 million on Flora sales in excess of £125 million, whilst Anchor Foods spent slightly more – £5.3 million – against an estimated £115 million sales of Anchor butter. In the same category, Dairy Crest spent £4.1 million against sales of between £50 million and £55 million for Clover, whilst St Ivel spent only £2.3 million on Gold, with sales of between £45 million and £50 million.

In the snack foods market, Walkers Crisps – the overall brand leader – spent £6.9 million defending sales of over £388 million. Pringles, the P&G brand, received £2.7 million against sales of £65–70 million. However, Quavers, with only slightly smaller sales of £55–60 million received only £1.4 million. Two other roughly comparable brands show the disparity of advertising support: whilst Golden Wonder spent £1.8 million on sales of £45–50 million, Wotsits received £846,000 against sales of between £40 and £45 million.

The primary issue is that of determining the reasons for this wide variation in expenditure patterns, and of determining an effective approach to the setting of a budgetary level. It should be clear that the determination of the correct level of expenditure must depend on proper analysis of the situation, rather than the use of 'norms', rule of thumb, or 'gut-feel'.

According to Simon Broadbent (1989), author of *The Advertising Budget*, the amount to spend is determined by a process, not a formula. Hence, there is no simple solution. Various methods of budget determination have been suggested, and the issue is one of deciding which approach is right for the situation.

The determination of the marketing communications budget cannot be considered in isolation. It is merely a part of the overall budgeting process which affects all aspects of the company's operation. Ultimately, any company must ensure that it remains in profit (at least in the longer term) if its business is to remain viable. As such, there will be a number of demands on the company's income and capital reserves. It may be necessary to improve the quality of production, which will require a significant investment in plant and machinery; to augment the sales force in order to achieve better distribution for the products it manufactures; to invest in research and development to ensure that the brand portfolio is maintained and is successful in a competitive environment, and so on.

Marketing communications budgets, in this context, are part of the overall marketing budget. Inevitably, companies must consider the variety of demands for expenditure from a wide range of different sources, and demands for expenditure on marketing communications must compete with all these other areas. Arguably the most important 'competitor' for funds comes from the desire to maintain a competitive price at the point of purchase. Inevitably, if prices are reduced, either to the retailer or the end-consumer, there will be a consequence for the overall level of revenue. In many companies, the source from which expenditure is most likely to be withdrawn is that of advertising and other forms of marketing communications.

The following section sets out most of the ways used to determine the budget.

Marginal analysis

Several attempts have been made to transfer the learning from the principles of economic theory to that of budget determination. In essence, the principles of marginal analysis suggest that a company should continue to increase its marketing communications expenditure until the point where the increase in expenditure matches, but does not exceed, the increase in income which those expenditures generate. This can be shown graphically (Figure 5.2).

Unfortunately, the application of the theory of marginal analysis does not transfer readily into the real-world situation. The first problem to deal with is the fact that the theory assumes that sales are a direct function of marketing communications expenditures. Whilst it is possible to postulate situations in which this might be the case – for example, in the area of direct marketing – even here this may be somewhat wide of the mark. The level of expenditure is only one of the variables which needs to be considered. The theory makes no attempt to consider, for example, the location of the activity in terms, say, of media placement, or of the copy content of the advertisement or sales promotion tool. It simply assumes that every pound spent is likely to achieve the same impact on the market. Clearly, other marketing activities will have an impact on the level of achievement which will render the formula almost incalculable.

Importantly, most marketing communications activities rely on a built-in time lag. Even in the area of direct marketing, where a more precise correlation can be established between patterns of expenditure and achievement, it will be necessary to make an allowance for other indirect variables. The nature of the message, its placement, the competitive environment and other factors will all have to be allowed for if the theory is to stand up in practice. Certainly, until the advent of rapid response computer programs, the amount of detail which would need to be built into such a calculation proved unwieldy at best.

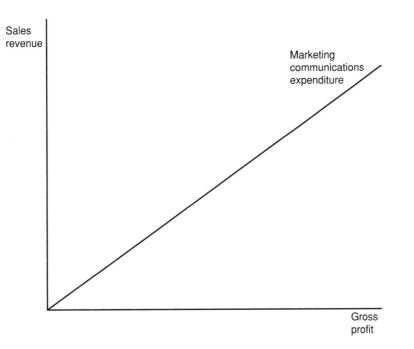

Figure 5.2

Several attempts have been made to build econometric models against which to 'test' different levels of expenditure. Suffice it to say that at best they provide some guidance as to the likely impact of the proposals in the real world.

Percentage of sales

Probably the most widely used method of budget determination is the calculation of a ratio between past expenditure and sales, sometimes referred to as the advertising/sales (A/S) ratio. The calculation itself is quite straightforward. The previous year's expenditures are calculated as a percentage of total sales, and the resultant figure is used to calculate the budget for the coming year. Thus, if £12 million worth of sales was achieved against a communications budget of £300,000, the percentage would be 2.5 per cent. Assuming that the sales forecast for the coming year was £15 million, this would yield a budget of £375,000. Whilst the process is a quick and easy one, there are flaws in the argument.

In the first place, the data used will be considerably out of date by the time that it is implemented. Since we do not have a full picture of current year sales, we must rely on, at best, the latest twelve months for which we have information on which to base our calculations for next year's activity. Secondly, it creates a situation in which the budget only increases against an expectation of higher sales. If sales are expected to decline, then the future communications budget must be reduced to bring it into line with the defined ratio. The inherent danger is that a brand that is under threat – and losing volume – actually reduces its budgets rather than increasing them. Thirdly, it fails to recognize that marketing communications activity can create sales volume for a brand. The application of the principle, in fact, operates in reverse – with sales being the determinant of expenditure levels.

However, it does demand a close examination of the relationship between the costs of marketing communications, the price charged for the product and the level of profit which is likely to be generated. This is particularly important when considering the specific nature of the ratio to be applied to the calculations. It may be possible, for example, to examine competitive ratios to determine whether the company is operating at, or near, the norm for the product sector.

The most important consideration, however, remains the basis on which the ratio itself is established. Many companies set a norm which is rigorously applied. In some cases, it becomes the established company practice, and though it may have been determined after a full consideration of competitive environment, the conditions obtaining at the time of setting the 'norm' will have changed considerably over time. The problem with this approach, therefore, is that there is a tendency to ignore many of the other important variables which may have a direct bearing on the possibility of achieving the desired objectives. Unless the ratio is regularly and consistently reviewed, it may become irrelevant to the contemporary situation which the brand faces.

Percentage of product gross margin

This approach is, essentially, similar to the previous one, except that the gross margin rather than the level of sales is used as the basis for calculating the future level of expenditure. Here, a percentage of either the past or expected gross margin – net sales less the cost of goods – is used.

It has particular relevance to brands with comparatively low production costs set against high unit prices. The manufacturers of such products will be concerned with maintaining the size of the margin as much as with unit sales volume. The consequence will be to enable such brands to spend more on marketing communications than would necessarily be the case with an A/S ratio in order to maintain their premium price in the marketplace.

As with other ratio methods, it is extremely easy to apply once the specific relationship has been established. But it carries with it many of the same advantages and disadvantages discussed above in the context of the percentage of sales approach.

Residue of previous year's surplus

This method is based entirely on prior performance, whereby the excess of income over costs in the previous year is designated as the budget for the following year. Although simple in principle, it clearly demands that a surplus is achieved in order for monies to be spent in any future period. It fails to recognize the need for investment in growth brands or, for that matter, the impact of competitive activities.

Percentage of anticipated turnover

This approach is based on the allocation of a fixed percentage of future turnover to the marketing communications budget.

Unit–case–sales ratio method

This method, sometimes referred to as the case rate, requires that brand volumes for the next year are estimated and a fixed sum per unit is allocated towards marketing communications expenditure. It is then a simple process of multiplying the expected sales volume (in units or cases) by the fixed allocation to arrive at a total communications budget. In some instances, comparisons are made between the company's own case rate and those of its competitors to explore the relationships between them.

Obviously the approach is a simple one, but it begs the question as to how the case rate itself is calculated. In some instances, it may be based on past experience. Usually, it is a company or industry norm. Here again, as with other ratio-based approaches, expenditure patterns reflect past achievement or anticipated sales. As such, it tends to benefit growth brands and disadvantage those which are declining. It ignores the fact that a brand which is suffering in the marketplace may need to increase its levels of expenditure to arrest the decline, rather than reduce the budget, which would be the automatic result of applying the method.

Competitive expenditure

Another approach frequently used is to base a brand's expenditure levels on an assessment of competitors' expenditures.

Often, a calculation is made of the level of category expenditure, and a percentage – usually related to a brand's share of market – is chosen as the basis for calculating that brand's expenditure levels. In other instances, an attempt is made to achieve parity with a nominated competitor by setting a similar level of expenditure to theirs. At the very least, this approach has the benefit of ensuring that brand expenditure levels are maintained in line with those of the competition. However, it suffers from the obvious difficulty of being able to determine an accurate assessment of the level of competitive spend.

Whilst it is obviously possible to obtain a reasonable fix on advertising spend from published information – sourced from *Register MEAL* – the same is not true of sales promotional spend and other categories of marketing communications. Figures for the latter are rarely published. Moreover, it fails to recognize that the expenditure patterns of a competitor may well be dictated by a totally different set of problems and objectives.

Desired share of voice

This approach is an extension of the previous one where the management may relate the volume share of the product category to expenditure within the category as a whole, and is primarily related to advertising expenditure. Thus, if a brand has a 15 per cent share of the market in which it competes, and total advertising expenditure for the category is £8 million, in order to retain a proportional share of voice it would need to set a budget of £1.2 million. By the same token, the company would have a benchmark against which to establish the levels of expenditure required to drive a brand forward. Hence, it might decide to increase its share of voice to, say, 20 or even 25 per cent in an attempt to gain a greater level of visibility for its brand and a greater share of the overall category.

Media inflation

This approach makes the simple assumption that a budget – usually the previous year's – should be increased in line with the growth in media costs to ensure a similar delivery of the message to the target audience. At the lowest level, this approach ensures that the real level of advertising expenditure is maintained. However, it fails to acknowledge any of the other variables which will have an impact on the achievement of the marketing objectives. Most importantly, it removes the desire to consider other, more meaningful, media efficiency approaches.

Media, as with most other things, presents a competitive environment to the company. When a particular medium increases its price, this should be the cue to re-examine its role within the overall context of the communications programme, rather than simply increasing the budget to reflect the high price being charged.

Objective and task method/DAGMAR

This method is based on a more realistic examination of the specific objectives which the marketing plan needs to meet, and was established as an attempt to apply a more scientific approach to budget determination. The basis of the approach was a paper commissioned by the American Association of National Advertisers and published in 1961.

In the paper 'Defining Advertising Goals for Measuring Advertising Results' (DAGMAR) the author, Russell Coley, proposed that advertising should be specifically budgeted to accomplish defined goals or objectives. The DAGMAR approach – also known as the objective and task method – requires that specific objectives for the campaign are defined at the outset. These may be expressed in terms of, for example, increasing brand awareness, encouraging sampling and trial, promoting repeat purchase and so on. In each case a finite numerical target is given, and the costs of achieving this target are calculated. The resultant budget is thus based on a series of goals rather than on past or future results, and is thus the most realistic in marketing terms.

It offers the benefit of being able to monitor the campaign achievement against the targets set, and provides a more accurate guide to budgetary determination for the future. The limitation on the accuracy of the method is the ability to access sufficient information to ensure that all of the relevant variables can be considered. Although the original paper dealt specifically with the task of establishing advertising budgets, the method is equally applicable to other areas of marketing communications.

Experimentation

A guiding principle for budget determination, as with other aspects of marketing, is the need, on the one hand, to protect the company investment whilst, on the other, ensuring that sufficient new and innovatory approaches are taken to drive the brand forward. It is for this reason that most major marketing companies utilize an experimental approach at various times. Having established the overall marketing communications budget by the normal or most appropriate means, it is possible to create a mini 'test market' for the purposes of experimenting with a variation. By isolating, say, one region of the country, it is possible to

experiment with alternative budget constructions. In many cases, and in the absence of definitive data, it is useful to determine the impact of, for example, an increased level of media expenditure or a particular sales promotion technique.

The benefit of this approach is that the main sources of business are 'protected', in the sense that they receive the 'normal' support levels. Hence, the position of the brand is not unduly prejudiced. By 'hot-housing' a different approach, real experience can be gained and the budgetary process enhanced with the additional knowledge. It is an attempt to apply an empirical approach and, thus, a more scientific method to the process of budget determination. However, it is important to restrict the number of 'experiments' in order to ensure that the data is readable against the norm, and that the individual variables can be properly assessed within a real market environment.

What we can afford

This approach is based on a management assessment of either the brand itself or the overall company position. In effect, management determines the level of profit desired, or the return on investment, and the marketing communications budget is the amount that remains after calculating that level. Of course, it fails to recognize the contribution of marketing communications itself, and ignores other environmental factors, such as competitive pressure, which might militate against the profit level being achieved. Although this is a somewhat arbitrary approach to the budgetary process, it has to be recognized that the issue of affordability plays an important part within any financial procedures. There will always be competing demands for funds within the company – to support the activities of other brands within the portfolio, to fund areas such as production capability, to finance research and development, and so on. It is a fundamental role of management to determine company priorities and to allocate funds accordingly.

New products

One area that demands a separate mention is that of developing a marketing communications budget for a new product. Clearly, past data will be unavailable and, hence, many of the usual budgeting approaches cannot be applied. At the simplest level, the approach to new products is similar to that of the objective and task method, described above. Calculations must be made of the amount of money required to achieve the objectives established for the brand.

It must be recognized that, in most instances, new products require investment in advance of sales performance. Indeed, without the appropriate levels of investment in marketing communications, most new products are unlikely to succeed. A realistic time frame for the achievement of the goals must be established at the outset. It is unrealistic to expect a new product to make a major contribution in the short term.

It is important to re-state that there is no hard and fast formula for defining a marketing communications budget. It is important to experiment with a number of the methods described above, and to ensure that the appropriate use is made of previous company experience, industry data and experimentation. The imperative for all companies is to ensure the building up of a database of information – both within the company and from competitor knowledge – which can be used to enhance the process.

Budgeting for integrated marketing communications

Whichever method or methods are adopted, however, our task must be to consider the process of budget determination itself. Broadbent (1989) suggests that the process is made up of six separate stages, as follows.

Stage 1: Brand objectives

Here, we must consider the role of the brand within the company and the importance of the brand to the achievement of the overall objectives. Consideration should encompass both the short-term time frame of the plan (e.g. the year ahead), as well as the longer-term considerations (e.g. over the next three to five years). It is also important to examine the relationship between volume and profit contribution.

At this stage also, the source of the brand's sales should be identified. The larger the audience, the greater the likely budget requirement. By the same token, by adopting a more concentrated approach, the media budget may be lowered.

Stage 2: Review the brand budgets

It is important to consider how the brand has performed in the past, since this will have significant implications for its ability to perform in the future. If a brand has been in decline, then the previous budget will need to be increased if the decline is to be arrested or reversed.

Stage 3: Marketing history and forecasts

As well as a consideration of the brand itself, it is important to consider the market category which will help to put the brand into context. This will reveal a number of important facets which will assist in the brand planning process.

Although volume sales may be increasing, it is important to determine whether they are keeping pace with the category as a whole. In fact, the brand may be losing share of market which, in the longer term, could endanger its position.

It is vitally important to maintain a record of brand performance over time within the market sector in which it operates. That implies maintaining data about competitive brands, advertising and other promotional expenditures, and so on. There are, as has been mentioned, a number of sources which will be important in this context. Nielsen will provide data on retail sales volume; AGB, similarly, will provide a commentary on sales over time, but from the perspective of consumer purchases; whilst media expenditure levels can, within certain limitations, be obtained from MEAL Media Register. By examining this databank, along with other information streams, it may be possible to identify particular relationships, trends, and the dynamics of the product category.

Stage 4: Assess expenditure effects

Examine the effects of previous advertising and promotional expenditure to determine the level of brand responsiveness to marketing communications activity. Previous experience is a valuable guide to likely future performance. And remember, in this respect it is possible to learn as much from competitor performance as from your own brand.

Stage 5: Set budgets

Consider the application of a number of the standard approaches to budget determination (these are set out in detail above). This is very much a preliminary exercise in budget determination, since it will suggest a range of possible amounts to be spent, with affordability and feasibility being checked in the final stage.

Stage 6: Check feasibility

The final stage of this proposed process is ensuring that the budget determined is feasible and practical within the context of the established objectives.

The budget contingency

It may be an axiom, but it remains true that anything that can go wrong, will! It is, therefore, both sound practice and prudent to identify a sum of money (usually expressed as a proportion of the overall budget) to be used to remedy deficiencies in the performance of the marketing communications plan. Inevitably, much of the planning process takes place in advance of the implementation of the details of the plan. Whilst steps will be taken to anticipate likely changes which might occur in the marketplace, it is clear that there will be a variety of unforeseen circumstances which may impair the achievement of the desired goals. Competitive product introductions, price changes, alterations in competitive expenditures, may be just a few of the variables which alter once the plan is put into effect.

The sensible marketer recognizes that his plans must operate in a dynamic rather than a static environment. Simply because a plan has been created and approved at senior management level should not imply that it is to be implemented without change. There needs to be constant monitoring and feedback built into the marketing communications plan, to ensure that it reflects the situation which actually obtains rather than the one that was envisaged when the plan was created. Only in this way can the process be amended and adapted to mirror the real market environment.

Allocating the promotional budget

It is not just the resolution of how the overall budget is calculated, but the allocation of funds within the budget which must be addressed. Again, the emphasis must rest with integrated marketing communications and the identification of the most appropriate and cost-effective communications channels to achieve the specific task. That having been said, however, it must be recognized that there are no set formulae for allocating budgets between competing communications approaches.

According to research conducted by PIMS Europe, the business of allocating a marketing budget is not only a complex task but, if done incorrectly, can have a devastating impact on a brand's overall profit. The company conducted a study of some 500 US and European fmcg in companies, an attempt to determine whether a 'correct' marketing mix exists. The study identifies seven key factors which influence the optimum marketing mix: brand rank; concentration of the trade; pace of innovation; market growth; sister brands; breadth of offering; and historic brand image.

It would appear that whatever a brand leader does with its mix, it will always generate better profits than number twos or threes. It suggests that if brand leaders spend less than 50 per cent of their budget on media, they will earn, on average, a 39 per cent return on capital employed over four years; whereas a 70 per cent ad spend will cause returns to rise slightly, to 43 per cent. However, if a number two brand spends between 50 and 70 per cent of its budget on media advertising, it earns its highest possible return at 28 per cent. If it increases this to 70 per cent or more, the profitability is likely to be exactly halved. For also-ran brands, the difference between the optimum and non-optimum mix is the difference between a maximum return of 11 per cent or losses. The penalty for getting the mix wrong is correspondingly greater for brand followers.

However, it is difficult to attach too much importance to the findings. On the one hand, the analysis is somewhat superficial, since only two variables – advertising (including direct marketing) and promotion – are considered. On the other, there are confusing correlations between cause and effect. It cannot determine, for example, whether brands are investing heavily in their futures, or if companies are using their brands as cash cows (*Marketing Week*, 24 April, 1997).

The marketing communications budget should be allocated against an identification of the identity of the target customer and how effectively we can reach him or her. The key decisions should relate to the state of the market (growth or mature), the state of the competition (few or many competitors) and an understanding of the cost/reward relationship for marketing communications within the industry.

We have already looked at the various methods by which the overall marketing communications budget may be determined. In turn, a series of key strategic decisions must relate to the deployment of that budget against the various elements of the campaign.

The consumer continuum

As we have seen, the potential market for any product or service is made up of different groups of individuals who display varying degrees of loyalty towards the brand. This can be depicted as a continuum, as in the chart below (Figure 5.3).

The starting point is to define each target audience and identify strategic requirements. It is important to note that the broader the base of the audience, the less costly per head the campaign is likely to be. The narrower the identified target, the more costly per head it will be to reach these individuals. However, the cost of reaching each individual within the

Figure 5.3   Continuum of potential target audiences

target audience is only one consideration. Of greater importance is the potential for conversion. Even if it is expensive to reach potential customers, this may be worth while if they can be persuaded to switch their purchases to the brand. Cleland (1995), writing in *Advertising Age*, suggests that it takes six times as much money to attract a new customer as it does to retain an existing one.

In many instances, the appropriate channels will be self-identifying, by a careful examination of the objectives, and the techniques which can best meet them. Since all marketing communications tools have identified roles in the communications process, it will be apparent that a careful consideration of the needs will, similarly, identify the areas likely to be most appropriate.

If the task is defined as generating high levels of awareness among a wide target audience, then it is probable that advertising will absorb a substantial proportion of the communications budget; if the task is to generate trial and sampling, the budget will need to be apportioned primarily between sales promotion and advertising; if the need is to promote the corporate identity, the budget is likely to be spent on corporate advertising and public relations; if the task is to reach a narrowly defined and readily identified group of consumers, direct marketing techniques will come to the fore.

The imperative in all cases is the need for integrated marketing communications. We have seen, from the beginning of this text, that the consumer does not discriminate as to the source of the message. Our fundamental objective is to deliver the brand proposition in the most cost-effective manner to the defined target audience. As such, we need to identify and integrate those marketing communications techniques which best achieve this goal.

Rossiter and Percy (1997) suggest that this is best achieved using a matrix approach, which is itself an extension of the objective and task method, described earlier. By describing the various tasks required to be fulfilled by the separate tools of marketing communications, it is possible to consider these against the suitability and effectiveness of the tools available. Inevitably, the process itself is a complex one, involving several revisions to the budget plan. However, it will avoid unnecessary duplication of expenditures and provide for the integration of the overall marketing communications campaign.

References

Arnold, D., *The Handbook of Brand Management*, Century Business–The Economist Books, 1992

Broadbent, S., *The Advertising Budget*, IPA/NTC Business Books, 1989

Cleland, K., 'Few Wed Marketing Communications', *Advertising Age*, 27 February 1995

Nielsen, *Category Management*, 1992 NTC Business Books

Rossiter, J. R. and Percy, L., *Advertising, Communications and Promotion Management*, 2nd edition, McGraw-Hill, 1997

Additional reading

To understand the interface between marketing communications and the broader issues of marketing management, the following will aid understanding:

Arnold, David, *The Handbook of Brand Management*, 1992, Century Business

Lancaster, Geoff and Massingham, Lester, *Marketing Management*, 1993, McGraw-Hill

Doyle, Peter, *Marketing Management and Strategy*, 1994, Prentice Hall

Broadbent, Simon, *The Advertising Budget: The Advertiser's Guide to Budget Determination*, 1989, IPA/NTC Business Books

CHAPTER 6

Choosing and using marketing communications agencies

Aims and objectives

- To examine the nature of the UK advertising agency scene;
- To gain an insight into agency structures;
- To consider the various functions within the agency;
- To learn about alternative agency structures;
- To develop an understanding of agency/client relationships and agency remuneration;
- To determine the process of selecting agencies.

The structure and roles of marketing communications agencies

Marketing communications agencies play a varied role in terms of the contribution they make to their respective clients' businesses. Indeed, this is the focus of much of the debate which is currently raging within the marketing communications industry. In some instances, this is a reflection of the structuring of the specific agency or consultancy which the company uses – its range and breadth of skills, and the relationship which exists between the organizations. In others, it depends to a substantial degree on the role which the client company perceives the agency or consultancy to be capable of fulfilling. We will explore these and related issues in the pages which follow.

The UK agency scene

The top ten UK advertising agencies are truly global, with representation through wholly-owned subsidiaries or partner agencies in most of the major marketing regions of the world.

Their growth has been the result of acquisition and the organic development of new business. Often, reflecting the move to provide a greater range of services to their clients, agencies have formed substantial groups, comprising not only the functions of advertising, but also major subsidiaries operating in the fields of media specialization, sales promotion, direct marketing, public relations and other areas.

The current top ten agencies in the UK are shown in Table 6.1.

It can be seen that, over recent years, there has been considerable stability in the respective agency positions, although inevitably there has been some slight movement among them. The most significant change has been the meteoric rise of M&C Saatchi, following

Table 6.1   Agencies ranked by A. C. Nielsen MEAL billings

Rank 1996	Rank 1995	Rank 1994	Rank 1993	Agency	1996 billings* (£ million)
1	4	2	4	Abbott Mead Vickers BBDO	306.81
2	2	3	3	J. Walter Thompson London	278.15
3	3	4	2	Ogilvy & Mather	254.63
4	5	5	6	BMP DDB	237.00
5	1	1	1	Saatchi and Saatchi	224.34
6	6	6	5	D'Arcy Masius Benton & Bowles	186.86
7	12	11	9	Publicis	186.46
8	20	–	–	M&C Saatchi	174.95
9	7	9	8	Lowe Howard-Spink	169.54
10	8	8	7	Bates Dorland	168.38

* UK billings only

Source: *Campaign* magazine, 28 February 1997; 1 March 1996; 24 February 1995

the much publicized break-away from the original Saatchi & Saatchi agency.

Agency structures

The structure of marketing communications agencies will have a marked impact on the range of skills and services which they can offer their clients. It has to be said, however, that there is no single prescription for agency structuring. A key factor will be the scale of the agency. The larger it is, the greater the range of specialist skills it can afford to employ. By the same token, smaller agencies necessarily tend to employ personnel who are more 'generalist'. A further factor will be the underlying nature of the agency itself which, in turn, will largely determine the nature of the people it will need to employ to provide the necessary services which its clients expect and demand. As might be expected, the specialist skills of, say, an advertising agency will demand a different pattern of recruitment from, say, a public

relations or sales promotions consultancy. Equally, if the agency specializes in a particular type of advertising, for example, retail, medical or high-tech accounts, then it will need to employ the skills of people who have a particular understanding of or aptitude for that field of activity.

From the outset, agencies tended to be generalist in their approach, that is, they attracted a wide variety of clients whose accounts demanded different inputs. However, as competition between advertising agencies intensified, so they began to concentrate their efforts into particular fields. To some degree, this was self-fulfilling. If an agency already had a portfolio, for example, of fast-moving consumer goods, then it would tend to attract clients from similar fields. It would be better able to demonstrate its expertise and achievements for existing clients and thus attract more, similar accounts to the agency. By the same token, however, the effective fulfilment of clients' briefs often requires very specialist knowledge. A copywriter who has the skill to develop impactful consumer campaigns is unlikely to possess a knowledge and understanding of more technical areas. Accordingly, such clients will tend to be attracted to agencies that can provide the appropriate inputs.

Recent years have seen an increasing degree of specialization within the field of advertising, although there will inevitably continue to be some degree of overlap between the different agency provisions. Much will depend on the overall nature of the client's business. If the account is predominantly recruitment based, that is, the advertising is designed to recruit staff to their client's companies, then, not unreasonably, the client will tend to be attracted to an agency which can demonstrate expertise in that area. However, such clients may often have a requirement for other forms of advertising. Whether they use their specialist recruitment agency to develop such advertising will depend, to some degree, on the scale of their budget. If the advertising spend, in this case for non-recruitment advertising, is small, the client may prefer to remain with a single agency which, over time, will develop a substantial understanding both about the nature of the client's business and the specific advertising requirements. If the budget is substantial, however, the client may divide the account between two or more agencies, to achieve a better match between the skills offered and the specific advertising requirements.

The result has been the development of a very complicated advertising scene. Some agencies will operate within comparatively narrow fields, such as those indicated above, together with others such as financial specialisms, retail, business-to-business advertising, direct response, charity, tourism and so on. Such agencies will continue to develop their expertise within these areas, which serves to attract a number of clients operating within related areas. Some examples will serve to illustrate:

Primary Contact, which specializes in business-to-business advertising, recorded billings of £12.2 million in 1996.*

The Smith Jones Communications Company, whose business is largely in the fields of computers and high technology, achieved 1996 billings of £7.25 million.*

Dewynters is primarily concerned with clients in the fields of entertainment and leisure, and recorded billings of £8.56 million.*

PTK Healthcare, as its name suggests, is involved in medical and pharmaceutical accounts, with 1996 billings of £6.78 million.*

Dewe Rogerson specializes in financial advertising, with billings of £13.22 million.

WWAV Rapp Collins is a specialist in direct marketing, and recorded billings of £40.85 million.*

*(Campaign Report, 1997)

In the same way, the specialist tools of marketing communications have equally given rise to the development of agencies and consultancies which tend to concentrate their efforts within more narrowly defined limits. Some, for example, have developed reputations as specialist sales promotions consultancies, others operate within the field of public relations, whilst yet others offer specialist services within the area of direct marketing. However, in some instances, such 'specialist' agencies will be grouped together to provide a wider range of services to the client base. This is particularly true of the large advertising groups which have been created by the acquisition and merger between several such specialists. The Cordiant Group comprises Saatchi and Saatchi Advertising, Zenith Media, etc.; WPP owns J. Walter Thompson, Ogilvy and Mather; D'Arcy Masius Benton & Bowles consists of DMB&B, DMB&B Financial, IMP (a substantial specialist in the field of sales promotion), MediaVest, MS&L.

The advertising agency

Even within a specialist field such as advertising, the individual practitioners will have their own views of how best to structure themselves to meet the needs of their clients.

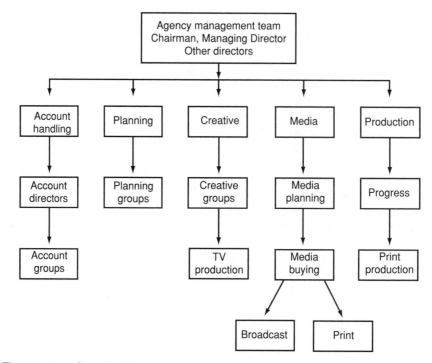

Figure 6.1   The structure of an advertising agency

In particular, agencies have an individual personality, and this will be reflected in the way that they set themselves up to deal with their clients' requirements. However, there are some common threads which run through most of them, as can be seen in Figure 6.1.

The agency management team

Providing the overall guidance and strategic direction of the agency will be a senior management team. They will come from a variety of different backgrounds and will offer a broad base of experience to the team. Commonly, the management team will comprise most or all of the heads of the various departments shown above, together with a financial director. They will fulfil a variety of different functions. On one level, they will

provide the essential cohesion which the agency requires. They will be responsible for establishing the central policies which will provide the basis upon which the agency operates with its client base. On another, they will provide the essential point of contact at the senior management level of the client company. This function is particularly important since, in other respects, the senior client management may not have regular contact with the agency and need to be apprised both of issues relating to their own business and other factors which will govern the working relationship between the companies.

The core functions of the advertising agency will be provided by a team representing the four major departments, each of which must work closely with each of the others to ensure the successful development of effective advertising and communications campaigns (Figure 6.2).

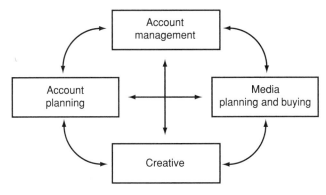

Figure 6.2 The core agency team

Account management

The account management team will vary considerably, depending on the nature of the business for which they are responsible. Most agencies will have one individual who maintains overall management responsibility for the account management function within the agency. The head of account management will have a key responsibility in maintaining the ongoing relationships with the clients and will hold frequent meetings with the senior client management team. He or she will be responsible for ensuring that the clients' needs are reflected in the performance of the agency, the recruitment and guidance of the account management team, and for setting the 'style' of the agency in relation to its account handling role.

Each account of the agency will be led by an account director, who may be a member of the main board of the agency. That individual will have the key responsibility of guiding the relationship with the client or clients (in many instances, the account director will be responsible for leading more than one piece of business) and providing the focus for the day-to-day handling of the business. In a simplistic sense, they are the clients' representatives within the agency and will be responsible for the guidance of the work which is produced by the agency.

Beneath the account director, in structural terms, will be a number of account handlers, variously referred to as account executives, account managers and so on. They will provide the day-to-day liaison with the client company and will be responsible for ensuring that the essential work required by the client is fulfilled both on time and within budget. Most importantly, they represent the channel through which the dialogue between the client and the agency is conducted. They convey information between the two parties, providing the necessary interpretation to 'translate' client language into agency-speak and vice versa. They have a co-ordinatory responsibility in terms of bringing together members of the agency team whose inputs will be required to satisfy the client's requirements at the various stages in the development of an advertising or communications campaign. They also have the responsibility for presenting the resultant work of the agency back to the members of the client team.

Agencies vary considerably in terms of their account handling structures but, in essence, their objective will be to mirror the client's own internal structure and provide appropriate contact points between the organizations at all relevant levels.

Planning

The role of planning is a comparatively new function within the advertising agency, but one which has evolved dramatically to change the nature and function of the agency response to its clients' communications needs.

Two individuals, above all others, can lay claim to having created this important agency function: Stanley Pollitt, who later went on to found an agency called Boase, Massimi, Pollitt (now BMP DDB, the fourth largest agency in the UK, with UK billings of £237 million in 1996) – and Stephen King at J. Walter Thompson (in 1996, the second largest agency in the world – its UK billings stood at £278 million) (Campaign Report, 1997). So, how did they change the nature of advertising? Most significantly, they made the first real attempt to integrate the process of understanding the consumer with the function of creating advertising messages.

Several factors have contributed to the emergence and growth of the account planning function, not only within this country but within most major advertising agencies throughout the world. In part, it represented a response within the agency to the changing needs of their client companies. The increased understanding of the marketing function necessitated a closer focus on the consumer. Hitherto, dialogue with the consumer audience was provided by the research department of the agency, although its contribution was relatively minor and comparatively late in the advertising development process. Most often, research was used to test advertising rather than integrated into its development. The result was the creation of friction with the creative department, who saw their ideas condemned by what they saw as inadequate research techniques.

The research departments themselves realized that their contribution to the development process was under-utilized. Their responsibilities were largely limited to providing an overview of the marketplace – often using the internal resource of a desk research or library facility – and evaluating the results of creative development. A major part of their function was that of copy testing – using prompts such as commercial scripts or storyboards to evaluate the consumer's response to an advertising message. Since the research department was considered a backroom function, it was rarely represented at the key meetings, either internal with the people responsible for creating the advertising, or with clients to provide an advocacy role of the material that the agency was presenting. At the same time, agency management began to appreciate the cost of misdirected creativity. Without adequate guidance, the creative department might waste enormous amounts of time – a precious resource – on the development of advertising which was irrelevant to the true needs of the consumer or, at best, misunderstood.

The development of account planning changed all that. Account planners have an important strategic responsibility within the agency. They are required to provide a far deeper understanding of both the consumers and the brands which they purchase. Often, it is their responsibility to guide the strategic direction of the advertising, isolating the positioning which the product or service should adopt to most closely correspond with the identified needs of the consumer. They are fully integrated with the creative process and work closely with the creative teams at all stages of the advertising development, not merely in terms of its final evaluation. They have a key voice in the agency–client dialogue. Unlike their research predecessors, they are represented at all key meetings and contribute to the development of the broader issues of strategic development being addressed by the client company. They occupy senior management roles within the majority of agencies, and address similar issues on behalf of the agency itself. Ultimately, however, it is their ability to identify the critical consumer insight to the client and agency team alike which makes their contribution so important.

Lisa Fortini-Campbell (1992), in her book *Hitting the Sweet Spot*, defines five key functions of the account planner.

1 Discovering and defining the advertising task

The account planner is the person who has the responsibility for organizing information regarding the consumer and the marketplace. He or she uses a variety of inputs, including both existing client and agency data as well as specific primary research which he or she initiates.

2 Preparing the creative brief

The account planner is the person within the agency who prepares the creative brief which will both inform and inspire the creative process. We will discuss the creative brief itself in Chapter 8, but suffice it to say at this stage that this document provides the focus on the key issues – most importantly, the critical consumer insight – which will guide the creative development process.

3 Creative development

The account planner is integral to all stages of creative development, from the initial thoughts and rough ideas to the final work which is presented to the client. He or she represents the custodian of the brand values and, critically, interprets these in the context of his or her understanding of the needs and wants of the consumer. In many instances, account planners may well go back to the consumer at a number of intermediate stages to ensure that their reaction to the advertising proposition is an appropriate one. This will provide additional guidance to the creative team to enable them to hone the proposition to its most effective level.

4 Presenting the advertising to the client

Advertising may 'sell' itself to the client, but usually needs some interpretation to demonstrate how the advertising works with the consumer. It is the planner's function in this area to identify how the advertising campaign will work in the marketplace and to pinpoint the broader implications of the advertising approach in terms of the objectives – both short- and long-term – which have been established for it. Account planners provide the essential rationalization and justification for the advertising approach, often utilizing information about the advertising from research conversations with consumers. Their role is to provide an objective evaluation of the consumer response to the agency proposals.

5 Tracking the advertising's performance

After the implementation of the advertising campaign, the planner continues to monitor consumer reaction to it. This process will provide important feedback to the agency and client teams, not only about the impact of the campaign itself, but also information which will guide the subsequent development of the campaign.

The creative department

The creative department represents the public face of the agency. It is their responsibility to create the advertising messages which are ultimately seen by the target public or publics. The larger agencies employ a considerable number of people within their creative department who not only possess the specific skills of art direction and copywriting, but may also have built up extensive specialist experience within particular market sectors. Sometimes, if an agency has a number of different clients in a particular area, for example, retailing or pharmaceuticals, it may employ specific creative staff who have demonstrated a clear understanding of those respective markets.

In most agencies, the creative department is headed up by a creative director who has built up a wide range of experience. Not only is the creative director responsible for the final evaluation of the work produced by the members of the department, but he or she is also responsible for the smooth running of the creative function within the agency. Often, the position will be held by someone who has established a strong reputation within the industry, since that reputation will contribute to the desired image of the agency in the minds of its clients and prospective clients.

It is most common for creatives to work as a team, usually comprising two people, one with art direction skills, the other with copy-writing skills. Their role is to interpret the creative brief and translate it into an effective advertising message. In many cases, these teams work so closely that their individual contribution to the final work is indistinguish-able. Either or both will contribute equally to the determination of the final idea – the copywriter contributing to the visual compo-nent as much as the art director suggesting the copy approach. Indeed, so close do these relationships become that they will often change jobs together and join a new agency as an established team. Here again, reputations become progressively important. Teams that have consistently produced effective advertis-ing campaigns may well be a major reason why clients are attracted to the agency at which they work.

The creative process is often augmented by a number of other functions within the agency. Since it is not an essential requirement that an art director can draw, he may need to call upon the services of a specialist visualizer, who can translate his ideas into a form which others can readily recognize. Similarly, some agencies employ typographers, whose responsibility is to ensure the appropriate use of typefaces that can contribute to the overall communication of the advertising message. Increasingly, however, this manual task is being replaced by those with computer skills, with the availability of a wide variety of software packages which can be used to assist the process.

The media department

The media department fulfils the essential role of ensuring that the messages created by the agency are communicated in the appropriate media at the right time and at a realistic cost. The issue is complicated by virtue of the fact that there may well be multiple media solu-tions, and the media department must use its skills and experience to ensure that the medium selected contributes to the effective-ness of the communications process.

The media department usually consists of several people, each possessing discrete spe-cialist skills. Central to this is a research and planning function. There is a vast array of data available to the media planner which will assist in the determination of the appropriate media for the task in hand. It is the planner's responsibility to interpret the available infor-mation and identify the route most relevant to the needs of the campaign. We will see later that, although cost-effectiveness is an impor-tant consideration, it may be overridden in certain circumstances by the need to ensure that the media environment is the most appropriate for the effective communication of the specific message to the identified target audience.

Most media departments will also employ specialist buyers, whose responsibility it is to implement the agreed media solution. Through the establishment of close relation-ships with their own designated area of the media – television, radio, press, posters, etc. – they are the people who ultimately conduct the negotiations designed to purchase time or space at the most cost-effective level. The fragmentation of the media has increased the number of specializations within the depart-ment. In the larger agencies, for example, there will often be a number of media special-ists who deal exclusively with the regional or local media, usually reflecting the specific needs of their client base.

The media function is an important one within the agency environment, but it is an area which has been complicated by the comparatively recent trend towards the sepa-ration of this function from the rest of the agency with the creation of media indepen-dents and dependants. The former exist solely to provide their clients with the essential functions of a media department; the latter similarly fulfil these functions but operate as a wholly-owned subsidiary of an advertising agency or other communications group. Specialist media agencies such as TMD Carat and CIA Medianetwork operate completely independently of any advertising agency grouping. Zenith, the largest of the media dependants, operates as a wholly-owned subsidiary of Cordiant. However, as well as fulfilling the media function for many of the clients of that agency, they are also retained by a number of companies whose creative and advertising development is the responsibility of an advertising agency outside the Cordiant Group of Companies.

MediaVest occupies a similar relationship to DMB&B. Again, it serves to plan and buy the media requirements for several of the clients of that agency but, additionally, works directly or indirectly for a number of clients who have no relationship with DMB&B.

It has to be recognized that scale has become an important facet of negotiating effectively with the media sellers. The larger the media agency, the greater the potential discounts that it can achieve on behalf of its clients. And, by removing the restriction of working for an individual agency and its clients, a media independent or dependant can, effectively, aggregate the business of several agencies or client companies. The latter facet has become increasingly important, with a number of large companies centralizing their media planning and buying function within a single media specialist. The existence of these specialist agencies has meant that, in some instances, agencies maintain only a 'skeleton' media staff, with the main task of media fulfilment being contracted out.

Production

The production department have the critical responsibility of ensuring that creative ideas are correctly translated into the final form

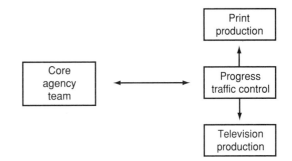

Figure 6.3 Services to the core agency team

appropriate to their appearance in the designated media (Figure 6.3). One function within the production department which has a special role is that of the progress or traffic manager. This individual (and there may well be several within the larger agencies) has the specific responsibility for ensuring that the various stages of the creative development are completed at an appropriate time to ensure that the advertising appears in the correct media on the due date. In many cases, the development of the conceptual advertising campaign, which was presented to the client by the agency team and subsequently approved for appearance in the form in which it is required by the media, is a lengthy and complicated one. Individual elements will need to be brought together within an agreed time frame. For example, specific photography may be required, using selected models. Whilst the creative team will have the responsibility for choosing both the photographer and the artists required, it will be the task of the progress manager to ensure that each stage of the production process is completed within an agreed time frame to meet the copy deadline. In this respect, it is vitally important that the progress manager works closely with the media department to identify such timetable requirements. The same principle applies equally to the production of television advertising.

It is important to note that most of the final components of any advertising campaign are sourced outside the agency. It will be essential for any campaign to utilize the skills of outside photographers, television commercial production teams and so on. This is an important consideration, since it will have a significant bearing on the charges that the client will be called upon to pay during the development of the advertising campaign.

Other services to the agency team

The information department

No agency can function effectively without a constant flow of relevant information (Figure 6.4). Every day, articles will be published which will have a bearing on the way in which the agency understands its client businesses.

In the larger agencies, an internal function would be a library or information management service, which would cull relevant journals and other periodicals in order to build an effective database of information from which agency staff could draw. In other instances, the department might be given the task of sourcing information pertinent to a new project from appropriate sources (industry associations, governmental bodies, etc.).

In smaller agencies, this function would be fulfilled by some external resource. Several

companies exist which can provide this input on an hourly, daily or other basis, obviating the need for the agency to tie up its resources in a function which might only be drawn upon at irregular intervals.

Personnel

Like any other business function, an advertising agency must be capable of dealing with a wide variety of personnel issues: recruitment, remuneration, dismissal and so on. An internal personnel or human resources department provides these functions, although in some instances the responsibility may be fulfilled by a senior member of the management team assisted by other dedicated members of staff.

Finance

As organizations grow, the financial provisions of their operation have to be considered as a separate entity. Clearly, there is a close interrelationship between the financial function and that of personnel management, and often these departments are combined. However, whichever structure is employed, the agency must be capable of managing its cash flow, ensuring the prompt payment of its invoices and discharging of its debts to other organizations which it uses from time to time.

Other agency/consultancy structures

The above sections dealt extensively with the broad structure of the advertising agency, although, in many respects, the model could equally well be used to describe the structure of many sales promotion consultancies, direct marketing agencies, public relations agencies and so on. Where they differ is in the specific nature of the functions they fulfil and, hence, the nature of the personnel they employ. It is fair to say, however, that there is an increasing

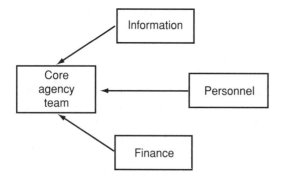

Figure 6.4   Other services to the core agency team

structural convergence between all forms of marketing communications agencies and consultancies, whatever the services they provide.

Because of the increasing demand for the strategic consideration of the issues which confront their organizations, many client companies expect a broader strategic input from the various agencies with which they work. To that end, therefore, the function of planning, for example, is spreading widely throughout all areas of marketing communications and is no longer restricted to the advertising fraternity.

There are certain specific skills which will be required uniquely by dedicated agencies in particular fields. The copywriting skills within a public relations consultancy or direct marketing agency will be significantly different from those required by a conventional advertising agency, as too will be the understanding of the mechanical aspects of production. By the same token, the interpersonal skills possessed by those within different fields of marketing communications may also be different.

Regional agencies

Although a large number of clients work closely with their main agencies, often centred on London or another major city, there are also a substantial number of regional agencies which have developed to provide a more local service to their clients. Some of these exist as subsidiaries of the major international agencies. Indeed, the largest regional agency in 1996, with media billings of slightly under £49 million, was McCann Erickson Manchester, part of the McCann Erickson Group. However, others, such as BDH Advertising (placed second regionally, with billings of £41.51 million) and Faulds Advertising (third regional agency, with £38.61 million), operate independently.

The changing role of marketing communications

One important issue which must be considered is the nature of the fundamental changes which all forms of marketing communications agencies are being called upon to address.

We have already seen the underlying move towards integrated marketing communications. Perhaps more than any other single issue, this is resulting in significant changes to the nature of the agencies and the services that they seek to provide. This has manifested itself in a number of different ways. In some instances, agency groupings have been formed which provide their clients with access to a wide range of specific skills not usually associated with the world of advertising. If we look, for example, at several of the major international agency networks, many of them have established formal links with other companies within the field of marketing communications. In some cases, we are seeing the establishment of single, integrated agency structures which seek to provide the totality of marketing communications input under a single 'roof' – effectively providing 'one-stop' shopping to their clients.

Ironically, of course, this has often been the nature of the service provision of several of the regionally based 'advertising' agencies. The inherent nature of their relationships and, perhaps, the size of the companies with which they deal has resulted in them being regarded as the major source of input, and certainly the 'guardians' of the communications process on behalf of their clients. At the same time, we are also witnessing moves in the opposite direction. Rather than providing the 'full service' of the larger advertising agencies, many companies have established themselves within comparatively specialized fields.

À la carte

In some instances, responding to the needs of their client base, some agencies provide an à la carte service, in which client companies are invited to access only those services which they require. Often, a client will require a specific range of inputs from an agency corresponding to their position in the market-place. This may be in the form of advice in the strategic area, involvement in the new prod-uct development process, the development of creative materials and so on. In most cases, the agency is remunerated in the form of a fee related to the volume of the work. Most importantly, the client has access to those inputs which it requires at a particular moment of time, but with the knowledge that, as its business or demands grow, so the agency can continue to service the expanding requirements of the business.

Media specialists

This has been the important growth sector of recent decades, and has significantly elevated the contribution of media to the communica-tions mix. In response to the demands of their clients, most of the major agencies have separated the media function and can now provide a dedicated service distinct from its other functions.

There may be several different reasons for a company to use a single media source for its media planning requirements. Clearly, there are significant benefits to be derived from placing the totality of their media planning and buying requirements into a single media company. The economies of scale which can be obtained from negotiating the entirety of its spend will often represent significant savings to the client company. It can ensure con-sistency of approach, despite using several different agencies to provide the creative and planning inputs.

Some companies appoint an independent media specialist to evaluate the performance of their advertising agencies, who retain the direct responsibility for the planning and buying of the media in their area of the client's business.

Creative boutiques

In the same way that media has become a specialist function, so too creative develop-ment has, in some areas, been separated from the rest of the advertising agency role. In some cases, creatives who have developed a strong relationship with the company have estab-lished themselves as independent operators who continue to provide the input in this area. In others, the client gains access to a pool of talented individuals who can be used either to supplement the creative work of their agency or to enable them to draw on these skills without the need to appoint a full-time agency.

Specialized agencies

The specialist nature of some specific business areas has resulted in the development of agencies with parallel skills. Often, because of the particular nature of a market, the com-pany will need to gain access to a number of individuals who have developed an under-standing of the special requirements. This may result from the specialist nature of, for example, the regulatory requirements or the technical nature of the business area. In recent years, specialist agencies in the fields of high technology, medical and pharmaceutical products and financial services have all emerged to provide specialist inputs to their clients. Apart from the obvious differences in terms of their knowledge base, there is a further difference which distinguishes these agencies from their mainstream counterparts. The convention has long been established that the major agencies do not handle competing clients. Recently, BMP DDB resigned the John Courage account in order to take on Bud-weiser world-wide.

Some companies insist that their agencies do not handle any business in those areas in which they operate, even though the particular agency may not handle that aspect of the client's business directly. This is becoming an increasingly difficult stance, as major agencies would find themselves precluded from large areas of business potential. The involvement of major conglomerates in a wide variety of business areas might prevent an agency from handling major areas in which they would otherwise wish to become involved.

In the specialist agencies, no such restrictions exist. Client companies accept that, in order to gain access to the specialist skills, they must sacrifice the non-competition rules.

The agency/client relationship

All agency/client relationships are different, often reflecting the culture of the companies involved. Some companies attempt to establish enduring relationships with their advertising partners which, in many cases, are sustained for many years. J. Walter Thompson has handled the Kellogg's account since the 1930s. WCRS recently published a monograph celebrating fifteen years of advertising for BMW (the paper won the Grand Prix in the IPA Advertising Effectiveness Awards in 1994). Levi's was the first account awarded to Bogle, Bartle, Hegarty and remains with that agency today.

Yet others tend to change on a more frequent basis, perhaps reflecting their insecurity with the area of advertising expertise, or because they perceive that change will enhance other aspects of their overall business performance. Periodically, companies feel the need to check out what is available to them. In some cases, this is the direct result of some deficiency – real or perceived – in the performance and contribution of their agency. At other times, the agency review may be a reflection of management changes within the client company, and the resultant desire to reflect those changes by selecting an agency

with a similar personality. Yet again, some reviews are built into the process. Some organizations specifically adopt a time-limited relationship with their agency – say, three to five years – at which time a review of the current agency scene is implemented, irrespective of the performance of the incumbent.

Many senior managers maintain a 'watching brief' to be alert to changes in the marketing communications scene. The spate of mergers and take-overs during recent years has, inevitably, resulted in some conflicts of interest, with clients having to remove their business to another agency at relatively short notice. By maintaining an awareness of agency performances, clients can at least identify potential contenders for their business should they decide to move.

There are a wide variety of reasons why a client/agency relationship breaks down. A survey conducted for *Campaign* magazine (23 September 1994) identified several causes for the account move.

'It has lost its enthusiasm for your product/service'	85%
'It is not devoting enough time/resources to your account'	87%
'It lacks integrated communications skills'	32%
'It lacks the technology to service your account'	15%
'It is working on a conflicting account'	61%
'There is a personality clash'	44%
'You change agency regularly as a matter of course'	2%

Agency personalities differ substantially, and these have an important bearing on the client relationship. The inherent nature of the agency stance, its reputation in areas of creativity, account planning and handling, the style of its involvement with its clients' businesses, and other factors serve to distinguish any one agency from its competitors. Not surprisingly, agencies tend, in the main, to attract clients with similar personalities to their own.

Agency remuneration

An important dimension of the relationship will, inevitably, be a reflection of what the company is charged for the work that the agency produces and, with this, an agreement as to the ownership of this material. There are a variety of different bases for agency remuneration, and it is important that, whichever method is used, agreement should be reached at the outset.

However, before examining the various remuneration systems, it is important to make a distinction in terms of the work that an agency is involved in. It is important to make a separation between above- and below-the-line activities. In simple terms, *above-the-line* expenditure relates to media expenditure – that is, the cost of advertising on television, in the press and magazines, on radio and outdoors, and cinema. It is these areas from which the agency receives its commission payments. *Below the line* covers all other areas of marketing communications, whether on sales promotion, public relations or elsewhere.

Commission

The traditional commission system continues as the most common basis for calculating agency income. For many decades, the principle has been established that agencies receive the bulk of their income *not* from their clients, but from media proprietors. (Indeed, this gives rise to the use of the word 'agency'. They were the agents of the media companies.) Historically, agencies have received 15 per cent of the monies spent in the media as a direct discount from the television contractors, radio stations, media titles and other sectors. You may sometimes see the figure of 17.65 per cent used. This is the amount required to uplift the net media expenditure to yield 15 per cent commission.

The important thing to remember is that this commission is already built into the media rates. If, for example, a poster campaign is quoted as costing £100,000, it will already contain an agency commission of £15,000. When you are preparing budgets, remember not to double-cost this element. Some students show the gross cost of media plus an agency charge of 15 per cent. This is wrong!

It is also important to remember that this commission payment covers only the cost of the internal charges – staff salaries and other overheads, predominantly – and that charges incurred by the agency for the production of items or the commissioning of any work on behalf of the client will be passed on, usually uplifted by a similar rate of 15 per cent.

Negotiated commission

For several years, pressure has been applied on agencies to adjust the commission rate to more accurately reflect the volume of work involved in handling a client's business. Client companies, especially the larger ones, have long recognized that their account represents a highly desirable income source for an agency. Moreover, there will usually be several agencies well equipped to handle the business, whatever its nature. In these situations, they can well afford to apply pressure to competing agencies to reduce the overall costs of their advertising activities.

Today, many agencies are prepared to negotiate a level of commission lower than 15 per cent. Sometimes this will be a straight reduction on the entirety of the business, say to 12 per cent or 10 per cent. In other instances, it will be based on a sliding scale. In these cases, the first £1 million of billings might be charged at the full rate of 15 per cent, the second million at, say, 12 per cent, and so on down to an agreed level. In part, this is a reflection that agencies, like other businesses, achieve economies of scale and that, as income rises, the associated costs rise at a slower rate.

It is also important to recognize that the calculation of commission can go the other way. In the case of a highly labour-intensive account, with a relatively low level of expenditure, the agency may require a higher level of commission to compensate it for the level of work involved. Some agencies, especially the larger ones, may operate on a minimum level of billings which they are prepared to service. This is a direct reflection of the fact that large agencies carry large overheads which have to be recouped from the activities of their clients, either in the form of billings or fees. Often, however, a company with comparatively small billings may wish to retain a large agency in order to have access to the skills and knowledge base that the agency possesses. The company may feel that the level of input, particularly of a strategic nature, may only be obtained by working with a large domestic or international agency. If a client wishes to retain one of these large agencies, then he may be called upon to remunerate the agency by way of a supplementary fee.

However, whatever method of commission calculation is agreed, it is vitally important that it is formally agreed, in writing, at the outset of the relationship. Seldom is there more ill-feeling than when either party feels aggrieved either that it is being overcharged, or that it is being underpaid, for the level of work required.

Fee-based

Some agency/client relationships are based on a level of fee being calculated and agreed at the outset. Here, some assessment of the level of work involved in handling the business is agreed and a fee reflecting this is determined. It is argued that, by removing the commission element, agencies are no longer predisposed to recommending increased levels of media expenditure on the basis of their own increased income needs. By the same token, since the agency receives no more (or less) for its large recommendations than its smaller ones, the client can feel more comfortable that

these are based on a proper consideration of the strategic issues.

In some instances, a retainer fee is offered by the client to its agency where, for example, the company wishes to secure the input of an agency although, because of limited media expenditure, it recognizes that the agency would not receive adequate compensation for its services. However, for the fee method to work smoothly, periodic reviews must be included within the contractual arrangements to ensure that both parties remain comfortable with the level of fee charged.

Time-based

In a few instances, the remuneration of agencies is based on similar principles to that of other professional bodies. Since often a great deal of time is involved in, say, the development of creative concepts, or media campaigns which for some reason do not run, an agreement is based on the time required to develop the work.

The system is based on the maintenance of accurate time-sheets by all those personnel involved with the client's business, and the salary and associated costs raised by an agreed factor to deliver an appropriate level of profit.

Cost-based

An alternative approach is to apply the same principles as above to the costs of developing the associated work for a client. Again, an agreed percentage uplift is applied to all costs to ensure that the agency receives a profit for its efforts.

Performance-based

In a very few instances, the agency is rewarded on the basis of the results it achieves for its clients. Specific targets are established and agreed, and the agency is compensated for either achieving or exceeding the targets set. By the same token, the agency reimburses the client if it fails to reach the agreed levels of performance. Although this method of remuneration may become more widespread in those areas, such as media, where the buying performance of the agency can be directly measured, comparatively few full service advertising agencies are prepared to accept such a basis of compensation. Clearly, advertising is only one component of the overall mix and, if other areas of the company fail to reach their goals, this will impact negatively on the agency income without their being able to control the level and nature of the activity.

Production costs

The issue of production costs remains a thorny problem, and is often the source of unsettling established relationships.

As noted above, whether the agency receives commission, a fee, or income based on time or costs, clients must expect to pay the costs of production for the materials required to implement a campaign. Whether this is in the form of a television commercial or a direct mail piece is, in itself, immaterial. The principle is that rarely do agencies maintain in-house production facilities.

When an agency has agreed the finished concepts for implementation, these will be passed on to some outside company for final production. This may involve, for example, the production of film and video, the casting of artists for a commercial or press advertisement, the photographer's charges, typesetting, any print items and so on. A proper approach is to agree cost estimates at an early stage in the process, so that the client company has a complete understanding of the likely costs involved in communications materials. Some, like those of a television commercial, may be extremely high. Inevitably, the more complicated the materials, the higher the relative costs. A complicated mail piece will cost considerably more than a simple letter.

If both parties know the 'ball park' costs of production early in the process of creative development, subsequent difficulties can, substantially, be avoided. There is no point continuing with the development of a complicated brochure involving expensive location photography if the need is for a simple communications item! Some latitude must be built into cost estimates. Almost inevitably, some changes will take place during the production phase, and these must be paid for. But, at minimum, the likely cost parameters will be clearly understood by both parties, and the shock of receiving a production bill of £400,000, when the client was expecting to pay, say, £250,000, will be largely overcome.

An issue which surfaces at regular intervals is that of the ownership of the creative work produced by agencies. So long as the relationship between an agency and its client is sustained, this is not an important consideration. However, when a client moves on, for whatever reason, attention must be given to the transfer of the copyright in the advertising and related materials. Often, this problem is resolved by an examination of the contract between the two parties. In most instances, certainly in terms of the relationships between the larger companies, the agreement between them provides for the transfer of copyright either upon the payment of a supplementary fee or in consideration for a percentage of subsequent billings during the period in which the creative work continues to be used.

The agreement is important for two reasons. On the one hand, it protects the agencies and recognizes that a major contribution is their ability to produce effective creative work. On the other, it provides for the client to continue to use the material whilst the new agency is 'bedded in'. Even after a company appoints a new agency to handle its business, the process of developing new materials may take several months. By continuing to have access to the work produced by the previous agency, the client can continue to support his business during the period in which the new work is being developed, researched and implemented.

The criteria for agency selection

The starting point in any agency selection process must be the definition of the services which you require them to provide. Different agencies fulfil different specialist roles, and it is important to isolate which services you will require. The range is certainly broad enough to provide the flexibility to meet any circumstances:

1 Full service agencies offering directly or indirectly (often through subsidiary companies) a comprehensive range of marketing communications inputs.
2 Broad-based specialist consultancies in the fields of media planning and buying, sales promotion, public relations and direct marketing.
3 Narrow-based consultancies offering, for example, creative services (copywriting and art direction), planning, new product development, and so on.

It is important to identify the particular *services* that will be required in order to isolate the nature of the organization or organizations to be employed. If the needs of the organization are predominantly in the area of sales promotion or public relations, for example, there is little point attempting to secure the services of an international advertising agency. Not only are the main skills likely to be under-utilized, the senior management are extremely unlikely to become involved with the management of your business. Having identified the services, the next step is to identify the qualitative and quantitative criteria that will be used to evaluate performance:

- Do you require the agency, for example, to be skilled in areas such as market research; is planning a key requirement; what type of creative skills do you require?, and so on.
- Should the agency have prior experience of your market sector; what size should the agency be – do you wish to be a major player, or are you content to be 'a small fish in a big pond'; should the agency be part of an international network, or are you content with a domestic agency?

You can then begin the process of identifying a shortlist of agencies that can fulfil your brief. In this respect, it is important to consider a wide variety of inputs to help you in the selection process. Certainly, it is important to examine recent issues of the trade press, which will help you identify which agencies are 'hot' and which are not. It may provide you with examples of work that they have produced for other clients, so that you can consider aspects such as creative performance. There are a number of specific publications which will also help you identify the current clients and other aspects of the agencies you might be considering. Among these are the *Campaign* publication *Portfolio*; the British Rate and Data (BRAD) *Advertiser and Agency List*; the *Blue Book*; and similar titles. You might consider consulting the *Advertising Agency Register* or the *Sales Promotion Register*, both of which maintain current portfolios of agencies in the respective fields and can help guide you towards a shortlist by offering advice based on their experience of agency structures and 'personalities'.

There is little doubt that rumours of an 'account change' are particularly unsettling to the working relationship with the incumbent agency. You should avoid publicizing any impending review until as late as possible.

It is important that you visit a number of agencies to get to know the personalities involved – relationships with agencies are dependent on 'people' factors. These meetings will provide them with the opportunity to set out their credentials and, hopefully, to identify the personnel who would be working on your business, should they be appointed. At this stage, try to discriminate between the 'A' team of senior management who will be responsible for new business presentations and who (unless your account is of major significance) will be unlikely to work on your business, and the day-to-day team. It is the latter with whom you will have to develop a working relationship.

Some companies issue a preliminary questionnaire to agencies they are considering, which contains a number of specific questions to assist the process of 'shortlisting'. This may be used to ensure that the criteria you have established are met by the possible contenders and that other important areas, including agency remuneration, are covered before the shortlist is finalized. Similarly, there are a number of specialist selection companies who will undertake the preliminary stages on your behalf. The benefit of using such consultants rests in their experience, gained from an involvement in the process over many years – unlike your own, which is likely to be somewhat limited – and the fact that the identity of the company seeking to appoint may be protected for somewhat longer.

Whatever approach you adopt, the next stage is the creation of a shortlist and the issuing of a specific brief. The brief to the agency is used to enable them to demonstrate a specific response to your requirements. As such, it needs to provide the contenders with as much information as can be provided – bearing in mind that the more vague you are at this stage, the less able they will be to provide a full response to your requirements. As far as possible, you must be prepared to allow the agencies to access the same information as you would require for the development of your marketing communications plan. Security can be maintained by inserting a confidentiality clause into the briefing document. Allow sufficient time for the agencies to absorb and analyse the information provided, and to carry out their own research, if necessary, when considering the date for the 'pitch'.

If there is insufficient time between the briefing and the presentation, the response will, inevitably, be somewhat shallow.

Finally, establish some form of objective assessment against which to measure the agency presentations. Define the formal criteria, so that all involved in the process can participate in the decision on the same basis. Whether the presentations will be assessed on the basis of strategic recommendations, or on the basis of preliminary creative work, is a somewhat subjective decision. Equally, it is important that, as far as possible, the key people at the company end should be involved in the selection process. It is they, rather than the senior management, who will need to establish good working relationships on an ongoing basis. The importance of these interpersonal relationships cannot be stressed enough.

The *Campaign* survey (September 1994) referred to previously, and conducted among 117 marketing directors, identified several important factors which were sought from an agency during a pitch:

'Quality of thinking'	94%
'Good chemistry between both parties'	90%
'Evidence that the agency understands and can enhance your brand'	5%
'A powerful creative idea'	68%
'Strategy that offers value for money'	73%
'An agency culture that fits your own'	64%
'Presence of senior agency staff who will stay on your account'	81%
'Evidence of sound business/ management skills'	75%

Once the agency selection has been made, it is important to ensure that there is a smooth and efficient handover between them and the previous incumbent, so that there is no interruption to the flow of work on your business. Contacts need to be formalized and the winning agency announced.

The *Campaign* survey identified seven important dimensions which were sought from a new advertising agency:

'It has previous experience working in
your market sector'   46%

'It offers a fully integrated service,
including below the line'   35%

'It offers international resources'   16%

'It offers a remuneration system based
on fees, not commission'   41%

'It is fundamentally committed to creative
excellence'   74%

'It has embraced new technology and
uses it'   38%

'It is able to advise you on the
information superhighway'   22%

In some instances, as we have already seen, the reasons behind an agency change have more to do with the breakdowns in personal relationships and the perceptions of the agency service, than with the quality of the creative work produced by the agency. In other instances, the cause of the move will be an international realignment of the agencies on the client roster. There will be occasions when the client will wish to continue to use the creative material which has been previously produced, despite a change in the agency appointed to handle the business. Most agencies have made provision for this in their contracts. Usually, the client will be required to pay a compensatory fee which will ensure that the rights to the creative output are transferred to the company on the cessation of the agency contract.

Recently (November 1995), the Incorporated Society of British Advertisers (ISBA) and the Institute of Practitioners in Advertising (IPA) issued a guide to best practice in the management of the pitching process. It embodies a ten-point pitch guide covering many of the key points made above. It makes the strong recommendation that the pitch list should be limited to three agencies, or four if the incumbent is included, and that all agen-

cies participating should be informed of the number on the list. It also makes the suggestion that client companies should make an overt financial contribution to the costs of the presentation as a sign of commitment. Although it recognizes that such payments are unlikely to cover the costs of the agency's involvement in the presentation process – often, the costs run into many thousands of pounds – nevertheless, it does serve to demonstrate the seriousness of the intent towards the agencies involved.

References

Campaign Report, Top 300 Agencies, *Campaign*, 28 February 1997

Fortini-Campbell, L., *Hitting the Sweet Spot: How Consumer Insights Can Inspire Better Marketing and Advertising*, The Copy Workshop, 1992

Additional reading

To gain an insight into the advertising agency scene is somewhat scantly covered in most texts, despite the importance of the topic. Several excellent American texts exist, but the scenario they depict is significantly different from that operating in the UK or, for that matter, the rest of Europe.

One compilation which will shed some light on areas covered in this chapter is:

Butterfield, Leslie (ed.), *Excellence in Advertising: The IPA Guide to Best Practice*, 1997, Butterworth-Heinemann

Students are also recommended to read the trade publications, *Campaign*, *Marketing* and *Marketing Week*, which regularly carry articles on specific aspects of agency management, client perceptions and similar issues.

Part Two

Part Two

CHAPTER 7

Advertising

Aims and objectives

- To examine the diverse nature of advertising;
- To consider the functions of advertising;
- To understand the advantages and limitations of advertising;
- To gain an insight into the different types of advertising;
- To develop an understanding of the advertising process;
- To grasp the importance of the theoretical background to advertising;
- To determine the strategic dimensions of advertising planning;
- To explore the development of the advertising plan.

Advertising is one of a variety of marketing communications tools that companies can utilize to achieve their defined objectives. Historically, advertising has always played the lead role in terms of communications activity, although that position is being eroded dramatically as the other tools of marketing communications gain more widespread usage.

In a recent paper presented by John Philip Jones (1995) he demonstrates the trend in marketing communications in the USA:

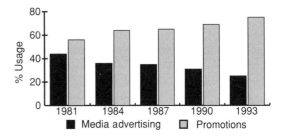

Whilst a similar trend is observable in the UK, it is significantly less marked. Not only does advertising continue to play a greater role in overall terms, it continues to dominate strategic thinking regarding the application of marketing communications in many areas of marketing.

The diverse nature of advertising

It would be wrong to consider advertising as a single entity. There are, clearly, several different types of advertising, and it is important to understand the role and purpose within the context of the specific advertising campaign.

One simple way of discriminating between types of advertising is to examine the target audience at which the advertising message is aimed. Here we can distinguish between advertising aimed at the consumer, and that which is aimed at some other audience. Much of what we see on a day-to-day basis consists predominantly of advertising targeted specifically at different consumer groups. For example, Sainsbury's aim their campaigns at shoppers who, they hope, can be persuaded to use their outlets in preference to those of their competitors for their regular purchases. Pedigree Petfoods (part of the Mars company) target specific pet owners. They are, for the most part, less concerned about where consumers buy, rather that they purchase a brand from the Pedigree portfolio. Similarly, Kellogg's mount different campaigns to promote the sales of each of their breakfast cereals.

Against this form of advertising, however, can be contrasted that aimed at the 'trade' audience. The same products may well be involved, but the underlying nature (and, of course, the content) of the advertising will be different. Brands will use trade advertising to communicate the advantages of their brand to particular retailers, to encourage them to stock and display their products alongside competitive products, including the retailer's own. A considerable amount of advertising is designed to communicate between businesses, either in the instances like those above, or where the target audience is the end-user of, say, the raw materials which the company processes. This category would also include advertising by 'professional' companies such as solicitors and accountants, promoting their services to potential users. Yet another target audience will be the financial community. Such advertising will, for the most part, appear in the broadsheet newspapers and the specialist magazines (although it is by no means restricted to these areas). Here the purpose will be to communicate some aspect of the company's performance, such as its financial results.

An alternative way of describing advertising is in terms of its specific purpose. Most advertising takes the form of commercial activity designed to promote the particular products or services which the company produces. Whilst brands receive the majority of the expenditure on advertising, there are instances where the company seeks to develop an image for itself beyond that of the brands it manufactures. Corporate advertising, as we will see in Chapter 14, is attracting increasing attention, with the recognition that many consumers wish to identify the values of the company from which they buy products and services. Similar campaigns may be mounted by industry groups, designed to promote a category of products. Recently, the Meat and Livestock Commission, representing the farming community, mounted a campaign to encourage people to eat more meat, against the adverse publicity of the BSE scare. In the same way, although for different reasons, the video industry has developed advertising to encourage video rental in general rather than promoting any particular film title or even the outlets from which the videos can be obtained.

But against this is the considerable amount of non-commercial advertising, undertaken by governmental bodies and charitable organizations. These latter are often designed to affect people's attitudes and opinions rather than sell anything specific.

The functions of advertising

The particular roles that advertising can play are many and varied, although they fall within three broad areas:

- To inform
- To persuade
- To sell

To inform

In certain instances, advertising simply seeks to provide the public with specific pieces of information. In many cases, this has a neutral content, such as public announcements, or some forms of governmental advertising. In other instances, manufacturers may use advertising to inform previous consumers of some deficiency in their product. This is apparent in the case of product recalls, where the manufacturer uses advertising to communicate the particular problem to the widest possible audience in order to ensure a speedy dissemination of information and an equally rapid response on the part of the owners of such products.

In the case of a manufacturer introducing a new product, there is a need to inform potential consumers about the new product. This may take the form of a simple announcement, or may provide details about the product, its functions and some form of comparison or claim about the product in the context of existing product offerings.

In order to extend the appeal of an existing product, manufacturers may attempt to use advertising to suggest new uses for a product. In many instances, responses to consumer research will identify different ways in which the consumer uses the product, and these may assist in the identification of new opportunities. A manufacturer may wish to inform the market of a price change or some other aspect of the product proposition. Recently, for example, Mars have focused advertising on the new formulation of their eponymous brand. The national daily newspapers frequently mount promotions wherein the price is reduced to encourage greater levels of trial.

Sometimes it will be necessary to provide some form of explanation of how a product works. When Dyson introduced its revolutionary new vacuum cleaner, it needed to explain to potential purchasers the operating differences between its product and those of its competitors (the Dyson cleaner does not use a bag and claims to filter out more dust than rival manufacturers' products). Service companies may need to provide information concerning the range of available services to the consumer. This is clearly seen in the context of banking services, where a company may offer the ability to maintain a current account with a cheque book, credit card facilities, domestic and foreign services, such as the ability to withdraw funds whilst on holiday abroad, together with deposit accounts, investment programmes and so on. The list of services may be quite extensive.

If the manufacturer identifies a dissonance between the product performance and consumer perceptions, it may be necessary to use advertising to correct false impressions. Similarly, when a product deficiency has been identified, it may be necessary to reduce consumer fears. Following the withdrawal of the Perrier brand, the brand owners used advertising extensively to inform customers of the steps that they had taken to remedy the problem and to reassure them that the new product was safe and reliable. In fact, most manufacturers do little more than use advertising to recall the defective product, and fail to respond to consumer fears which might result from the identification of a problem.

As we will see, it is not only brands that are important. An increasingly important element of reassurance derives from the image of the company which produces the product. Advertising can assist in the process of building a company image.

To persuade

Either because of changes to the product formulation or because of a previous miscommunication, manufacturers may wish to change customers' perceptions of product attributes or benefits. Following the reformulation of many products within the soap powder market, and the removal of the bleaching agent, it was important to provide a new basis for product comparisons. Advertising stressed the products' powers to ensure colour fastness and de-emphasized their ability to get clothes whiter.

Much 'cause' advertising attempts to persuade consumers to alter their attitudes towards a particular issue. Political parties utilize this form of advertising, especially during the run-up to an election, to persuade the audience that their policies are the most appropriate and to motivate them to vote for a particular party. Similarly, charities often attempt to focus attention on a specific concern. For several years, the RSPCA has campaigned to improve conditions for animals and has used a variety of advertising approaches to alter public opinions. Government departments sometimes use this form of advertising to bring about a change in attitudes towards issues of general concern. Over many years, for example, the Department of Transport has used advertising messages to influence attitudes towards drink driving or child road safety.

In some market sectors, advertising may be used as a precursor to other activities. It may, for example, attempt to provide specific information to the target audience in order to persuade potential customers to take a sales call.

To sell

Most advertising seeks to promote the sale of particular goods or services. To achieve this objective, the advertising provides the potential or existing customer base with information about the product or service. In the majority of instances, such advertising seeks to reinforce existing attitudes by explaining how the product is appropriate to the potential users' existing needs or lifestyle.

Some advertising, particularly that of a promotional nature, will attempt to persuade the customer to make a purchase now, rather than delay it until some later time. The advertising will convey a sense of urgency, often by placing some form of time constraint on the offer being made. This is particularly the case with 'sale' advertising. Potential customers are notified of the sale dates and reminded that they can only obtain the particular 'bargains' at that time. Similarly, retailers will make 'time-limited' offers which impose restrictions as to when customers can take advantage of the offer price.

A key role of advertising is to bring about the building of brand preferences and to encourage brand switching. This is the form of most advertising campaigns, and the advertiser will stress aspects of brand superiority and will sometimes make direct comparisons with competitive products. Often, it will not be sufficient merely to inform consumers of the existence of the brand. It will be important to direct them to those outlets which stock the product and to remind them where to buy it. Many campaigns feature a list of stockists and this serves two purposes. On the one hand, it provides consumers with the necessary information to enable them to locate the product. On the other, it provides an incentive to the featured outlets to continue to stock the brand.

Some products have a distinctly seasonal appeal. Advertising may be used to remind consumers that the product may be needed in the future and to ensure that the brand is kept in mind during the off-season. Finally, even dominant brands have to ensure the maintenance of 'front of mind' awareness. The consumer has a comparatively short memory and, even with familiar brands, needs to be reminded of the benefits and advantages they provide.

The advantages and limitations of advertising

Many organizations, both commercial and those in the not-for-profit sector, use advertising to achieve their goals. It is important to recognize that the users of advertising can control the specific nature of the message and, to a large degree, the composition of the audience to whom that message is addressed.

Advertising offers a number of benefits to the user:

1 It can create images of products which serve to differentiate them in the marketplace. Since,

as we have already seen, the increasing convergence of technology has resulted in a situation in which many products cannot be differentiated in physical terms, manufacturers must utilize other methods to create some distinction for their products or services. In many product categories, consumers are unable to discriminate between competing brands in 'blind' tastings, yet they express preferences for particular brands. The basis of their selection, in many instances, is the positive associations of the brand in terms of the image or appeal of the product derived from the style and content of the advertising supporting that brand.

2 Advertising can assist in the creation and maintenance of brand equity. Today's brands have a real financial value which is significantly greater than the investment required to produce them. De Chernatony and McDonald (1992) report the addition of some £127 million to the balance sheet of Reckitt and Colman following their acquisition of Airwick Industries. This sum was attributed solely to the intangible benefits of 'goodwill, heritage and loyalty conveyed by the newly acquired brand names'.

3 Advertising can create a unique personality for a brand. It is undeniably true that it is the brand personality which is the key to sparking consumer desire. Advertising creates specific impressions of a brand which are left beyond the actual message being communicated. There are many examples of this, including Levi's, Tango, John Smith's Bitter and Nike. All of these demonstrate the important part played by the personality created through advertising as a major contributor to the consumer's propensity to purchase the brand.

4 Advertising can be used to reduce overall selling costs. Imagine a sales force attempting to communicate with millions of potential consumers of a product category without access to conventional media!

Against these advantages, it is important to recognize the limitations inherent in advertising:

1 It has to be recognized that advertising is not a universal panacea. Whilst it can introduce consumers to a new product concept and may encourage them to try it, if the product fails to live up to expectations, even the most powerful advertising campaign will seldom overcome consumer rejections of an ineffectual product or service.

2 Advertising is inherently an expensive means of communicating with a desired target audience, at least in capital terms. With some exceptions, advertising media costs are extremely high and involve varying degrees of wastage. Even the best planned media schedule will reach consumers who have little or no interest in the product category.

3 As a vehicle for communication, advertising essentially represents a one-way medium. Increasingly, marketers are recognizing that there is a need to establish a two-way dialogue with the potential consumer. Unless some form of feedback mechanism is built into the execution, such dialogue is inhibited. Advertising tends to be somewhat impersonal. Whilst it is effective in communicating simultaneously to large numbers of people, the specific needs and wants of the individual cannot be recognized and responded to.

The other tools of marketing communications, which will be explored in depth in the chapters which follow, offer alternative means of communication with both existing and potential consumers. Each of these tools has distinctive advantages which advertising may not be able to match.

Types of advertising

Pioneer advertising

This serves to inform consumers about the existence of a new product category. The purpose of such activity is to stimulate primary demand for a product which was previously unknown in the marketplace, rather than identifying the particular attributes of a specific brand. However, many new products are specifically introduced by manufacturers with a strong branding presence, in the hope that they will continue to 'own' the category even when joined by other, similar products. The portable tape player continues to be known as the 'Walkman' even though it is manufactured by several companies other than the originator, Sony.

Competitive advertising

This seeks to persuade consumers of the particular benefits and advantages which derive from a particular brand. The intention is to increase selective demand by providing information regarding the product attributes and benefits which may not be available from competitive products, or, even where the attributes are shared, to create the impression that they are the 'property' of the advertised brand. Intel, the manufacturers of computer chips, have used this approach to successfully brand a component within another manufacturer's product with such success that it is almost impossible to sell a computer without 'Intel inside' in the mainstream market.

Comparative advertising

This relates to specific campaigns which directly compare one product's attributes with those of its competitors. It is important to recognize that, in the UK at least, such advertising is a relatively new phenomenon. Under the provisions of the Trade Marks Act 1938, the trade mark of a brand was protected from infringement and could only be used with the express permission of the owners of the mark – hardly likely to be given to a competitor for use in such advertising. Under the new Trade Marks Act, introduced in October 1994, the restrictions on comparative advertising have been lifted. The result has been the appearance of a number of new campaigns making direct and overt comparisons between brands. Many campaigns now

directly name competitors and make overt comparisons between the various products, services offered or prices charged, in order to develop a competitive advantage. Hardly a day passes without the technique being employed by companies within the mobile phone sector, for example.

Currently, Eurostar are mounting a campaign to assert their advantages over the airlines using a comparative approach. The advertising identifies two major advantages on the London–Paris route for the business market. In the first instance, Eurostar claims a ten-minute check-in facility (compared with the conventional thirty minutes for the airlines). Secondly, they identify the fact that, whilst Eurostar terminates in the middle of Paris, the airlines arrive at Charles de Gaulle airport, several miles from the centre of the city.

The advertising process

The development of advertising is a sequential process which must reflect the marketing strategy. Only when the marketing strategy has been determined can the development of advertising strategy begin.

In broad terms, the process of advertising development follows a series of individual steps which are depicted in Figure 7.1.

It must be clear that there is an intimate relationship between the marketing and the advertising strategies. The former will determine the broader marketing goals to which all of the elements of the marketing mix will contribute. The latter will determine the specific goals that can be fulfilled by advertising. Only when the specific advertising strategy has been decided upon can the budget be determined.

This is an important part of the development process, since the scale of the advertising budget will impact substantially on the achievement of the defined strategy. This is particularly the case if the budget allocated is

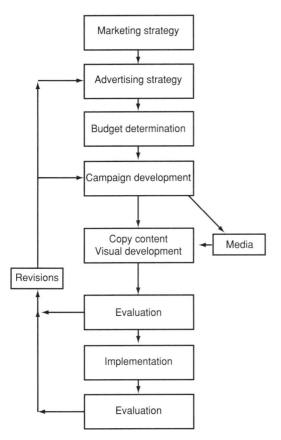

Figure 7.1   The stages of advertising development

too small for the goals determined. A limited budget may constrain the advertising into media which are inappropriate to the task, as we have seen in Chapter 5, which covers the important dimensions of budget determination.

Once the budget has been agreed, the team responsible for the campaign can proceed with the campaign development. In outline terms, this will consist of determining the specific objectives for the campaign and considering the copy and visual content of the appropriate message. In turn, there will need to be an assessment of the media most suitable to the delivery of the message.

In most cases, the agency will explore a number of potential routes to identify the one which will have the most beneficial commu-

nications impact. Market research, particularly of a qualitative nature, will be employed to ensure both that the outline executions convey the correct image and, importantly, are clearly understood by the target market. Often, a series of revisions will be required to reflect the findings of this research and to hone the advertising to achieve the most impactful and relevant campaign.

Only when the agency and the client are confident that the proposed advertising route fulfils the advertising objectives will they proceed to final execution. Clearly, the production of advertising entails very considerable expense, and it is imperative that the risks of error are minimized as much as possible. Here again, market research will play an important role in ensuring that there is an appropriate fit between the advertising message and the interpretation placed on it by the desired target audience. There is often a considerable variation between the rough drawings, which will be used in preliminary research to assess consumer response, and the final execution. It will be important to ensure that elements such as the casting of the artists who appear in the advertising, the 'props' used in a photograph or commercial, and even the music and voiceover, convey the right values.

The penultimate stage is the implementation of the advertising campaign. This stage will include, for example, the negotiations for the media time or space to ensure the best placement of the advertising message, the final elements of production, such as the delivery of the advertising to the media and the appearance of the advertising.

The final stage of the process is the evaluation of the campaign, to determine the extent to which the defined objectives have been met. As previously, market research techniques will be employed to assist in the evaluative process. Most commonly, advertisers will use devices such as tracking studies to monitor the performance of the advertising over time and to gauge the impact on the desired target audience. Even at this stage, it may be necessary to make additional revisions to ensure that the advertising meets the objectives set for it. Whilst the earlier use of market research may make a valuable contribution to the understanding of the advertising, it is only at the time when the advertising 'goes live' that its true impact on the target market can be properly assessed.

Understanding the advertising process

It is clear that advertising is but one of the elements of marketing communications. Although it is capable of fulfilling a number of different roles, the specific function must reflect the objectives contained within the marketing plan. In the development of any advertising campaign, the starting point for the planner must be to determine the specific objectives. As we have already seen, a key determinant of the nature of the advertising campaign will be the available budget, since this will affect the type of media which can be afforded.

Over the past fifty years or so, several attempts have been made to determine the nature of the advertising communications process, and to assist the planning of effective advertising campaigns. Perhaps the earliest model of advertising which gained widespread attention was that known as AIDA (Figure 7.2). Essentially, this proposed a simple hierarchical structure to identify the stages of the communications process. Originally proposed at the turn of the century to explain the process of personal selling, it was rapidly adopted as a model to explain the process of communications in advertising.

The basic tenet was that, in order to have effect, the first task of any campaign was to gain the *attention* of the viewer or reader. From the outset, it was recognized that a fundamental aim of communication was to cut through the surrounding clutter and arrest the

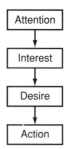

Figure 7.2   The AIDA model of the process of communication

attention of the potential purchaser. Moreover, it suggested that the process of communications required the audience to pass through a series of sequential steps, and that each step was a logical consequence of what had gone before. The principle of sequential activity or learning is used commonly in many marketing models, and is often referred to as a *hierarchy of effects*. The attention phase is key to the process, since whatever follows will be of little value if the attention of the audience has not been achieved.

The second stage is the stimulation of an *interest* in the proposition. In most cases, it would be reasonable to assume that if the first requirement – attention – had been met, the second would follow on almost automatically. Indeed, if the communications message has been properly constructed, this will be true. However, in some instances, particularly where an irrelevant attention-getting device has been employed, the potential consumer does not pass fully to the second stage.

The third stage is to create a *desire* for the product or service being promoted. Often, this will take the form of a 'problem–solution' execution in which the advertiser seeks to position his product as the answer to a problem which he has previously identified. Soap powder advertisements often follow this sequence of events, although many other examples can be found from contemporary marketing activity. Personal care, hair care and do-it-yourself products are other areas where this approach is currently employed.

The fourth and final stage of the AIDA model is the stimulation of some form of response on the part of the audience – the *action* stage. Most advertisements have a specific call to action, and many are linked with promotional offers designed to induce a purchase of the product or some other desired end-result.

Many other hierarchical models have been developed to identify and explain the process of advertising communication. Two of these models are worthy of specific consideration. The first was developed by Lavidge and Steiner (1961) and offers a number of points of difference against the AIDA model. Their model can be depicted as shown in Figure 7.3.

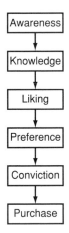

Figure 7.3 The Lavidge and Steiner model of the advertising process

A major premise of this model is that the receiver of the advertising message must pass through a series of distinct stages in a defined sequence in order to ensure a purchase of the product or service that is being advertised. The implication is that if any of the stages are missed out the desired outcome will not be achieved. The starting point, and one which is held in common with many of the other models, is that the consumer must be stimu-lated to become *aware* of the product or service being advertised. Given the previous commentary on the general clutter of commu-nication – both of a general and of an advertising nature – it is clear that the mes-sage must be capable of breaking through to gain the receiver's attention.

Following this, he or she needs to be provided with specific information about the product which improves their *knowledge* and understanding of the brand. This may relate to the attributes, features or benefits of the product or service or, as we will see later, may relate to some emotional facet of the brand proposition. This state of knowledge must then be developed into a *liking* for the product or service. At the very minimum, the task is to ensure that the consumer includes the product alongside other known brands within the product category. We have already seen (in Chapter 5) that most consumers identify a 'portfolio' of brands which satisfy their broad needs.

The next stage is that of creating a *preference*. The task of advertising must be to offer some point of distinction to create a separation in the mind of the consumer between the prod-uct being advertised and others within the category, provided that this point of difference can be established. Implicit in this statement is the assumption that there is a correspondence between this point of difference and the consumer's needs and desires.

The penultimate stage of *conviction* is the result of the consumer forming a specific purchase intention towards the advertised product or service. Lavidge and Steiner sug-gest that only when all of these stages have been concluded will the consumer convert intention into action and *purchase* the brand.

In the early 1960s, Russell Colley proposed a new approach to advertising planning enti-tled Defining Advertising Goals for Measured Advertising Results, often referred to by the acronym DAGMAR. Unlike some previous models, the DAGMAR approach proposed a precise method for the selection and quantifi-cation of communications tasks which, in

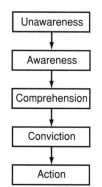

Figure 7.4   Russell Colley's hierarchy of effects model

turn, could be used as the basis for measuring performance. Like his predecessors (and many others subsequently), Colley also used a hierarchy of effects model to describe the advertising process, seen in Figure 7.4.

It is not proposed to describe the individual stages of the Colley model, the elements being self-explanatory. However, Colley's main contribution to the advertising process rests in his identification of a procedure to ensure that the goals established for advertising were precisely formulated and capable of being monitored.

An imperative of the approach was to ensure that the objectives established were capable of unbiased measurement. This is not simply a question of, for example, quantifying levels of awareness, or of trial, but rather of defining precise levels to be achieved for specific aspects of comprehension of the message. At the same time, Colley suggested that precise time scales be determined for the achievement of the objectives set. In order to enable such measurements, it was suggested that a series of benchmarks should be identified. Apart from the obvious benefit of providing the base against which subsequent achievements could be measured, the benchmarking process has a far more important role in the process of strategy determination. It provides a major contribution to the overall planning process by indicating areas in which marketing communications activity might be appropriate. Importantly, the proponents of the DAGMAR approach argue that benchmarking is an essential prerequisite of the planning process.

Targeting is a further dimension of DAGMAR, whereby a detailed understanding would first be developed regarding the target audience(s). Again, it is argued that, without such knowledge, the impact of the message is likely to be weakened. By understanding exactly who (age, sex, class, usership patterns, lifestyle factors, etc.) represents the best prospect for the proposition, not only can they be targeted more effectively by careful media selection but, similarly, the message can be made to appeal directly to them, rather than to potential users as a whole.

Needless to say, Colley recommended the adoption of a written approach to the procedure, partly to impose a discipline on the process – the need to express thoughts clearly and precisely in written form demands far more care and attention to the meaning given than the verbal expression of an idea – and partly to ensure that all participants in the process are both aware of, and committed to, the task.

Although the DAGMAR model continues to be widely used, it is often criticized for implying that consumers are essentially *passive* in the marketing communications process. Whatever the criticisms made of it, however, it is the essential nature of his process of defining objectives which has ensured the enduring appeal of the DAGMAR process.

Although considerable progress has been achieved in the measurement of results, with new techniques being developed, it has to be recognized that some aspects of the marketing communications process remain unclear. Frequent attempts are made, for example, to determine the precise way in which advertising works. In a book by Colin McDonald (1992), some 150 pages are devoted to an examination of current theories and, although the author makes some valid recommendations, there is no definitive answer to the question of how advertising works. Indeed,

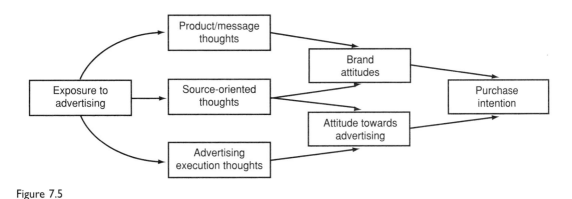

Figure 7.5

since its publication, several new theories have been propounded, which add to the debate, but fail to resolve it.

A particular model of advertising response, which summarizes the key facets of the process, is that used by George and Michael Belch (1993) in their book on advertising and promotion (Figure 7.5). This model proposes that the consumer is influenced in the construction of his or her opinions of a brand by a series of interacting factors. Following exposure to the advertising message, three important areas exert an influence on the consumer's attitudes. The first are a series of thoughts which relate specifically to the message contained in the advertisement. The advertiser may seek to make reference to particular facets of the brand, its performance, its attributes or some other dimension which will enhance perceptions of the product. To these are added source-oriented thoughts, which relate to the environment in which the advertising is seen. Some media will enhance the credibility of the message, whilst others will have the opposite effect. Finally, there are a series of issues which relate to the advertising execution itself.

It has long been recognized that consumers are as much influenced by the nature and content of the advertising itself as the message it seeks to convey. Recently (December 1995), the advertising agency Lowe Howard-Spink conducted a survey of television viewers which suggests that the content of advertising may actually cause viewers to 'turn off'

(reported in *Campaign*, 8 December 1995). Their work claims to identify a third of the population who actively avoid advertising.

The combination of the three factors establishes a series of attitudes in the mind of the consumer, both towards the brand and the advertising itself, which, in turn, have a decisive impact on their purchase intention.

An alternative model to explain the process of advertising communication is that of 'Heightened Appreciation' (Yeshin, 1993). The model, depicted in Figure 7.6, suggests that the responsibility of the planner is to identify the specific dimension of the brand which has significance to the consumer in order to focus attention on it. By stressing a particular aspect or attribute of the brand in advertising, the consumer becomes more aware of that attribute in a use situation, resulting in an enhanced image for the brand.

The most recent model is one proposed by Professor Andrew Ehrenberg (1997). Essentially, Ehrenberg rejects earlier models based on the principles of persuasion. He argues that the notions of persuasion and conversion before the action of purchase takes place are not supported by empirical evidence. In their place, he proposes a new model based on four dimensions (Figure 7.7).

The *awareness* stage reflects the fact that the consumer has, first, to become aware of and interested in a new brand. This, he suggests, can be achieved in a number of different ways – through advertising, retail

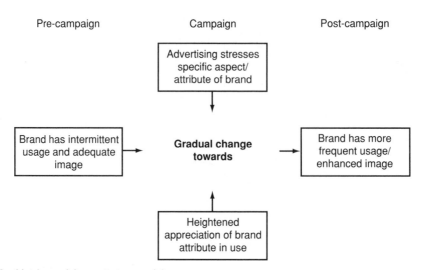

Pre-campaign   Campaign   Post-campaign

Figure 7.6   The Heightened Appreciation model

displays, promotions, media mentions, direct marketing, word of mouth, and so on. For an existing brand, the consumer will already have some familiarity, and the various tools of marketing communications will be required to persuade the consumer to take a closer look, especially where an existing brand is repackaged or reformulated.

Curiosity may inspire *trial* and an exploratory purchase may, therefore, be made. Such trial purchases are, he argues, prompted by advertising, word of mouth and retail availability, and so on.

The third stage of the model – *reinforcement* – is a further area where advertising and marketing communications can play an important part. Advertising, for example, can

maintain awareness of the newly purchased brand and, in some instances, provide brand reassurance. It is here that positive beliefs about the brand may develop, with the brand entering the consumer's brand repertoire.

The final stage of *nudging* is where consumers, both those who have already tried the product, together with those who have yet to try it, can be persuaded to buy it or purchase it again. This stage is designed to reinforce a steady habit on the part of the consumer. Although 'reminder' advertising will often be used by established brands to fulfil this role, in some instances, more concerted efforts will be required. It is here that relaunches and similar devices may be employed, to draw specific attention to the brand and encourage potential consumers to think about it afresh.

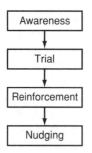

Figure 7.7   The Ehrenberg model

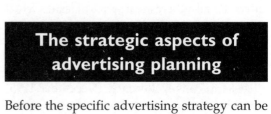

The strategic aspects of advertising planning

Before the specific advertising strategy can be determined, several key factors need to be considered in some detail. The important dimensions of branding have been referred to earlier in this book (see Chapter 3). Advertising plays a critical role in the context of the maintenance of the brand image or, in some instances, the creation of a new brand image, if that is the objective:

'The purpose of developing a statement of creative strategy is to make the advertising more effective by channelling the efforts of the creatives in the most productive direction.' (Murphy and Cunningham, 1993)

The role of communications activity, including advertising, over a number of years is not merely to ensure that a brand has a high level of awareness among its target audience, but also to bring about brand preference. By creating positive perceptions in the minds of prospective consumers, the brand may be elevated to a position of leadership within its market sector. It will become the norm against which all other competing products are compared. Creative strategy helps advertising to do its job in different ways – perhaps by creating perceptual differentiation, focusing on core competences, transcending perceived or practical barriers, and translating concepts into meaningful images. All of these will contribute to a product or service's position, either formed independently by the consumer or driven by the advertising message.

Leslie Butterfield (1997) has suggested a distinctive format for the determination of advertising strategy (Figure 7.8). The device adopted is the shape of a diamond, in which the vertical dimension indicates the sequence of steps involved in the overall strategy development process. The horizontal dimension represents the variable nature of the breadth of consideration, analysis and research involved at each of those stages.

The important differences between this and other strategy development models occurs in the latter part of the analytical process. In the analysis of the consumer's relationship with the brand, Butterfield suggests that it is important to consider what the product offers the consumer, both as a product and a brand, what they bring to it, and the purchase

Figure 7.8   The Butterfield diamond framework for strategic analysis

decision process and mechanism. The role for advertising is defined as what advertising can do that will best help to sell the product and how it can go about doing that.

In the determination of creative strategy, the important aspects of brand positioning and target audience identification are considered simultaneously. It is vitally important that segmentation and positioning strategies must fit together seamlessly. Once the strategy has been agreed (usually in the form of the creative brief), management should withdraw from the creative process.

It is clear that brand awareness is an important facet of brand loyalty. Whilst brand awareness alone cannot ensure brand loyalty, it follows that the reverse must be true. It is for this reason that so much advertising seeks to generate both a positive level of awareness for the brand as well as an inextricable link with the category of product within which it is promoted. It is also clear that once consumers develop an image of a brand, they tend to retain it for a long period of time. In some instances, these image dimensions may be linked to specific attributes of the brand; in most cases, however, they represent dimensions of perception which differentiate the product from its competitors. Indeed, in some instances, it is not the product which is the 'best' which occupies the position of leadership in its sector, rather, the one that has created the most positive associations for itself in the minds of consumers.

Sometimes these positive associations derive from a particular association which the brand has. Two tea brands have been promoted effectively using specific devices which create a positive identity in the minds of consumers. Tetley Tea has used the Tea Folk for many years, whilst its direct competitor, PG, is inextricably linked with the executional device of the chimps, who have featured in their advertising for more than thirty years.

Brand positioning

Equally important to the determination of the advertising strategy is the positioning of the brand. Here we need to identify the role that it plays in the minds of its current and potential customers. It is important to develop a solid brand benefit positioning. This, importantly, requires an identification of the consumer's needs and wants and a matching of what the product has or does in the form of a brand benefit positioning.

Robin Woods (1993), head of the US company, Segmentation Marketing, suggests that there are five specific requirements of a distinctive brand benefit position:

1 The position must be based on primary consumer needs used to select one brand rather than another.
2 It is important to convey why the brand meets those needs better than the brand with which it competes.
3 No other brand can be substituted with the same consumer message or proposition.
4 No other product class can be substituted and still leave consumers with the same message.

5 The message must be precisely and specifically communicated to consumers.

Some examples will serve to illustrate the nature of brand positioning.

The positioning of Häagen Dazs ice-cream targets a young, hedonistically oriented audience. In turn, the audience's response and perceptions underpin the brand's status – and so reflect its positioning and subsequent appeal. The creative strategy was to associate the dimensions of sexiness, fun and indulgence with the pleasure of eating Hägen Dazs ice-cream (Holbrook and Hirchman, 1991).

Coca Cola's creative strategy is designed to ensure that the brand is always portrayed as the classic and original cola. Their advertising messages continue to reflect this brand positioning – 'Always Coca Cola', 'You Can't Beat the Real Thing', 'Eat Football, Sleep Football, Drink Coca Cola'.

Subaru Cars enhanced its status by making an overt comparison with an established brand in the field, Volvo, and even challenging its position: 'Volvo has built a reputation for surviving accidents. Subaru has built a reputation for avoiding them. Subaru Legacy – We built our reputation by building a better car.'

Various authors have identified different positioning dimensions which may be adopted by brands:

1 A brand may be distinguished as a result of particular product characteristics or benefits. For many years, Jacob's Club biscuits were differentiated from competitive products with the statement 'If you like a lot of chocolate on your biscuit, join our club'. The proposition served to associate more chocolate with the brand, inferring a superiority over competitors' products.
2 The brand positioning may reflect a positive price/quality relationship in the minds of prospective consumers. The John Lewis Partnership has become inextricably linked with the proposition 'Never Knowingly Undersold', whilst the Asda price check underpins their claimed price superiority.

3 Some brands are differentiated by the nature of the product user. By associating the brand with particular consumer groups, the brand seeks to fulfil a unique role relative to its competitors. Recently, Audi used this approach to differentiate its customer from the 'flash, yuppie driver' who would not be content with the understated nature of the car.

4 A similar process can be achieved by associating the product with a particular use or application.

5 In some cases, brands are differentiated by their position as a cultural symbol. They represent certain important dimensions of behaviour or self-expression, e.g. Levi's.

6 Finally, brands may adopt a particular position relative to an identified competitor. Avis have long been seen as the main challenger to the brand leader (Hertz), although in some markets this is far from being a reflection of their true position in the marketplace.

Many brands are not where they wish to be in the consumers' minds. Identifying the desired positioning will determine both the content and nature of their communication. In the case of Boddingtons, the objective was to heighten appreciation of the product and its characteristics. The creative approach was to condition drinkers to appreciate the large creamy head and to associate this with good quality. The various executions used for the brand employed a variety of humorous metaphors to underpin the endline – 'The Cream of Manchester' (Boddingtons Case Study, 1995).

We have already seen that there are a number of different types of buyer behaviour. Understanding the process of buying behaviour will have important implications for the determination of advertising strategy. Product categories exhibit differing levels of involvement for the consumer. Clearly, a frequently bought impulse item – such as ice-cream or confectionery – requires little thought on the part of the consumer. In response to the felt need, the consumer will simply purchase a product which satisfies that need. Sufficient information will already be stored in the consumer's memory to facilitate the choice between different brands and to enable the purchase to be made with only a low-level consideration of the alternatives. At the other end of the spectrum, major purchasing decisions which involve significant sums of money, or items which are only infrequently purchased – such as a new car or a holiday – will create a high level of involvement in the purchasing decision.

The involvement level of different product categories can be regarded as a continuum – from low level to high level – and understanding where a product is located on the scale will be important in deciding the nature of the advertising message. Advertising which is designed to support frequently purchased fast-moving consumer goods or services will, often, serve only to reinforce and underpin existing values. Advertising for expensive consumer durables will, in many instances, supply a great deal of information to provide a framework for an understanding of the product's features and benefits.

A further consideration will be the extent to which the decision is based on rational or subjective factors. *Rational* decisions are those which are based on a careful consideration of the functional values of a product or service, and in which the perceived performance will be the primary criterion for choice. *Subjective* decisions are those which are based on such factors as taste or image. An important consideration in both areas is the role of the brand. Some brand names project an image of quality and performance, which will impact on the consumer's purchasing decision process. By the same token, other brand names are synonymous with style and fashion.

It is possible to create a simple matrix to depict these factors, and on which any product or service can be plotted (Figure 7.9). Identifying the position on this scale (using objective measures such as market research) will be important to the development of an effective advertising strategy.

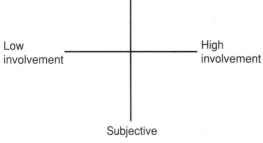

Figure 7.9

Implications for strategy development

It is clear that advertising can fulfil fundamentally different strategic roles in the communications process.

Routine problem solving

For products and services which are bought routinely, the fundamental role of advertising is to reinforce the values associated with the brand, and to ensure a high level of pack recognition at the point of purchase. Consumers will not spend much time evaluating the available alternatives. They will already possess adequate information on which to make the purchase decision, and advertising must ensure that the brand values are sufficiently well known and 'front of mind' to ensure that the brand, at the very least, is included on the shortlist of products to be considered.

Limited problem solving

For products and services which are purchased on a less regular basis, the primary task of advertising is to provide the necessary levels of reassurance to the consumer that the purchase is an appropriate one. Since the purchase itself is undertaken less frequently, the advertising will need to remind the consumer of the benefits associated with using the brand, and to establish clear advantages relative to the competition. Sometimes these will be tangible benefits relating to particular attributes of the brand, such as taste, quality, economy and so on. In other instances, they will be emotional benefits, such as good motherhood (caring for the needs of the family); or social values (the type of people who use the product or service).

Extensive problem solving

In the context of products which require more extensive problem solving – as we have seen previously, normally associated with expensive and very infrequently purchased items – the role of advertising will be both to establish the specific values of the brand, and to provide much of the necessary information upon which the purchase decision will be made.

Sometimes advertising in such instances will attempt to establish the evaluative criteria which the consumer will use in the making of brand comparisons. It will indicate suggested criteria for choice and, not unreasonably, demonstrate how it performs better than the competition against these given criteria. It is important to make a distinction between the dimensions of purchasing behaviour. Not all products are purchased for rational reasons, although these may be important in the context of justifying the particular purchase to others.

Rational decisions

Some purchasing behaviour is conditioned by the need to take rational decisions as to the nature of the purchase. In those instances, it is important to provide consumers with hard factual evidence which will occasion their purchase. This may take the form of a promotional device, such as a lower price or extra product free. In other instances, it may be some statement of the functional performance of the brand, such as lasting longer than its competitors. In the case of more expensive purchases, this may take the form of long copy advertising, factual comparisons, etc.

Image decisions

Many products and services are purchased more because of the image that is associated with them than because of the purely functional benefits. In such instances, it is important to consider the style and the image which are conveyed by the advertising, or the possibility of developing an association with famous names or personalities.

The following are some indications of possible strategies that might be considered.

Generic strategy

Sometimes, where a brand is in a dominant position in the market, it will simply make a straight claim of product benefit. Heinz Baked Beans and Tomato Ketchup both use advertising which has, over a number of years, established them as being synonymous with the category.

Competitive strategy

In the majority of instances, an advertiser will seek to establish a point of difference between his own and competitive products. In some cases, this will be based on a specific dimension of the product (e.g. 'Persil Washes Whiter' or 'Nescafe – Best Beans, Best Blend, Best Taste'). In others, it will derive from a positioning of the brand which sets it apart, such as 'Avis – We Try Harder'. In all instances, the objective is to establish some point of advantage which distinguishes the product or service. It is important to remember, however, that such competitive strategies should not be taken to imply that only the particular brand possesses the attribute – rather, that they have used the advertising medium to make it their own.

Brand image dimensions

Here the advertiser will use other associations to ensure that the product or service is separated from its competitors. Häagen Dazs does not use basic claims in its advertising to reinforce its quality positioning; rather, it associates the brand with desired lifestyle imagery. The long-running Levi's campaign communicates the values of 'freedom', 'individuality' and 'originality' rather than asserting that they wear better than rival jeans. Such advertising is a reflection of the desires and aspirations of its consumers, rather than a reflection of specific aspects of the product itself. As such, the advertising will seek to convey such dimensions as sensory and pleasurable benefits (as with Häagen Dazs); intellectual stimulation (as, for example, with *The Economist* or *The Sunday Times*); or social approval (Burberry's advertising). Table 7.1 identifies alternative advertising strategies.

Advertising strategy and the product life cycle

The appropriate advertising strategy will be a function of the stage which the product occupies in terms of the product life cycle (Figure 7.10). The pre-stage will require a rigorous examination of the product in the context of its market and the target consumer audience that needs to be informed about its existence. This will entail a thorough analysis of the various alternatives which are available to the consumer, a detailed consideration of the consumer segments, their needs and wants from the product category, and the determination of a match between these and the product or service offering.

At the introductory stage, the fundamental need will be to create product awareness and to stimulate trial of the new product. At the same time, specific trade advertising may be utilized to increase awareness of the product among potential stockists and, thereby, create

Table 7.1

Strategy	Description	Application	Creative implications
Generic	Straight product or benefit with no assertion of superiority	Monopoly or extreme dominance of product category	Serves to make advertiser's brand synonymous with product category; may be offset by higher order strategies
Pre-emptive	Generic claim with assertion of superiority	Most useful in growing or awakening market where competitive advertising is generic or non-existent	May be successful in convincing consumer of superiority of advertiser's product; limited response options for competitors
Unique selling proposition	Superiority claim based on unique physical feature or benefit	Most useful when point of difference cannot be readily matched by competitors	Advertiser obtains strong persuasive advantage; may force competitors to imitate or choose more aggressive strategy
Brand image	Claim based on psychological differentiation, usually symbolic association	Best suited to homogeneous goods where physical differences are difficult to develop or which may be quickly matched; requires sufficient understanding of consumers to develop meaningful symbols or associations	Most often involves prestige claims that rarely challenge competitors directly
Positioning	Attempt to build or occupy mental niche in relation to identified competitor	Best strategy for attacking a market leader, requires relatively long-term commitment to aggressive advertising efforts and to understanding consumers	Direct comparison severely limits options for named competitor; counter-attacks seem to offer little chance of success
Resonance	Attempt to evoke stored experiences of prospects to endow product with relevant meaning or significance	Best suited to socially visible goods; requires considerable consumer understanding to design message patterns	Few direct limitations on competitors' options; likely competitive response: imitation
Affective	Attempt to provoke involvement or emotion through ambiguity, humour or the like, without strong selling emphasis	Best suited to discretionary items; effective use depends upon conventional approach by competitors to maximize difference; greatest commitment is to aesthetics or intuition rather than research	Competitors may imitate to undermine strategy of difference or pursue other alternatives

Source: Patti, C. H. and Frazer, C. F., *Advertising: A Decision Making Approach*, Dryden Press, 1984

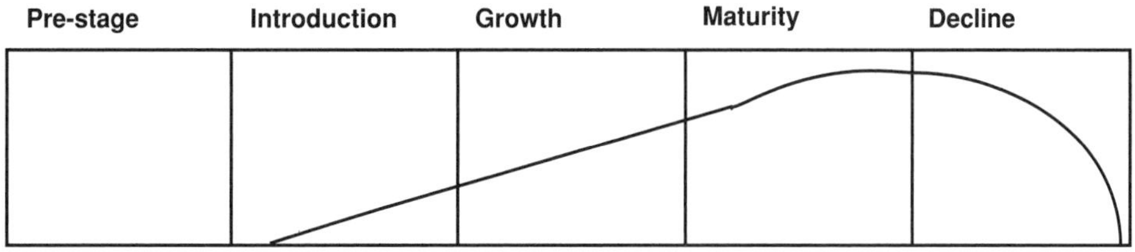

Pre-stage	Introduction	Growth	Maturity	Decline

General promotional objectives

Define objectives and plan the promotional campaign	Develop product awareness, stimulate demand and attract distributors	Create product acceptance and brand preference	Maintain and enhance brand loyalty, convert buyers and distributors of competitive brands	Phase product out

Advertising strategy

Screen concepts, create ads and plan media selection	Primary demand advertising to get potential purchasers to try product	Extensive advertising expenditures, emphasizing advantages of the product and brand	Reminder and emotional advertising and promotions to promote repeat purchases and differentiate brands	Minimal ad expenditures, emphasizing low price to reduce inventory
	Trade ads to introduce product			

Figure 7.10   Advertising and the product life cycle
Source: Zikmund, W.G. and D'Amico, M., *Marketing*, 4th edition, West Publishing Company, 1993

a wider base of distribution. Subsequently, some of the trialists will go on to become brand loyalists and proceed to repeat purchase of the product; others will simply include it within their personal brand portfolio; and yet others will reject the brand.

Once the product has reached the growth stage, it will be important to use advertising to maintain consumer demand and to ensure that the consumer's attention is focused on the advantages of the brand relative to its competition.

In the maturity phase, the advertising will be required to maintain customer loyalty. Together with other promotional devices, such as sales promotion, the strategic intent will be to ensure that the existing consumers make repeat purchases on a regular basis whilst encouraging customers of competing brands to switch their custom. Existing consumers will, substantially, be aware of the product's inherent benefits and will not need to be reminded of them. Rather, advertising will take the form of providing some emotional reinforcement of the brand proposition to ensure continued loyalty. Alternative advertising may also be required to stimulate trial among those who, for whatever reason, have rejected the brand. Often, this will involve some form of re-presentation of the product proposition, for example, expressing the brand as new or improved.

Finally, during the decline phase, advertising expenditures will be reduced significantly, reflecting the decline in brand volumes. The essential requirement will be to ensure that the decline can be slowed, although expenditures may well be directed towards reducing the stocks in the trade. Most often, this period will be associated with a series of price-led promotions which will ensure the maintenance of offtake.

It will also be important to understand the nature of the consumers of the brand. Clearly, at the introductory phase, all consumers will be trialists, some of whom may subsequently become loyal purchasers of the brand. At this stage, as we have seen, advertising will need to provide specific reasons to purchase.

New category users are non-users of the product category. Some will have a positive attitude towards the category; some will be unaware and have no attitude towards it; yet others will be negative. Needless to say, those who are positively disposed towards the category will be easier targets for an advertising message than those who are unaware or, certainly, those who are negative towards it. In reality, most consumers exhibit a varying degree of loyalty towards individual brands, as can be seen in Figure 7.11. Nevertheless, many established brands retain a small percentage of users who will, under most normal circumstances, be unwilling to switch from their preferred brand to some alternative, even when incentives are offered to them (this is exemplified by the Daz Challenge).

Many consumers are loyal to a comparatively small number of brands which represent their personal portfolios of preference. In effect, they have determined (possibly as a result of prior experience) that several alternative brands meet their personal criteria. They may well exhibit a specific preference towards one of them but where, for example, their preferred brand is out of stock or, alternatively, where a comparable brand is on special offer, they will choose to buy an alternative and be content with it. These consumers may also be referred to as 'brand switchers'.

The final category comprises those consumers who can be regarded as promiscuous buyers. For the most part, they are prepared to accept the brand which, in their terms, represents the best value for money at the moment of purchase. They are highly responsive, therefore, to promotional offers. They may also exhibit some levels of loyalty, i.e. prefer brands, for example, to private label or vice versa.

Research by Ehrenberg (1972) suggests that, for buyers of the average supermarket product, some 15 per cent will switch brand within a single week of purchase, 70 per cent will switch over a period of six months, and 90 per cent by the end of a year. If we examine these figures from a different perspective, it suggests that the average brand enjoys only 10 per cent of hardcore loyalists, although these will invariably be responsible for a significantly larger percentage of the brand's unit sales.

Advertising will have a differential impact on each of these groups of consumers and, in some instances, the advertiser may develop specific campaigns to respond to the differing needs of the groups.

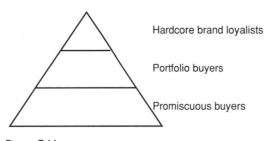

Figure 7.11

Determining the advertising objective

Defining the advertising objective is the starting point for campaign development. In simple terms, the advertising objective is a specific statement of what the advertising is designed to achieve. This will define, in measurable terms, the role of the advertising, for example, in the context of awareness, brand choice, image change, loyalty or some other aspect of advertising communication. Casting the objectives too wide, or attempting to achieve too much within a limited budget, will undermine the effectiveness of the advertising message:

'Advertising objectives are simply statements describing what is to be accomplished by advertising to capitalise on opportunities and/or overcome problems facing the advertiser during the planning period.' (Murphy and Cunningham, 1993)

The issue of determining the appropriate objectives is an essential part of advertising campaign planning, following the principles established by Russell Colley in his 1963 paper on DAGMAR. It is clear that the objectives establish the essential direction for the campaign. Moreover, as Colley suggests, clear measurable objectives are essential for the subsequent managerial evaluation and control of the advertising effort. Without such a clear, concise definition of what it is that the advertising is attempting to achieve, it will be impossible to determine whether the campaign has succeeded after its completion.

One issue to be discussed is the link between advertising and sales. Not unreasonably, most companies continue to invest money in advertising in order to stimulate demand for their products. The consequence of this belief is that the additional sales, and the revenue derived from them, will serve to offset the costs of the original investment. The corollary of this belief will be that sales may be considered the arbiter of success.

Unfortunately, there are two important factors which, in most situations, suggest that sales measurement is a less than appropriate evaluation device. Firstly, advertising does not work in isolation of other components of the marketing communications mix, or even the marketing mix. Because all of the elements are inextricably linked, a lack of performance in some areas may well result in sales targets

not being achieved. This does not mean, however, that the advertising campaign has failed to achieve its specific goals. Secondly, in many instances, there is a delay before the impact of advertising is felt. Evidence for this delay is provided in a study of the effects of advertising conducted by Millward Brown (1991).

Developing the advertising plan

Since the advertising plan is an integral part of the marketing plan, it is imperative that the marketing plan forms the basis of all advertising planning. In many instances, both the marketing plan and the advertising plan will be developed together. However, in some cases, the advertising plan will be developed separately. As such, it must contain a number of specific elements. Although there is no formal prescription, it is likely that the advertising plan will contain the following items:

- a review of the background situation;
- a competitive analysis;
- an overview of the brand;
- an analysis of the consumer;
- a statement of the marketing goals;
- a summary of advertising recommendations;
- a summary of media recommendations;
- a budget determination;
- a summary of evaluative procedures.

It is important to remember, however, that advertising does not and cannot exist in isolation of the other elements of marketing communications. For any marketing communications plan to work to its maximum demands the total integration of all communications activities. Obviously, not every marketing communications plan embraces all of the elements. However, it is highly likely that the marketing plan will demand the use of, say, sales promotion, sales force incentives, and point of sale material. Care must be taken to ensure that all of these, and any other elements, are fully integrated to ensure the maximum impact on the target audiences. This is especially important in the context of the nature of the organizations which may contribute to the fulfilment of marketing communications activities.

Since the early 1970s, there has been a progressive fragmentation of the consultancy sector. Prior to that time, a client could reasonably expect that all of the elements of a marketing communications campaign would be developed in conjunction with the advertising agency. There followed the emergence of specialist companies within the fields of sales promotion, direct marketing, media planning and others, each of which provided a high level of both input and expertise to the planning of the specific elements of the campaign. Inevitably, with this fragmentation of activities, and the more narrow focus adopted by the specialist agencies, the responsibility for determining the most efficient use of resources became a primary responsibility of the brand management team.

Although the ultimate aim of most advertising is to ensure continued sales of the product or service, there are a wide variety of factors which may exert an influence on the outcome. The strength of the sales force and their ability to achieve appropriate levels of distribution will impact upon the advertising's ability to generate consumer sales. However effective and influential the advertising campaign, it cannot achieve the desired objectives if the product is not available at the point of purchase. Similarly, the timing of the campaign relative to the establishment of stocking levels will have an important bearing on the achievement of the desired goals. Advertise too early, and the product will not be available; advertise too late, and the product will have been sitting on the shelf for some time, with the consequent disillusionment of the retail stockists. Competitive factors will also influence the effectiveness of any advertising campaign.

For the most part, advertising development takes place in isolation of the competitive environment. That is not to say that competitive activity is ignored; rather, that its specific nature will not be known in advance. In most cases, competitors will not simply stand by and watch a new campaign diminish their share of market. They may well retaliate with new activity of their own, designed to undermine the effectiveness of the campaign.

As noted earlier, the primary aim of advertising is the achievement of specific communications objectives, any of which may contribute to the creation of a positive purchasing intention. Depending on the position of the brand, advertising may set out to create a basic awareness of the brand, to ensure improved knowledge of the brand and its attributes, create a more favourable image, stimulate positive attitudes, and so on. Ultimately, its function is to sustain the brand as a profitable entity. This is reinforced by the quote from John Bartle (1997), the Managing Director of Bartle, Bogle, Hegarty:

'Although advertising can be, and is, used in a variety of different ways, its prime contribution is in helping to build and sustain brands for commercial benefit, often leading this process.'

Advertising can, therefore, fulfil a number of roles. As such, the objectives which advertising may be required to fulfil are somewhat diverse. The following is a list of some advertising objectives.

Awareness

At various times in the life of a brand, it is important to raise the level of awareness among target consumers. Inevitably, this is most often associated with the introduction of a new product. However, either because of competitive or other pressures (perhaps the reduction in the levels of advertising support), the levels of awareness of a particular brand may fall, and advertising will seek to improve the levels. In some instances, although the consumer may be aware of the product itself, he or she will need information as to where to purchase it (particularly if it is in limited distribution). Advertising will seek to identify stockists of the product.

Reminder

Reminder advertising can take a number of forms. In some instances, it serves (as with awareness advertising) simply to ensure that the brand is brought towards the front of the mind. In others, it will seek to communicate specific benefits or uses of the brand which may have been forgotten (Kellogg's have used this approach with their campaign for Corn-flakes, with the endline 'Too good to be forgotten'), or, perhaps, to suggest new uses which will make it more relevant to the consumer's needs.

Changing attitudes, perceptions and beliefs

From time to time, market research will reveal a dissonance between the stance of the brand and the desired positioning. Perhaps the image of the brand has become 'old-fash-ioned', or more recently introduced com-petitor products are seen to have greater relevance to current needs. Although advertis-ing will be designed to counteract these influences, it should be recognized that the task of changing attitudes and perceptions is far more difficult to achieve, but one in which advertising can make a valid contribution.

Both Lucozade and Hellmann's Mayon-naise are examples of advertising campaigns which dramatically changed consumer per-ceptions of the brands.

Reinforcing attitudes

Often, the role of advertising is to remind consumers (particularly in the case of routine purchases) of the original reasons why they chose the product. In some instances, such advertising will reassert the original values of the brand, either to offset competitive pres-sures, or simply to reassure consumers that those brand values have not been changed. Kellogg's, for example, ran a campaign with the broad theme 'If it doesn't say Kellogg's on the box, it isn't Kellogg's in the packet' to reduce the encroachment of retailer products which might otherwise be confused with the leading brand.

Product line building

In some instances, the volumes for individual product lines, although profitable, will be insufficient to sustain advertising. Here, the manufacturer may seek to communicate values which are common to all product lines which bear the brand name (even though they may well have different functional benefits). Sometimes, although not always, this will take the form of corporate advertising, to associate a series of positive values with the parent name in order that it serves to endorse the products with which it is associated.

Relating product to consumer needs

Although a brand may be in common use, the underlying reasons for its purchase may have become confused. Advertising will seek to ensure that the product is seen as being directly relevant to contemporary consumer requirements.

Image

Advertising may seek to convey particular image dimensions in order that the product will be better perceived by the target audi-ence. As we will see in the following chapter, many brands are bought primarily for the image they portray, rather than because of their functional benefits. Much perfume advertising is of this nature, as, of course, is that for Levi's.

Business-to-business advertising

The principles applied to the development of consumer advertising are equally appropriate in the context of business-to-business campaigns. However, there are important differences, and these need to be recognized in terms of the strategic understanding of the campaign requirements. In business-to-business campaigns, it must be remembered that the purchaser is not paying directly for the goods or services. He or she has a corporate responsibility to make the correct decision. Moreover, the purchaser may be required to justify his or her decision, both factually and emotively. The scale of the purchase decision is often large, not just in terms of costs, but in both commitment to the particular supplier over an extended period of time, and in terms of the implications of the purchase decision to the company.

In the business environment, the purchaser is much more likely to develop a personal relationship with the supplier, and the advertising needs to reflect or reaffirm the part that personal contact makes in the decision-making process. Importantly, the purchaser may or may not be a user and, in some circumstances, may well be a consumer of the same company's goods in an individual capacity. Many companies are suppliers both of industrial goods and consumer products (e.g. Lever Bros. have an industrial division, whilst KGF have a catering division which supplies similar products to those sold in conventional retail outlets in a repackaged form).

The notion of integration is just as important in business-to-business communications as it is in consumer marketing. Since there will often be many people involved in the purchasing decision, it is important to recognize that the process of communications is significantly more complex than in the consumer field. Since members of the decision-making unit may be exposed to different components

of a single campaign, it is essential that all elements convey, in broad terms, the same message – although there will often be a need to tailor that message specifically to respond to the needs of the individual within the overall target audience.

References

Bartle, J., The Advertising Contribution, in Butterfield, L. (ed), *Excellence in Advertising*, Butterworth-Heinemann, 1997

Belch, G. E. and Belch, M. A., *Introduction to Advertising and Promotion: An Integrated Marketing Communications Perspective*, 2nd edition, Irwin, 1993

Boddingtons Case Study, in Baker, C. (ed.). *Advertising Works*, Vol. 8, IPA/NTC, 1995

Butterfield, L., Strategy Development, in Butterfield, L. (ed.), *Excellence in Advertising*, Butterworth-Heinemann, 1997

de Chernatony, L. and McDonald, M., *Creating Powerful Brands*, Butterworth-Heinemann, 1992

Ehrenberg, A., 'How Do Consumers Come to Buy A New Brand?', *Admap*, March 1997

Ehrenberg, A.C.S., *Repeat Buying – Theory and Applications*, North Holland Publishing Company, 1972

Holbrook and Hirchman, 'The Consumer's Ability to Process Brand Information from Ads', *Journal of Marketing*, October 1991

Jones, J. P., Advertising's Impact on Sales and Profitability, Advertising Effectiveness Conference, 16 March 1995

Lavidge, R. J. and Steiner, G. A., 'A Model for Predictive Effects of Advertising Effectiveness', *Journal of Marketing*, 1961

McDonald, C., *How Advertising Works, A Review of Current Thinking*, The Advertising Association/NTC Publications, 1992

Millward Brown, *How Advertising Affects the Sales of Packaged Goods Brands*, Millward Brown International, 1991

Murphy, J. H. and Cunningham, I., *Advertising and Marketing Communications Management*, Dryden Press, 1993

Woods, R., 'Why Has Advertising Gone Blank', *Brandweek*, 22 February 1993

Yeshin, T. (ed.), *Inside Advertising*, Institute of Practitioners in Advertising, 1993

Additional reading

Parente, Donald, Vanden Bergh, Bruce, Barban, Arnold and Marra, James, *Advertising Campaign Strategy: A Guide to Marketing Communication Plans*, 1996, The Dryden Press

McDonald, Colin, *How Advertising Works: A Review of Current Thinking*, 1992, The Advertising Association/NTC Publications Ltd

Aaker, David, Batra, Rajeev and Myers, John G., *Advertising Management*, 4th edition, 1992, Prentice Hall

Students should also consult the superb *Advertising Works* books, representing a compilation of the successful papers in the IPA Effectiveness Awards produced biannually. The 1992 and 1994 volumes were both edited by Chris Baker, with the latest edition, Volume 9, 1996, edited by Gary Duckworth

CHAPTER 8

The development of advertising

Aims and objectives

- To examine the role of the creative brief;
- To develop an understanding of creative strategies and tactics;
- To distinguish between rational and emotional advertising appeals;
- To consider the diversity of advertising approaches;
- To examine the varying styles of advertising;
- To learn about the contribution of personalities and music;
- To examine the nature of creativity;
- To appreciate the importance of establishing guidelines for the evaluation of advertising.

In the previous chapter, we considered some aspects of the theoretical background which assists us in the understanding of the advertising process. In this chapter, we will examine the way in which advertising is developed from a practitioner standpoint. Before proceeding, it will be worth making a distinction between some of the terms which will be used.

The communications objective

This is a statement of the messages, images or information that the campaign is required to communicate.

The creative platform

The particular device chosen to convey the message.

The advertising execution

The nature of the advertising appeal used to communicate the message to the target audience.

The creative brief

Most advertising agencies use a very precise format for the purpose of briefing creative work. Although the topic headings may differ from agency to agency, the fundamental need is the same in all cases – to provide the creative department with the appropriate guidance to the development of creative materials, in a succinct and easily comprehensible form. The creative brief is the basis of all advertising development and should encompass, in summary form, the major findings of research and other inputs upon which the advertising will eventually be based. A contemporary example of a creative brief used by a leading advertising agency is reproduced in Figure 8.1.

SAATCHI & SAATCHI
ADVERTISING

CREATIVE BRIEF

CLIENT	BRAND	PROGRESS CONTROLLER	DATE

ACCOUNT GROUP	CREATIVE GROUP	PLANNER	MEDIA PLANNER

JOB TITLE		DEVELOPMENT BUDGET £	PRODUCTION BUDGET £

TV	RADIO	PRESS	POSTER	DIRECT COMMUNICATION
PROMOTION IDEAS	SPONSORSHIP / EVENTS	IN-STORE	NEW MEDIA	

CAMPAIGN REQUIREMENT

TARGET AUDIENCE. WHAT THEY CURRENTLY THINK AND DO

WHAT SHOULD THE ADVERTISING MAKE THE TARGET AUDIENCE THINK AND DO

THE SINGLE MINDED PROPOSITION

SUBSTANTIATION FOR THE PROPOSITION

DESIRED BRAND CHARACTER

MANDATORY INCLUSIONS

DATE FROM CLIENT	CORE GROUP MEETING	INTERIM REVIEW DATE	DATE TO CLIENT

SIGNATURES GROUP DIRECTOR	PLANNER	CREATIVE SERVICES DIRECTOR	CREATIVE GROUP HEAD

Figure 8.1   Saatchi & Saatchi creative brief (produced by kind permission of that agency)

The briefing form consists of two separate sheets of A4: a cover sheet which is designed to provide the background to the briefing process, and the briefing form itself. The former requires the planner to answer three specific questions.

1 Why are we advertising?

It is here that it is important to provide the context in which the advertising campaign is to be developed. This will include an identification of the current brand situation, the competitive environment. The imperative is to summarize the underlying reasons for doing the advertising and the main tasks which the campaign will be required to perform.

2 What territory do we want to own with this brand and why?

Here, the planner has the opportunity to identify the main distinguishing characteristics of the brand, either physical or emotional, and the factors which will ensure that the brand is clearly differentiated from its competitors.

3 How are we going to judge the success of this campaign?

The planner will need to identify the way in which the campaign is intended to work, and the means by which the achievements will be measured. These might include, for example, the impact on sales, the way in which the campaign might affect consumer behaviour and attitudes, the effects on the trade, the company sales force, internal morale, and so on.

After supplying specific information which will guide the creative process, the first important task is to define the campaign requirement. This is designed to isolate the specific task which the creative department is expected to fulfil. This may, for example, take

the form of a campaign which builds on the previous advertising heritage of the brand, and which will be used to refresh and update particular aspects of the communication. The PG Tips tea television commercials are among the longest-running British advertising campaigns. Periodically, new advertising executions will be developed, to communicate a desired attribute of the product, or some other emotional value. The context of the commercials, however, will remain the same, with all the major characters being represented by chimpanzees.

It may demand the development of a completely new campaign, sometimes for a new product, as, for example, when Dyson introduced their innovatory vacuum cleaner. The advertising requirement, in this instance, was to differentiate their product from their major competitors and to demonstrate a competitive advantage. On other occasions, advertising will be used to represent a change in the strategic direction of the brand. Recently, for example, after many years of running advertising which was based on puns on the word *eau*, Perrier adopted a totally different stance in the marketplace, using a youth-based, lifestyle execution. (They have since appointed a new advertising agency, and returned to the original *eau* device.)

It may require the development of a single advertisement for some specific purpose, such as a tie-in with some retailer activity. The major perfume companies often utilize press advertising in this way, with a consumer offer being made available at identified retail outlets. In other instances, the company may wish to announce a new store opening. B&Q recently ran a television campaign across London to unveil their new Ealing store. There may be a need to make an announcement of an immediate nature to the target audience, as was the case with the recent advertising for Johnson's Wax, recalling a specific product line.

In some instances, the advertising component will reflect some other form of marketing communications activity which has already been developed, or is in the process of development. Here the other activity will take the lead, and advertising will provide the means by which the proposition is communicated to a wider audience. Often, this will feature a sales promotion offer, such as a competition or on-pack lottery, which otherwise would only present its message at the point of purchase and then, predominantly, to existing purchasers of the brand. This approach is frequently adopted by the fast-food chains to feature promotional tie-ins with current blockbuster films, such as Jurassic Park, or the M&M's campaign featuring the Mr Bean character to coincide with the launch of the film.

The next important stage in the process is the identification of the *target audience*. Clearly, some of the information will be available in the form of specific demographic data (age, sex, class, etc.). However, wherever possible, it is important to go beyond these tight (and somewhat restrictive) definitions. If the creatives can be helped to understand the dimensions of the audience (young, old, attitudinal values, lifestyle factors and so on), they will be able to reflect these in terms of the tone and style of the message. Advertising aimed, for example, at a youth market will probably employ different language and tonal values than a campaign designed to support the introduction of a product to an older target audience. By the same token, this information will provide the media department with the key factors by which to isolate the appropriate media to provide the most cost-effective coverage of the defined target audiences.

The identification of the appropriate media to communicate the message to the target audience is an important dimension of the advertising process. Each of the available media not only has a series of unique characteristics that make it more or less appropriate for the task in hand, but they also represent an environment for the message which will serve to enhance or diminish aspects of that message.

Elsewhere in the brief, there will be an identification of the *budget*, which will provide an indication of the likely *media* options. Budgetary factors may preclude the use of certain media, such as television, on the simple grounds of cost (either of the medium itself or the production of the associated commercials). Sometimes the brand will choose to reflect its image in particular media – often to the exclusion of others. It is important that both the creative and media departments are made aware of these issues to avoid the wastage of time involved in the development of proposals which are inappropriate. These, and other important dimensions of media and media planning, will be considered in greater depth in Chapter 9.

It is important to recognize, however, that the creative brief should not be unnecessarily restrictive. It is not the job of the planner to predetermine media selection which, itself, may be an important facet of the creative message. The selection of the appropriate media environment for the advertising is often as important as the message itself. A good example of this was the launch advertising campaign for Häagen Dazs ice-cream, which exclusively used upmarket, quality colour magazines which were chosen to position the brand in the minds of potential consumers. For a full discussion of the Häagen Dazs case history, which develops this and other issues, students might like to refer to *Advertising Works, 7*, edited by Chris Baker and published by the Institute of Practitioners in Advertising with NTC Publications Limited, 1993. A similar example of the importance of media planning in the generation of impact is demonstrated by the highly praised Wonderbra campaign created by TBWA. Although limited to a media budget of just £330,000, the campaign generated an estimated £18 million of coverage in the media, resulting in an increase in sales of some 41 per cent (Baker, 1994a).

This is followed by a definition of what the advertising should make the audience think and do. This is the response which the advertising should elicit from the target audience and, importantly, should be realistic within the confines of the available budget.

The next area in which information is required is 'single-minded proposition'. Effective advertising must be based on a careful study of the important consumer dimensions. (What can the brand say about itself which will create a clear separation in the minds of consumers between it and its competitors?) Although summarized into a very short form (there is only space on the brief for, at most, two short sentences), this is a critical aspect of the creative briefing process. It will almost certainly be the culmination of a great deal of research activity and analysis, which has provided the agency with an understanding of the important consumer perceptions of the brand's characteristics.

This will be accompanied by some – again, short – substantiation of the reasons why the consumer should believe the proposition. This may relate to some physical characteristic of the brand. In many instances, it is a direct consequence of the emotional values which the brand represents. If the creative department understand the purpose of the advertising, they can better fulfil the brief.

The 'desired brand character' is the opportunity to indicate whether the advertising proposition is to be authoritative and serious or amusing and light-hearted, fashionable and stylish or down-to-earth and approachable, and so on. Similarly, there may be specific elements of the advertising which need to be carried over from previous campaigns. Perhaps a particular personality spokesperson is used to represent the brand; on other occasions, an underlying theme needs to be reinforced (as in the case of the Safeway advertising, where the campaign has evolved through a series of child 'presenters', giving the retailer a unique executional device). Certainly, there may be specific requirements to identify the brand with a logo, and perhaps the identity of the parent company.

The final requirement is to define the 'mandatory inclusions'. This will consist of information which must be supplied to the reader, listener or viewer of the advertising. In some instances, this will be a reflection of some legal or other code of practice. For example, all cigarette advertising must carry a health warning, whilst financial advertising will be required to indicate the terms and conditions which apply within the sector. In other instances, there may be a specific client requirement to include a telephone number or list of stockists, or there may be particular 'rules' about the depiction of the logo.

Some agencies, such as Bogle, Bartle, Hegarty, make an important distinction between the actual product and the brand in terms of the creative briefing form, as the following examples demonstrate:

Häagen Dazs Ice-Cream
The product: Super-premium, fresh-cream, ice-cream
The brand: The ultimate sensual, intimate pleasure

Boddington's Ale
The product: Cask-conditioned ale from Manchester
The brand: The smoothest drinking bitter – with a Mancunian point of view

Levi's 501s
The product: Five-pocket, Western, heavyweight denim jeans
The brand: The original and definitive jeans. The embodiment of jeans values (freedom, individuality, rebellion, sex, masculinity, originality and youth)
(Bartle, 1997)

The creative brief fulfils a vital role in the strategic development of advertising. Although much of the work will have been done separately, it is the framework for the determination of the strategic approach which the advertising will take. As such, it fulfils many of the key requirements of the DAGMAR approach described earlier. However, it is also important to recognize that the briefing document fulfils other functions.

From the management perspective, it is the distillation of the major part of the preliminary strategic development which will guide the entirety of the creative process which follows. For the creative department, it provides an indication of the important directions and the thrust of the communications message which they will be required to develop. The responsibility of management in this context is to establish the broad areas in which the creatives should operate. It should provide a sense of focus and discipline within which they can operate. For the media planners, it will provide the key dimensions of the target audience, which they will seek to reach in the most cost-effective way possible. It will avoid the unnecessary waste of time, energy and cost on developing creative messages which are inappropriate to the brand or the target audience. And it serves as the benchmark against which the creative work can be assessed.

An alternative description of the briefing process is the paper by Charlie Robertson in *How to Plan Advertising* (Cooper, 1997).

Creative strategies and tactics

The determination of the creative platform

According to Winston Fletcher (1994), the average 35-year-old British adult will have seen some 150 000 different commercials, most of them half a dozen times or more. Achieving distinctivity is, therefore, a paramount consideration and is the driving force behind the creative process. Bland advertising, at best, fails to attract the attention of the consumer. At worst, it can undermine the image associated with the brand and result in consumers shifting to a brand which has more up-beat and positive associations.

A survey conducted by Lowe Howard-Spink concludes that as many as 56 per cent of consumers are 'avoiding' advertisements in magazines, 54 per cent say that they are ignoring posters, whilst 44 per cent zap out of TV commercials altogether. The findings of the survey suggest that as much as 13 per cent of the money spent on TV advertising (almost £500 million) was wasted due to the phenomenon it called 'advertising avoidance'. One bad ad in a break can put people off the remainder. The analysis was based on BARB data from which three broad segments emerged, all of which were of roughly the same size: non-avoiders, who rarely missed commercial breaks; moderate avoiders, who saw about 20 per cent fewer ads than non-avoiders; and avoiders, who saw only about half as many ads as non-avoiders.

This would appear to correlate with the findings from TGI. In 1991 it recorded that 33 per cent agreed with the statement 'I enjoy the TV ads as much as the programmes'. That figure is now down to 23 per cent. The research further identified that there is a strong correlation between advertising 'likeability' and awareness. This is reinforced by a variety of previous studies conducted throughout the world by, among others, Haley and Baldinger (1991), Du Plessis (1994) and Millward Brown. A survey conducted by *Adweek* in the United States indicated that more than 40 per cent of Americans actively refuse to buy a product if they do not like the advertising.

The key factors which make people notice advertising are:

1 When the product itself is inherently different.
2 When the advertisement is sufficiently unusual.
3 When the advertisement has some particular personal relevance.
4 When they seem to keep seeing it, and eventually it penetrates their consciousness.

There are contrasting views of what makes for good advertising. Just as brands exhibit different personalities, so too do the agencies which create the advertising that supports those brands. Most often, the choice of which agency to appoint to handle a particular account will be determined as much by the intrinsic approach adopted by the agency as any other factor. Some agencies adopt a 'hard sell' approach; others can be typified as preferring 'soft sell' advertising.

'Hard sell' advertising is an approach in which the advertiser uses specific facets of the product or service to convince the target audience that it is the best available. It often employs comparative techniques to display the particular advantages. This approach is seen commonly in many of the executions used to support the brands of Procter & Gamble. It is often accompanied by a specific injunction to buy now. The advertising within this category utilizes a series of logical appeals to the target consumer to communicate the product benefits or attributes. It provides information based on the performance of the product, the particular features it possesses, or its ability to provide the means of solving problems with which the consumer has to deal.

'Soft sell' advertising, by contrast, uses a somewhat more subtle approach to the differentiation of its products. The essential ingredient is the desire to create an image in the minds of the consumers which will, ultimately, lead them to a purchase. Such advertising rarely promotes a specific facet of the brand – seldom do such ads feature particular product attributes to communicate a reason to buy. Most commonly, they deal with images and product associations which will result in the consumer considering the product or service in a more favourable light.

There can be no prescription as to which approach is superior. Indeed, the very simplistic categorization of advertising into these two groups suggests a more extreme differentiation than actually exists. Most forms of advertising contain elements of both logical and emotional appeals. However, particular clients tend to favour one or other of the approaches in the support of the brands within their portfolio. Both styles of advertising are evidently effective in the creation of

brand support. This is an area where the combination of the culture of the client and the role of the account planner are brought together in the creation of an advertising message which will best serve to communicate the role of the brand and contribute to the overall marketing and marketing communications objectives.

The creative challenge

The primary task facing the creative department is to take all of the inputs and transform this information into a creative idea or advertising execution. Rather than simply stating the attributes or benefits that a product or service possesses, they must ensure that the advertising message takes a form which will gain the attention of the potential consumer, arouse his or her interest, and make the advertising memorable. A key consideration will be the extent to which the advertising will be based on a rational or an emotional appeal.

Rational appeals

Many communications messages are based on rational appeals to the consumer. These provide the viewer or reader with specific information relating to the product. These may identify specific features which are found in the product (for example, Club Biscuits have 'more chocolate'); certain attributes which the product or service possesses (e.g. Fairy Liquid washes more dishes than cheaper brands); or benefits which the consumer will derive from using the product (e.g. Neurofen Plus adopts a problem–solution approach in which the commercial associates the problem (back pain) with the ease and comfort delivered by the use of the product).

Rational advertising appeals tend to be used when the manufacturer wishes to convey particular information to the potential consumer. Sometimes, when the product is either superior to its competitors or where the manufacturer wishes to achieve a position of superiority by virtue of being the first or only product in the category to make a particular claim, he will also use a rational appeal to the consumer. This is commonly seen with the 'first among equals' positioning. These appeals are most commonly used where the product is particularly complex, or in those situations where the consumer will require specific information in order to reach a purchasing decision. The computer market is a perfect example of where rational appeals are commonly used. Much business-to-business advertising tends to be of this type, since the buyers involved in the purchasing decision will often possess a high degree of knowledge regarding the products available to them and will require specific information to justify their decision to change the target of their purchasing decision.

In some instances, rational advertising utilizes some form of comparison between the company's product and those with which it competes. The Royal Bank of Scotland, for example, directly compares the interest rates charged on its credit card with those of other financial institutions. Similarly, mobile telephone providers often compare their call rates with those of their competitors. In the UK, however, comparative advertising is far less widely used than in the United States, where the format tends to be commonplace. A commonly used format is what might be considered 'generic' comparisons. In these advertisements, the advertiser compares his product with an unidentified competitor – the consumer being left to decide the identity of the 'other' product. This can be seen in such campaigns, for example, as the Daz Challenge.

Such comparative advertising is particularly beneficial to new brands, since it enables them to position themselves alongside other well-established products. This device can be effective in attempting to ensure the inclusion of the product within the consumer's purchasing portfolio. A recent press advertisement for a new brand of vacuum cleaner, manufactured by Dyson, uses the comparative approach. For most brands, however, this comparative route will tend to be rejected, since there is a risk that the rival's product will be promoted by the advertising and will derive additional consumer exposure. A wide variety of rational motives can be used as the basis for advertising appeals. These might include convenience, economy, health, sensory benefits (such as taste, smell, touch), also quality, performance, comfort, reliability, durability, efficiency, efficacy, etc.

Emotional appeals

Increasingly, advertising utilizes emotional appeals as the basis of the message to the consumer. We have already seen that the result of convergent technology is the minimizing of differences between products within a given category. Clearly, in these situations, any attempt to achieve product differentiation on the basis of a logical appeal to the consumer will fail to achieve sufficient distinction between the manufacturer's brand and its rivals. Moreover, in a crowded media marketplace, it is clear that consumers like and enjoy advertising which, in turn, enhances their liking of the featured product or service.

David Ogilvy (1964), in *Confessions of an Advertising Man*, argues, 'The greater the similarity between brands, the less part reason plays in brand selection. . . . The manufacturer who dedicates his advertising to building the most sharply defined personality for his brand will get the largest share at the highest profit'. In a similar vein, John Bartle, the Managing Director of Bartle, Bogle, Hegarty, argues that as the USP (unique selling proposition) is fast disappearing, then what becomes correspondingly more important is the ESP – the emotional selling point.

Advertising appeals

'Few purchases of any kind are made for entirely rational reasons. Even a purely functional product such as a laundry detergent may offer what is now called an emotional benefit – say the satisfaction of seeing one's children in bright clean clothes. In some product categories, the rational element is small. These include soft drinks, beer, certain personal care products and most old fashioned products.' (Ogilvy and Raphaelson, 1982)

We can look in more detail at the variety of appeals, both rational and emotional, which are used in contemporary advertising. Indeed, advertising can be classified by the style of appeal used to communicate to the consumer. The advertising appeal refers to the basis or approach used in the advertising to attract the interest and attention of consumers and influence their feelings towards the product.

Feature appeal
Ads that use a *feature* appeal focus on the dominant attributes or characteristics of the product or service. Flymo employs a product demonstration – 'Squeezing this much grass into this much space' – to establish a clear product benefit. Tetley use the long-running cartoon characters to demonstrate their new 'drawstring' teabag.

Competitive advantage appeal
When a *competitive advantage* appeal is used, the advertiser makes either a direct or indirect comparison to another brand or brands and usually makes a superiority claim on one or more attributes (Daz Challenge, Dyson).

Price or value appeals
Price or value appeals are often used to persuade consumers that they are receiving more for their money or making a saving. Price appeals are at their most impactful when combined with some other benefit, such as when a company offers high quality at a reduced price. Dixons have recently used the

'price check' principle, underpinned with the promise that they check to ensure that no-one offers the same items cheaper than them. Similarly, the Esso Price Watch – 'We never stop watching' – provides the consumer with the same benefit.

Quality appeals
Quality is the basis of a separate appeal, such as with Sainsbury's 'Fresh Food – Fresh Ideas' campaign.

News appeals
News appeals are those where some form of new information is provided about the product or service. This approach is commonly used by new products or existing products which have made changes such as improvements or modifications. Currently, Mars are using this approach to transfer the values of 'Opal Fruits' to their new name, 'Starburst'.

Popularity appeals
Product or service popularity appeals focus attention on the wide existing customer base or the market position occupied by the brand, e.g. Hertz No. 1.

Appeals to ego or self-esteem
Fear or anger Appeals are sometimes designed to create an element of shock for the consumer which, in turn, provokes impact and recognition. The possible danger, however, is that as well as shocking the target audience, it may also serve to alienate them. Some of the early anti-smoking advertising suffered from this problem. A current anti-smoking press advertisement depicts two cigarettes arranged in the form of a cross, with the copy 'A quarter of a million people pack it in every year'. American Express travellers' cheques have consistently used the fear factor as the basis of their advertising (the fear of losing travellers' cheques highlights the potential consumer risk of a spoilt holiday). Over-the-counter medicines sometimes use a similar fear factor: Diocalm, an anti-diarrhoeal product, uses the

fear of contracting a funny tummy whilst on holiday as the platform for its product sale.

Social acceptance The current TV licence campaign depicts non-payers as 'spongers'.

Star appeals and testimonials These enable consumers to identify with their favourite celebrities. The approach attempts to establish empathy among the target audience by presenting the personality in a situation to which the consumer can relate. Seeing a product being endorsed by a famous person can capture attention and convey authenticity for the advertising message. Dolland & Aitchison are using Burt Reynolds in a TV campaign to underpin the proposition 'where everybody gets star treatment'.

Sensory appeals These are designed to create a particular image or evoke a response in the mind of the consumer. This approach is commonly taken by drinks manufacturers evoking a sense of thirst, or food manufacturers evoking taste in their advertising.

Novelty appeals These offer potentially the greatest opportunity for creativity. These ads attempt to catch the attention of the viewer by presenting original perspectives on their proposition. Smirnoff Vodka has used this approach, whilst the current cinema advertising for Diamond White cider uses a surreal approach to convey that the world is turned on its head by the brand. John Smith's Bitter uses Jack Dee in a series of humorous commercials to differentiate the brand from its competitors.

Although the above examples serve to illustrate many of the most common appeals used in advertising, it is important to remember that, in many cases, advertising executions contain a combination of both rational and emotional appeals. The imperative is to identify a memorable stance for the brand which will serve to differentiate it from its competitors. If consumers can readily identify with the advertising, more often than not, they will buy the brand.

Styles of advertising

The different styles of advertising can, similarly, be divided into a relatively small number of groupings. The creative execution style refers to the manner in which a particular appeal is turned into an advertising message, that is, presented to the consumer.

Product as hero

This is advertising which focuses directly on the product and identifies a series of attributes or benefits which can be derived from using the brand. Primarily, it uses a straightforward presentation of information concerning the product or service and is often used with informational and rational appeals where the focus of the message is the product or service and its specific benefits or attributes. Pears soap 'attracts water and softens skin', whilst Aristoc poster advertising features the statement 'It's not my legs that are amazing, it's my tights'.

Product demonstration

This advertising is designed to illustrate the key advantages or benefits of the product or service by showing it in actual use or some contrived or staged situation. Such campaigns are very effective in convincing consumers of the utility of the product or the advantages of owning the brand. Examples can be seen in a variety of market sectors and often include domestic cleaning products. A similar approach has been taken by the Bosch Power Drill and Dulux Once paint. A poster campaign for Peugeot 506 uses chewing gum to underpin the proposition 'It sticks to the road'.

Problem–solution

Here, the advertising takes the form of a demonstration or identification of a problem to which the product represents the ideal solution. Pepsid AC is the remedy for indigestion, whilst Head and Shoulders eliminates dandruff.

Slice of life

These campaigns usually involve a problem–situation format in which the advertiser seeks to portray a real-life situation involving a problem that consumers might face. The advertising focuses on how the product resolves the particular problem. Ariel Automatic features incidents in the life of the Skinner family, whilst UPS uses a similar approach to depict a business-to-business situation. It is important in such advertising to relate the situation as closely as possible to consumer perceptions. If the scenario is seen to be contrived or unrealistic, it will fail to have the desired effect.

Testimonial

In this, a person speaks on behalf of the brand, describing his or her personal experience of using it (as in the current Oil of Ulay advertising). This approach is very effective when the spokesperson is someone with whom the audience can identify closely. Testimonials must be credible and must be based on actual use of the product or service. DHL is currently using this device, featuring senior executives from leading international companies to depict how their companies rely on DHL to deliver their needs.

Spokesperson presenter

This uses an apparent or established authority to lend credibility to the brand message. In some instances, this takes the form of the proverbial 'man in a white coat' to provide 'scientific authority' for the product claims; in other cases, it will be a real individual whom the viewer or reader trusts to provide reliable information.

Endorsements

These appear in a variety of different forms and rely on the fact that the viewer identifies with the person, company or body which supplies the endorsement. Clearly, their effectiveness depends on the degree of 'credibility' possessed by the presenter and the extent to which the target audience associates with the chosen individual. Some of the different applications of this approach are:

- *Professional endorsement* and the provision of scientific and technical evidence. This approach uses an 'authoritative' presenter to communicate information about the brand. A variation on this theme is the provision of specific scientific or technical evidence to the consumer. For many years, washing machine manufacturers have been used to endorse washing powder brands, often presented by the 'man in a white coat'. Now Miss Selfridge, among other retailers, recommends Ariel Futur.
- *Media endorsement* as in the cases of Pantene Pro V, and the vehicle selected by specialist car magazines as 'Car of the Year'.
- *The use of a personality character.* Harry Enfield is used in a variety of his character roles to support a number of different brands, such as Dime Bar and Hula Hoops. Most recently, the notion of character endorsement has been extended into the field of cartoons, with a commercial depicting Homer Simpson eating Doritos.
- *The personality as individual.* Gerard Depardieu represents the Courvoisier brand, Eric Cantona has featured in Eurostar commercials and Tim Henman uses Kellogg's Sustain.

The commercial which featured the greatest number of celebrities was one for the *Sunday Times* to mark the occasion of the paper's re-launch after a long dispute. The Benton & Bowles-produced commercial featured no fewer than twenty-three personalities in a 60-second commercial, and included John Gielgud, Ralph Richardson, Glenda Jackson, Richard Attenborough, Joan Collins, Dame Edna Everage, John Thaw and Edward Fox among others.

Opportunistic advertising

Seasonal or other events often provide the basis on which to develop short-term advertising campaigns. The last general election showed the process in action. Tango developed a 'Vote Orange' commercial; John Smith's Bitter adapted the Labour party slogan 'Britain deserves better' into 'Britain deserves bitter'; whilst British Airways used its own 'Where is Everybody' slogan in an ad depicting all three main party leaders standing in front of a ballot box.

People like me

The use of 'real' people interviewed in front of the camera, and using the technique known as 'vox pops' (the voice of the people), is a device designed to achieve identification with the target audience. If viewers or readers identify with the people used in the campaign, they are likely to perceive the featured product or service as being appropriate for themselves. This approach is currently being used in the Always campaign.

Mini-drama

Both Oxo and Gold Blend have involved the consumer in a developing 'soap' drama which has been extended over many years and has seen considerable changes to reflect the development of consumer lifestyles. The Gold Blend campaign, which was originally launched in 1969, demonstrates the ability of a campaign to evolve whilst retaining the emotional bond with the audience. According to the case study presented in *Advertising Works*, Vol 9 (Duckworth, 1997), the result has been an increase in brand volume of around 60 per cent at a time when the market was static or declining.

Continuing character

Included in the storyline, is a central character or personality symbol to deliver the advertising message and with which the product or service can be identified. This approach is often used to transfer the distinctive identities of the characters and create an associated personality for the brand. An example of this approach is that adopted by Renault for the Clio in which Nicole and Papa have been retained over an extended period and, in the process, have created a unique personality for the car. Sadly, that campaign has now ended.

Brand heritage and history

The approach can be seen in a variety of advertising campaigns, such as Heineken Export, Thornton Chocolates – 'Chocolate Heaven Since 1911' – and Clerical and Medical Insurance.

Pastiche

Many commercials are derived directly from scenarios established in major films. Indeed, many creatives spend an enormous amount of time watching contemporary movies which are a guide to contemporary taste and moods. Illustrations of the application of the device are Yorkie, which derives from 'The Fugitive', and the Nationwide, using a device from 'Four Weddings and a Funeral'.

Spectacular, musical, stage show

Commercials using this approach often involve a 'cast of thousands' and, inevitably, are costly to produce. Halifax uses this technique in several of its executions.

Non-verbal

This is increasingly important approach, especially where commercials are intended for use across a variety of different markets, where the use of language to describe the product or its benefits would prove difficult. Examples include Land Rover Discovery, Vauxhall Vectra and Gordon's Gin.

Infomercial

This approach adopts a 'news-style' presentation in which the execution is very similar to that of a foreshortened television programme. Currently employed by Standard Life.

Teaser advertising

This is commonly used by new products to create an element of intrigue and curiosity and build excitement and anticipation. A good example is the launch campaign for the Nissan Micra (Baker 1994c) and the initial campaign for Cable and Wireless.

Animation

This involves various executions using drawn or computer-generated illustrations. It offers important advantages in enabling creation of situations which might be impossible to film in real life. Claymation, the technique used in the 'Wallace and Gromit' films, has been used for British Gas, for example.

Fantasy

This approach is often used where emotional appeals are relevant. Product or service becomes a central part of the storyline; for example, Pirelli uses images and symbolism to associate with the brand.

Shock advertising

Benetton adopted a shock approach to its advertising. Initially, the images used were uncontroversial, but the campaign evolved progressively to use images that were both startling and, to some, offensive. Perhaps the two images which caused the greatest concern were the poster showing a leading American Aids campaigner on his deathbed, and the picture of the newborn baby, still covered in blood. Both ads elicited large numbers of complaints. The former included many from Aids charities, who felt that the image used

was gratuitous and demeaning; the latter attracted the greatest number of complaints received by the Advertising Standards Association (ASA) in its history (BBC Television, My Greatest? Mistake, March, 1997).

Using celebrities

Advertising has long recognized the value of using identified spokespersons who are easily identified by the consumer. It recognizes the fact that the celebrity has the ability to draw attention to the advertising message. Here again, this adds a point of difference to the advertising and assists the process of breaking through in a cluttered media environment. It is hoped that the popularity, respect and admiration that the consumers hold for the celebrity will be transferred to the product or service he or she is advertising.

However, the use of celebrities carries with it a variety of risks. There is the danger that the personality will overwhelm the product and its message. This was seen in the campaign for the video producers. Viewers were readily able to recall the personality – Dawn French – but less able to remember what she was advertising!

- *Overexposure.* If the celebrity is identified within a number of different commercials or associated with a variety of brands, the consumer may perceive him or her as lacking in integrity.
- *Liking.* There will inevitably be different perceptions of any personality within a given audience. Some people will like the celebrity, others will dislike him or her. The latter may well associate their dislike of the individual with the brand.
- *Negative associations.* In some instances, celebrities, by their very nature, may be associated with negative actions. To avoid the risk of this negativity being associated with the product, advertisers will cease to use the personality – often at very considerable cost.

However, despite his public fall from grace, Nike continued to use Eric Cantona and featured the specific issue within their advertising campaign.

There is an overriding need to ensure that there is a close match between the brand, the target market and the celebrity. Consumer research is important in this context.

The high cost of celebrity endorsements can be evidenced with a number of examples. M&G featured the former Chancellor of the Exchequer, Lord Lawson of Blaby, in a campaign to support its PEPS offer. Reportedly, he received somewhat less than £100,000 for his appearance in the advertising. Helen Mirren features in the current campaign for Virgin Airlines. She received a fee estimated to be around £300,000 for her role. Hugh Laurie received a reported £500,000 for his involvement in the current BT campaign.

Music in advertising

Music is often used to set a mood and create favourable associations with a brand. The largest study concerning the effect of music on advertising was carried out by Stewart and Furse in 1986. They analysed over 1000 commercials and discovered that there was a positive relationship between the musical factor and the level of recall and comprehension. There is considerable evidence that, where music has been used before by a brand, then the advertising is more easily understood and there is better identification and awareness of the brand being advertised.

A study by Branthwaite and Ware (1997) identified the common functions of music within advertising:

Indicates branding	7%
Sings message	7%
Borrows a lifestyle	15%
Gives pace	34%
Background music	38%
Creates mood	54%

Levi's have used musical underpinning extensively in their advertising campaigns, with great success both for the brand and the artists featured. The approach has been continued since the first BBH commercial in 1986 known as 'Laundrette', which featured the Marvin Gaye track 'I Heard it Through the Grapevine'. Several of the backing tracks used by Levi's have reached number 1 in the charts; these include, among others, 'Stand by Me', Ben E. King in January 1987; 'The Joker', Steve Miller in June 1990; 'Boombastic', Shaggy in September 1995; and Babylon Zoo, also in 1995.

Speaking of the use of music, John Hegarty (1995) stated, 'We are surprised, however, that it took the record industry so long to wake up to what advertising can do. We give a narrative and a stronger sense of image to a song than a film of the band could ever do'.

The variety and diversity of music tracks featured in commercials can be seen from the following examples: The Hollies, 'He ain't Heavy', used by Miller Lite; Desmond Dekker, 'The Israelites', used by both Vitalite and Sony Tapes; Rover 200, using 'An Englishman in New York' by Sting; Hovis using a Dvorak motif; and The Mamas and Papas, 'California Dreaming', used in the Carling Premier Lager commercial.

Music is sometimes used as a signature to provide an audible identification of the company's messages. By identifying a unique piece of music which can be associated with the advertising, the company can achieve an almost immediate recall of its messages, for example, Allied Dunbar's 'There May Be Trouble Ahead'. Sometimes, however, confusion can result, especially when more than one advertiser selects the same piece of music. This occurred recently when both Cheltenham and Gloucester and Delta Airlines selected the same background music.

Non-verbal communications

The use of non-verbal communications is an increasingly important consideration, especially to overcome language difficulties associated with international advertising. However, the approach is equally popular in domestic advertising, designed to differentiate the campaign from other advertising approaches.

Examples of this are campaigns by Locketts Throat Lozenges, the Nissan Micra, Sony In-Car Entertainment, and the Ford Mondeo campaign. Gordons and Tonic features a series of surreal images accompanied by a music track, whilst Alpen contains subtitles and music, but again, no voiceover. The latest Diamond White cider commercial takes a somewhat surreal approach, designed to convey that the world is turned on its head by the brand. The cinema film, part of an overall £7 million campaign, is cut to the music of the 1960s group, the Bonzo Dog Doo Dah Band. Levi's used predominantly non-verbal communications in its campaign across Europe (Baker, 1994b). The advertising campaigns developed for the brand consistently use moving pictures and music and avoid the use of the spoken word.

However, great care needs to be taken in the production of such commercials, especially where they are intended for international use. Although signs and gestures may be used to augment the meaning of language, they may not have the same meaning in other cultures. For example, the traditional gesture for OK symbolizes a willingness to give money in Japan. Elsewhere, the gesture has a more offensive meaning. Similarly, hand holding between members of the same sex has a different meaning in some countries, whilst the inappropriate touching between sexes may be considered offensive in some regions. It would be considered an affront in many Arab countries, for example, to see a man and woman embracing in public. Similarly, great care needs to be taken in the selection of models. Their ethnic 'look' may affect the acceptability of the advertising message in particular markets. Gillette, for example, re-shoot their campaign to ensure that the artists reflect the local 'look' for each market area. By the same token, attention must be given to ensuring that the setting is consistent with local requirements. An American-designed kitchen, for example, may evoke a different reaction from a UK kitchen to an English audience. Marieke de Mooij (1994) suggests that all aspects of a commercial must, as far as possible, be neutral. Everything, from landscapes and buildings to road signs and car number plates, have a national appearance, which will be inconsistent and unconvincing to someone from a different country from the one in which the advertising was shot.

Creativity in advertising

Much debate centres around the role of creativity in advertising. There is little doubt that there is a need for 'The Big Idea' – essential to break through the surrounding clutter and to arouse interest in an otherwise dull product category, as was the case with Tango. However, just because an advertisement is 'creative' does not mean that it will increase sales or turn around a brand which is already in decline. Creativity must be relevant and serve to differentiate the product or service from its competitors in a way that consumers find meaningful. Moreover, the problem is that consumers have become more advertising-literate, requiring more innovative concepts to impact on their awareness.

In a paper written in 1984, Mo Drake indicates the extent to which consumers have become advertising-literate: 'Consumers talk about advertising in much the same way as they talk about television programmes. It is a component of their media diet and they are increasingly familiar with the tricks of the industry. In effect, consumers are not only

Table 8.1	Dimensions of viewer response	
Schlinger	Wells, Leavitt & McConville	Aaker & Slayman
Entertaining	Humorous	Amusing/lively/clever
Relevant	Relevant	Informative/effective
Alienating	Irritating	Irritating/silly
Empathetic	Sensual	Warm
Familiar	Unique	Familiar
Confusing		Confusing
Brand reinforcing		

Source: du Plessis, E., 'Likeable Ads Work Best, But What is Likeability?', *Admap*, May 1994

consumers of products, they are also consumers of advertising.'

This process is accelerated by the number of programmes which explore the tricks of the advertising trade. Almost every programme in the BBC series 'How Do They Do That?' goes behind the scenes of a particular advertising execution and explains how the effects were achieved.

Bovee Thill *et al.* (1995) describe creativity as 'the ability to produce original ideas or original ways of looking at existing ideas', whilst Shultz and Tannenbaum (1989) argue, 'What all too often passes for creativity has very little to do with presenting a cogent selling message. Something that is creative is new or different or unique. But advertising that is simply innovative is not necessarily effective in helping motivate customers and prospects to buy ... it must present the sales message more effectively, not just dramatically or in a more entertaining way'.

Creativity encompasses all of the original ideas that are used to develop a campaign. It represents the application of original thinking to establish a particular point. Creative advertising seeks to provide a new and fresh dimension about the brand's proposition. Various attempts have been made to define what elements contribute to an effective advertising campaign (Table 8.1).

It can be reasoned that each of the components contained in the above studies represents an element of creativity designed to encourage consumer response. As we can see readily from any of the established models of advertising effectiveness, achieving an impact on the consumer is an integral and vital part of determining the success of any campaign. In order to achieve this impact, advertising must first break through the surrounding 'noise' and achieve some form of sensory reaction. Moreover, in a competitive environment, it is especially important that potential consumers are able to distinguish between competing messages from rival brands. If one brand establishes a particular proposition or benefit, for a second brand to break through, it must provide an even greater stimulus and establish a greater empathetic link for it to be recognized. It is this particular need to achieve a bigger impact than competitors that fuels the drive for creativity.

The American Advertising Research Foundation demonstrated that 'likeability' of an advertisement (see du Plessis article, in *Admap*, May 1994) is the best predictor of advertising effectiveness. However, others feel that this term is too broad to be used as an accurate measure of advertising effectiveness. Among these is Terry Prue, writing in the foreword to *Advertising Works* (1994a). He

Table 8.2   Fundamentals of creativity

The role of advertising is to communicate a selling message	Persuasion
The role of creativity is to make the selling message compelling to the consumer	Intrusion/interest
The quality of creativity is dependent on the quality of the brief	Clear thinking/planning

Source: Saatchi and Saatchi, *Developing Effective Creativity*, 1995

indicates that many ads can be effective without being 'liked'. He proposes the use of an alternative word, 'involving'. To demonstrate his thinking he cites road safety and AIDS campaigns, both of which can be shown to be effective without necessarily being liked by the target audience. It is reasonable to assume, however, that effective advertising both involves and persuades the consumer.

Saatchi and Saatchi (1995) have developed a series of criteria for the development of creative advertising (Table 8.2).

There continues to be considerable debate about the credibility of the various 'Award' schemes within the advertising environment, such as those of the Creative Circle and others. In order to dimensionalize advertising effectiveness related to awards, David Gunn (1995), Creative Director at Leo Burnett, conducted a survey which invited agencies to evaluate their award-winning campaigns against their own predefined objectives. The assessment has been spread over a number of years and provides some interesting findings: 'In 1989, 78% of cases were associated with market success. In 1993, 80% did well in the marketplace and in 1995, 86% of the award-winning campaigns increased market share.'

However, there are a number of important points to be made about this study. At best, it is unscientific, in so far as the award winners themselves are the arbiters of measurement of success. Moreover, the obvious difficulty, even assuming that the associated brands were successful within the time frame of the advertising campaign, is the

fact that the advertising effect cannot easily be distinguished from the other elements of the campaign.

The two sides of the argument are illustrated in a quote from Nissan Europe's Vice President of Marketing: 'The agency will say that creativity is the most important thing, but obviously to us an increase in sales is most eloquent' (*Sunday Times Culture*, 16 July, 1995).

It is argued that the best practitioners are those who are able to help a client company satisfy its stakeholders' interests for earnings, whilst also creating a strong demand for its products. An excellent example of the value of creativity in advertising can be seen from the turnaround of the Tango brand. The introduction of the 'You've Been Tangoed' advertisements by Howell Henry Caldecott Lury led to sales over the campaign period rising by an initial 26 per cent, brand awareness increasing from 42 per cent to 72 per cent, and agreement that there was no mistaking the orangey taste of Tango by 65 per cent.

Steve Gatfield (1995), Chief Executive at Leo Burnett, suggests that the co-ordination of creativity 'is not a mechanical process, but a fragile art', whilst White (1994) argues that 'The idea is the most elusive, intangible and important product of an advertising agency . . . campaigns can succeed or fail on the strength or weakness of the idea'.

Speaking on creativity, John Hegarty, Creative Director of BBH, writing in *Admap* (December 1994) says, 'It's always good to learn about how others have been successful, even if it's only to learn how to do it differently'.

Advertising and the brand personality

Advertising can best provide the awareness breakthrough, the emotional resonance and the differentiation which will endure and without which even the best product does not leave the factory in any real volume (Bartle, 1997).

Advertising can be used at different stages to establish or reinforce a brand's personality.

1 For new brands, the role of advertising is to create a distinctive new image which will serve to distinguish the brand from its competitors.
2 For mature brands, the advertising can reinforce the existing brand proposition.
3 For ageing brands, advertising can be used to achieve a repositioning in order to reach different target audiences.

Guidelines for evaluating creative output

At its minimum, effective advertising must satisfy the following conditions:

1 It must derive from a sound marketing strategy.
2 Effective advertising must take the consumer's viewpoint – consumers buy product benefits, not attributes.
3 Effective advertising is persuasive.
4 Advertising must find a unique way to break through the surrounding clutter.
5 Good advertising prevents the creative idea from overwhelming the strategy.

A series of important questions need to be answered in this context:

- Is the creative approach consistent with the brand's marketing and advertising objectives?
- Is the creative approach compatible with the creative strategy and objectives, and does it communicate what it is supposed to?
- Is the creative approach appropriate to the target audience, for example, does it have street cred, as with the Sega campaign?
- Does the creative approach communicate a clear and convincing message to the consumer?
- Does the creative execution overwhelm the message?
- Is the creative approach appropriate for the media environment in which it is likely to be seen?
- Is the advertising legal, decent, honest and truthful?

Measuring advertising effectiveness and campaign evaluation

As we have seen, the underpinning of any successful advertising campaign will be the use of market research. As markets become increasingly complex, it is beyond the scope of advertising planners, or even the most highly paid creatives, to base their work entirely on some form of intuition.

The IPA have run the Advertising Effectiveness Awards continuously since 1980, which seek evidence of advertising effectiveness against a series of rigorous criteria. Indeed, the model has set a trend which has been substantially reflected in the schemes run in other countries. Importantly, as the awards have developed, so too the evaluative criteria have changed, reflecting the changing role of advertising within the marketing communications mix. The awards recognize that the process of advertising evaluation is continuously evolving because of the complexity of the decision chain and the fact that consumer 'interaction' with the brand prior to purchase is usually much more

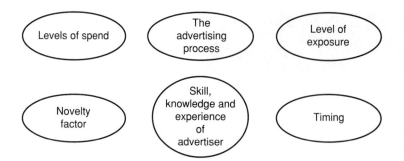

Figure 8.2 Factors influencing advertising effectiveness. Source: Krugman, H., 'Advertising: Better Planning, Better Results', *Harvard Business Review*, March–April 1975

lengthy and involved (Duckworth, 1997). Despite this, the debate as to the determinants of effective advertising continues to rage, especially within the advertising trade press.

The success of advertising in the future seems likely to depend on the advertiser's knowledge of the social and temporal context in which his advertisements are being consumed. For example, are consumers likely to be channel surfing, the target group's attitudes towards advertising *per se*, and their familiarity with its conventions (Goodyear, 1994). Moreover, with the costs of making a mistake increasing alarmingly, few advertising professionals would fail to seek guidance from the marketplace.

Market complexity is increasing and market transparency is decreasing. The constant flow of technological innovation, product adapting and service improvement result in short product life cycles, an increasing knowledge gap between manufacturers and consumers, and a reduction in the physical and psychological differentiation of brands (Poiesz and Robben, 1994).

There are a wide range of factors which influence advertising effectiveness (Figure 8.2).

In addition, other factors may play an important part. These will include brand name prominence; brand image; advertising recall; persuasion; the search for information; buying intention; and, of course, the purchase decision process.

Effectiveness should mean achieving objectives. Communication must be developed with an objective in mind. This might include: to build a brand image, or to strengthen the brand in people's minds, to defend the position against other brands, or to steal brand share. Objectives are of little use if they are not involved in the communications plan. Solid planning is the key to success in advertising. Once the advertiser has obtained a solid understanding of the marketplace and has determined the marketing objectives, he must address three important issues to develop a marketing communications plan:

1 Who do I want to communicate with – who are the target audience, what are their characteristics and where can I find them?
2 What message do I want to communicate to them?
3 How will I communicate with them – what is the most cost-effective medium available?

In his paper 'Measuring Sales Response to Advertising', Karin Holstius (1990) examines a mathematical correlation between the two forces and demonstrates how they interact with external forces. The results of the study showed that increases in advertising boosted sales and, whenever there was a peak in advertising expenditure, there was a corresponding peak in sales volume.

In the development of an effective advertising campaign, research input is likely to be sought from a number of key areas.

Consumer research

There are a number of important areas of information which will be required on which the advertising campaign will be based. The planner will require detailed information as to the nature and behavioural patterns of the consumer to whom the message is to be addressed (who are they; where are they; how, when and where do they buy the product; how do they use the product; what specific attitudes do they hold?; and so on). It is important to build up a finite picture of the target consumer in order that the message can be properly constructed and focused.

According to a study conducted by Brown and Staymen in 1982, attitudes towards advertising, the message and the brand are constantly changing. Advertising is now having to face the uncertainty of functioning within a largely competitive environment (Dyer, 1982). In today's competitive climate, customers are having to process three times as much information as was the case fifty years ago, and this is an important issue in the context of the way in which potential customers process advertising information.

- Customers are increasingly selective in what receives their attention.
- Customers pay increasingly less attention to communications.
- Customers process communication at a shallow, more superficial level.
- Customers are starting to 'consume' more pictures at the expense of words.
  (Franzen, 1994)

Competitor information

It will be vital for the development of advertising to understand the nature of the competitive environment. Who are the competitors and what are their offerings? How are their products or services positioned to the consumer, and what images – either positive or negative – do they possess? What advertising approaches do they use? And so on.

Strategy development

Depending on the amount of information which the planner already possesses, it may be necessary to conduct specific research to aid the process of strategic development. This will be specifically concerned with the nature of the message, and is designed to identify the strongest possible positioning and consumer proposition which can be made. It is quite likely that the planner will explore a number of different alternatives at this stage, in order to identify the single proposition which is likely to achieve the highest level of impact on the target consumer. Part of this process will involve an exploration of competitor positionings in an attempt to determine whether there is a gap in the marketplace which can be adopted by the brand.

Monitoring research

In most instances, the planner does not start from scratch. Since most products and services already exist in the marketplace, it is reasonable to assume that they will have benefited from previous advertising support. It will be important to understand the workings of previous advertising campaigns and to explore the image which that advertising will have created in the minds of the consumers. Indeed, such research, often conducted on a regular periodic basis, will not only yield considerable information about the company's own brands, it will also provide a valuable insight into competitor brands. Additional research is likely to be used at various stages in the development of the advertising campaign, and this will be explored in more detail later in Chapter 8.

Wilkins (1997) suggests that the diagnostic measures of any TV campaign may include:

- likeability of the campaign;
- persuasion;

- message communication;
- campaign image.

There are four key factors which lead to and facilitate the measurement of an advertising campaign:

- *The strategic impact* – this should compare the brand against pre-existing market psychology, and not only anticipate the needs and responses of the audience, but exceed them.
- *The executional impact* – the message should not only be delivered well, it should attract the audience's attention and imagination.
- *The media impact* – this is concerned with the effectiveness of the media used and relates to the cost efficiency and innovation of the media deployment.
- *Integration* – ensuring that the campaign fits well with the other marketing tools used and achieves cohesive communication to the target audience.
(Baker, C., 1994c)

In an article in *Admap*, Terry Prue (1994b) suggested key points for the achievement of success through advertising:

- *Persuasion.* The campaign told the target group something that was both interesting and relevant. The BMW campaign effectively persuades through the communication on various product benefits (the whole being more than the sum of the parts).
- *Involvement.* The building of a closer relationship between the brand and its target audience through the establishment of 'emotional ties' within the advertising. The Boddington's campaign is involving, having been built on 'persuasive truths' about being a smooth-drinking pint. Emotional links are made through the identification of product qualities that are evoked throughout the communication: the creamy head and bright colour.
- *Salience.* The use of creative advertising that is so memorably different that it registers the brand as more significant and worthy of purchase consideration (irrespective of the

communication content). The Pepperami campaign utilizes this approach, and has forced the brand into the consciousness of its youth target group.

Brand salience is a complex factor. It is more than simple brand awareness. It is the result of past, present or future aspirations and relationships with a brand and involves strength of feeling in terms of an inclination to use, buy, try, re-use or re-try it (Gordon, 1992).

A series of criteria for measuring advertising effectiveness have been developed by Giep Franzen (1994):

- Advertising must be perceived with the senses;
- it must succeed in gaining and retaining our attention;
- it must be likeable and not irritating;
- it must contribute to the difference we perceive between the advertised brand and alternatives;
- it must influence our choice in favour of the advertised brand;
- its central message must be stored in our memory.

There is increasing evidence that certain measures used in pre-testing correlate weakly with measures of persuasion or effectiveness and, indeed, with sales. Recall of ads shown in reels or folders is a measure of short-term memory, and does not predict the impact and memorability of an ad when eventually run in real life. The procedure for pre-testing has, for a long period, consisted of measuring impact, recall, communication, believability, likes, dislikes, product advantages and disadvantages, and persuasiveness. New measures include enjoyment, noticeability, attention holding, confusion, and branding strengths/weaknesses.

Increasingly, there is justifiable pressure to demonstrate the effectiveness of advertising campaigns. Clients need to make the most of their scarce resources and justify the value of their advertising to (sometimes cynical) internal audiences. However, whilst there is a strong need to ensure that the appropriate techniques are utilized for advertising research, there are situations in which such activity can be counter-productive.

Paul Feldwick (1994), the Executive Planning Director of BMP DDB Needham, writing in *Admap*, suggests a number of situations which need to be avoided:

1 When it monopolizes resources, often using a disproportionate share of the brand's total research budget at the expense of other projects which are likely to have a greater impact on, for example, understanding the consumer; or when it sets simple yardsticks to measure complex objectives. Many organizations have complex and, sometimes, mutually conflicting objectives which require to be met. Most research techniques are better at measuring and monitoring some aspects of performance than others, with the result that a 'dominant' element becomes the primary source of measurement over all the other important dimensions.

2 When it reduces agency involvement and damages the agency/client relationship. Sometimes the process of evaluating the advertising becomes confused with an evaluation of the performance and contribution of the agency.

3 When it is used to avoid independent decision making. Unfortunately, there are no research procedures which can eliminate risk completely. Often, companies, perhaps to ensure that they have something or someone to blame for their decision in the event of things going wrong, await the outcomes of specific research upon which to base their decisions. This slows down the process of decision making and impairs entrepreneurial decisions.

John Philip Jones (1994), a professor at Syracuse University in the USA, writing in *Admap*, makes a number of observations regarding the short- and long-term impacts of advertising, based on considerable experience and evaluation of brand performance:

1 A short-term advertising effect is a pre-condition of a long-term one. To a large degree, a long-term effect is a repetition of a series of short-term effects.

2 The ability of a brand to generate repeated short-term effects depends on the continuity of its advertising schedule.

3 The long-term effectiveness of advertising is also influenced by the brand's internal momentum.

4 50 per cent of advertising campaigns have a noticeable sales effect both in the short and long term.

5 A further 20 per cent of ad campaigns have a noticeable short-term sales effect but no long-term effect, which Jones attributes to the lack of media continuity.

6 30 per cent of campaigns actually result in sales going down. The campaigns are simply too weak to protect the brand from the superior effectiveness of competitive advertising.

The underlying problem of measuring advertising effectiveness is that virtually all of the methods available for measuring and attributing sales variations to advertising are only possible in the short term. In the longer term, advertising becomes lost within other influences, and its effects become direct and inferential (McDonald, 1992). Against this, Winston Fletcher (1992) argues, 'No advertiser waits for a year for their advertising to take effect. Advertising must work both immediately and residually. It must generate response both today and tomorrow. Unless short-term results are achieved the long-term benefits will never materialise. Advertising could not possibly work in the future if it does not work in the present'.

According to Lillien and Kotler (1993):

'No one knows what advertising really does in the marketplace. The purpose of advertising is to enhance buyer responses to the organisation and its offerings by providing information, by channelling desires and by supplying reasons for preferring a particular organisation's offer. For advertising, even more than for other elements of the marketing mix, it is important to keep in mind that advertising decisions and their effectiveness are influenced to a great extent by their interaction with marketing objectives, with product characteristics, and with other elements of the marketing mix.'

References

Baker, C., *Admap*, December 1994a

Baker, C. (ed). 'Jeans Sans Frontières', *Advertising Works*, IPA/NTC, 1994b

Baker, C., *Advertising Works*, Vol 8, IPA/NTC, 1994c

Bartle, J., The Advertising Contribution, in Butterfield, L. (ed.), *Excellence in Advertising*, Butterworth-Heinemann, 1997

Bovee, C., Thill, J., Dovel, G. and Wood, M., *Advertising Excellence*, McGraw-Hill, 1995

Branthwaite, A. and Ware, R., 'The Role of Music in Advertising', *Admap*, July/August 1997

Cooper, A. (ed.), *How to Plan Advertising*, 2nd edition, Cassell, 1997

de Mooij, M., *Advertising Worldwide*, Prentice Hall, 2nd edition, 1994

Drake, M., 'The Basics of Creative Development Research', *International Journal of Advertising*, 1984

Duckworth, G., *Advertising Works*, Vol 9, IPA/NTC, 1997

Dyer, G., *Advertising as a Communication*, Methuen, 1982

Fletcher, W., *A Glittering Haze: Strategic Advertising in the 1990s*, NTC Publications, 1992

Fletcher, W., 'The Advertising High Ground', *Admap*, November 1994

Franzen, G., *Advertising Effectiveness*, NTC Publications, 1994

Gatfield, S., 'Brand Building and the Agency', *Admap*, January 1995

Goodyear, M., 'Keeping Up With The Jones', *Admap*, September 1994

Gordon, W., 'Advertising Research', *Admap*, June 1992

Gunn, D., 'Do Creative Commercials Sell', *Campaign*, 22 September 1995

Hegarty, J., 'Factors Behind Success: The 1994 IPA Award Winners', *Admap*, December 1994

Hegarty, J., BBH in 'The Bottom Line', *Culture* magazine, *Sunday Times*, 26 November 1995

Holstius, K., 'Measuring Sales Response to Advertising', *International Journal of Advertising*, No 1, 1990

Jones, J. P., 'Advertising's Woes and Advertising Accountability', *Admap*, September 1994

Lillien, G. L. and Kotler, P., *Marketing Models*, Prentice Hall, 1993

McDonald, C., *How Advertising Works*, Advertising Association NTC Publications, 1992

Ogilvy, D., *Confessions of An Advertising Man*, Longman 1964

Ogilvy, D. and Raphaelson, J., 'Research on Advertising Techniques that Work and Don't Work', *Harvard Business Review*, July/August 1982, 18

Poiesz, B. C. and Robben, H. S. J., 'Individual Reactions to Advertising', *International Journal of Advertising*, 1994

Prue, T., *Advertising Works*, Vol 6, IPA/NTC, 1994a

Prue, T., 'How Advertising Works: the 1994 IPA Advertising Effectiveness Awards', *Admap*, November 1994b

Saatchi and Saatchi, *Developing Effective Creativity*, 1995

Shultz, D. E. and Tannenbaum, S. I., *Essentials of Advertising Strategy*, 2nd edition, NTC Business Books, 1989

White, H. *How to Produce Effective TV Commercials*, 3rd edition, NTC Business Books, 1994

Wilkins, J., TV or not TV?, MRS Conference Paper, March 1997

Additional reading

Schultz, Don E. and Tannenbaum, Stanley I., *Essentials of Advertising Strategy*, 2nd edition, 1994, NTC Business Books

Schultz, Don E., *Strategic Advertising Campaigns*, 3rd edition, 1994, NTC Business Books

Bovee, Courtland, Thill, John, Dovel, George and Wood, Marian, *Advertising Excellence*, 1995, McGraw-Hill

Davis, Martyn P., *Successful Advertising: Key Alternative Approaches*, 1997, Cassell

Trout, J. and Rivkin, S., 1996, *The New Positioning*, McGraw-Hill

Cooper, Alan (ed.), *How to Plan Advertising*, 2nd edition, 1997, Cassell

Butterfield, Leslie (ed.), *Excellence in Advertising*, 1997, Butterworth-Heinemann

Franzen, Giep, *Advertising Effectiveness*, 1994, NTC Publications

CHAPTER 9

Media and media planning

- To become familiar with the role of media planning;
- To examine the changing face of the media;
- To identify media characteristics;
- To gain an insight into the media planning process;
- To consider the importance of media strategy and objectives;
- To become familiar with sources of media information;
- To explore the issues of media scheduling.

If any area of advertising development has changed over recent years, media and media planning must be at the forefront of those which have experienced the greatest changes. On all fronts, any discussion of media has become progressively more complex.

1 The underlying media scene has become dramatically more complicated, with changes in both the number and scope of the available media outlets.
2 The task of the media planner and, with it, the responsibilities for 'getting it right' have become more involved.
3 The improvements in technology have provided access to an ever increasing volume of data. The tasks of media analysis have become more sophisticated.

4 The media role has become, in many instances, a discipline separated from other aspects of advertising planning – not in the sense that media considerations can be divorced from the overall context of advertising planning but, rather, that the primary responsibility is increasingly moving away from traditional agencies into the hands of media specialists.
5 The need for media planners to adopt an innovative approach to break through the surrounding clutter is becoming increasingly important.
6 The requirement for the media function to be accountable is greater than at any other time.

The consequence is that the contribution of media planning has been recognized as being more important to the strategic process:

'Media is already far more centre stage, media planners can come up with innovative and effective solutions and media planning can break new ground.' (Bulman, 1994)

The role of media planning

We have already seen that one aspect of the creation of effective advertising is the determination of the appropriate message to communicate the benefits – real or perceived – of the product or service to a defined target audience. The role of media planning is to identify the most suitable media to carry those messages to that audience.

The process of media planning must be seen as overlapping and being concurrent with that of developing the creative message. The inter-relationship between the two strands is an inevitable facet of the overall communications process. For obvious reasons, a key influencing factor will be the scale of the overall media budget. The proposed level of expenditure may preclude certain media channels from being utilized. However, it is equally important to consider the nature of the message itself. Identifying what the advertiser needs to say about the product or service will play a major role in the selection of the most appropriate media outlets.

The determination and fulfilment of media strategy involves a number of separate and distinct tasks:

• Identifying the appropriate target audience.
• Determining media objectives.
• Specifying the media categories and vehicles.
• Determining the optimum time to advertise.
• Negotiating for and buying media.
• Evaluating the performance of the media plan.

The media planner is confronted with a wide variety of options – television, radio, print media, posters, ancillary media – several of which may reach the defined audience. The challenge which confronts the media planner is the identification of the most relevant and cost-effective media to fulfil the tasks defined.

The changing face of the media

Recent years have seen a progressive increase in the number and range of the media available to the planner. In the UK alone, we have three terrestrial commercial television stations (ITV, Channel 4 and Channel 5); numerous satellite and cable stations, all of which accept paid-for advertising or programme sponsorship; a wide range of national daily and Sunday newspapers, each vying with the others to provide effective reach of a group of readers; regional and local newspapers, designed to serve the interests of smaller communities; weekly and monthly magazines which respond to the specific interests of particular groups within the population; national and regional commercial radio stations; cinema; poster sites which can be bought on a local, regional or national basis; ancillary media in the form of transport advertising such as that which appears on buses, trains, and even taxi cabs; and an increasing diversity of 'new' media, ranging from the Internet to till receipts. Finally, as well as 'conventional' advertising, most of these media outlets offer opportunities for sponsorship activity.

The inevitable consequence of this explosion in media availability has been the fragmentation of the audiences which each of them covers. When commercial television commenced in the UK in 1955, a single ITV channel provided the only outlet for the advertisers' messages within the medium. Programmes competed for viewership with the output of the BBC, but the consumer's choice was restricted and the advertiser could be reasonably confident of substantial audiences for the programmes in which he advertised. The arrival of BBC2 and, more significantly from the standpoint of paid-for advertising, the commencement of Channel 4 in 1982, provided the consumer with a greater range of programme choices and effectively reduced the numbers viewing any individual programme.

Moreover, it rapidly became apparent that each programme attracted a different sort of audience, depending upon its nature and content and the time of day. Some were more likely to attract a male rather than a female audience, some younger rather than older viewers, and so on. The greater the availability of programmes, the more likely that the audience would be spread across them, simultaneously reducing the number of viewers but, correspondingly, enabling the media planner to use more sophisticated research techniques to identify the precise nature of the viewers and ensure a correspondence with their targeting needs.

This process has continued progressively. Although the penetration of cable and satellite viewership remains at a comparatively low level within the UK, currently around 30 per cent, its reach is expected to grow in the years ahead, accelerating audience fragmentation. This is particularly important given the natural tendency of terrestrial television to appeal to the comparatively old and downmarket audiences.

A similar process can be seen in other areas of the media. In 1991 there were only fifty-three regional commercial radio stations, compared with the current number of 180 covering the whole of the UK. Vast numbers of 'dedicated' magazines and periodicals have exploded onto the scene, each of which is targeted to a specific target audience. Here, perhaps more than any other area of the media, titles come and go with great regularity, adding to the complexity of media selection. Even if a particular title achieves an effective coverage of a desirable audience, its success is not guaranteed and its disappearance may require the media planner to seek alternative means of reaching that group of consumers.

Table 9.1 Changes in European media 1991 and 1995

Country	No. of TV stations		No. of radio stations		No. of newspapers		No. of magazines	
	1991	1995	1991	1995	1991	1995	1991	1995
Austria	2	2	4	4	100	200	200	900
Belgium	7	11	805	300	41	32	600	700
Denmark	4	6	270	303	62	365	41	50
Finland	3	4	61	63	439	240	84	172
France	6	6	1 612	1 288	808	880	2 400	2 023
Germany	9	13	162	230	576	600	1 986	1 800
Greece	6	6	500	420	280	280	67	73
Ireland	2	2	22	28	62	54	65	108
Italy	669	700	689	2 500	98	125	894	1 128
Netherlands	4	16	23	315	61	57	74	1 300
Norway	3	7	250	390	206	200	233	347
Poland	3	17	5	119	34	100	37	300
Portugal	2	4	339	287	290	318	900	628
Spain	13	13	1 400	1 500	125	115	800	4 500
Sweden	5	7	195	260	177	175	200	200
Switzerland	3	5	46	44	221	263	124	124
UK	5	25	53	171	1 032	2 030	2 161	2 485

Source: MRS Conference Paper, 1997, Cooke, M. and Pounds, J., *Market and Media Segmentation*.

This phenomenon is not unique to the UK. Table 9.1 illustrates some of the changes which have taken place over recent years in the context of media availability across Europe.

Despite this audience fragmentation, costs have not moved in the same direction. Despite the smaller audiences which the individual media attract, in general, costs have accelerated at a rate faster than inflation. Although this may seem to be a contradiction, in fact it is a simple reflection of the forces of supply and demand.

Although, at face value, it may seem desirable for the advertiser to reach the widest possible audience with his commercial messages, in fact this is rarely the case. The fundamental problem is that all media carry with them a degree of wastage, that is, readers, listeners or viewers who are inappropriate to the advertiser's message. In an ideal world, the advertiser would wish to target his message exclusively to those individuals who might be persuaded to purchase his product or service. Audience fragmentation may offer the opportunity to limit the exposure of the message to those consumers who most closely correspond to the desired target audience. Media proprietors are aware of the function they fulfil, and charge the advertiser accordingly. Moreover, where competition for the same audience exists, as it does in most cases, the rates which the media can charge are increased by direct competitive demand for the same space or airtime among a number of different potential advertisers. The more successful media owners are now better than ever at controlling their inventory.

Access to media and their characteristics

Each of the available media not only has a series of unique characteristics that make it more or less appropriate for the task in hand, they also represent an environment for the message which will serve to enhance or diminish aspects of that message.

Media can, therefore, be considered against three separate dimensions:

1 Does it enable the communication of the advertising message?
2 Does it provide cost-effective coverage of the target audience?
3 Is it the appropriate environment in which to place the message?

Television

Television, traditionally, has provided a major means of communicating to a mass market and, as such, is frequently used for the promotion of fast-moving consumer goods. However, as might be expected, the associated costs are extremely high. Not only is airtime expensive, but so too are the costs of producing a commercial for airing. As an indication, a 30-second peak-time commercial (between 7.30 and 10.30 p.m. on Carlton Television – covering the London area alone) would cost around £55,000. An off-peak spot of the same time length in the same region would cost some £7,500. The comparable rates for Channel 4 in London – which attracts significantly smaller audiences – would range from £26,000 for a peak-time spot down to £1,000 for an off-peak one. By comparison, a peak spot in the Grampian region – covering Scotland – would cost around £14,000, with an off-peak spot for as little as £250.

The advent of satellite-based television stations has introduced a new dimension to television buying. A peak spot on Eurosport, for example, costs around £12,000.

Production costs are similarly high. It is realistic to expect to spend anything from £250,000 upwards for a 'simple' commercial, and something of a slightly more spectacular nature, such as those for British Airways or The Halifax, could cost £1 million or even more. Similarly, using a personality to endorse a brand does not come cheap. A famous name might add a further £100,000–£200,000, and a music track – especially if it is in the charts – could cost the same again!

Programme sponsorship on commercial television has gained in significance, representing, as it does, a new way of communicating with the viewers and providing a context for the brand. Cadbury's £10 million deal to sponsor 'Coronation Street' has recently been renewed; 'Going Places', the retail travel agency, has linked with 'Blind Date'; Tizer with 'The Chart Show' and Texaco has concluded a three-year deal worth a reported £12 million to sponsor ITV's coverage of the Formula 1 Grand Prix series.

The key factor is not just the *size* of the audience but its *composition*. Inevitably, almost any advertiser using television as a medium will have to accept a degree of wastage – that is, viewers who are not interested in his particular message. The task, therefore, is to identify the programmes which are most closely targeted to the desired viewing audience. The consequence is that an advertiser may accept a smaller audience on, say, Channel 4 or for one of the satellite stations, because the viewership is more in line with the profile of the brand. The use of viewing data from such sources as BARB will enable the refinement of the television schedule to ensure that, as far as possible, the viewing audience corresponds with the brand's target group.

The share of total viewing figures (based on BARB for September 1997) reveals the following breakdown of all adults' (15+) viewing:

BBC1	31.8%
BBC2	10.0%
ITV (inc GMTV)	34.2%
Channel 4/S4C	9.9%
Channel 5	3.4%
Others	10.7%

New figures released by the IPA and BARB indicate that cable and satellite viewing is gaining significant ground, particularly on ITV. Satellite viewing is set to overtake BBC2 and become the third largest 'channel' behind BBC1 and ITV. Satellite recently broke the 25 per cent penetration of all homes, with 5.9 million now owning a satellite dish. According to a survey conducted by European Media and Marketing, Eurosport is the most watched pan-European TV channel. It now reaches 45 per cent of the top European households each month, whilst CNN is in second place with 27 per cent (*Campaign*, 2 May 1997).

Press

The print media can be subdivided into a number of separate areas for the purposes of media planning. There are a series of national daily and Sunday newspapers which appeal to different social groups, enabling the advertiser to reach significant segments of the population who at least can be segmented on socio-economic grounds. To these can be added a variety of regional titles, which offer coverage on a geographic basis (although their stature is somewhat less). Further, there is a wide range of over 3000 media titles which enable the targeting of 'special interest' groups. Whether they are interested in fishing, car maintenance or antiques collecting, there will be a number of titles specifically targeted towards the group.

As noted earlier, print media offers the ability to develop a long copy message to the target audience, and similarly sophisticated research tools such as the National Readership Survey (NRS) and the TGI will enable a profiling exercise to be undertaken. A few cost indications are given in Table 9.2 to dimensionalize the implications of using the print media.

Radio

Commercial radio, often regarded as a support medium only, is gaining credibility in its own right. In fact, more people listen to a

Table 9.2

Title	Circulation	Readership	Cost – page B&W (£)
The Sun	3.6m	10.1m	29 500
The Times	0.6m	2.0m	16 000
Mail on Sunday	2.0m	6.2m	28 500
Car Magazine	132 318	0.6m	2 642
Antique Collector	13 878	–	2 190
Computer Shopper	123 318	–	2 635
Woman's Own	731 348	3.6m	1 550

commercial radio station than to the BBC, as the following figures show.

Radio Listening	1997
All BBC	48.4%
All commercial	49.4
Atlantic 252	2.4
Classic FM	3.3
Talk Radio	1.5
Virgin Radio	2.6

Source: Rajar/RSL in *Marketing*, 8 May 1997

As we have seen, for the most part, consumers cannot recall the source of the advertising message. Indeed, there is considerable evidence that some radio advertising will be recalled as having been seen on television!

Radio may provide the means of achieving comparatively low-cost coverage of an identified target audience, since not only are the rates for using the medium relatively low, so too are the associated production costs. With four national radio stations and over 180 local radio stations in the UK, the ability to target specific audiences is improving rapidly. The diversity of programming (from jazz to classical; from rock to pop; and a variety of speech-only programmes) for listeners can be targeted on a variety of interest dimensions, both nationally and regionally.

The recent allocation of frequencies to new radio stations will extend the opportunities for listener segmentation even further, once they are all on air. Historically, audiences for radio are young, downmarket and biased towards men. It offers very good regional coverage, although the reach of media is less, and markedly so, compared to TV, newspapers and posters. As with television, radio is purchased on the basis of time length. A 30-second commercial on Capital Radio (London) would cost around £1,800, against a similar spot on Isle of Wight Radio at only £22.

A new dimension in radio advertising is the sponsorship of programmes. From the outset, the commercial radio stations have recognized an important new revenue opportunity, and one which potentially allows the sponsor to achieve a greater level of affinity with the target audience. Beamish Red now sponsor the Breakfast show on Virgin following the arrival of Chris Evans at the station, whilst Woolworth's are the sponsors of The Chart Show on the same station. Whilst these are comparatively long-term relationships between manufacturers and programmes, there is an increasing trend towards 'short-term' sponsorship. Several of the radio stations offer daily or weekly opportunities for companies to promote their products and services through sponsorship of an 'event' such as a prize give-away or phone-in competition, and to augment their conventional use of the medium.

Radio listeners are far less promiscuous than TV viewers. In the UK as a whole, according to figures from RAJAR, some 35 per cent listen to a single radio station each week, with a further 29 per cent listening to only two. Despite the availability of increased choice, and the proliferation of radio stations, loyalty tends to be significantly higher than in many other media areas. This, of course, has significance for the production of radio commercials. The average radio listener is much more likely to be exposed to a radio campaign than the average TV viewer. More importantly, frequent repetition, a consequence of the relative cheapness of the medium, can eventually 'turn off' even the most avid listener. Today, comparatively few advertisers have got the message that it is important to create a pool of commercials when advertising on radio in order to keep the campaign fresh and interest alive. Given the low costs of radio commercial production, this is not expensive to achieve.

Cinema

Cinema is continuing to attract substantial audiences, with a profile that is significantly younger than for other mainstream media. After the commencement of commercial television, cinema admissions experienced a significant decline, but that situation has now been reversed, as the following figures show:

UK cinema admissions

1984	54 million
1990	89 million
1996	123 million
1997	130 million
1998	163 million
2000	180 million projected

Source: CAA/Gallup

Cinema is normally purchased on a screen-by-screen basis. This enables very tightly focused advertising campaigns down to the smallest geographic regions. Additionally, it can be bought by town, TV area, nationally, by film title and by guaranteed audience. An average campaign, providing national coverage, would cost around £30,000 per week. The latest research into the medium reinforces the view that cinema advertising is the most impactful medium among those who go.

However, it is important to remember that production costs will make the investment in cinema considerably higher. Not only are the costs involved in producing a cinema commercial as high as those for television, but each screen on which the commercial is to be shown requires its own copy.

Posters

Outdoor media is available in a variety of different forms and sizes. Poster sites are available most often in 96-, 48-, 32- and 16-sheet sizes. The medium also encompasses a range of options, from taxi cab sides to supermarket trolleys.

Predominantly, posters and other outdoor media provide the opportunity of reminder advertising, reinforcing an aspect of the campaign which is developed elsewhere (on television, on radio or in the press), but enable a tight focus on the brand identity with the featuring of the pack, the logo, and similar devices. A great advantage of the medium is the fact that sites can be purchased close to the point of purchase, underpinning the brand message close to the moment of purchase. A national campaign of around 1000 48-sheet sites would cost around £300,000 for a month's duration.

The new media

The scope of media availability is enormous. The latest area to which attention is being

Table 9.3 A comparison of media advantages and disadvantages

Media	Advantages	Disadvantages
Television	Mass coverage High reach Impact of sight, sound and motion High prestige Low cost per exposure Attention getting Favourable impact on image	Low selectivity Short message life High absolute cost High production costs Clutter VCRs Disappearing in commercial break
Radio	Local coverage Low cost High frequency Flexible Low production costs Well-segmented audiences	Audio only Clutter Low attention-getting capabilities Fleeting messages
Magazines	Segmentation potential Quality reproduction High informational content Longevity Multiple readership	Long lead times Visual only Lack of flexibility
Newspapers	High coverage Low cost per reader Short lead times Ads can be placed in interest sections Timely (currency of advertising message) Reader controls exposure Can be used for coupons	Short life Clutter Low attention-getting capabilities Poor reproduction Selective reader exposure Limited colour availability
Cinema	Very young audience profile Impact of sound and motion Attractive media environment High attention value Can be tightly focused	High production costs Comparatively long lead times
Outdoor	Location-specific High repetition Easily noticed	High cost per contact Poor image Clutter

given is that known as 'ambient media'. This area encompasses non-traditional areas, such as supermarket trolleys and floor mats, take-away box lids, using lamp-post posters (as Nike did as part of the guerrilla tactics during Euro 96), or Snickers during the same event, which took over Wembley Park tube station and painted it 'Snickers Green'. The company also covered all available surfaces – walls, beams, bins and posters – with the Snickers logo. The brand had a heavyweight presence on lamp-posts leading to the stadium and also used taxi cab sides, the most common and well-established version of ambient media. It is estimated that around 62 per cent of all London taxis now carry an advertising message. Petrol stations offer other opportunities to communicate with the consumer, through advertising on petrol pump nozzles, and it is anticipated that this area may well benefit from the proposed tobacco advertising ban since ambient media is likely to remain outside the scope of the restrictions. Marlboro is already using petrol pump nozzles.

A new form of ambient media is set to present a new opportunity for advertisers. The device is based on a new form of technology which allows the real-time placement of advertising messages on posters surrounding sporting events. With the increasing complexity of international regulations, governing which product categories are allowed to advertise in which countries, the technology may well overcome the difficulties for internationally screened events. Formula 1, for example, is screened worldwide, although certain countries preclude the use of cigarette advertising. The technology will allow for the reinstatement of the brand message only in those countries where such advertising is permitted. Similarly, Anheuser Busch considered the technology in order to overcome the problems of the Loi Evin (which bans alcohol advertising in France) which undermined their sponsorship of the 1998 World Cup, which was staged in that country. It will also enable local advertisers to participate on a national level in events which receive international coverage and where the fees of involvement would preclude them.

There has been considerable discussion about the potential media applications of the Internet. Whilst there is little doubt that the medium will offer significant opportunities in the future, this position is still a long way from being realized. The value of Internet advertising in the UK in 1996 was only £2 million according to accountants KPMG, representing only 0.2 per cent of the total advertising market. A similar study by New Media Communications placed the value at £1.7 million. The latter group have estimated Internet media sales over a five-year period as follows:

1996	£1.7 million
1997	£3.9
1998	£8.2
1999	£15.6
2000	£26.5
2001	£39.8

One of the difficulties associated with the measurement of Internet media is the fact that it is often offered free with conventional media. For example, a recruitment ad booked into the *Daily Telegraph* will automatically go onto the electronic *Telegraph*.

The media plan

The planning process is, essentially, a cyclical one. It consists of following a series of distinct stages, although in some instances these may overlap and, indeed, the identification of new information will require the return to previous stages to consider whether changes should be made.

Iain Jacob (1997) depicts a model for the generation of a media plan, shown in Figure 9.1.

As can be seen, the development of a media plan is a complicated task. It involves several different stages and the use of research data to ensure that the plan is properly constructed, cost-effective and capable of delivering the desired impact on the chosen target audience. Moreover, it is a task which cannot be carried out in isolation of the other parts of the advertising planning process.

But there is a series of additional factors which the planner will need to take into consideration. Some of these will be objective and based on available data analyses; others

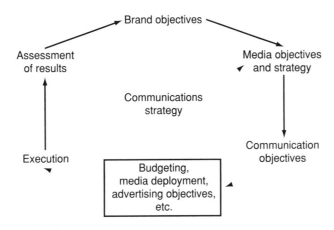

Figure 9.1 Generating a media plan

will be more subjective, such as a consideration of the media environment.

Here, factors might include an understanding of the differing patterns of readership or viewership. The point was made earlier that the planner seeks to minimize the wastage

involved in the purchase of any media outlet. Inevitably, the broader the appeal of a media channel, the greater the degree of potential wastage, resulting from the fact that members of the audience to which the advertising will be exposed will not be an appropriate target

Table 9.4 Viewing profiles of selected TV programmes

	The Bill		Friends		Channel 4 News		Blind Date	
	Audience size (000's)	Index	Audience size (000's)	Index	Audience size (000's)	Index	Audience size (000's)	Index
Men	7 541	95	3 032	93.2	2 487	122.1	3 583	73.7
Women	8 806	104.7	3 664	106.4	1 706	79.1	6 443	124.9
Age 15–24	2 325	93.1	2 938	287	280	43.7	1 738	113.5
Age 25–34	3 044	94.8	2 027	154.2	522	63.4	1 765	89.8
Age 35–44	2 390	85.3	949	82.7	620	86.3	1 286	74.9
Age 45–54	2 389	90.8	443	41.1	727	107.7	1 525	94.5
Age 55–64	2 134	107.3	180	22.1	758	148.5	1 387	113.8
Age 65+	4 065	126.4	159	12.1	1 285	155.8	2 315	117.5
ABC1	6 937	86.6	3 703	112.9	2 418	117.7	4 306	87.7
C1C2	8 064	98.1	3 585	106.5	1 941	92.1	4 806	95.4
C2DE	9 410	112.9	2 992	87.6	1 774	83	5 709	111.8

Source: 1997 TGI (April 1996 – March 1997)

for the message. By conducting an analysis of the viewers of particular television programmes, it will be possible to determine the make-up of the audience to ensure that it is aligned with the desired target as far as possible. For example, by examining TGI data, we can see a significant difference between the viewing patterns of 'The Bill', 'Friends', 'Channel 4 News' and 'Blind Date', as can be seen from the somewhat abridged data in Table 9.4.

The same principle will be applied to other media opportunities since, in turn, this will have an impact on the overall cost and cost-effectiveness of the campaign. But, as with other aspects of media planning, there is a trade-off. In many instances, it is possible to reach a dedicated audience who, for example, read a relevant magazine or watch a targeted television programme. Unfortunately, it is also likely that the absolute size of these audiences will be significantly smaller than for more general media activity. Again, it is important to understand the specific nature of the media environment and the extent to which the selected medium not only reaches the desired audience, but serves to act as an endorsement of the message to them.

The importance of media strategy

In many respects, media strategy is as important to the achievement of the overall objectives as the creative approach. However powerful the advertising message, it will be ineffective if it fails to achieve exposure among the appropriate target audience. The development of an appropriate media plan commences with a statement of media objectives. But first, a definition. *Media objectives* are the translation of marketing and advertising objectives and strategies into goals that can be achieved by media. The *media strategy* is the translation of those objectives into general

guidelines that will control the planner and the use of media. These need to cover the following points:

- What target audience should be reached by the media?
- What is the message that the advertising wishes to convey?
- To what geographic market(s) should the message be directed?
- How far into the target audience can the advertising reach, given budgetary constraints?
- With what frequency should the message reach the target audience during the campaign period?
- At what times should the message reach the target audience? This needs to address day, time and seasonality issues.
- What type of medium provides the best match between the intended market and the actual audience?

The setting of media objectives in a careful and precise way is essential to the success of the media component of the advertising campaign.

Sissors and Bumba (1993) have identified a series of specific questions to be considered in the setting of media objectives (Table 9.5).

Each of the available media will need to be considered in the light of these considerations. The process consists of two separate stages. Initially, the planner must determine which class of media best fulfils the criteria. This involves a comparison and the selection of the broad media classes, for example, television or radio or press, etc., or some combination of these. Table 9.6 depicts some of the important variables which will need to be examined.

Only when this category analysis has been completed can the planner move on to select the specific media within classes. This involves a comparison and evaluation of the best media within the chosen category in order to differentiate, using a series of predetermined criteria, which is the best newspaper, television or radio station and so on.

Table 9.5

Media objectives	Media Strategies
What reactions should we take as a result of media used by competitors?	Should we use the same media mix as competitors? Should we allocate weight as competitors? Should we ignore competitors?
What actions should we take as a result of our brand's creative strategies?	Which media/vehicles are best suited? Any special treatments? Which dayparts?
Who should be our primary and secondary targets?	Which product usage patterns should we consider? Heavy/medium/light users? What distribution of strategic impressions? Which dayparts?
What balance of reach to frequency is required?	What levels of reach and frequency? What levels of effective reach/frequency?
Do we need national and/or local media?	What proportion should go into national media? What proportion into local media?
What patterns of geographic weighting should we use?	Should we weight by spend or ratings points? Where should we place weights? When should we weight (weeks/months)? What weight levels for each market?
What kind of scheduling pattern suits our plans? Continuity/flighting/pulsing?	Should we use one or the other? When should we weight more heavily?
Does media have to support promotions? How?	What proportion of the budget should be used? What media mix?
Is media testing needed? How should it be used?	How many and which markets?
Is budget large enough to accomplish objectives?	Do we need to set priorities? Which must we achieve? Which are optional? Do we need more money than available?

Source: Sissors, J. L. and Bumba, L., *Advertising Media Planning*, 4th edition, NTC Business Books, 1993

Media information sources

To guide the media planner in the determination of the appropriate media, there are a variety of dedicated information sources. Either in their original form, or when subjected to special analyses, these provide substantial information on viewership, listenership and readership of the various media outlets.

- BRAD – British Rate and Data provides comprehensive details of the rate card costs for all media outlets. Updated monthly, it provides necessary production information and copy dates.

Table 9.6 Media outlet

Considerations	Terrestrial television	Cable & satellite television	Newspapers	Magazines	Radio	Outdoor	Cinema
Audience coverage	High, with considerable selectivity of audience profile	Moderate, but good profiling opportunities	Very tight focus on socio-economic groupings	Can isolate interest-specific groups	Moderate coverage, but high loyalty	Reasonable coverage but can be tightly focused	Low but selective
Geographic availability	Available on national and regional basis	Stations received across Europe	National, regional and local availability	Mostly national, but some regional titles	National, regional and local availability	Can be purchased nationally or down to single location	National, regional and local availability
Attention and interest	Variable	Variable	Moderate	High	Moderate	Low	Highest of all
Intrusive nature of media	Potentially high	Potentially high	Moderate/low	Moderate/low	Moderate	Low	Highest of all
Media environment	Good, potential for 'endorsement'	Good, potential for 'endorsement'	Good reference value	High level of endorsement	Variable	Low	High
Ability to demonstrate product	Very good	Very good	Limited	Limited	Poor	Poor	Very good
Availability of colour	Yes	Yes	Sometimes available	Mostly	None	Yes	Yes
Availability of sound	Yes	Yes	No	No	Yes	No	Yes
Creative flexibility	Very high	Very high	Good	Good	Good	Moderate	Very high
Lifespan of message	Short	Short	Medium	Long	Short	Short	Long
Long copy availability	Limited	Limited	Good	Good	Limited	No	Limited
Production costs	High	High	Medium	Medium	Low	Medium	High
Production requirements	Lengthy	Lengthy	Short	Lengthy	Short	Medium	Lengthy
Planning requirements	Reasonably flexible, minimum two months	Reasonably flexible, minimum two months	Moderate copy dates	Long copy dates, minimum three months	Very rapid availability	Moderate copy dates, minimum one month	Moderate, minimum two months

- A. C. Nielsen MEAL – provides a summary of mainstream media expenditures which can be analysed by product category down to brand level. Although based on rate card costs, it provides comparative guidance as to the expenditure patterns of competing products by month and with annual moving totals.

There is now a successful rival providing a similar service called MMS.
- ABC – The Audit Bureau of Circulation is the source of circulation data regarding newspapers and magazines. It is important to note that readership of publications is usually significantly higher than levels of circulation.

- NRS – The National Readership Survey provides comparative data on readership. Currently provides information on reading frequency and average issue readership. This latter is important, in that it provides an indication of the number of people who claim to have read or looked at a given publication within a specific period of time. This AIR is currently provided from some 244 publications, and is subdivided by age, sex, socio-economic groups and geographic regions. Readerships are also shown by weight of TV viewing, education, holiday taking, employment and occupational status, shopping expenditures, major expectations, and car and home ownership.
- JICREG – The Joint Industry Committee for Regional Press Research provides information relating to regional media, with information on average issue readership, cumulative readership and readership duplication.
- CAVIAR – The Cinema and Video Industry Audience Research provides audience data based on age, frequency of cinema-going, social grade and sex.
- OSCAR was the comparable data source for the outdoor industry. Now replaced by POSTAR II, to provide more relevant and reliable information. Measuring people who actually see a poster (rather than those in an arbitrary catchment area) will provide information on coverage and frequency on a site-by-site basis.
- AIRC – the Association of Independent Radio Contractors provides regular data and other information on listenership. Important information sourced by RAJAR – Radio Joint Audience Research – provides comparative data for commercial and non-commercial stations, both local and national. A representative sample of the total population is interviewed on a regular basis.
- BARB – The Broadcast Audience Research Board is the provider of research data evaluating television audiences, based on the viewing patterns of almost 4500 households across the UK. BARB provides valuable quantitative information, including the profiles of viewers of specific programmes, TV ratings, coverage build-up and frequency of viewing.
- TGI – The Target Group Index is the source of detailed media analysis, enabling an examination of the audience composition by socio-economic and geographic dimensions.

Identifying target audiences

A critical phase of the media planning process will be the identification of the appropriate audience or audiences for the intended message. We have already seen that this is equally important in terms of defining the overall marketing communications objectives. We have already considered the various methods by which target audiences can be identified (see Chapter 2), so we will not restate the process here. Suffice it to say that the media planner will use a variety of approaches, utilizing demographic, geodemographic, psychographic, lifestyle and product usage information to ensure that the various audiences can be identified properly. Whilst each of these variables, depending on the source of the information, may be used individually, it is more likely that they will be used in various combinations, again depending on availability of information within the particular market or sector.

Strategic options

Media mix strategies can take a variety of different forms, although they can be broadly identified as two variations. Media mix strategies may be concentrated or assorted.

A *concentrated* media mix is one in which the budget is concentrated, typically, within a single media type (or at most, a very limited number of media vehicles). It offers a variety of benefits:

- By concentrating the media effort in a limited area, there is a strong chance of dominating that medium compared to competitors. The result is that the advertising expenditure is likely to have greater impact on those consumers exposed to that medium.
- By limiting the range of media, retailers (especially if directed) will be more aware of the media effort. This will potentially enhance their readiness to support the campaign.
- Similarly, by concentrating expenditure into a single or comparatively few media areas, there will often be a negotiating advantage. Remember that media are in competition with each other and will be more likely to offer attractive prices if they feel that they can secure the bulk, or all, of your expenditure in the process. And, by restricting the number of media outlets, there may be considerable savings in terms of production costs.

An *assorted* mix is one which uses several media types. This is particularly likely if the target audience is subdivided into several discrete groups which can only be reached by the use of separate media channels. Here again, there are a number of advantages to be considered:

- An assortment of media types enables the delivery of different messages to different target groups. It is an inevitable consequence of the increasing number of media channels.
- The assortment of media environments may provide a range of opportunities which can be exploited within the media and creative strategies. For example, one medium may be used to create impact, drama, movement, etc. (TV) whilst another may be used to deliver a longer copy message (press).
- Using an assortment of media channels often provides a means of increasing coverage of the selected target groups (although this is mostly achieved at the cost of frequency).

Media scheduling issues

Media planning essentially revolves around two key issues: the balancing of coverage, and frequency. However large the advertising budget, there will never be enough money to maximize both elements, and the planner must determine the balance between the two. Inevitably, some form of trade-off will have to be made, between a campaign which achieves the maximum level of coverage but provides few opportunities for the target audience to see or hear the advertising message, and one which narrows the coverage to enable a greater frequency of exposure.

Coverage or *reach* is the measurement of that percentage of a given target audience who might be exposed to an advertiser's message in a given period through the use of a particular medium. Conventionally, coverage is not concerned with the number of times each individual sees the message, only with the total number of individuals who may see it. As we have seen, specific tools are available to provide the media planner with information in this area.

Frequency is specifically concerned with the number of times that people within the defined target group might be exposed to the message during a given time period. An important consideration here is the word 'might'. Although reach and frequency measures can provide information on the potential that the medium can provide, they can offer no guarantees that any given individual will notice the advertising. Inherently, there are a number of factors which will need to be considered in this context.

The intrusive nature of the message

Some advertising is innately more 'visible' than other campaigns. All advertising has to compete for the attention of the consumer, not merely with other advertising messages, but also with the general 'noise' within the media environment. Most consumers read newspapers or magazines, watch television or listen to the radio for the intrinsic benefits that the medium will provide. For an advertising message to communicate effectively, it must break through the surrounding 'noise' in order to impact upon the consumer.

If the reader of a newspaper or magazine article is involved with the subject matter, he or she may well turn the page without noticing your advertisement. Similarly, the viewer of a television programme may use the commercial break to leave the room for other purposes. The person may well use the opportunity to 'channel cruise' or, with the increasing penetration of video, to fast-forward the tape to continue watching the programme which they are watching. In all of these cases, the placement of the message will play a significant part in drawing the attention of the individual towards it. This may affect the design and content of the message as well as its position within the medium.

The competitive environment

A further consideration will be the comparative level of competitive expenditure. At times when competitors are spending heavily, the weight of their activity may reduce the effective communication of your message. It may be preferable to seek to plan to advertise at times when competitive presence will be lower, in order to gain a greater awareness of your own campaign.

The nature of the message

Advertising which seeks to remind the consumer of knowledge it already possesses demands a lower frequency of exposure than a campaign which seeks to create awareness in the first instance. Moreover, the more complicated the message which the advertiser wishes to communicate, the greater the number of times it will need to be exposed to the audience for the message to penetrate.

Message length

Some advertisers can build the effective frequency of their message by the utilization of different time lengths or space sizes. At the outset of a campaign, longer commercials or larger advertisements may be used to achieve the desired level of penetration through the surrounding clutter and 'noise'. Subsequently, shorter time lengths or space sizes may serve to assist the consumer in recalling the overall message, or to focus the attention of the consumer on a particular facet of the message.

The number of exposures

There is no consensus as to the 'correct' number of exposures that an advertising campaign should seek to achieve. Although various studies have been conducted in an attempt to ascertain the incremental value of consecutive exposures of an advertisement, the debate continues as to the desired level for any given campaign. Two differing views illustrate the argument.

Herbert Krugman (1972) suggests that three exposures of the advertising message is the minimum requirement to achieve effective impact. He argues that the first exposure generates a response of 'What is it?'; the second 'What of it?'; whilst the third and subsequent exposures serve as reminders of what has gone before.

In contrast, John Philip Jones (1995) argues that sales are generated by a single advertising exposure. His study claims to demonstrate that the extra sales effect of more advertisements becomes progressively smaller as the number of advertisements is increased. He concludes that it is therefore uneconomic to concentrate media into heavy bursts during the period before a consumer buys a brand, because of those diminishing returns. It is more sensible, he submits, to stretch the available funds by buying low frequency over a longer period. This ensures

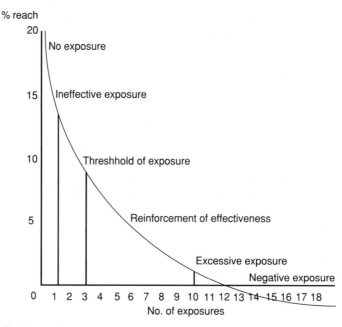

Figure 9.2   Graph of effective reach

that there are fewer gaps in the brand's advertising schedule, avoiding the danger of the brand becoming vulnerable to competitive encroachment.

The impact of successive exposures of an advertisement is shown graphically in Figure 9.2. The authors suggest, as with Krugman, that effective exposure is achieved with the third exposure to the brand and that, thereafter, further advertising serves to reinforce the brand message.

It is important to remember that whilst each medium is capable of achieving significant impact on the target audience – depending, of course, on the quality of the message – there will remain groups of consumers who will not be exposed to advertising within a single medium. Some people, for example, who listen to the radio or read newspapers and magazines, may not be exposed to a campaign which is only on television. Inclusion of these media will inevitably increase the reach of the campaign (Wilkins, 1997).

Wilkins illustrates this premise with a hypothetical campaign, based on three media – television, press and radio (Figure 9.3).

Indeed, many media plans are developed using different media channels in order to reinforce the advertising message in different ways. For example, television might be selected to achieve initial impact and raise awareness of a brand proposition, whilst print media such as newspapers might be added to the schedule to provide more detailed copy and, therefore, an explanation of what the brand offers.

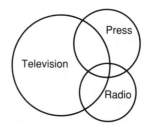

Total reach:

TV 65%
Press 20%
Radio 8%

Combined reach 76%

Figure 9.3

The status of the brand

Brands which have already established themselves within the marketplace will tend to attract more attention than those which are unknown. Accordingly, they can, as a generalization, operate at a lower level of frequency and concentrate more on the reach of their message.

Seasonality factors

In many market categories, the volume of sales differs on a monthly basis, either because of inherent trends within the sector or because of the brand's propensity to respond to, say, changes in weather conditions. Many products are given as gifts, and peak around Christmas and other gift-giving occasions (Father's Day, Mother's Day, etc.); D-I-Y products tend to experience a seasonal boost in the spring, as the weather improves and people turn to home improvement activities; ice-cream and soft drinks sales increase dramatically as the temperature rises. In each instance, the media planner will want to capitalize on the market opportunities which these changes represent.

Purchasing patterns

Especially in the area of fast-moving consumer goods, there may be a propensity to purchase products on particular days of the week. Much shopping activity takes place at the weekend, and planners may wish to concentrate advertising in the days immediately beforehand to stimulate both awareness of the proposition and the consequent sales.

Alternative approaches to media scheduling

In the vast majority of instances, it is apparent that a single exposure of the advertising

message will be insufficient to communicate effectively to the target audience. The more often consumers are exposed to the message, the greater the likelihood that they will understand it. However, this inevitably results in a reduction in the potential for achieving a high level of coverage of the desired audience, since the two facets of media planning work inversely. This can be seen graphically in Figure 9.4.

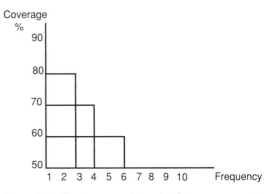

Figure 9.4   The inverse relationship between coverage and frequency

Although a great deal of work has been done to research the balancing of coverage and frequency, as we have seen, there are no definitive answers. Even today, much depends on the skills and experience of the media planner in assembling a media schedule which will achieve the objectives that have been set. However, there are a series of important factors which will affect the overall planning process and raise specific considerations regarding the necessary frequency of the advertising. These will involve a consideration of the marketing background, creative dimensions and the media environment.

Marketing factors

- *Brand history.* Is the brand new or well established? New brands require much higher frequency in order to achieve impact on the consumer, as, indeed, may a new message from an established brand.

- *Brand share.* The higher the brand share, the lower the frequency required.
- *Brand loyalty.* The higher the level of loyalty, the lower the level of frequency required.
- *Purchase cycles.* The shorter the purchase cycle, the higher the required frequency to maintain front-of-mind awareness.
- *Usage cycle.* Products used on a very regular basis will be used up and need to be replaced comparatively frequently. A high level of advertising frequency is desirable in order to maintain 'front-of-mind' awareness, as in the case of, for example, soap powders.
- *Competitive share of voice.* Higher frequency is required when a high level of competitive 'noise' exists and when the goal is to match or beat competitors. This may vary by season, e.g. the car market pre-August.
- *Target group.* The nature of the target group in terms of their ability to learn and absorb messages has an effect on frequency levels.

Creative factors

- *Message complexity.* The simpler the message, the less frequency required.
- *Message uniqueness.* The more unique the message, the less frequency required.
- *New versus continuous campaigns.* New campaigns require greater frequency to register the message.
- *Image versus product sell.* Creating image demands greater frequency.
- *Message variation.* Single messages require less frequency than multiple messages; however, the trade-off is that multiple messages may reinforce values of brand and maintain level of interest in overall proposition.
- *Wearout.* High frequency may lead to message wearout, as when the target consumer becomes bored with the advertising message and further insertions not merely cease to have an impact but can actually result in a diminution of interest in the brand. Tracking studies can be useful in identifying campaign wearout. The point was made earlier that, based on experience with radio, the audience tends to be more dedicated. Given the comparatively low

costs of using the medium – both airtime and production – it is possible to achieve a comparatively higher level of frequency of exposure, even on a limited budget, and there is, therefore, a greater propensity for wearout.

Media factors

- *Clutter.* It is increasingly true that advertising must compete, within its media environment, for the attention of the viewer, reader or listener. Media outlets which carry a high volume of advertising may well diminish the likelihood of the consumer remembering a particular advertisement for a brand. In the context of television, there are additional considerations. The factors of 'zapping' and 'zipping' mean that many commercials are never seen by their potential audiences. The survey conducted by Lowe Howard-Spink, detailed in the previous chapter, suggests that as much as 44 per cent of the audience zap out of commercials completely.
- *Editorial environment.* An ad that is consistent with editorial values will require less frequency.
- *Attention.* The greater the attention-getting values of the ad, the less frequency required. Conversely, low attention-getting ads require greater frequency. This is an important factor to consider in the context of international and global campaigns, since the attention-catching nature of a particular campaign may well be culturally bound and, hence, have less impact in some countries than others. Moreover, as we will see in Chapter 15 (International Marketing Communications), the level of understanding of the 'language' of advertising in different markets may impose different requirements.
- *Scheduling.* Continuous scheduling requires less frequency than flighting or pulsing (described below).
- *Number of media used.* The lower the number of media used, the lower the level of frequency required.
- *Repeat exposures.* Media that allow for repeat exposures require less frequency, for example, monthly magazines.

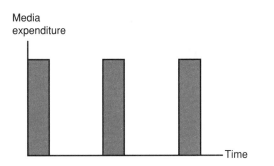

Figure 9.5   Burst pattern of media expenditure

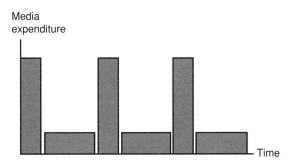

Figure 9.7   A pulsing campaign

These considerations will often be reflected in the way in which the media campaign is laid down. In some instances, in order to achieve the maximum level of impact, media expenditure will be concentrated into a relatively short period.

Often associated with awareness objectives, the *burst* campaign (sometimes referred to as *flighting*) compacts media activity into a series of relatively short time frames, with relatively long periods of absence from media activity in between (Figure 9.5).

An alternative approach, mostly associated with reminder campaigns, is to extend the time scale of the advertising message over a long period. The *drip* campaign provides continuity of the message, although at the cost of impact (Figure 9.6).

A compromise between the two is the development of a *pulsing* campaign (Figure 9.7). Here, a comparatively low level of media activity is maintained over a long period of time, with periodic increases in the expenditure pattern, often associated with seasonal or other influences on buyer activity.

A third consideration is that of the impact of the message within a given medium. The media environment will be a critical factor in terms of the way that the message is received and interpreted by the target audience. In some instances, as noted earlier, the nature of the advertising campaign will, itself, determine the broader issues of media selection (television versus press or radio, and so on). However, it is in the area of the specific selection of the timing of the appearance of the commercial, the press titles or radio stations selected, that will have the greatest level of influence on the advertising message.

Implementing the media plan

No media schedule is ever perfect. The aim must be to maximize the effectiveness of the campaign elements by the careful determination of the format in which the schedule is planned and the specific content of the media in which the advertising will appear.

Here again, a number of factors will be important, especially the nature of the media buying process.

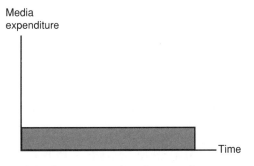

Figure 9.6   Drip pattern of media expenditure

All media outlets have what is known as a *rate card cost*. This is the amount of money that the media proprietor seeks to earn from the sale of a particular time slot or space in a newspaper. Every month, BRAD publishes a comprehensive listing of all media opportunities and their respective costs. From this it is possible to determine the rate card cost of, say, a page in the *Sunday Times*, or a 30-second TV spot on Carlton Television at different times of day. In practice, few media buyers will pay the asking price, but will negotiate down to a lower level. This will be dependent on the value of that audience to different potential buyers. Since all media have a finite amount to sell, they can only achieve the greatest price when the demand for what they have to sell exceeds the supply. If the demand is at a lower level, the media proprietor will offer a discount to attract buyers who would otherwise not be interested at the full price. In some instances, such discounts will be available in return for making a commitment to the media outlet; for example, agreeing to place a series of consecutive advertisements in the same magazine or on the same radio station, or in return for an agreed share of the overall brand expenditure.

The negotiating skills of the media buyer are of extreme importance to the delivery of a cost-effective schedule. By understanding the media environment, it may be possible to negotiate savings of as much as 15 or 20 per cent of the rate card cost which, in turn, will have a major impact on the overall delivery of the complete schedule.

Other media considerations

The placement of the advertising must reflect the advertising objective. We have already seen that the media environment is one of the important considerations in this context. However, there may well be other considerations.

There is as much creativity in media planning as there is in advertising content. Identifying a suitable but unusual media vehicle may well provide the element which differentiates a manufacturer's advertising from that of his competitors. Several examples, taken from recent campaigns, illustrate the application of creativity in the media context.

Recently, Pretty Polly adopted an unusual stance to its poster buying by negotiating a format which had not previously been used. They took a conventional landscape format and turned it on its side. Despite the fact that the company had to negotiate the building of special poster sites to house the advertising message, the campaign achieved both distinctivity and noticeability – both essential components of any advertising campaign – together with major PR exposure. The same format has, interestingly, been adopted by Peugeot for its latest 406 campaign.

When Häagen Dazs entered the UK market in 1991, they adopted an unconventional approach to media planning. Unlike other manufacturers in the sector, they identified the need to use the selected media to assist in the positioning of the brand. By examining the interests of their target consumers, they matched these with titles that reflected them. Accordingly, their initial schedule consisted of national newspapers – albeit with a regional bias to reflect their pattern of retail distribution – together with a selection of upmarket women's magazines (such as *Vogue*, *Tatler* and *Cosmopolitan*). The impact of seeing unconventional advertising in an unconventional media environment played a significant role in establishing the unique identity which became the property of the brand. (The case study on which this example is based is available in a more detailed form in Baker, C., *Advertising Works* 7, IPA, NTC, 1993.)

Nike dominated a recent issue of FHM (*For Him* magazine, March 1997) with a campaign designed to launch its new range of footwear. There were a series of separate elements which set the campaign apart. Firstly, it was designed to be interactive. Accompanying every issue of the magazine was a CD on which were the recorded voices of the sports personalities which the brand uses to endorse the products in its range. The CD also had a series of music tracks which provided a context within which the message was delivered. On separate pages within the magazine were a series of depictions of different footwear styles, designed to accompany the voice on the CD. Finally, there was a listing of stockists of the new Nike range.

Recently, a movie bought an unconventional package. To promote the film 'Scream', the producers bought two 1-second spots together with a 3-second time length in a single break on Channel 4.

In 1993, Diesel Jeans focused their advertising exclusively on MTV and achieved a dominant presence within the medium. In effect, they turned the limitations imposed by a small budget into a virtue. They achieved a high level of visibility among their desired target audience and, in the process, became a significant player within the market sector. Interestingly, Levi's adopted a similar approach with their 'Washroom' campaign in 1996. They turned their back on the media strategy that had been employed for the previous ten years to focus on tighter targeting of the youth market via satellite. At the time, Roy Edmundson of Levi Strauss said 'We have to take the risk of taking terrestrial TV away for a while in order to learn whether we can do without it'. Subsequently, Levi's have returned to a more conventional laydown of their media monies.

A further innovative media approach is that known as 'road blocking'. This is a device whereby a commercial is aired simultaneously on all available or relevant channels to ensure coverage of the whole audience, including channel switchers. Recently used by Peugeot, a single commercial could be seen on all available television channels.

Contingency planning

In all instances, it is important to have a contingency budget to respond to circumstances which represent change from the planning phase. Since the planning process takes place before implementation, significant changes may occur within the relevant variables which affect the effectiveness of implementation. Such changes may include:

- *Changes in economic conditions.* The sales of many products respond specifically to changes in economic circumstances. These may be broadly based (for example, a downturn or improvement in the general economic environment), or may be more specific (such as a budget which increases or decreases the tax on a specific product category).
- *Changes in sales.* The brand may achieve greater or lower levels of sales than those anticipated. These may require a re-deployment of support, especially if there are strong regional variations in performance.
- *Changes in the competitive environment.* It is important to remember that media planning takes place in the absence of specific knowledge of competitor plans. They may take the decision to, say, up-weight their media expenditure at specific times of the year, or to introduce a new product. The brand will obviously need to respond to these changes.

The need to retain flexibility is important in media planning. Sometimes the opportunity to take advantage of market opportunities is only possible if part of the budget remains unspent and uncommitted. Periodically, media outlets will be left with unsold space or time and will offer it to existing or desired advertisers at 'bargain' rates.

Evaluation of the media plan

To ensure that the media campaign continues to deliver against its targets, a proper evaluative process must be implemented. Whether this takes the form of periodic *ad hoc research* activity to investigate specific dimensions of the advertising effectiveness, or continuous market research in the form of a *tracking study*, is somewhat less important than the fact that appropriate objective measurements are taken.

Increasingly, however, it has become apparent that there are new considerations, especially in the context of evaluating television as a medium. Engel (1994) suggests that consumers have become more active zappers – switching channels during commercials or using the mute button – and zippers – using the fast-forward button on the VCR – and are regularly taking action to avoid unwanted commercials. This view is reinforced by research suggesting that as many as nine out of ten commercials are not evaluated for content before they are zapped. To some degree, the placement of a commercial in an ad break – a factor over which there can be only limited control – will be an important influencer. If an ad is placed between a bad set of commercials, then the risk of being zapped remains high.

Another factor which affects viewers' watching of commercials is what Kaufman and Lane (1994) refer to as Polychronic Time Use: 'People tend to combine several different activities within the same amount of clock time.'

Media planners have identified deficiencies in BARB's assessment of television viewing. Whilst presence in front of a TV set accounts for nearly 25 hours per week, the time spent actually watching TV accounts for less than 17. Research studies into viewing habits have revealed that much TV 'viewing' is more likely to be characterized by a semi-attentive glance rather than the enraptured gaze. Many people are actually engaged in some other activity whilst 'watching' TV, e.g. reading a newspaper, book or magazine, pursuing some form of hobby, chatting, preparing food, etc.

The changing face of media implementation

As mentioned earlier, the development of the media independent and media dependants has been one of the most important factors within the overall advertising environment. Initially, perhaps to gain more recognition and status for their areas of responsibility, small groups of media specialists broke away from their parent agencies and established independent media consultancies, whose sole contribution to the advertising process was the development and evaluation of media campaigns.

However, as the pace quickened, clients saw the advantages of having the media function separated from the others. In the first place, they could receive independent advice divorced from the creative process. The media specialist could be remunerated on a different basis – that of achievement – and, indeed, many media companies were rewarded for their efforts on the basis of the percentage improvements over agreed targets that they could achieve. In some cases, these specialists were used to assist in the evaluation of the performance of one or more conventional agencies, assessing the achievements of each of them in order that the client could determine which was performing best. And, of course, there was the possibility of achieving significant cost savings. Not only could the basic level of remuneration for the media specialist be reduced, but by placing all of the media planning and buying into one specialist agency, the company could achieve bulk buying discounts. Instead of having separate agencies buying on behalf of different brands within the company's portfolio, one agency could be appointed to handle all of the buying. And the aggregation of the budgets made the negotiating position ever stronger.

In some respects, the process has now come full circle. Traditional agencies, not wishing to

Table 9.7 Top ten media specialists by billings, 1996

Media agency	Associated advertising agency	Billings (£m)
Zenith Media	Saatchi & Saatchi	554.29
TMD Carat		400.66
MediaVest	DMB&B	357.69
BMP DDB (Optimum)	BMP DDB	311.07
Mediaopolis	Y&R, RSCG, WCRS	233.03
CIA Medianetwork		230.36
New PHD	Abbott Mead Vickers BBDO	227.66
Initiative Media	Lintas	226.94
Universal McCann	McCann Erickson	220.78
The Network (O&M)		211.15

Source: A. C. Nielsen – MEAL, published in *Campaign*, 10 July 1997

lose out on the media revenue, have, progressively, taken stakes in or bought out the independent media operators. Today, many of them are wholly owned subsidiaries of the major advertising agency groups. Table 9.7 shows the top ten media specialists and the agencies with which they are associated.

However, the face of media planning and buying is now wholly different from that of, say, ten or twenty years ago. Today's media specialist has the advantage of highly sophisticated IT-based facilities which enable the interrogation of media data on a level never previously imagined. What at best was a long and laborious exercise several years ago can now be completed rapidly and provide the planner with information to guide the media planning process.

References

Belch, G. E. and Belch, M. A., *Introduction to Advertising and Promotion*, Irwin, Homewood, Ill, 1993

Bulman, J., MD of B&J Media Services in *Campaign*, 16 September 1994

Engel, J. F. et al., *Promotional Strategy*, 8th edition, Irwin, 1994

Jacob, I., Making the Most of Media, in Butterfield, L., *Excellence in Advertising*, Butterworth-Heinemann, 1997

Jones, J. P., Advertising's Impact on Sales and Profitability, IPA Conference Paper, March 1995

Kaufman, C. and Lane, P., 'In Pursuit of the Nomadic Viewer', *Journal of Consumer Marketing*, 1994

Krugman, H. E., 'Why Three Exposures May Be Enough', *Journal of Advertising Research*, 12, 1972

Sissors, J. L. and Bumba, L. *Advertising Media Planning*, 4th edition, NTC Business Books, 1993

Wilkins, J., TV or Not TV?, MRS Conference Paper, March 1997

Additional reading

Bogart, Leo, *Strategy in Advertising: Matching Media and Messages to Markets and Motivations*, 2nd edition, 1990, NTC Publications

Broadbent, Simon and Jacobs, Brian, *Spending Advertising Money*, 4th edition, Business Books, 1994

Butterfield, Leslie (ed.), *Excellence in Advertising*, 1997, Butterworth-Heinemann

CHAPTER 10

Sales promotion

Aims and objectives

- To consider the growing role of sales promotion;
- To identify the benefits and disadvantages of sales promotion;
- To grasp the importance of the determination of objectives;
- To become familiar with the techniques of sales promotion;
- To recognize the role of point of purchase display;
- To appreciate the strategic dimensions of sales promotion;
- To consider the evaluation of sales promotion and the use of market research;
- To learn about the use of sales promotion agencies.

The growing role of sales promotion

Over recent years, sales promotion has become a particularly dynamic area within the overall context of marketing communications. Although accurate figures are difficult to come by, most industry pundits agree that, today, more money is spent below the line than above it.

The only major study to attempt to quantify the levels of expenditure was conducted jointly by the Institute of Sales Promotion and the Advertising Association in 1988. At that time, it was estimated that the overall level of UK sales promotion expenditure was of the order of £2.5 billion. By comparison, in the same year, the Advertising Association estimated advertising expenditure to be at a level of £6.57 billion. Extrapolating that data, Mintel, in a special survey of sales promotion (1996) (Mintel Marketing Intelligence, April 1996), have suggested that expenditure in the field has increased to around £4,900 billion by 1995 (versus £10.98 billion on advertising in the same year).

Since the impact of sales promotion is, primarily, geared to the short term, it is inevitable that the area should enjoy considerable growth at times of economic recession. Pressure on personal levels of disposable income tends to make consumers significantly more price-sensitive, and price-oriented sales promotions reflect this consumer pressure. Moreover, consumers have become increasingly price- and value-sensitive. Instead of simply purchasing a particular brand, many consumers use the basis of price in order to make their purchasing decisions. In many categories, consumers have become increasingly used to the offer of some form of incentive. Increasing numbers of brands are effectively forced to continue providing such incentives to satisfy the needs of consumers. However, it is also true that this growth has been influenced by changing attitudes among marketers.

In an increasingly competitive retail environment, and with the concentration of buying power into relatively few hands, manufacturers have turned to sales promotion to achieve on-shelf differentiation between their own products and those of their competitors. We have seen earlier that the opportunity for real product differentiation is diminishing as a result of the convergence of technology. As soon as one manufacturer improves his product offering, he is likely to be followed rapidly by his competitors offering the same, or a similar, benefit. The variety of sales promotion techniques provides manufacturers with a comparatively easy method of distinguishing their product from those of the competition within the retail environment.

The retail trade have also imposed other pressures on manufacturers to focus their attention on promotions. Rising sophistication on the part of retailers and, importantly, direct access to brand sales data collected at the point of purchase, have resulted in retailers demanding higher levels of promotional support from their suppliers in return for continued distribution and display levels. Retailers are now more aware than ever before of the financial contribution which an individual brand can make towards its overall profitability. In their efforts to improve their own margins, pressure is brought to bear on manufacturers to increase their rate of sale by the use of sales promotional devices. Manufacturers have little choice but to agree, or face the possibility of having their product removed from the shelves.

Moreover, since the appeal of retailer products is often based on price, sales promotion has provided manufacturers with the ability to adjust the retail price to the consumer – in the short term – and minimize the differential.

Undoubtedly, a major influence has been the desire for short-term sales achievement in

its own right. The consequence of the adoption of mass-production techniques in many industries has, in many instances, heightened the level of competition for market share. Sales promotion techniques are often seen as a means of achieving these increases in sales volume with the benefit of improved market share and, importantly, the ability to utilize excess manufacturing capacity.

In many companies, the performance of product management may be monitored by their ability to deliver volume sales. Since sales promotion potentially has an immediate impact on consumer sales, there has been a tendency for product managers to turn to these techniques in order to achieve their sales objectives. At the same time, pressure on margins has made for closer attention to the detail of the achievement of cost-effective sales volume. Since the results of the application of many promotional devices can be predicted with a high degree of accuracy, product management can be confident in their volume forecasts. Similarly, with the increasing costs of other forms of marketing communications, especially that of advertising, management has turned to areas which are perceived to be more cost-effective – especially for the achievement of short-term sales. The progressive fragmentation of audiences and the increase in media costs have tipped the balance in favour of sales promotion techniques which are more likely to deliver demonstrable results.

A further factor is the growing belief of product and sales management in their ability to handle the techniques of sales promotion. Unlike other areas of marketing communications, sales promotion is rarely subjected to the same level of internal debate as would be the case with, say, advertising. This enables product managers to be more 'independent' and self-motivated in the determination and implementation of sales promotional activities.

The growth of specialist sales promotions agencies has also contributed to the increased recognition of the importance of the area, and the growth in credibility which the application of sales promotion techniques has enjoyed. Historically, sales promotion has been viewed as an adjunct to other marketing communications techniques. Today, it is recognized that the use of sales promotion has an important impact on marketing strategy. The tactical and strategic implications of sales promotion will be explored in this chapter.

Varied though the array of sales promotions are, together they represent a variety of methods to achieve an aspect of the total strategy for the brand.

The benefits of sales promotion

Undeniably, sales promotion offers manufacturers a series of benefits which few other forms of marketing communications activity can deliver. Price promotions enable manufacturers to adjust to variations in supply and demand without changing list prices. Often, price promotions can help even out peaks and troughs in consumer demand to lower average operating costs. By reducing prices during periods of comparatively slow sales, manufacturers can entice more consumers to purchase their products. An extreme example of the impact of reduced price was seen recently during the BSE scare. Following a period of dramatic reduction in beef sales, several retailers reduced their prices to almost half the previous levels. Within a matter of days, sales had recovered to their former position. In addition, list prices are often set high as a defence against price controls, rapid increases in commodity prices and to test sustainable price levels.

Because sales promotion costs are variable with volume, they enable small regional businesses to compete against brands with large advertising budgets. Whilst a small manufacturer may not be able to afford the high costs associated with media-based activity, those companies will be able to afford on-shelf promotional activity. The same point applies equally to new products targeted at segments too small to warrant large-scale advertising spend. Sales promotions may well be the only marketing communications support a new product introduction receives. Particularly in those markets where the underlying product proposition is familiar to potential purchasers, a store-based promotion may be all that is required to induce desired levels of trial and offtake. This is, similarly, important from a retailer perspective. By inducing consumer trial of new products and clearing retail inventories of obsolete products, price promotions reduce the retailer's risk in stocking new brands.

Sales promotions encourage different retail formats, thereby increasing consumer choice. In almost any product category, there will be more on-shelf differentiation by virtue of the divergent promotional techniques being employed than for any other reason. And, because different items are on promotion weekly, consumer choice is enhanced and shopping for otherwise mundane products becomes more exciting.

Short-term sales promotional activity may serve to encourage the retail trade to bring forward their purchases, reducing the incidence of out-of-stock situations on retail shelves. Promotions also encourage the trade to provide temporary displays, price cuts and/or advertising features, all of which may contribute towards increasing sales to consumers. Such activities are often used to add excitement at point of purchase to otherwise mundane products.

Sales promotions may increase consumer demand by encouraging trial in new categories and improving the attention-getting power of advertising. Often, advertising and promotions are linked together to ensure the maximum impact of the message upon the desired target audience. Buying on deal is a simple rule for time-pressured consumers. If there are no other factors on which to base a purchasing decision, price may well have a significant bearing on the brand chosen.

In contrast to some of the other marketing communications tools, however, sales promotion predominantly works on a short-term basis. And, unlike advertising or public relations, for example, it may have no lasting impact on the brand. Research by Ehrenberg *et al.* (1991) indicated that 'Consumer promotions have large immediate sales effects, but do not appear to be brand building'. In a study of twenty-five grocery brands across four countries, the authors found the following:

- For an established brand, sales do not remain high once the promotion is over. The benefit is only very short-term, and post-promotional sales only show a 1 per cent increase.
- Buyers coming in because of price promotions had bought the brand before.
- Price promotions only reach a limited percentage of the customer base, typically 10–20 per cent.

They concluded that promotions provide no sustained impact on sales, i.e. promotions offer temporary effect only. Equally, they found that there is no discernible after-effect on consumer loyalty because the majority of extra buyers in a sales blip will have already bought the brand previously (80–90 per cent during the last twelve months).

The limitations of sales promotion

A key objective of much sales promotion activity is to encourage brand switching and to counter the franchise-building effects of competitive brands' advertising. Few manufacturers deny that increasing promotional expenditures have diminished the strength of brand franchises and brand loyalties and have resulted in an increasing level of 'promiscuous' buying on the part of consumers:

'As a rule, promotions can never improve a brand image or help the stability of the consumer franchise.'
(Jones, 1990)

Many promotions are developed independently of the overall brand strategy and may, therefore, impact negatively on the desired brand image. Unless the promoting company ensures a consistency between the nature of the promotional device and the product position, there may be a conflict which undermines the effectiveness of image-building advertising for the brand.

Frequent price promotions make both trade customers and consumers significantly more price-sensitive, not just towards the brand on offer but towards all brands in the category. Some consumers become unwilling to make any purchase unless the product is on special offer. Some consumers may infer that a promoted item is not selling well, is about to be discontinued, or has been reduced in quality to finance the incentive. Some retail accounts may claim promotion allowances without providing the appropriate levels of support, thereby increasing the costs of sale to the manufacturer without the benefit of expanded consumer exposure. Although unquantified, it is believed that some part of the promotional allowance may, in certain instances, be retained by the retailer rather than passed on to the consumer.

Ehrenberg (1994) argues that price-related promotions are picked up only by a brand's existing customers. He suggests that an average of 93 per cent of those buying during a price promotion had already bought the brand before.

Some consumers tend to stock up during a promotional period rather than purchasing during the normal cycle, with the result that whilst the brand enjoys a short-term increase in sales and market share, this may be achieved at a lower margin and, in effect, be obtained at the cost of future 'full price' volume.

The over-use of sales promotion within the marketing communications mix may reduce the overall profitability of the brand. This is evidenced by a comprehensive PIMS study conducted in 1991. A total of 749 businesses involved in consumer goods and services were assessed on the basis of the differing advertising and sales promotion ratios. The companies which used dominant sales promotion activity within their communications programmes achieved a return on investment (ROI) of some 18.1 per cent. Those with a more balanced ratio enjoyed an ROI of 30.5 per cent.

The determination of objectives

Although sales promotion has an important role in the context of ensuring the speedy achievement of sales objectives, to consider sales promotion in this way is somewhat limiting. It is clear that the techniques available are capable of fulfilling a wide range of specific objectives.

Before exploring the nature of those objectives, it is important to establish the key principles.

Sales promotion objectives must be defined clearly and succinctly

It is vital to define precisely what is expected of the campaign and over what duration it will be run. Few promotions are open-ended, and a time scale must be established for the fulfilment of commitments. Promotions which, for example, are designed to establish consumer loyalty will cause consumer alienation – and will almost certainly fail – if the time scale is too far beyond normal consumer purchase patterns. By the same token, however, promotions should not be allowed to

continue for too long a period of time, as they will lose the enthusiasm both of the retail trade and of the consumer.

Sales promotion objectives must be capable of measurement

Some numerate value must be attached to the objective. Is the campaign, for example, designed to achieve a 40 per cent level of trial, or re-purchase among 25 per cent of existing users? Not only will this establish the parameters for the campaign, it will enable a proper evaluation once the campaign has been completed. By monitoring the results, it will be possible to determine whether the objectives have been met or exceeded, over what time scale the results have been achieved, and the cost-effectiveness of the expenditure.

Apart from the immediate benefit of evaluation, the process will add to the sum of knowledge to ensure the efficient use of resources and the selection of the most appropriate techniques in the future. This is an important facet of promotional planning. Many companies build up a 'database' of experience in the promotional field. Previous experience of the impact of specific promotional formats will enable them to predict, with a reasonable degree of accuracy, the likely outcome of a new implementation of that format.

Sales promotion objectives must be achievable

There is an inevitable temptation to set grand objectives for any form of marketing communications activity. Whilst it obviously makes sense to establish real targets, it is also important that they are felt to be realistic within the constraints of the budget available, the organization's structure, and the competitive environment. A promotion which, for example, sets unrealistic targets for the number of sales force contacts will, inevitably, fail. By the same token, a reduction in the on-shelf price of a particular product will only achieve consumer impact if it is meaningful. Reducing the price by one or two pence is unlikely to result in large increases in the levels of offtake.

Sales promotion objectives must be realistically budgeted

Few companies have a bottomless financial pit. Almost all activity will be constrained by budgetary limitations. It is imperative that the objectives are related to the financial resources and not set at an unrealistic level.

By the same token, it is important that the organization is aware of the likely cost impact of the achievement of the objectives. All promotions cost money, and if the level of consumer demand for the promotional offer exceeds the level of affordability the consequence will be disappointed consumers and a failure to meet the requirements of the campaign. The alternative, if consumer demands are to be satisfied, is that the cost of mounting the promotion will far exceed the available budget. The Hoover experience is a perfect example of such an outcome.

A considerable level of consumer alienation will inevitably follow the withdrawal of a promotional device if substantial numbers of consumers have collected vouchers or other proofs of purchase but have been unable to collect sufficient to redeem the incentive offered.

Sales promotion objectives

Undeniably, used properly, the extensive range of sales promotional techniques enables companies to fulfil a wide range of objectives. We will consider below some of the objectives which specific sales promotion campaigns can be addressed to achieve. It is important to recognize that sales promotions can be designed to achieve defined consumer objectives, trade objectives, or both.

Consumer objectives

Enquiries/list building

An increasing concern among manufacturers is the desire to build accurate lists of actual and potential consumers. Promotions can be designed specifically to ensure that consumers provide this information. Traditionally, a variety of sales promotions have used a mail-in or phone-in facility as the means by which the consumer gains access to the promotion incentive. However, comparatively little use was made of such information. Today, as the costs of conventional media increase, companies are seeking more cost-effective ways of reaching their target audiences. Access to lists of names and addresses enables the subsequent communication to these named individuals with a minimum of wastage.

H. J. Heinz has developed a sophisticated database of brand users and is increasingly using direct mail as a means of maintaining contact with those consumers.

Product trial and sampling

A key area of sales promotion rests in its ability to generate product trial and sampling, either of an existing or a new product. A properly constructed promotional offer will have an immediacy of impact which will attract the potential consumer. Here, the key requirement is to overcome consumer objections to using the product – most often associated with risk. By reducing the consumer's level of risk, the desired levels of trial can be achieved. Most commonly, price-oriented promotions are used for this purpose, although an alternative expression of price reduction – additional free product – will have a similar impact.

Product re-purchase/loyalty

The generation of repeat purchase, and, in the longer term, the establishment of consumer loyalty to a product, is a major facet of sales promotion activity. Such promotions can be targeted specifically to recent trialists, for example, to encourage them to purchase on another occasion. Long-term promotions are frequently used to provide an overlay to the purchase which provides the consumer with a valid reason – over and above the specific product benefits and performance – to purchase the brand on a number of separate occasions. However, it is important to recognize the work of Ehrenberg *et al.* (1991) mentioned above, in this context.

Increasing rate/frequency of purchase

A similar requirement will be that of increasing the rate and frequency of purchase. This may be achieved by the presentation of new usages for the product, or the suggestion of new use occasions. Kellogg's ran a television campaign which suggested that 'breakfast' cereals are also appropriate for consumption at other times of day.

Sometimes the objectives may be fulfilled by overcoming the consumer's 'out-of-stock' situation. By encouraging multiple purchase of a product, the manufacturer will also achieve more frequent usage simply because the product will be there when the consumer requires it.

Trading up

Often, and particularly at the time of introduction of a new product, the manufacturer will make available a smaller size of the product for trial purchases. Subsequently, however, they will wish to encourage the consumer to purchase larger quantities. This will be encouraged through the use of a variety of promotional techniques.

At the very least, the manufacturer will ensure that purchases of the product are brought forward. In many cases, however, this will also be accompanied by a greater fre-

quency of use simply because the product is immediately available to the consumer. As with the increasing of the frequency of purchase, the manufacturer removes the consumer from competitive attack for a period of time.

Introducing a new product

Sales promotional techniques, because of the immediacy of their impact, are conventionally used at the time of a new product introduction. Often, either through the use of successive promotional executions, or the specific nature of the execution, the manufacturer will incentivize the consumer to pass through the various initial stages of the product life cycle.

Trade objectives

In the same way that sales promotions can be targeted specifically towards the consumer – although there is an inevitable trade impact – various techniques are available to target the trade.

Traffic building

Some techniques, particularly those which involve, for example, in-store sampling, may also serve to increase the volume of traffic for the retailer. Although the consumer will be motivated to visit the outlet because of the specific incentive, it is highly likely that he or she will make other purchases whilst in store – to the benefit of the retailer who participates in the promotion.

Inventory building

In precisely the same way that the manufacturer might seek to encourage the consumer to purchase larger packages of the product, so he might also wish to ensure a deeper inventory on the part of the retailer. There are a variety of stock-loading techniques which will be discussed later and which may be employed for this purpose.

Stock reduction

At certain times, the manufacturer may wish to ensure that there is effective pull-through of his products and, thereby, reduce the level of stock held by the retailer. Such activity may be particularly associated with the introduction of a new product.

Offsetting impact of competitive activity

One great benefit of sales promotion over other forms of marketing communications is its speed of implementation. Certain forms of promotional activity can be introduced, literally, within days of determining the need. For this reason, sales promotion will often be employed to minimize the impact of competitive activity.

Promotional support to trade

In certain instances, promotions will be designed to provide either general or specific support to the trade. Some of the objectives which can be fulfilled by such activities are feature pricing; the provision of displays and display incentives; and in-store demonstrations, which will provide for trial of a product and will often be accompanied by some additional incentive to the consumer, e.g. discounted price, to purchase the product.

Other in-store support may provide the opportunity to build on special events, for example, a new store opening; some themed activity in which the brand can participate (e.g. Italian Week, Cookery Week, etc.); seasonal activity to promote sales (such as Spring Cleaning Event, Midsummer Sales, etc.); or cross-promotion, where two products are sold together (Safeway have recently mounted a large campaign in which pairs of one branded product together with an appropriate Safeway own label product were sold together at a discount – among many others, Dolmio sauce with Safeway pasta).

As noted above, the motivation of the sales force, dealers, etc. by the use of incentives – often linked to sales targets – is an important area of sales promotion activity.

Sales promotion strategy

Sales promotions can, and should, be considered as having a significant strategic role. In many instances, such activity can achieve objectives which no other form of marketing communications can deliver. Importantly, sales promotion can improve the level of manufacturer profits because they permit price discrimination and because they can, in other ways, influence trade and consumer behaviour.

Price discrimination

Promotions enable manufacturers to operate a policy of price discrimination, by charging different prices to different consumers and trade accounts that vary in terms of price sensitivity. Recently, for example, the author failed to renew a subscription to a computer magazine. Shortly afterwards, he received a mailing offering him a 'loyal subscribers' discount. Still failing to renew, he received yet another mailing with an even greater discount. Finally, he received a telephone call, offering him an even more advantageous price. Clearly, this system was established practice for the publication and, no doubt, previous subscribers were recruited at each of the differing price levels.

The same principles can also be seen at the retail level. Coupons and special prices are often aimed specifically at the price-sensitive consumer, who will make the effort to obtain such discount offers. Sometimes they will be accompanied by point-of-sale material, flagging the existence of the reduced price offer and inducing the consumer to go to the appropriate part of the store where the offer is available.

Certainly, it is apparent that different prices may be charged for the same product in different retail outlets. Designing promotions that enable more price-sensitive retailers and their consumers to pay less usually generates more contribution than if one price were charged to all. Using this approach, manufacturers can tailor their pricing to meet the particular needs of the retail outlets they serve. We have already seen that sales promotion activity can also enable the modification of manufacturers' effective prices over time, without necessitating a change in the list prices. Short-term promotional price reductions can be used to reflect variations in consumer demand and minimize the impact of such fluctuations.

Consumer behaviour

Short-term promotional activity can be used to create a sense of urgency in consumers, persuading them to stop comparing alternatives and buy earlier, or in greater quantities, than would otherwise have been the case. If consumers believe that the price reduction will only be available for a comparatively short period, they may be induced to 'bulk buy', to the obvious benefit of the brand. This is an increasing facet of the retail environment, with some major supermarkets, for example, offering periodic three for the price of two offers to achieve this objective. It is for these reasons that temporary promotions often produce greater sales increases than equivalent price cuts.

A further application of the technique is to place price offers or coupons within a specific advertising campaign. This can serve to enhance the impact of the advertising message and convey a brand benefit as well as price information. The mobile telephone market is a good example of this application of the promotional device.

Promotions may also be used to convey specific brand information by stimulating trial use. The consumer is informed of a specific product benefit, perhaps through advertising, and his or her interest in the feature or benefit is heightened at the time of usage. It is important to recognize that sales promotions enable manufacturers to communicate directly with those consumers who are specifi-

cally stimulated by an 'offer' and encourage the switching between brands. Particularly in today's pressured purchasing environment, it has to be recognized that many consumers use promotional pricing as a simple rule of thumb for making the purchase decision.

Sales promotion techniques

As much as we have seen that there are many different objectives which can be established for sales promotion activity, so too there are a wide variety of executional techniques which can be employed to meet these objectives. The following section details some of the major techniques and describes both the advantages and disadvantages in use.

Reduced price offers

Money off

Money-off promotions, in their variety of implementations, remain the most commonly employed promotional device. Often referred to as price packs or RPOs, these promotions offer the consumer the most powerful incentive to purchase – money! In essence, the promotion consists of a price reduction which is communicated either on or off the pack. The size of the price reduction will be determined by an assessment of the brand requirements and the competitive environment.

Most often, the offering consists of a flash on the pack detailing the size of the price reduction, either as an absolute price or as a reduction on the normal price. However, it may be communicated to the consumer with a notice at the point of purchase. By providing an *immediate* price reduction, a manufacturer makes the most impactful offer. All consumers will be made aware of the offer and will receive the benefit at the time of purchase.

An obvious disadvantage to be considered is the fact that *all* consumers receive the incentive, despite the fact that some – the loyal users – would probably have purchased at the normal price. Equally, such promotional offers are easily, and potentially speedily, matched by the competition. Moreover, they lack distinctiveness, since all products and services can offer money off.

A further, and possibly the most important, disadvantage is the fact that frequent use of money-off techniques may result in a reduced price expectation on the part of the consumer (the reduced price becomes the norm), and may denigrate the image of the brand.

Against these must be set the obvious advantages.

Money-off promotions can be speedily implemented. If the offering is a simple price reduction on-shelf, the promotion can be implemented within a few days. Moreover, since most companies have built up considerable experience of the technique, there is little need for testing and the results can be predicted with a reasonable level of accuracy.

The impact of the technique is considerable. It has a universal appeal and both the trade and the consumer like the promotion. Importantly, the promotional device is available to all manufacturers and service providers. Not only are there no specific economies of scale (which would otherwise restrict the use of the device to larger companies), but a means of transmitting the offering to the end-consumer is similarly available to all – the pack is not the only vehicle.

Coupons

There are a number of different ways of transmitting a money-off offer to the consumer. Although the manufacturer's product is an ideal vehicle for carrying the coupon, there are many alternative carriers and means of communicating with the end-consumer.

On some occasions, a manufacturer will use another product within the range to carry the coupon. This has the dual advantage of providing an incentive to purchase product A, whilst encouraging trial of product B. This is sometimes referred to as *cross-couponing*. On other occasions, a manufacturer will negotiate with another to carry his coupon on their product. This has a similar benefit to the carrier, since the value of the purchase is enhanced. However, it may also ensure that the two products are related in the consumer's mind (for example, money off toothpaste when you buy a toothbrush; or money off butter or jam when you buy bread).

Although far more costly, money-off coupons can be distributed within the media, or even on a door-to-door basis. These may be used to target new users (who might not be aware of the offering in-store) or to employ a more cost-effective carrier to reach the target audience.

Obviously, on-pack coupons will take longer to implement, since the revised pack design containing the flash will need to be fed into the production pipeline. And, if another carrier is to be used, negotiations will be required before the offer can be implemented. Coupon offers are significantly more expensive and time-consuming in terms of implementation. But sometimes they offer a particular benefit.

Where the coupon is designed to be redeemed at the time of a *subsequent* purchase, such offerings have a similar appearance of immediacy and impact although, in practice, many consumers forget to redeem the coupon! Hence, money-off coupons may have a similar visual impact to that of an immediate money-off offer, but will represent a lower real cost, since the level of redemption will be lower. They thus represent an effective way of inducing sampling and, because they can be transmitted via alternative carriers to designated groups of consumers, they are particularly effective in encouraging new users.

The pack

A third form of promotion, which has the same effect as reducing the price, is that of bonus or multi-packs. These offers represent an alternative expression of the money-off proposition, by providing the consumer with additional product at no extra charge.

As noted, there are two forms of the offer. The *bonus pack* consists of an enlarged pack size, although the price charged is that of the 'normal' pack which it replaces. In some instances, such packs are specially produced and provide the consumer with 10, 20 or more per cent extra product free. In other instances, partly to offset the additional manufacturing costs and difficulties, the manufacturer simply offers a larger size for the small size price. An alternative execution, especially important to manufacturers whose product format precludes the bonus pack offer, is that of the *banded pack*. Here, two or more packs are banded together at a reduced price – 'Save x per cent when you buy two'; 'Three for the price of two'; and so on.

Both promotional formats reflect the fact that there is a differential between the cost of the product and the consumer's perception of value. Indeed, such is the relationship that these promotions can sometimes offer greater consumer value at a considerably lower cost to the manufacturer. Both devices can encourage the consumer to increase the frequency of purchase, or, in the case of the bonus pack, to trade up to a larger size. They obviously have a high perceived value and can offer considerable on-shelf impact.

The choice between the two devices will depend on manufacturing circumstances. Bonus packs require a flexibility of packaging and manufacturing which is not available to all manufacturers. The latter requires minimal production changes, although it must be recognized that the process of banding may be both labour-intensive and time-consuming to implement.

Free gifts

Many manufacturers seek to incentivize the purchase by the offering of a free gift item at the time of purchase. Once again, there is the advantage of immediacy in that, if the consumer is attracted by the gift, he or she is more likely to purchase the product. There are four distinct forms of free gift offer.

1 The *on-pack free gift* is any item of merchandise which is presented to the consumer by affixing it to the external surface of the product. The application of the technique is commonly seen in a wide variety of areas (a free spoon attached to a jar of coffee, for example, or a computer program affixed to a magazine). Indeed, it is in the latter area where the promotional device is most frequently available. The obvious disadvantage is that of pilferage. If the free gift is missing, the consumer is less likely to purchase the promoted product.

2 The *in-pack free gift* is used by a number of packaged goods manufacturers, with a description of the gift on the pack surface, and the item only available once the packaging has been opened. Cereal products are regular users of this promotional tool. An obvious problem with this form of promotion is the possibility of contamination between the product contents and the free gift item, and great care needs to be taken to avoid this occurring. Some manufacturers seal the free gift prior to its insertion into the pack, but this adds considerably to the price of the promotion.

3 The *with-pack free gift* is an execution which relies on the co-operation of the retailer, since the free item of merchandise is not attached to the purchased item. However, it offers the advantage of not requiring any changes to the manufacturing process and is, therefore, available both to manufacturers of products and providers of services alike. The application of the technique is particularly popular within the cosmetics trade, and free gifts of substantial value are frequently offered by the makers of perfumes and aftershaves.

4 The fourth important area of free gift is the *pack itself*. Once it is recognized that the packaging, or some alternative presentation, may represent added value to the consumer, it can be appreciated that this is an area of considerable potential. This format has been used by a variety of packaged goods manufacturers, either with reproductions of previous packaging – history has value – or to

present the consumer with some re-usable container device that will be retained after the product has been consumed. Most mustards in France, for example, come to the consumer in small glass containers which can be used as drinking glasses once the mustard has been used. Nestlé recently offered a series of re-usable containers with its Nescafé instant coffee brand. Each canister bore a different legend, reinforcing the brand proposition of best beans, best blend and best taste. In this case, even after the product was consumed, the canister reminded the purchaser of the brand benefits.

All of these varieties of gift incentives have the attraction of immediacy and, if well selected, can add considerable value to the brand. Often, their use serves to extend the brand values by a close association of the free gift with the primary product, for example, offering a tumbler with a bottle of spirits.

A variation of the theme is for the manufacturer to offer sequential free gifts over time, which serve to deliver loyalty over an extended period. These often take the form of a collectable series of gifts, which encourages the consumer to continue purchasing the promoted product in order to collect the set.

Above all, all forms of free gift offer represent a distinctive form of promotional activity which will serve to differentiate the brand from its competitors. They have obvious on-shelf impact which may induce the consumer to purchase the brand ahead of its competitors.

The key problem associated with free gifts is that of identifying items of sufficient perceived value at an appropriate cost to the brand. Low-cost items may be of poor quality and value, and thus serve to detract from the brand rather than add value to it. A good decision basis is to ensure that the quality of the free gift is perceived to be at least the same as that of the brand itself. The costs of a free gift promotion may be quite high if the quality requirement is to be met.

Other disadvantages of the technique are associated with the different executions. As already noted, on-pack free gifts are subject to pilferage, and this may annoy the real purchaser. Overcoming the problem by seeking to insert the free gift inside the packaging may require significant alterations to the packaging machinery and, particularly with food products, may themselves require additional packaging to avoid contamination of the contents. With-pack free gifts require a substantial level of trade co-operation, which may make their implementation more difficult to achieve.

Free mail-ins

An alternative to the free gift item offered at point of purchase is to invite the consumer to send in an appropriate number of proofs of purchase for a gift item. Although somewhat more complex in its implementation, the technique has a number of direct advantages.

Since the free gift may be occasioned by multiple purchases of the product, the gift item can be more expensive and, hence, more attractive to the consumer. As such, it may add to the differentiation of the brand from its competitors. There is an obvious loyalty aspect to the execution, since the consumer will have to make several purchases in order to obtain the necessary proofs of purchase. And, as with some couponing techniques, although motivated to buy the brand with the intention of redeeming the free gift, many consumers forget to do so.

Similar problems are present with free mail-ins as with other free gifts in terms of the difficulty of obtaining suitable merchandise to offer. Additionally, however, it must be remembered that the extra costs of postage, packaging and handling may make the promotion too expensive to run.

The promotional device lacks immediacy, and consumers will be far less motivated to buy the brand if they are expected to collect wrappers and wait to receive the free gift (to a large extent, this will depend on the nature and perceived value of the free gift being offered).

Finally, the technique has relatively low appeal to the trade.

As with all forms of free gift merchandise, it is important to test the items, both to ensure the level of acceptance of the gifts as well as to anticipate the likely levels of redemption.

Self-liquidating offers

As the name suggests, these incentives are 'paid for' by the consumer. In effect, the manufacturer uses his bulk-buying power to purchase gift merchandise, which is then offered to the consumer at cost. Obviously, depending on the item to be offered, and the skills of negotiation, it is possible to offer such items at considerably less than their perceived retail value. The resultant offer – for example, a free cutlery set with a retail value of xxx, yours for only half xxx and x proofs of purchase – is thus attractive to manufacturers. The promotional costs of self-liquidating offers are low – the consumer bearing the costs of the item itself, whilst the brand bears the cost of distribution and display. They afford the opportunity to create an offer of apparent value without having to bear the associated costs. As such, they represent useful vehicles for the creation of a presence at the point of purchase and, as with other gift-based promotions, represent the opportunity to provide 'dealer loaders', where the manufacturer gives samples of the merchandise to retail staff in exchange for display space or some other consideration.

However, as a general rule, they are unlikely to generate major trade enthusiasm. Retailers are aware that self-liquidating promotions generate relatively low levels of consumer redemption and, hence, are not likely to create significant increases in sales volume.

Recent years have seen an unusual application of the principle of self-liquidators. On a regular basis, media proprietors use the device of telephone-based competitions to reward participants in competition formats. Readers, viewers and listeners are invited to phone a dedicated phone line with the answer to a question. Although it is sometimes made explicit, in some instances the participant is not informed that the phone call will be charged to his or her account. The revenue generated will, often, more than cover the costs of the promotional offer.

Contests and competitions

This is an area which has enjoyed considerable growth over recent years, especially with the development of pseudo lotteries, in which the consumer is, apparently, offered the opportunity to win a prize of sizeable value.

Contests and competitions are good point-of-sale vehicles, as they represent an opportunity to add to the brand aura. The offer of a substantial prize fund in cash or merchandise is likely to attract the attention of the potential consumer. The chance to win, say, one of ten cars, or a luxury holiday, will be likely to motivate considerable numbers of consumers to fulfil the competition entry requirements. However, set against the sales volume, the costs of such activities are relatively low.

The disadvantages of the promotional format is that it lacks the immediacy of other forms of incentive. Once again, the retail trade is aware that they will often generate only low levels of consumer participation. In many respects, the success of the format will be dependent both on the creative treatment and the scale and nature of the prizes offered.

One word of caution, however. Most countries require that participation in competition formats be dependent upon the exercise of some form of skill. The absence of inherent skill in a competition may render the promotion illegal. An alternative option is to remove the purchase requirement on the part of the consumer! Although this sounds less than sensible, the reality is that most consumers intending to enter the competition will continue to buy the brand as if it were a requirement of entry.

Table 10.1

Technique	Money-off packs	Money-off coupons	Banded packs	Bonus packs	Free gifts	Free mail-ins	Self-liquidators	Contests & comps.	Sampling
Objective									
New product launch	**	*	*	*	*				**
Induce trial	**	**	*	*	*				**
Encourage new usage	*	*	*	*	*				**
Gain new users	**	**	*	*	*				*
Retain existing users	*	*	**	**		*	*	*	
Increase frequency of purchase		*			**	**			
Increase purchase size				**	*				
Increase distribution	*	*	*	*	*				*
Increase inventory	*	*	*	*					*
Reduce inventory	*	*							
Activate slow-moving lines	*	*	*	*				*	
Gain special featuring in store							*	*	*
Increase shelf facings	**			*	*				

A recent 'World Cup' promotion mounted by Coca Cola on a world-wide basis to reinforce their sponsorship activities of the event is a perfect example of the implementation of this form of pseudo lottery. The 'instant win' prizes are obtained by revealing the identity of the prize by removing the ring-pull from the can. The rules of the competition provide, however, that anyone can enter the competition simply by sending in their name and address to the handling house, who will open a can on their behalf.

In-store sampling

Although relatively expensive, in-store sampling may provide the opportunity to provide a direct interface between the product and the consumer. Especially in those instances where the product is, perhaps, complicated to understand, or new, the opportunity for a sales person to explain the functions of the product and to enable the consumer to sample it may be very desirable. The trade like such promotions, since they generate in-store activity which tends to encourage a higher level of all product purchases – not just the product which is being sampled.

Table 10.1 can be used as a simple checklist to establish the specific nature of a promotional technique to meet a defined objective. It must be remembered, however, that the list is not exhaustive and that, in some instances, several objectives may be combined.

Promoting to consumers

A consideration of brand loyalty factors

An important dimension of sales promotion, which is sometimes overlooked, is the fact that certain forms of activity reward all users with the incentive, irrespective of whether or not they would have purchased the product anyway. It has to be remembered that the consumers for any product or service make up a continuum, ranging from loyal users to promiscuous buyers. Loyal users would be those consumers who purchase regularly or on all occasions, whilst promiscuous buyers will be those who usually purchase only in response to some form of incentive. Most promotional techniques are indiscriminate in this context, and tend to reward all purchasers. Thus, whilst a promotional device may be attractive in terms of attracting new users, it will also be received by those users who would have purchased the brand without the incentive. When costing out the benefits of promotional activity, this factor must be taken into account. Although comparatively few brands can boast a high level of loyalty, this may account for 15–20 per cent of purchasers and, on the Pareto principle, these customers may account for up to 80 per cent of all product purchases. By definition, therefore, the incremental benefit of the promotion may only be the remaining 20 per cent of purchases which might not otherwise have been bought.

There are a number of other factors which need to be considered in the determination of promotional strategy.

Level of involvement with purchase

There is some evidence that, where consumer involvement with the product category is low, promotions which have an immediacy of impact will work better than those which impact over time. Thus, clearly identified money-off promotions, or the offering of bonus-free product, will have a high level of impact compared with money off next purchase and similar offers. In this regard, it is important that the discount or offer is clearly 'flagged' to the consumer. Since many consumers are not aware of absolute prices, an on-shelf offer which effectively reduces the price, but which is not clearly identified to the consumer as such, will have far less impact.

Purchase frequency

It is important to understand the nature and frequency of purchase for the target consumer. Ideally, incentives should be timed to coincide with the patterns of purchase of the heavy user, so that they are encouraged to buy within their normal rate. If a phased incentive (with, say, on-pack vouchers that need to be saved) has too short an interval, even heavy users will not be able to buy sufficiently often to achieve their goal. Petrol promotions in the past, which have offered vouchers for items, or collectable free gifts (World Cup coins, car badges and so on), can result in considerable consumer irritation if insufficient time is allowed for them to complete their set.

By the same token, a differential impact can be achieved by addressing the issue of pack size. It is reasonable to assume that regular users will, in the main, tend to buy a larger pack size. If an incentive is offered on a smaller size, it will tend to attract more new users than existing ones.

Coupon distribution

We have already seen that all recipients of a promotional incentive will be rewarded, irrespective of whether or not they would have purchased the product at the 'regular' price. By targeting discount offers, for example, by including the coupon in a newspaper or magazine advertisement, or by the use of direct mail, it can be more effective in attracting new users than those who are loyal to the brand.

Brand franchise

Much has already been said about the potential risks of short-term promotional incentives undermining the desired imagery of a brand.

Careful consideration needs to be given to the likely impact which a promotion will have on overall consumer perceptions, as much as to the assessment of its ability to achieve short-term volume goals. Too great a reliance on price-based offers will tend to encourage consumers to focus on the price not only of the preferred brand, but also of potential competitors – sometimes to the detriment of the brand.

Point of purchase communications

The creation of impactful displays at the point of purchase is a major dimension of promotional planning. It provides the brand with an increased level of visibility and, particularly in impulse purchase situations, may be the necessary trigger to motivate a purchase of the promoted item. In the crowded retail environment, point of sale material may be an important element in distinguishing one brand from its competitors. Importantly, such material provides the opportunity to extend the brand proposition to the point of purchase, and serves, for example, to remind the potential consumer of the key message from the advertising. It augments the impact of the promotional proposition which might otherwise be limited by, for example, the size of the pack and allows for a more colourful and creative treatment. Whilst such material is comparatively expensive, it may avoid the greater costs associated with changing the pack design which, in turn, might reduce the consumer's recognition of the brand. Bearing in mind that the material is likely to be displayed in areas of the store other than where the product is displayed, it helps remind the consumer of the brand promotion.

However, it is important to recognize that many retailers now adopt strict design codes to minimize the confusion which would result from a wide variety of treatments appearing in their outlets. Most often, such material will need to be discussed at an early stage with potential stockists to ensure that the design is consistent with their own requirements. Importantly, this affords the opportunity to ensure the active participation of the retailer, who will enjoy the potential benefits of increased offtake of the brand through his outlets.

After many years during which manufacturers have been denied the ability to place point of sale material in retail outlets, many retailers are beginning to feature it again. In part, this is a reflection of the increased competition on the high street. The somewhat restrictive approach adopted by many retailers resulted in their outlets becoming somewhat boring. Today, manufacturers are being encouraged to provide more support at the retail level to enhance the shopping experience and increase the differentiation between retail brands. Banks and building societies are increasingly turning to point of sale to enhance their retail branches as part of a recognition that their customers respond more positively to a less formal and impersonal environment.

An increasingly important aspect of point of sale promotion, which follows on from the previous point, is the ability to 'tailor-make' promotions with one or more retail chains. By developing material in conjunction with one or more retail groups, the promotion is more likely to achieve its desired objectives. Indeed, several retailers may be likely to insist not only on personalized point of sale, but also personalized promotional activity to provide them with a competitive advantage over other similar retailers.

Strategic dimensions of sales promotion

As with any other form of strategy determination, the starting point must be the correct assessment of the situation or need. What is

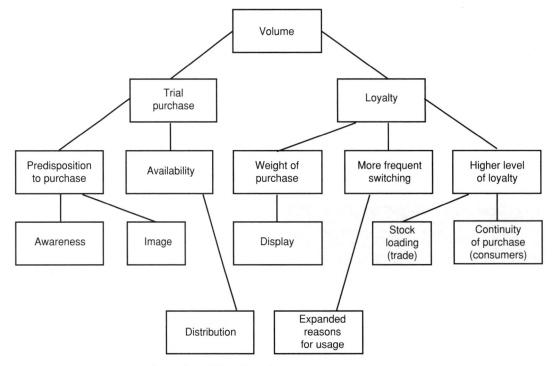

Figure 10.1   Promotional goal hierarchies (Chris Brown)

the promotion designed to achieve and what is the problem that needs to be rectified? In this respect, it is important to analyse the situation of the brand relative to its competition to identify the true cause of the problem (e.g. low sales volume – is it caused by some deficiency in the product or is it, perhaps, the result of competitive activities?). Sales promotion may help in the latter situation but is unlikely to remedy the former. Indeed, it may accentuate the problems, as more trialists will become aware of the imperfections in the brand!

Chris Brown (1991) offers the following diagram (Figure 10.1) to indicate the hierarchy of promotional objectives in his book, *The Sales Promotion Handbook*, Kogan Page, 1991.

As with other forms of marketing communications, it is important to *set precise objectives* for the activity. Is the promotion expected to increase trial and sampling, or reward loyal users? Not only must the objectives be spe-

cific, they should also be measurable. What level of trial is to be generated – 10, 20 or 30 per cent or higher? If no value is given to the objective, it will be extremely difficult to determine whether the goal has been achieved on its completion!

Having determined the objectives, the next stage is to *identify the potential solution*. We have already seen that a number of promotional techniques can achieve similar objectives. Selecting the appropriate promotional technique is a vital part of the process, and Table 10.1 (page 205) provides some guidance in this respect.

Pre-costing the promotion must be an important element of the process. Perhaps, with the usage of market research techniques, it will be possible to identify the likely take-up of a consumer free gift offer or coupon promotion. At the very least, it will be important, for budgetary reasons, to be able to anticipate the likely costs of the exercise. In the instance of merchandise offers, it will be important to ensure that adequate quantities of the items are available to meet expected levels of consumer demand (thereby avoiding consumer disappointment) – and, at the other end of the spectrum, not to over-order and thereby be left with unused stocks of the free gifts.

Control mechanisms must be established at the outset to ensure the smooth implementation of the promotion. How will the company respond to changes in the levels of consumer demand? Is there sufficient manufacturing capacity to cope, for example? What happens in the event that the promotion goes wrong? Are there adequate monitoring procedures to identify what is going on in the marketplace? And so on.

Finally, once the promotion has been implemented, the results must be carefully *measured*.

Joint promotions (or cross-promotions)

An increasingly important area of promotional activity is that of joint promotions, where two or more participants promote their brands together to obtain a mutual benefit. We have already seen that this form of promotional activity affords a major opportunity for close co-operation between brand manufacturers and retailer stockists.

There are a wide variety of joint promotions which encompass a range of different executions. Perhaps the most apparent are those promotions in which the brand proposition is advertised via other products and services (a free trial size of a new product, for example, banded to the packaging of an established brand). Such activity may offer significant advantages to both of the participants. For the promoter, the opportunity is to gain access to a group of new consumers, who are encouraged to associate the product with another

from a similar or related category. For the carrier, the promotion provides the opportunity to add value to his product in the form of a free gift or other incentive at a significantly reduced cost.

In some instances, such promotions are organized on an 'in-house' basis, in which two products from within a company portfolio are combined to offer additional benefits to the consumer. Recently, Nestlé offered a free sample of its new breakfast cereal, Shredded Wheat Fruitful, banded to packs of other regular Shredded Wheat. The promotion served to introduce the new product to existing consumers of the core brand and thereby extend the appeal of the latter product.

For such activities to generate the maximum consumer impact and, therefore, benefit to the participants, several important factors need to be considered. Of these, it may be argued that the most important is the degree of image match between the participating brands. It is clearly important that the two products or services should have similar images, otherwise one might serve to denigrate the other. Equally, there should be a similarity in the target market profiles of the participants. There would be little value to the carrier if the audience for the promoted product was different from its own. That applies equally to the nature of the distribution patterns of the two brands. In the majority of instances, it is important that the two brands are available from similar outlets. There are exceptions, however, where the brands will be similar in other dimensions, but the promotion will be used to carry a product into a retail environment where it is not normally found.

For established brands, it is normally desirable for the two participants to be of similar status in the marketplace in order that each complements the other. However, it may be possible to trade off the quality of one product against the quantity of the other, particularly where there is a good correspondence of the audience.

Joint promotions offer a wide range of advantages, as can be seen. Importantly, the costs involved in establishing the promotion, generating publicity and the necessary administration can be shared between the participants, both of whom will derive benefit from the activity. They enable the participants to build upon each other's customer base and, potentially, extend outwards to a variety of new customers. The participation of two players often results in greater visibility than if either of them promoted on a solus basis. And, of course, the risks involved in the promotion can be shared between the participants. In many instances, the carrier brand may enjoy the benefits of a promotion at a very low cost, or even completely free. Indeed, recognizing the power of their pack, some manufacturers charge for the privilege of being carried by them.

Against these advantages can be set a variety of potential disadvantages. Great care must be taken to ensure that there is an image match between the participants, since poor matches may be detrimental to the image of one or both partners. Such promotions are often both time-consuming to set up and relatively complicated to execute and administer. Also, particularly where the products are to be banded together, long lead times may be required, and they suffer the potential danger of pilferage, as with any other on-pack offer.

The evaluation of sales promotion

When evaluating a promotion, it is important to consider the specific objectives, since that will assist in the identification of the best approach. At the basic level, there is a need to quantify the impact of the promotional device on volume and contribution.

The volume sold on promotion, multiplied by the reduced contribution per pack, yields a contribution net of the cost of promotion. If there are any additional fixed costs, e.g. the provision of point of sale material, dealer incentives, etc., these should similarly be deducted. The resultant figure can be easily compared with the expected contribution if the promotion were not run.

If the objective is one of profit growth, then it is important to identify the promotion that provides the greatest increase in contribution levels. If the objective is volume, then promotions that yield the greatest increase per pound invested will be required. If it is to increase penetration, then the key is to identify the return from each of the different approaches to increasing penetration. In this context, it is important to consider the price-elasticity of the brand. Understanding the price-elasticity of a brand will help set appropriate discounts. Market leaders, more expensive brands and brands with very strong emotional benefits will tend to be less price-sensitive than the market average. If such a brand uses price promotions, it is unlikely that it will be able to generate the necessary additional volume to get back the costs of the price discount. Strongly elastic brands which respond to price cuts are the likely beneficiaries of such promotional activity.

The volume a brand achieves when on promotion can be divided into two component parts:

1 *Base sales*, which are those that would have happened irrespective of the promotional activity.
2 *Incremental sales*, which are those which are directly attributable to the promotional activity during the period. These derive from three consumer responses:

  • Competitor steal – where the promotion encourages switching from a competitor's brand;
  • Brand cannibalization – where the promotion of a particular brand results in consumers switching their purchases from another product within the company's product portfolio;

- Category growth – where the additional volume derives from new customers who would not otherwise have purchased either the promoted product or one of its competitors.

An estimate supplied by A.C. Nielsen from a study published in 1995 provides some quantification of the contribution of promotions to annual brand volume. Across all of the brands examined by the company, promotions activity accounts for 11 per cent of annual sales.

Attitudinal research conducted by A.C. Nielsen among a panel of 7000 households provides some important information on consumer attitudes towards promotional activity and their responses in terms of purchasing behaviour. In response to the statement 'I will buy a brand I don't normally buy if it is on special offer', some 43 per cent of respondents agreed with the statement. Equally, 57 per cent stated that 'If I see a special offer I like, I will buy more than I need'. This is important in the context of bringing forward future purchases of the brand and encouraging brand switching.

The promotions-aware consumer

Seventy-four per cent of consumers interviewed by A.C. Nielsen agreed that they look out for special price offers; 66 per cent look out for special displays, and 56 per cent cut out coupons. These figures provide tangible evidence of the consumer impact of sales promotion activity.

Promotional impact in the impulse sector

The impulse sector includes soft drinks, snacks and confectionery. On average, among the brands studied by A.C. Nielsen, a 10 per cent price cut generates a 30 per cent increase in sales volume; stores running a multibuy can expect a 112 per cent sales increase; extra fill boosts paid-for volume by 27 per cent; and special packs, which include a multitude of offers, provide an uplift of 67 per cent.

In communicating the offer, a shelf talker will boost the effect by 13 per cent, and secondary display by 44 per cent.

How long should a special pack last?

A.C. Nielsen have provided information on four brand categories, one from each of the liquor, grocery, impulse and personal care sectors. Figure 10.2 shows the increase in volume from the first week that a special pack appears in-store. The effect of distribution is removed, and this, therefore, reflects genuine consumer demand.

It is not uncommon for special packs to linger in the trade for a considerable time. And whilst the shape of the curve undoubtedly varies by brand and by offer, the inference is that most special packs start losing their appeal after three to four weeks. Over-production of special packs by manufacturers, or over-ordering by retailers, is likely to be introducing unnecessary cost into special pack promotions.

In the evaluation of any promotional activity, several important factors need to be borne in mind.

1 Does the promotional concept fit well with the brand, its desired imagery and its target audience?
2 Is the recommended solution the most likely to achieve the desired objectives?
3 Is the promotion easy to understand and credible to the target audience?
4 Is it easy to participate in, or does it create a series of unnecessary obstacles for the potential consumer to overcome?
5 Is the promotion likely to satisfy the needs of consumers? Ideally, promotional offers should not overclaim, since this is likely to result in post-purchase dissonance. Rather, they should

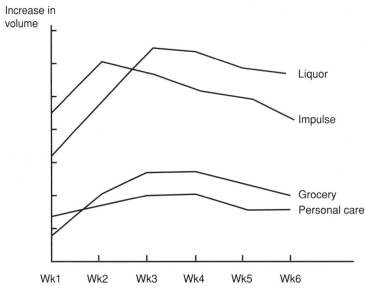

Figure 10.2   Impact of pack duration (A.C. Nielsen)

ensure that the customer remains satisfied and, if possible, deliver more than is expected.

6 Is the promotion dependent on a particular fad or fashion (such as a tie-in with a specific event), or does it provide a concept which can be repeated over time?

Based on their store level database, Nielsen (in *The Researcher*, January 1997) have pro-vided an indication of the average uplift achieved from sales promotion tools (Table 10.2).

The company estimates that an average of 16 per cent of the shopping basket is bought on promotion. The breakdown of the promo-tional component, by mechanic, is as shown in Table 10.3.

Table 10.2   Promotion effectiveness: average uplift

Promotion type	Percentage uplift
Shelf talker	10%
10% temporary price reduction	27%
Extra fill	28%
Display	44%
Multibuy	54%
Special pack	62%

Source: A. C. Nielsen Modelling Database

Table 10.3   Breakdown of promotional purchases, by mechanic

Temporary price reduction	34%
Additional quantity	13%
Price-marked pack	11%
Multiple purchase discount	13%
Send away	7%
Free item	5%
Banded pack	4%
Coupon	3%
Other	29%

Source: A. C. Nielsen Homescan Panel

Research into sales promotion

Sales promotion is an area where market research can amply repay the investment made in it, although, sadly, comparatively little use is made of the techniques available. Given the scale of the potential problems which can result from a poorly constructed or badly implemented promotion, it makes a great deal of sense to ensure that all possible steps are taken to avoid the many pitfalls which might otherwise occur.

The field of sales promotion is littered with examples of companies that have got it wrong. Hoover remains the outstanding example of the potential long-term damage that can result from a failure to understand the impact of the promotional mechanics on consumer demand. Customers who failed to receive free seats in the 1994 promotion continue to create adverse publicity for the company. Recently (*The Times*, 28 February, 1997) two customers were awarded damages in a move that opens up the way to thousands of other claims against the company, whilst *Marketing Week* (5 June, 1997) reported that a series of new legal challenges were due to be heard during the year.

However, other equally large companies have failed to ensure that the techniques they employ within the area satisfy the requirements fully. The *Daily Mirror*, for example, ran a scratch card promotion in July 1995 when, due to the poor construction of the wording, some 2000 readers thought that they had each won £50,000 – representing a potential liability of some £100 million. Similarly, Pepsi ran a competition in which the consumer purchasing a bottle with the number 349 printed under the bottle cap would receive £26,000. However, some 800 000 'winning' caps were printed, representing a potential liability of some £19 billion!

Market research can provide an important contribution to the understanding of sales promotion in two broad areas:

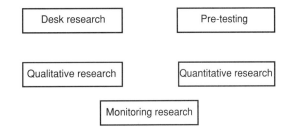

Figure 10.3

1 Testing
2 Monitoring

At the developmental stage, the appropriate use of the available techniques can provide an insight into the identification of objectives; enable focus and targeting of the offer to the desired consumer group; enable an informed choice between alternative executions; as well as assisting in the refinement of a promotion concept into an effective and workable proposition.

Figure 10.3 sets out some of the important areas in which market research can contribute to the development of more efficient and effective sales promotion activities.

Desk research

Most companies already possess a considerable amount of information which can be used to assist the promotional planning process. In many cases, there will be a body of knowledge built up from past promotional experience. Some companies maintain comprehensive evaluations of previous implementations which will provide guidance on their likely impact if repeated. Importantly, such dimensions as redemption rates and consumer and retailer participation are often monitored and recorded and will provide a benchmark for the development of new executions. The same may apply equally to competitive activities. Understanding the way in which competitive brands respond to promotional activity may also provide a guide to how similar promotions might work on the company's own brands.

There are a number of published sources which will also provide a valuable insight into promotional effectiveness. The annual Sales Promotion Consultants Association (SPCA) awards provide details of a series of promotions which have demonstrated their effectiveness in the marketplace. And, of course, the dedicated trade press regularly reports on promotional activities.

Pre-testing

Pre-testing of a promotional execution is an important part of the determination of its likely effectiveness. Using a variety of simulation techniques, promotions can be assessed for their likely appeal; the propensity to generate consumer awareness and offtake; the potential for generating repeat purchase; perceptions of value for money; and so on.

At this stage, it is possible to test a variety of different executions against each other and, where available, against a previously run promotion with a known outcome (to act as a benchmark). In this way, some finite results can be obtained which will add to the ability of predicting the likely impact of the intended promotion.

Qualitative research

Qualitative research methods can be used to assess such factors as the likely impact on the image of the brand of a particular range of promotional techniques. Identifying how consumers will react to an offer is important both in the tangible sense – how it will affect their propensity to purchase the brand – as well as the intangible aspects – such as how the promotion affects their overall perceptions of the brand (is a particular offer more likely to cheapen than improve the image, for example).

Techniques such as 'town hall tests', in which the purchase environment is simulated and the results of exposure to different consumer offers is monitored, can make a considerable contribution to the determination of the most effective incentive.

Quantitative research

Similarly, quantitative techniques can be used, in which consumers scale their preference for different forms of promotional offer. If possible, it is desirable to include some previous promotion, for which results are known, as a benchmark against which the performance of alternatives can be assessed.

In some instances, especially where the scale of the promotion is likely to be large, it may be advisable to stage a 'mini test market'. By running the promotion in a small region of the country, it will be possible to gauge the impact of the offering in a live environment, where the brand has to compete with real competitors.

Monitoring research

The close monitoring of consumer response once the promotion is implemented is, similarly, an important part of the process. By maintaining a constant feedback from the market it will serve to alert the company to any potential difficulties, which may be avoided with a speedy response. It has to be said that these techniques are often ignored or overlooked in the context of sales promotion activity. Market research will provide some assurance that the particular chosen technique is the appropriate one to fulfil the task set and, most importantly, to provide some indication of the likely outcome of the activity.

Throughout the sales promotion process, as with other parts of the marketing communications mix, market research can provide valuable insights into the likely impact of the activity as an independent variable but, more importantly, in terms of the impact which it will have on the brand as a whole. In this respect, a wide variety of research methods can be employed to gain additional knowledge about the brand (Figure 10.4).

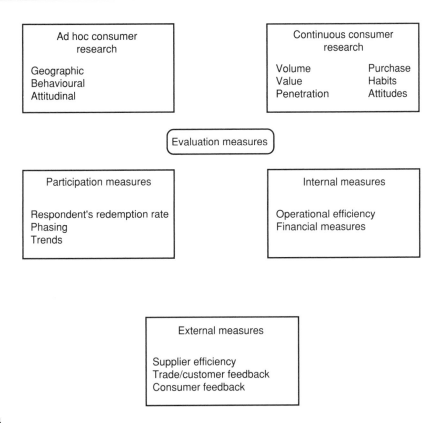

Figure 10.4

The legal framework for sales promotion

The field of sales promotion is governed by a number of both voluntary and legal requirements. The major practitioner bodies have jointly established guidelines for the implementation of sales promotional activities. The British Code of Sales Promotion Practice is published by the Committee of Advertising Practice (CAP) and the Institute of Sales Promotion (ISP) and provides an indication of best practice for the structuring of all forms of promotion.

Promotional activity is also embodied in a number of Acts of Parliament and other Directives. Among these are the Gaming Act 1968 and the Lotteries and Amusements Act 1976, which specifically set out the requirements for competitions and lotteries; the Trading Stamps Act 1964, which requires that any vouchers offered must have a cash value printed on them; the Financial Services Act 1986; and the Sale of Goods Act 1979, to name but a few.

Under normal circumstances, it is the Local Trading Standards Officer who polices pricing and trading issues, and who will investigate claims of unfair or illegal promotional practice. Price claims are the most frequent of the promotions issues. The various controls provide:

- Any price offer should be clear and not contain hidden extra charges;
- the promoter should avoid implying that the price is less than it really is, and where there is some form of restriction on the nature of

the offer, for example, money off next purchase, both parts of the offer should be made clearly and distinctly in the same typeface and size;

- where some form of comparison of value or worth is made, this must be justified in a way that consumers can understand.

We have seen that an alternative to money-off promotions is to provide additional 'free' product. These extra value claims must be justifiable and conform to the same basic rules as for price claims. It is important to note that, in some product categories, there are restrictions which govern the packaging sizes that must be used; for example, the Weights and Measures (Miscellaneous Foods) Order 1997 largely prohibits extra value on a wide range of food products.

It is vitally important that the codes of practice and legal frameworks are closely adhered to. Apart from the adverse publicity which may attach to an 'illegal' promotion (programmes like 'Watchdog' often feature promotional activity which, it feels, acts against the consumer's interests), it must be remembered that the Local Trading Standards Officer has the power to demand the removal from distribution of any packs which carry an illegal offer.

The use of sales promotion agencies

In the majority of instances, it is likely that companies will turn to specialist expertise to assist in the development of sales promotion solutions. The last twenty years have seen the emergence of several specialist agencies and consultancies in the field, which have built up a substantial body of knowledge and experience which can be brought to bear in the identification of a sales promotion solution.

In its annual survey of sales promotion consultancies, *Campaign* magazine (20 July

1995) lists some sixty-six separate companies, with turnovers ranging from £46 million (IMP turnover 1994, 167 employees) to £260,000 (Marketing in Action, with five employees). Clearly, therefore, the range of agencies is enormous, and so too are the variety of services which might be provided to their client companies. These will depend on the specific requirements of the client base, but are likely to include:

- strategic and advisory inputs;
- the development of consumer and trade promotions;
- promotional design and artwork production;
- copywriting services;
- print design and buying;
- the sourcing of merchandise;
- the design and development of sales literature;
- promotional administration, implementation and evaluation.

Somewhat more specialized services might include:

- project management;
- event management;
- sponsorship;
- staff motivation schemes;
- co-ordination between suppliers;
- locating and negotiating with third party contacts.

and several companies operate exclusively within one or more of these latter areas.

Selecting promotional agencies

The identification of a partner with whom to work is similar in many respects to the process outlined in Chapter 6 on choosing and using marketing communications agencies, although it is recognized that the selection criteria may be somewhat different.

A survey of some forty-seven client users of sales promotion conducted by *Campaign* magazine (25 February 1994) identified several important factors in the selection of a sales promotion consultancy. Critical to the decision-making process were three dimensions:

The need to maintain regular contact with clients	87%
Have a proven track record in the client's sector	85%
Principals and directors are readily accessible	81%

Somewhat further down the list of priorities were the following:

They are conveniently located	55%
They offer a wide range of services	39%

As with the selection of an advertising agency, the starting point will be a consideration of the specific requirements of the company. Given the range of scales indicated above, there is a wide choice of consultancies whose services may be considered more or less appropriate to matching the needs of the company.

At the top end, agencies including IMP, Wunderman Cato Johnson, Purchasepoint and KLP Marketing (ranked 1 to 4 in 1995) offer a totally integrated promotional facility, and the ability to provide almost all related facilities in-house. At the other extreme are a series of smaller consultancies, which aim to provide a responsive and fast service to their clients, but which have relatively few internal resources. For the most part, they maintain low staff levels, and tend to buy in all or many of their services.

Between these are the specialist agencies which operate in a niche promotional area. Some will specialize in sports sponsorship, others in conference organization and management, some in event creation and management, yet others in field sales operations and so on. The trade press will be an important

starting point for the review, providing up-to-date information on the performance of likely agencies. Similarly, it will be important to contact current and previous clients in order to obtain the views of others who have worked with them.

In each case, however, there are a number of important principles which need to be considered.

As the *Campaign* survey indicated, it will be important to consider the past work and experience of the agency. Some agencies offer specialist skills and knowledge, and may well have worked within the market sector on a previous occasion. Most agencies will be only too happy to provide a portfolio of past work or a credentials presentation which will enable the examination of demonstrable past achievements on behalf of their clients. Some will have won peer group awards (such as those offered by the SPCA) which will underpin their successes.

Such a meeting will also enable an assessment of their staff and the nature of the service the agency provides to its clients. To what extent will the company deal with the management of the agency, or will it be serviced by less senior employees? What specific qualities and experiences will the team bring to the relationship? And, since this area, as much as any other within the marketing communications business, depends on the relationship between people, what are their interpersonal skills, and is it likely that a positive chemistry will be established between them and the company?

The scale of the agency will need to reflect the scale of the company and the nature of the promotional inputs it requires. Do they have the necessary scale of resources to deal with the company's requirements? Can they operate in a variety of countries, if appropriate?

A further issue will be that of remuneration. Agencies derive their profit in two ways: by charging a fee, and making a mark-up on the services they provide. Charges usually relate to the scale of activity in which they are involved. Some will work on ad hoc assignments, or on a project basis, whilst others will only operate against a retainer income. The company needs to be satisfied that the method of remuneration is consistent with the way in which it wishes to do business.

The integration of sales promotion activities

It is important, in the planning of sales promotion plans, to ensure the continuity of communication with other elements of the marketing communications plan. There is little point running sales promotion activities which only serve to confuse the consumer's expectations of the brand. In this sense, it is vital to ensure that there is a consistency of image and functional values before a sales promotion technique is employed, and that it is fully integrated with other aspects of the marketing communications plan.

Increasingly, brands are seeking promotional devices which represent the achievement of integration. Tetley Tea, for example, has built up an equity around its brand by using the 'Tea Folk' within its advertising campaigns. In promotion terms, this has been reflected in the offering of a range of merchandise gifts which feature the characters and reflect the core values of the brand. Similarly, Tango offered an orange doll. It is interesting to note that both of these campaigns won Institute of Sales Promotion awards during 1996. Other companies have reflected the deeper values associated with their brands and the personality of their consumers in sales promotion executions. Häagen Dazs offered a 'Dedicated to Pleasure' CD, whilst Doc Martens used an 'Unlaced' CD.

Of course, the adoption of a strategic approach to sales promotion does not preclude the tactical use of sales promotion techniques. Its purpose is to provide a framework within which tactical planning can exist and be improved.

International sales promotion activity

The rules, regulations and codes of practice which govern sales promotion are far from being universal. Indeed, the application of the principles of sales promotion in the international context is fraught with difficulties. Free mail-ins, for example, are not permitted in Germany; promotions designed to encourage consumer loyalty with the offering of collector schemes are similarly prohibited in Austria, Germany and some parts of Scandinavia; self-liquidating offers may not be run in Norway and Switzerland and special permission must first be obtained in Holland.

The same problems exist with other forms of promotion and, whilst there are some movements towards common practices, at least within the EC, the situation for the moment remains somewhat confused.

It is imperative that any sales promotion planned for international implementation is checked for legal and other compliance on a country-by-country basis. It certainly cannot be assumed, as the examples above demonstrate, that simply because a promotion is 'legal' in one country it will be equally so elsewhere.

These, and other related issues, will be considered in greater detail in Chapter 15 on International Marketing Communications.

References

Ehrenberg, A. S. C., 'An Academic's Agenda for the Nineties', *Admap*, September 1994

Ehrenberg, A. S. C., Hammond, K. and Goodhardt, G. J., *The After Effects of Large Consumer Promotions*, London Business School, 1991

Jones, J. P., 'The Double Jeopardy of Sales Promotion', *Harvard Business Review*, September/October 1990

Additional reading

There are several texts which will provide a deeper understanding of the nature and scope of sales promotion:

Brown, Chris, *The Sales Promotion Handbook*, 1995, Kogan Page

Quelch, John A., *Sales Promotion Management*, 1989, Prentice Hall

Robinson, William and Hauri, Christine, *Promotional Marketing: Ideas and Techniques for Success in Sales Promotion*, 1991, NTC Business Books

Schultz, Don E., Robinson, William A. and Petrison, Lisa A., *Sales Promotion Essentials*, 1993, NTC Business Books

Toop, Alan, *European Sales Promotion: Great Campaigns in Action*, 1992, Kogan Page

CHAPTER 11

Direct marketing

Aims and objectives

- To examine the growth and impact of direct marketing;
- To explore the advantages and disadvantages of direct marketing;
- To grasp the importance and uses of the database;
- To develop an understanding of adopting a strategic approach to direct marketing;
- To consider the diversity of direct marketing objectives;
- To gain an insight into the management of direct marketing and the direct marketing planning process;
- To learn about the use of direct marketing consultancies;
- To consider media usage in the context of direct marketing;
- To understand the roles of testing and research in direct marketing;
- To become familiar with direct marketing applications;
- To explore the nature of relationship marketing.

The growth of direct marketing

The past decade has witnessed rapid growth in the field of direct marketing. Having said that, the principle of direct marketing is not a new phenomenon. Mail order companies, starting in the United States, have employed the fundamentals of direct marketing for the best part of 100 years to ensure their ability to sell their products directly to the consumer.

The main driving force has been the increased need to ensure a sharp focus on responding to customer needs, a requirement which can be better achieved by direct communication than through conventional retail outlets. The means by which this has been achieved has, undeniably, been the dramatic improvements in computer technology. The progressive improvements have enabled the realization of the potential of direct marketing. The underlying principles have not changed, only the means by which the objectives are achieved. The ability to programme the computer to respond to individual changes in consumer circumstances has meant that decisions as to when to take specific marketing actions can be determined without human intervention.

The problem, in terms of quantifying this growth, is defining precisely what is to be included within the sector, and of identifying the exact scale of the various components.

The British Direct Marketing Association defines direct marketing as

'an interactive system of marketing which uses one or more advertising media to effect a measurable response and/or transaction at any location.'

Table 11.1 Direct mail expenditure and volume 1986–1996

Year	Consumer volume (million items)	Business volume (million items)	Total volume (million items)	Total expenditure (£ million)
1986	976	425	1 401	474
1987	1 161	465	1 626	483
1988	1 221	545	1 766	530
1989	1 445	672	2 117	758
1990	1 544	728	2 272	930
1991	1 435	687	2 112	895
1992	1 658	588	2 246	945
1993	1 772	664	2 436	904
1994	2 015	715	2 730	1 050
1995	2 198	707	2 905	1 135
1996	2 436	737	3 173	1 404

Source: Royal Mail

An alternative definition is provided by Drayton Bird (1993):

'Any advertising activity which creates and exploits a direct relationship between you and your prospect or customer as an individual.'

Taking either of these definitions, the difficulties of isolating the components can be readily seen. Certainly, we must include the entirety of the area of direct mail which, according to the Advertising Association estimates, was worth some £1,404 million in 1996.

Within the overall usage of direct marketing, the direct mail sector has experienced substantial growth over recent years. Indeed, according to the Royal Mail, the sector has shown growth of some 126 per cent over the decade 1986–96. This can be seen from Table 11.1.

To that, we might add all, or at least the majority of, the expenditure on classified advertising, valued by the same source at £2,768 million. After all, most classified advertising is placed with the aim of eliciting some form of response from the reader.

It is at this point that the going gets tougher. Most other areas – whether in the press, on television or radio, or even posters – include some form of response mechanism (an address, a telephone number, etc.) in order that the viewer or reader can obtain further information. However, it is debatable whether this device is included to establish a *relationship* with the customer which, as we will see, is the key strategic reason for using the techniques of direct marketing.

According to market research carried out by BT and Channel 4, 19 per cent of all ads on ITV, C4 and satellite carry phone numbers (1995). This is an increase from the recorded level of 14 per cent in 1994 and 12 per cent in 1993. The study identified 177 direct response TV campaigns between January and March 1995, a growth of 67 per cent on the previous year. The sectors making the greatest use of DRTV are financial (32 per cent), automotive and travel (12 per cent each) and office and telecoms (around 5 per cent).

It is important to differentiate between brand response advertising – the depiction of the classic image with a phone number on the screen for a brief period – and lead generation commercials – lead first, close later, lots of repeat calls to action, lots of mention of consumer benefits – give evidence that the phone number is virtually omnipresent. The latter are often characterized by low production values and may have a negative impact on the brand image.

Whatever the true value, the importance of the process of the sector to marketing communications cannot be denied.

The impact of direct marketing

The average British household, which already receives an average of 7.6 items of direct mail each month, is set to see an increase as the total annual direct mail volume is expected to hit 3 million items for the first time. Figures from the Direct Mail information service for the second quarter of 1996 show an increase of nearly 10 per cent year on year. At the same time, direct mail expenditure has increased significantly, with second quarter year on year figures showing an increase of 22 per cent to £335.5 million, compared with £256.7 million for the same period in 1995.

The increase in direct marketing volume has come almost entirely from the consumer market, where mailings now account for around 77 per cent of total volume. The volume of direct mail within the business sector grew significantly during the 1980s. The recession of the early 1990s saw a decline in volumes; however, this has now been reversed, and volumes are increasing once again. The average businessperson is sent approximately fifteen items of direct mail each week, with most businesses maintaining a positive attitude towards the medium.

Included in the 'Others' category are entertainment, financial investment, FMCG and local government.

Table 11.2 Senders of direct mail, 1996

	% of volume	% requested
Mail order	15.3	7.1
Insurance	11.4	5.6
Credit card	6.2	2.6
Bank/Girobank	9.3	4.8
Building society	2.3	8.2
Retailers	8.9	11.2
Magazines	2.8	12.3
Estate agent	0.5	69.7
Manufacturer	6.1	11.3
Book club	5.2	14.9
Charity	7.3	5.2
Gas/electricity	2.4	9.2
Film co.	0.6	8.4
Others	21.7	12.8
Total	100	9.5

Source: The LetterBox File, DMIS, The Royal Mail, Spring 1997

The factors contributing to the growth of direct marketing

Recent years have seen fundamental changes in both consumer attitudes and behaviours which have, undoubtedly, contributed to the growth of direct marketing:

1 The desire for experimentation. As a result of foreign travel and changes in lifestyle generally, people are becoming more accustomed to the process of experimentation. The increased penetration of home computers and modems increases the potential for shopping in unconventional ways. Major grocery retailers, including Tesco and Sainsbury's, are experimenting with the

provision of computer-based shopping facilities.

2 New 'shopping outlets'. Although mail order has been around for a century or more, the convenience of shopping at a time when the consumer wishes to do so is beginning to reassert itself. This trend is likely to continue progressively with the development of direct shopping channels on television, such as QVC, and the advent of interactive television facilities through the medium of cable. The recently announced contract for digital broadcasting is likely to extend the reach of these facilities further.

3 The focus on the home, witnessed by various studies conducted by the Henley Research Centre, accentuates the desire to shop at home through mail order and shopping channels.

4 Underlying changes in society. More working women, changes in the composition of the family, and similar trends – have contributed to the desire for a more personalized service which is sometimes unavailable through conventional retail outlets. Importantly, this fragmentation of the audience represents a challenge to conventional marketing, as consumers want products and services which are more directly tailored to their own personal requirements.

5 Desire for greater shopping convenience. Changing lifestyles have dictated a need for new patterns of shopping to which, for a variety of reasons, traditional retailers have been slow to respond. With the increasing numbers of working women, for example, shopping can no longer be restricted to the normal 'daylight hours'. In the absence of conventional retailers responding to their needs, some consumers have turned to mail order catalogues, telephone marketing, and other forms of non-retail outlets to satisfy their needs. The same principle applies equally to the services sector. If the consumer wants to renew an insurance policy or pay a bill at 9 o'clock in the evening, he or she needs to access those services even if the retailers providing them are closed. Telephone response mechanisms provide the consumer with the potential of 24-hour shopping and, from the standpoint of the operator, avoids the need to invest in costly high street retail premises.

6 These have been paralleled by fundamental changes in the broader marketing environment. An important trend over recent decades has been the progressive growth of the service sector. As material standards have improved, individuals have turned to other areas to improve their lives. Services such as insurance, security and so on have directly benefited and, more importantly, have been able to utilize direct marketing approaches to achieve the most cost-effective coverage of their target consumers. The impact of direct marketing techniques can be clearly seen from the results of their application by companies such as Direct Line and their followers, which have decimated the traditional insurance brokerage business. Progressively, economic power in modern business is moving towards the service industries – and, in turn, these organizations have recognized that there is no longer the need for expensive retail outlets to service the needs of consumers.

7 The increasing costs of reaching fragmented audiences. With the increasing costs of media, and the inevitability of a high wastage factor, marketers have been encouraged to seek communications mechanics which are more precisely targeted and less wasteful. Even for a high-volume, fast-moving consumer goods product, many of the viewers of a particular television programme, for example, in which the product is advertised will not be interested in the product proposition. For slower-moving products and business-to-business propositions, the resultant wastage is likely to be considerably higher. The progressive splintering of media audiences, witnessed by the dramatic growth in all media channels, means that more sophisticated approaches need to be taken to reach the target audience in a cost-effective manner.

8 As marketing, and particularly market research techniques, have improved, it has become increasingly possible to segment markets along different lines. Because consumers are different, it is reasonable to assume that in many ways their needs, desires and aspirations will also be different. Direct marketing offers the opportunity to develop a line of communications with these identified market segments and to 'tailor' the message in ways that would not be possible using a conventional media approach.

9 The growth of the cashless society. Increasing numbers of consumers have become holders of bank accounts, credit cards and similar 'charging platforms'. These have become important in two respects. Firstly, cash is no longer the primary means of making a purchase. As more consumers become familiar with the principles of 'charging', so their patterns of purchase are likely to change. Since most cards, for example, offer the facility of spreading repayments for an expensive purchase over time, the consumer can consider making the purchase now, rather than waiting. And, as they become more familiar, they become equally more confident of the processes involved. Secondly, the possession of such charging facilities itself provides the basis for the creation of databases and the more precise targeting of prospective purchasers, since it is possible to identify previous purchases which indicate areas of interest.

10 The improvements in information technology, both in terms of computer facilities and other areas of IT, have provided the means for realizing the potential of direct marketing. The creation of databases, the processing of information, the possibility of conducting cross-analyses with other sources of information, the profiling of prospective consumers, and similar techniques are, potentially, made much easier with the widespread use of new technology. Most importantly, analyses can be conducted speedily – whilst the information is still fresh – and the prospective consumer can be contacted before his or her own situation has changed.

McCorkell (1995) suggests that there are three prerequisites for the continued growth of direct marketing:

1 The universal acceptance of direct marketing as a legitimate and logical marketing activity.
2 Widespread knowledge of its precise functions and how these dovetail with other marketing activities.
3 Availability of sufficient direct marketing physical resources and professional skills.

The advantages of direct marketing techniques

Targeting

One of the primary reasons for the increase in direct marketing techniques is the desire to target customers more precisely. By establishing a database gathered from previous customers, or profiled against the lifestyle of a typical customer, it is possible to target more effectively and profitably. The buying patterns of the customer base can be analysed and then used to seek potential customers who exhibit similar behaviour.

Some forms of direct marketing, especially those relating to direct mail, can be very precisely targeted. By accessing lists of named individuals who can be identified as having an existing interest in the market category, the advertiser can be reasonably sure that the recipients of his message will be more likely to be motivated by his offering. Business travellers, for example, can be offered, via direct marketing techniques, information on hotels, airlines, etc. which are directly relevant to their needs.

Direct marketing reaches class instead of mass. Direct response penetrates specific buyer groups (Lewis, 1992).

Relationships

A key aspect of direct marketing is the creation of relationships between the company and the prospect. Once a contact has been established, the ensuing messages can be directed and personalized to a *named individual*. The likelihood of securing a positive response is greater if the recipient of a message believes that it is geared to his or her specific needs. Each member of the target audience can be communicated with as an individual rather than as a member of a wider group. Not only can the mail piece be individually addressed, but its content can be modified to include the name, address or other details which relate strictly to the individual recipient.

In the UK, such activity has been substantially restricted to direct mail. However, advances in laser printing techniques in the United States have resulted in advertisements within specific magazines being targeted to named individuals. The USA edition of *Reader's Digest* already provides polythene bags with a personalized message to the reader printed on them. The service allows advertisers to use their databases to target areas by, for example, car dealership, bank branch or supermarket chain. The principle will be extended with the availability of videojet technology, which allows different names to be inserted into the headline or body copy of an advertisement in the magazine.

Interactivity

Unlike conventional advertising, which communicates with all prospective consumers in a somewhat indiscriminate manner, direct marketing has built-in response mechanisms which encourage a flow of information from the prospective consumer back to the manufacturer. The *feedback* of communication between the prospect and the company may be especially useful in avoiding, for example, post-purchase dissatisfaction, or identifying potential new product opportunities.

With general marketing, the communication is, in effect, a monologue. It is a one-way process in which messages are transmitted and received. But consumers are not asked or expected to engage in the communication process (Brown and Bruskirk, 1989). Direct marketing, on the other hand, asks for a response from the consumer, to participate in two-way communications.

Motivating action

Most direct marketing activity is designed to encourage a specific response, often using in-built incentive programmes. Whilst many other forms of marketing communications have a similar objective, it is the speed of monitoring the levels of response which provides direct marketing with its unique appeal to marketers.

Databases

By encouraging response, the company can build up a database of named individuals. Recognizing that many individuals will not make a purchase on their first exposure to a proposition, such individuals can be contacted at intervals with similar or varied messages in order to achieve the sales objective. Moreover, once a sale has been secured, those individuals can be re-contacted, either to encourage them to re-purchase, or to secure the purchase of another product or service from the same company.

Transactional information

Over time, it will be possible to build up specific profiles of customers. These might include, for example, the frequency of purchasing, the nature of purchases, differential responses to incentive programmes, characteristics of purchasers, and so on. Such information, which would not be available in the context of conventional marketing techniques, provides a basis for developing cost-effective sales among defined audiences.

Measurement

Because direct marketing produces a measurable response, it is possible to calculate the effectiveness of a specific campaign with a considerable degree of accuracy. Moreover, as enhancements are made to the database, it will be possible to predict levels of response to subsequent activities. Measurability is the central focus of direct marketing. It generates a response back to the advertiser; therefore the effect of any activity can be measured.

Predictability

'One of the greatest advantages of the direct mail medium is its predictability. If one has information about past direct mail efforts, then it is not only possible, but highly desirable to forecast the results of planned mailings.' (Nash, 1992)

To these can be added several other benefits which derive from the use of direct marketing techniques.

Comparatively low investment

Unlike conventional advertising, where the capital costs of both producing an advertisement and obtaining the space or time in which it will appear can be very high, the costs of direct marketing – especially direct mail – can be comparatively low. Companies can scale the level of investment to match the size of their businesses, and use the income generated to reinvest to further develop the business. Even small operators can, therefore, use direct marketing to reach their identified target audiences.

Controlled growth

Companies can develop their businesses on a progressive basis, rather than risking the potential of 'over-trading'. By limiting the number of mailings, for example, to manageable proportions, the company can ensure that it matches customer demand with an appropriate level and speed of response.

Testing

With the high degree of controllability of direct marketing, it is far easier to mount small-scale test exercises. The impact, for example, of different advertising messages, or of different mail pieces, can be assessed in advance of full-scale activity.

Costs

Whilst the costs of origination may be high, the fact that the audience can be more precisely targeted means that much wastage can be eliminated. Often, direct marketing is associated with comparatively low costs per customer purchasing.

Overall, the benefits of direct marketing can be summarized by a quote from Drayton Bird (1993):

'Direct Marketing:

- allows you to isolate someone as an individual
- allows you to build a continuing relationship with them
- allows you the ability to test and measure responses.'

The limitations of direct marketing

Image factors

In the context of the need to create and preserve the brand image, there is the potential danger of 'inappropriate' mailings or other direct marketing activities undermining the consumer's image of the brand. 'Junk mail' potentially undermines the image which may have been expensively acquired over many years through conventional media advertising. Purchase of cheap space or time may result in an inappropriate media environment. In the same way, low-cost production, especially of TV commercials, may undermine both image and response.

Content support

Advertising is, substantially, enhanced by the media environment in which it is placed. The same is not true of mail pieces, which inevitably must stand alone.

Brand familiarity

It is important to establish brand familiarity from the outset. Response levels tend to be higher when the target consumer is familiar with and confident in the brand.

Accuracy of lists

The use of the wrong list or one which has not been properly refined can serve to create a negative impact on the recipients of direct mail items. Moreover, the high costs of wastage associated with old lists adds to the overall cost of the direct marketing activity.

The importance of the database

At the heart of successful direct marketing activity is the database and, for that reason, the area is often referred to as *database marketing*. A fully functioning marketing database is a consumer database that includes both prospective and existing customers and, at its fullest range of applications, operates as a proprietary medium (Bickert, 1992).

Databases may be *internal* – created from the names and addresses of previous customers – or *external* – purchased from a third party or organization. In many cases, information may be derived from both sources.

Internal databases

Most companies have a great deal of information regarding previous customers. The primary issues are whether they bother to access this information and, if they do, whether they make the best use of the information available to them.

Almost without exception, the manufacturers of durable goods (fridges, freezers, toasters, cars, etc.) demand the return of some form of card following purchase. From the consumer perspective, the return of the registration or warranty card is the means of ensuring that they are logged on for the purpose of securing repair or replacement if the purchased product fails to perform properly during the warranty period. From the manufacturer's perspective, it is a primary means of compiling the names and addresses of the purchasers of their products and services. And, sadly, for many, that is as far as it goes. Despite the fact that these consumers have already evidenced their readiness to purchase products bearing the particular brand name, comparatively few companies recognize the importance of the marketing opportunity which this represents.

Not only does the list represent the means whereby a *relationship* can be established with existing customers, it also represents the means of selling them additional products from their range. Both of these dimensions may be of crucial importance in the longer term.

Next to a company's products or services, the mailing list is the most valuable asset. Using the database to establish a relationship with existing customers, potential difficulties which may be experienced with the product may be overcome. If, for example, some consumers find that the product does not perform as expected, they may experience dissatisfaction with the product, and make their views known to other potential purchasers. By maintaining a dialogue, the company will quickly learn of any problems and may take remedial action to minimize the impact of negative 'word of mouth'. The company may eliminate the source of these concerns by, for example, establishing a contact line where they can provide additional usage advice to purchasers. This, in fact, is a process which has been successfully adopted by many computer software companies. Even at this level, customer dissatisfaction can be minimized and those individuals converted into 'positive promoters' of the brand.

Since most companies manufacture a range of products and services, establishing a positive relationship with existing customers may be the key to achieving additional cost-effective sales to those same individuals. Moreover, by using market research to identify the elapsed period after which the consumer seeks to replace the purchase, the company can then re-contact him or her at the appropriate time to incentivize the consumer to buy from their range rather than from one of their competitors.

We need to distinguish between two forms of 'customer' who will provide information: *active* customers (those people with which the company has an ongoing relationship); and *inactive* customers (former buyers who have not purchased or responded for a defined period).

Sources of relevant information

Most companies receive a volume of unsolicited feedback, deriving from general and specific enquiries, complaints, and even letters and phone calls from satisfied users. Even at this this level, the information derived can provide valuable information to the planning process. Previous enquirers represent the opportunity of a subsequent conversion to a sale, in the same way that former 'near misses' may be encouraged to make a purchase at some future date. Past or lapsed users can provide valuable information on purchasing trends and, similarly, may be prepared to purchase again with an appropriate incentive.

The establishment of an effective and current customer database represents a valuable contribution to the process of understanding customer needs and the ability to develop the

company offering in a way that responds to those needs.

External databases

From time to time, companies need to supplement their own lists with those acquired from external sources. These range from general *compilations* (such as the electoral roll or the census) to those which are developed as the direct result of a relationship through membership of or subscription to an organization. The latter are more targeted to the extent that the list represents participation in some form of activity, which can be assessed for its relevance to the potential user. For example, a company offering some form of financial service may purchase lists of people who have previously responded to similar, but non-competitive, offers.

Although lists are widely available – a current advertisement in *Marketing Week* offers no fewer than 1500 separate lists which allow access to, for example, 551 716 people who are interested in fine art and antiques; 174 392 people who have a satellite TV; 27 979 people who have a 4 × 4 vehicle; and 108 549 who drink Heineken beer – it is vitally important to adopt a strategic approach in terms of their selection. In most instances, companies will need to use a list broker, who can provide access to a wide range of category lists, although it may be possible to deal directly with a third party organization whose database corresponds with the particular needs.

The use of external databases

Obtaining the appropriate list or lists is fundamental to the ultimate success of the campaign, and it is important to define a series of criteria to be met.

Source of list
As far as possible, it is desirable to identify the original source of the listings. This is important to avoid conflicts between the original

owner's use of the list and the purpose for which it is intended. Recently, one of the major supermarket chains was accused of releasing the names and addresses of members of its loyalty card scheme without authority. Inevitably, some recipients of third party mailings would be aggrieved that the information had been used in this way and would, potentially, reduce the effectiveness of such mailings.

At the same time, the way in which the list was originated will provide some guidance to its likely validity. For example, names and addresses of people who have *purchased* a product or service will tend to be more valuable than those collected, for example, as a result of entries to a competition.

Restrictions on use

It is important to identify any restrictions which may be applied to the subsequent use of the list by the original owners. These may cover such things as the categories of product or service for which the lists may or may not be used – to avoid offers of a directly competitive nature – or the use in certain areas which the owner deems 'inappropriate'.

When collected

The original collection date will be a guide to the accuracy of the list. The longer the time since its original compilation, the higher the incidence of 'gone aways'.

Frequency of use

If the list has been used often, this may affect the likelihood of achieving a positive response, especially if it has been used for a parallel market.

Size

It is important to dimensionalize the scale of the list. Often, small numbers may be sufficient to conduct a market test, but the overall numbers will be required to scale up the exercise to a partial or complete roll-out.

Profiling information

Many lists will contain only the titles, names and addresses of potential respondents. More sophisticated lists will be accompanied by profiling data, for example, ownership of particular goods and services; age and lifestyle details, and so on.

Other information

Apart from the obvious question of the cost of acquisition, it will be important to determine whether you will have direct or indirect access to the database, and the form in which the list will be supplied. You may wish to profile the information against your own database, or to de-duplicate lists to eliminate the possibility of more than one mailing being sent to the same individual, and so on.

Finally, you will need to identify when the list will be available to you, and on what terms. Some list suppliers, for example, discount the price to cover the cost of returns and 'gone aways', others don't! This may have a sizeable impact on the overall cost-effectiveness of the exercise.

Psychographic and lifestyle databases are increasingly becoming more sophisticated. Smaller, more precise campaigns have been found to generate a higher response compared with mass mailings to inadequately specified groups. Very precise segments can be identified by overlaying psychographic data on demographic and geographic databases, e.g. the 1991 Census.

Profiling the database

The process of profiling is an important part of gaining an understanding of the customer database. If it is possible to identify particular characteristics that customers share in common, then it is possible to apply those characteristics to other lists and, thus, identify additional targets whose potential for conversion will be greatest. There are a wide variety of profiling techniques, based upon analyses of the existing data in terms of, for example, demographic factors, location, type of housing, lifestyle characteristics, and so on. The greater the number of shared characteristics between existing customers and those names and addresses derived from other sources, the greater the potential for conversion.

Shaver (1992) identifies an approach to target audience profiling:

1 Start with your first profile, complete your analysis, and then move on to your next profile until you have analysed each profile on your list of potential customers.
2 Develop profiles of existing customers. Use database information to overlay demographic, psychographic and other special characteristics against your customer files based on their response history. In this context, attention needs to be given to the important factors of recency, frequency, monetary value and variety of products they have purchased.
3 Define each segment geographically in terms of any relevant distribution limits.
4 Use national database lists to 'locate' the different household densities of each of your customer profiles.
5 Evaluate each in terms of response potential versus cost-efficiency.

The use of the database

Once the database has been compiled, it represents a major opportunity to augment conventional marketing communications techniques. But, unlike conventional communications, the successful implementation of a direct marketing strategy is the repeated use and reinforcement of the database itself. In practical terms, it provides the ability to achieve some of the benefits of the one-to-one relationship normally associated with personal selling, without the attendant costs.

The database can fulfil important functions in two key areas. It offers a series of marketing applications, to assist in the determination of

the way, in which business is conducted; and it has a series of management applications, defining the way in which the company develops its policies.

Marketing applications

The database is a unique source of information to enable the identification of potential customers with particular needs. The analysis, for example, of previous purchasing information will enable far more precise targeting of potential consumers with a high propensity to respond to a particular type of product or service, or a particular type of offer.

These applications can be developed in a variety of different ways:

- Direct mail – selecting customers to receive appropriate offers;
- Response handling and fulfilment – recording customer responses, managing orders and despatches;
- Telemarketing – contacting selected customers (or allowing them to contact you);
- Recording the results of these contacts and initiating each step;
- Dealer, distributor and agent management systems – issuing information (e.g. names of enquirers, lists of prospects, etc.) and monitoring their performance;
- User group marketing – creating a membership scheme to provide additional benefits in return for loyalty;
- Consumer promotions – coupon distribution, redemption and analysis of results;
- Business promotions – managing sales force and customer incentive schemes;
- Credit card management – recruitment of credit card prospects, recording transactions, invoicing and promotion of ancillary offers;
- Targeted branding and sales promotion – delivering brand messages or specific promotions to prospects who are receptive or 'at risk' from competitive activity;
- Data marketing – selling or renting customer data.

Management applications

- Campaign planning – selecting customers with specific needs and identifying the kinds of offers to which they will respond;
- Campaign co-ordination – ensuring that individual campaigns run in a logical sequence rather than confronting prospects with clashing or inconsistent messages;
- Project management – managing the creation and delivery of promotional campaigns;
- Campaign productivity analysis – analysing which elements of the marketing mix are best for different customers, determining which campaigns are most successful;
- Campaign monitoring – receiving data on campaign performance in order that remedial action can be taken where necessary.

By its very nature, database marketing provides rapid feedback on the effectiveness (or otherwise) of campaign activities. By extrapolating the data it is possible to predict the ultimate achievements of the campaign, even at a very early stage. Importantly, if things are not going well, it is possible to take early remedial action to correct the situation. Moreover, it is possible to conduct regular analyses as to the individual performance of the various elements within the campaign mix. If individual components fail to deliver against targets and expectations, they can be modified without interrupting the overall campaign.

- Campaign evaluation – it follows from the above that, at the end of the campaign, specific and quantified data will be available to enable a comprehensive evaluation of all aspects of the campaign. If comparable data is available for previous campaigns, the differences in performance between these and current activities can be compared and evaluated. In this way, a long-term information source is created which will assist in subsequent campaign planning activities.

The strategic approach to direct marketing

As with other forms of strategic management, direct marketing needs to be considered in the context of the longer-term goals and objectives of the organization. The development of a cohesive and integrated direct marketing strategy follows a similar format to that of other aspects of marketing communications, and requires the sequential analysis of the organization and its environment.

We need to identify the specific *objectives* for direct marketing and, as we have seen earlier, these must be succinct, finite and measurable, agreed by all those involved in the process, and have mechanics for the monitoring and control of the activities built in. It is only at this point that we will be in possession of sufficient information to begin the process of *identifying potential strategies*.

Direct marketing, as we have already seen, provides the means whereby a relationship can be established between the company and its prospects to motivate a transaction. Thus, whilst direct marketing strategies may be similar to those of other forms of marketing communications, they are likely to be subtly different.

Most importantly, the strategic goals of direct marketing will be designed to ensure the *creation* of the most *effective database* for subsequent communications activities.

The objectives of direct marketing

Database marketing can fulfil a variety of objectives which build upon the market penetration achieved by other marketing communications tools.

Generating repeat purchase

Once the name and address of a purchaser have been captured, he or she can be re-contacted to achieve further sales of the same product. Some products will be restricted to direct marketing channels and, hence, the only opportunity to achieve additional sales will be by these means.

Recently, a number of CD and tape offers have been heavily advertised on commercial radio. Having logged a purchase, the prospect receives a series of follow-up mailings accompanied by an incentive to purchase additional 'exclusive' CDs.

It is important in this context to remember the 'Pareto principle'. This asserts that 80 per cent of revenue derives from 20 per cent of the customer base. It pays to focus on the loyal customers by providing them with a continuous incentive to purchase again and to remain loyal. Air Miles and Club Cards, such as those run by Tesco and Sainsbury's, are good examples of this device being applied. Holders of the card are given personalized membership numbers and are sent frequent newsletters and updates, with regular bonuses to reward regular customers.

New product introduction

Having established a database, it may provide the platform for the introduction of a new product or service which is likely to appeal to the same target audience. Importantly, a test campaign can be conducted with a high degree of security, and at significantly lower cost than would be associated with other testing formats.

A platform for cross-selling

As noted earlier, once a manufacturer has sold a single product or service (and assuming that the purchaser is satisfied with that purchase) the consumer can then be motivated to buy additional products from that company. The same principle applies to a supplier whose reputation rests in the selection and pricing of relevant merchandise. This may often encourage a previous purchaser to buy again. This principle is particularly appropriate to catalogue operations, such as Kaleidoscope, who have built up major business operations through direct marketing techniques.

Provide a new distribution channel

In some instances, a manufacturer will have the opportunity to create a direct distribution channel in parallel to conventional outlets. Products will continue to be available to 'all' consumers in the normal way, but the direct marketing channel will remain the exclusive preserve of the manufacturer, who can restrict competitive encroachment with the use of incentive devices.

Target minority markets

Conventional marketing communications may make the process of niche marketing unaffordable. We have already considered the high wastage factors associated with conventional media, for example. By precisely identifying niche opportunities, the manufacturer can continue to derive a profit even from comparatively small sales volumes – since the costs of achieving those sales will be far lower.

Establish loyalty

Through the establishment of a positive relationship with the consumer, the company can create a high degree of loyalty by providing additional benefits to the consumer, often not available through conventional channels. Sometimes this may involve the provision of a tangible incentive, such as a free gift or discount. In some instances, it may simply rely on periodic contact between the company and the consumer to provide additional new and relevant information. Many manufacturers create some form of 'club' for this purpose, for example, owners of particular makes of car, users of particular computers or software, etc.

Identify prime prospects

By isolating the best prospects within a database – people who spend most, or who purchase most frequently, for example – the company can direct its activities towards the achievement of the greatest return on its marketing investments.

Building relationships

The establishment of positive relationships is the primary aim of direct marketing. The process can be described as having five distinct stages.

The identification of prospects

The initial stage is to ensure the identification of prospects or, more effectively, to motivate potential purchasers to identify themselves. In many instances, a mass media approach will be used, with some built-in response mechanism. Often, although not always, an incentive to respond is also included. Most mail order catalogue companies, for example, use mainstream media to communicate their proposition and invite respondents to supply their name and address in return for some free gift together with the catalogue. A similar approach is adopted by many book clubs.

To qualify consumers

It is inevitable that not all respondents will want or be prepared to move to the second stage. Sometimes repeated activity, mailings or incentives will be required to motivate them to purchase. Where, however, consumers make an 'off the page' purchase, they are automatically qualified as future prospects. In all cases, some form of proof of initial purchase identifies the consumer as the basis for subsequent direct marketing activity.

To attract consumers

The third stage is that of increasing the consumer's knowledge of the products and services offered by the company. The Automobile Association (AA) periodically mail their members with details of merchandise and services which distinguish them from their competitors, and enhance consumers' awareness of the benefits of membership.

Other companies, such as computer software companies, mail owners with additional information to improve their image of the product. This may, for example, detail new or unusual usage which increases the reliance on the product, or it may be based on providing information about third party products which, similarly, augment the value of the base product.

To convert prospects

Here, the company targets existing users to try additional products. These may take the form of 'upgrades' on the existing product, which are offered to the existing user base at preferential prices. Recently, for example, Lotus, the makers of a wide range of software products, offered the users of any *one* of their products the opportunity to trade up to a suite of five programs at a massive saving against their individual retail prices.

Retention

The retention of existing customers is of vital importance to overall success and profitability. In all instances, customers are expensive to identify. Having found them, direct marketing affords the opportunity of developing programmes which will ensure their loyalty to the company's products or services.

A variety of mechanics can be used for this purpose. Some provide for the direct incentivization of loyalty through the offering of some form of collector device, for example, a display unit to house the items purchased. Others may offer a sequential discount, so that each subsequent purchase becomes progressively cheaper.

In the same way, 'club' magazines may provide a vehicle for both ongoing communication and incentivization. Exclusive free gifts, invitations to special events, and other forms of discount may be offered to customers to secure their loyalty in the longer term.

The essential difference between direct marketing and other forms of marketing communications exists in the use of four important elements:

1 The identification of prospects.
2 The creation of a database.
3 The ongoing management of the relationship.
4 The use of customized persuasion approaches.

Once a direct marketing programme has been established, it has all the elements of a customer loyalty programme.

Customer loyalty

The most recent trend in marketing communications has been the development of a substantial number of long-term consumer loyalty programmes, designed to attract consumers – predominantly to retail outlets – and to secure their ongoing loyalty over time. Although short-term schemes have been run for many years, it is only in the recent past that companies have adopted the premise of customer loyalty as a mainstay of their marketing programmes. In a comparatively brief period, supermarket loyalty cards have achieved high levels of both ownership and usage. Despite this, there is little evidence that they are helping stores to steal new customers or of even having a significant effect on the market share of participating outlets.

The desirability of achieving an increase in loyalty is underpinned by the findings of research conducted by Bain & Co. (reported in the *Financial Times*, 1 November 1996). Their work suggests that a 5 per cent increase in customer retention can significantly increase profitability – ranging from 25 per cent in bank deposits to 85 per cent in car servicing. A similar study by Price Waterhouse showed that a 2 per cent increase in customer retention has the same impact on profits as a 10 per cent reduction in overhead.

A survey conducted by NOP (reported in *NOP News*, December 1996) estimates that almost two-thirds of all adults have at least one card and that loyalty cards are used most frequently by heavy spenders on groceries. Some three-quarters of shoppers spending more than £75 on their main shopping trip claim to use their card every time they shop, compared with two-thirds of all card holders. However, there is less evidence of these cards having a major effect on how people choose between supermarkets, or what proportion of their shopping budget they attract. According to Pat Armstrong of NOP, 'shoppers seem to be one step ahead of the supermarkets – they take advantage of what the cards offer, but are not unduly influenced by them'. Certainly, it would appear that the fact that many people now hold multiple cards – representing membership in the loyalty schemes of competing outlets – demonstrates that such schemes are not really accelerating the process of individual store loyalty.

A further study, the Carlson Loyalty Monitor (reported in *Marketing*, 28 November 1996), was commissioned to obtain objective evidence into consumer perceptions of the top twenty-five UK loyalty schemes. Its findings make fascinating reading.

In terms of overall awareness, Tesco's Clubcard – with a claimed 8.5 million holders – was first with 66 per cent, followed by Sainsbury's Reward Card (56 per cent) and

Table 11.3 How important an influence on purchasing is the scheme?

Main influence/Important influence

BA Executive Club	74%	GM Card	23%
Forte's	65	Barclaycard	21
Diner's Club	47	Do-It-All	20
Beefeater Family	41	Homebase	19
Nat West Air Miles	41	Texas	18
Shell Smart	40	Granada	17
Mobil	33	Bhs Choice	16
American Express	27	Tesco	16
Beefeater Emerald	25	Safeway	15

Source: Carlson Loyalty Monitor, 1996

the Safeway ABC card (45 per cent). These were followed by British Airways Air Miles (38 per cent) and Mobil/Argos Premier Points and the Shell Smart Card (both with 27 per cent awareness).

However, when asked to grade how 'good' they thought each scheme was, BA Air Miles and Forte Privileges tied for first place, followed by the Beefeater Family Card and Diners Club Rewards. The bottom five (of the twenty-five surveyed) were the Sainsbury's Reward Card, Barclaycard Profiles, Do-It-All Bonus, Texas Spend & Save and Texaco All Stars.

Since a major reason for these card schemes is the encouragement of purchase, comparatively few cards appear to have a major influence on this dimension (Table 11.3). This would reinforce the NOP conclusion that, notwithstanding the fact that the companies operating loyalty schemes can achieve massive databases, from which to pursue other forms of motivation, multiple card holding by consumers reduces their direct loyalty effect.

The management of direct marketing

As with the other tools of marketing communications, the management of the process is vitally important to the achievement of overall success. The great benefit of direct marketing activity is the far greater ability to identify the outcome than in almost all other forms of marketing communications. Since all direct marketing campaigns have a response mechanism built in, the performance of the campaign can be speedily determined.

However, that benefit has a price attached. There is a far greater need for comprehensive management programmes to deal with the complexities of direct marketing. The very nature of direct marketing activity requires, in many instances, a large number of different suppliers and agencies.

To give just one example: An individual campaign might necessitate using a list broker to identify available listings; a computer bureau to conduct a profiling exercise to analyse the data against other criteria; an agency to de-duplicate the lists, which may be compiled from a variety of different sources; an agency to develop the creative proposition; perhaps a market research company to assess alternative treatments; a printer to produce the items; a handling house to effect the mailings; a fulfilment agency to ensure that consumer requests are met; and so on. And the above represents a much foreshortened version of the list of areas which must be covered and, in turn, suggests that project management itself is a vital ingredient of direct marketing activities.

The planning process

As elsewhere, the planning of direct marketing demands the adoption of a sequential process, which is depicted in a simplified form in Figure 11.1.

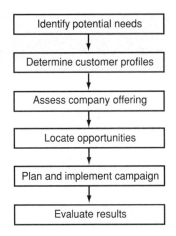

Figure 11.1

At the outset, it is important to identify the needs and wants which can be satisfied by the company's products and services. In some instances, it may be necessary to make alterations to the offering in order to ensure that it closely responds to consumer requirements. The distinctive opportunity provided by direct marketing is the opportunity to target precisely. It is, therefore, important to determine customer profiles which can be converted into market segments and new markets.

As elsewhere, it is essential to provide a point of difference between the company and its competitors. Accordingly, it will be necessary to identify the distinctive attractions and failings that the company has to its customers.

The nature of direct marketing is to enable unique offerings to different groups of potential consumers. In this context, it will be necessary to isolate emerging market segments, identify unsatisfied needs and competitive gaps and develop the propositions to respond to the separate needs. Since there will be a variety of ways in which the approach to target consumers can be made, it is important to conduct an assessment of the communications mix and potential distribution channels and to assess the real ability of the company to

service its customers. Concurrent with this will be the need to develop the specific nature of the campaign and its execution. Testing will be an important part of this stage, to determine the most impactful propositions to ensure the cost-effective implementation of the campaign.

The final stage, as with other areas of marketing communications, will be the assessment and evaluation of the results achieved. Part of the learning will have been derived from the testing stage, although it is only when the campaign is fully implemented that its real impact can be determined. And, of course, this knowledge can be applied to subsequent campaign implementations.

In this context, there are several important facets of direct marketing planning:

- Campaign design is important to effective direct marketing. It is important to remember that identifying the appropriate targets and ensuring accurate timing of the activity is as important as the campaign proposition. However powerful the message, addressing it to the wrong audience, or not ensuring that it arrives at an appropriate time, will impact negatively on the overall effectiveness of the campaign.
- The testing of all activity is especially important in direct marketing. One obvious advantage of the direct marketing approach is the comparative ease with which tests can take place.
- Direct marketing must be planned for the longer term. Often, it is necessary to plan a succession of contacts (sometimes through different media channels) in order to recruit a customer. Moreover, effective direct marketing campaigns inherently demand comparatively long lead times. To plan, test and evaluate takes time!
- Enquiries and orders must be handled efficiently and speedily to optimize customer satisfaction and to avoid the risk of dissatisfaction. This aspect of direct marketing management is vital to the establishment of long-term relationships with customers.

- Continuity of activity is an essential part of direct marketing. Activity must be planned to coincide with identified consumer needs and wants to avoid the risk of customers going elsewhere for fulfilment of their requirements.
- Analysis of results is important to achieve an enduring understanding of the elements which work effectively. The components of any campaign must be assessed individually and in conjunction to determine which worked and where improvements might be made.

As an integral part of the direct marketing planning process, it is important to assess the capabilities of the organization in a series of significant areas:

1 Order form and instructions
2 Receiving mail and telephone calls
3 Checking credit
4 Processing orders
5 Addressing and list maintenance
6 Controlling inventory
7 Billing
8 Reporting and controlling
9 Order filing and shipping
10 Handling complaints and adjustments.

It is important to recognize that it is impossible to achieve complete effectiveness in any of these areas, as the operation is substantially dependent on external factors. These will include customers, carriers and, in some instances, vendors. However, it is important to identify important deficiencies prior to the campaign commencing so that the issues can be addressed appropriately.

According to McCorkell (1995), the four cornerstones of good direct marketing practice are:

- Interaction
- Control
- Targeting
- Continuity.

Using direct marketing consultancies

The growth of the direct marketing sector has seen the parallel growth of specialist consultancies in the field. Although considerably smaller than the conventional advertising agencies alongside which they operate, the scale of some of these specialists warrants specific mention. Among the largest of these is WWAV Rapp Collins which, according to the 1997 Campaign Agency survey (*Campaign* magazine, 28 February 1997), had billings of £40.83 million. Others of substantial scale include Brann, Ogilvy & Mather Direct, and Wunderman Cato Johnson. Although many of these specialist organizations remain independent, the growth of integration has led many agency groups to develop or acquire direct marketing companies.

Alongside these are a number of more specialized companies, operating as computer bureaux, list brokers and telemarketing and fulfilment agencies. Equally, the specialism has its own professional body, the Institute of Direct Marketing. The difficulty for client companies entering the area of direct marketing is the selection of the appropriate partners with which to operate.

Dick Shaver (1992), writing in *The Direct Marketing Handbook*, suggests that effective direct marketing planning requires the establishment of a strategic planning 'core group' which can be made up of in-house specialists, consultants, freelancers and others. They should represent each of the functions of direct marketing – marketing, creative, media, financial, production, data processing, manufacturing, merchandising and fulfilment. He argues that, properly directed, this group can identify obstacles and create strategies that planning experts alone cannot.

One opportunity clients have to evaluate direct marketing agencies is to involve them in a 'live' pitch for the business. This approach was recently adopted by Racing Green, part of the Burton group, when the two short-listed agencies for the business each mounted rival campaigns on the back pages of the *You* magazine in the *Mail on Sunday*.

The use of media

It is fair to say that there are few *rules* to govern the selection of the most appropriate medium for use in a direct marketing campaign. Much will depend on a consideration of:

- the nature of the proposition;
- the nature of the target audience;
- access to targeting information.

Figure 11.2, adapted from H. E. Brown (1989), illustrates the diversity of direct marketing channels and their relationship to the business organization. The most significant of these channels are considered below (see also Table 11.4).

Television, in general terms, is a very expensive medium. The ability to target selected audiences is somewhat limited and, whilst it is capable of generating leads, the cost per contact is often quite high. However, with the advent of direct response television channels – already well established in the USA, and beginning to take off elsewhere – the situation is likely to improve.

Radio involves lower capital outlay and the facility to target is similar to, if slightly better than, that of television. Nevertheless, in general terms, the cost per contact remains at a high level.

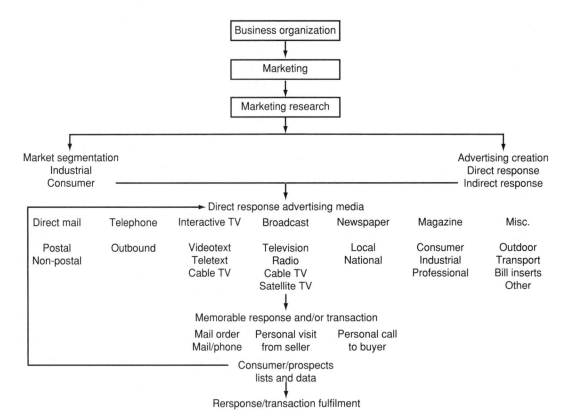

Figure 11.2   Marketing channels and their relationship to the business organization (Adapted from Brown and Bruskirk, 1989)

Print media, in its variety of forms, enables far better targeting. The existence of titles which are geared to the needs of specific interest categories ensures that the readers of such publications are, at the very least, predisposed to the product category. Provided that the appropriate titles are selected, the cost per contact can be extremely low.

Posters are of somewhat limited value. The ability to target, other than on a geographic basis, is extremely limited and, whilst the capital cost is not too great, the cost per contact is likely to be so. Despite this, it is estimated that expenditure on direct response poster ads has now reached some £45 million, with around 12 per cent of all poster campaigns having a direct response mechanism.

Public relations activities have an important role to play in this context. The placing of relevant releases with appropriate media – particularly in the press – and the building in of a response mechanism, such as a telephone number or address, is capable of generating significant numbers of enquiries. Unfortunately, the outcome is rarely predictable and the costs are, therefore, highly variable.

The two areas which are particularly responsive to direct marketing are, of course, *direct mail* and the *telephone*. Both offer extremely good potential to target precisely and, if used correctly, are very cost-effective forms of marketing communications activity.

A comparatively new medium to be considered for direct marketing is that of *door-to-door* activity. The advent of increasingly sophisticated systems based on the analysis of geodemographic data – such as ACORN and PiN, among others – has enabled more precise message targeting. This is an area which is proving to be of considerable value to fmcg products, where the opportunity to provide physical product samples and purchasing incentives to identified households is generating positive response levels.

Mail has, traditionally, been the mainstay of direct marketing. Increasingly, however, the better understanding of the media has ensured that it too can contribute to effective direct marketing campaigns. Technological advances in terms of computer technology, satellite and cable and fax machines increasingly provide new opportunities for the direct marketing planner.

Direct response TV has witnessed dramatic growth over recent years. According to Laser, the television sales house, advertisers are spending around £380 million on DRTV. DRTV ads now account for around 12 per cent of the total commercial TV audience. Laser also estimated that 16 per cent of radio campaigns contain a direct response element.

The use of market research in direct marketing

As we have seen, market research is at the centre of all effective marketing communications. Uniquely, however, in the field of database and direct marketing, direct access to existing and potential customers is already available on the database itself.

Until comparatively recently, little use was made of market research within the area of direct marketing. Perhaps because of the short-term nature of some activities, or because of the lack of recognition of the value of a database, limited efforts were made to take advantage of the potential integration with market research techniques. Some commentators have suggested that, because testing is part of the process of direct marketing, it was synonymous with market research and obviated the need for it. Indeed, for many practitioners, this still remains their position. They argue that because databases themselves are increasingly subjected to sophisticated examination and analysis, market research, and the techniques it employs, can offer little in the way of new information.

Certainly, it is true that the direct access to a database does make conducting certain *quantitative* forms of market research somewhat

Table 11.4 A comparison of major direct response media

Medium	Advantages	Disadvantages
Direct mail	Reaches all households Selectivity and personalization Most suitable for testing Most flexible Maximizes customer list income Second highest response rates	Second most expensive Long start-up time Profile analysis potential limited
Telephone	Powerful 'one to one' capability Fastest response time Selectivity Flexibility Excellent for research and profile analysis Can increase average order size substantially Highest response rates Powerful for cross- and upgrade selling	No visual appeal Highest cost per contact Telephone establishment defines reachability
Magazines	Ability to reach mass audience Ability to define target by readership Long ad life Low cost per contact Inexpensive to test Moderate lead time	Less space to tell story Less personal Slower response Less selectivity than mail or telephone
Newspapers	Shortest start-up time Fast response Wide variety of formats Broad local, regional or national coverage Inexpensive to test	Poor selectivity No personalization Rates variable Quality of reproduction and colour availability highly variable
Television	Powerful demonstration capability Fast response Wide choice of time-buying opportunities Can reach all households	Limited copy time No permanent response device Difficult to split test
Radio	High frequency Inexpensive Different profiles can be isolated by choice of station Short start-up times Powerful support medium	No response device Limited copy time No visual appeal

easier. The identification and location of target segments is simplified, as, indeed, is the access to difficult groups in conventional research terms. However, it is in the area of *qualitative* research that the usual market research procedures can provide considerable assistance.

Where, for example, there is a need to explore creative strategy or creative concepts, or to gain a deeper understanding of consumers' needs, the various qualitative approaches available to the marketer come into their own. The ability to judge consumer reactions to the various individual components of an overall proposition can be achieved far more readily, say, in the context of a group discussion. Similarly, the use of the various projective techniques can only be conducted with the direct participation of the respondent on a one-to-one or group basis.

Where the database can simplify the process is by providing speedy access to qualified respondents. Ordinarily, pre-interview procedures must be followed to identify, for example, people who have recently purchased a particular product, or who are contemplating such a purchase in the near future. Identifying

such individuals may be achieved by interrogating the database. These provide the basis of a sampling frame, with information being available about individual customers in the form of:

- name
- address
- postcode
- geodemographic code
- telephone number
- demographic and profile data
- promotion and response history
- customer value
- purchase history.

The other area in which market research procedures are normally employed, however, is that of market testing. There is little doubt that this may sometimes be carried out far more cost-effectively by conducting the test against the database directly. By extracting matched samples from the database, alternative propositions can be exposed to them and their response levels compared against each other.

Figure 11.3, taken from *The Direct Marketing Handbook*, illustrates the application of market

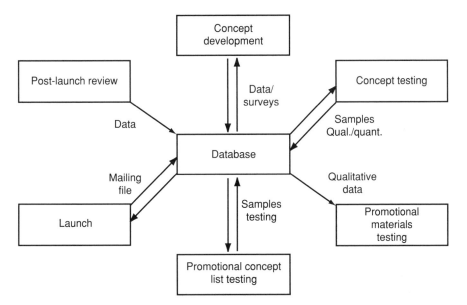

Figure 11.3 Application of market research techniques to stages of the direct marketing planning process (Adapted from Mouncey, 1995)

research techniques to the various stages of the direct marketing planning process.

The use of testing in direct marketing

Testing may be defined as

'The planned and scientific inclusion and measurement of alternative marketing elements (or combinations) in a campaign in order to improve systematically future campaign performance and profitability.'
(Forshaw, 1995)

Testing offers a comparatively low-cost approach to identifying relevant market data. Conventional market research, although relatively inexpensive, may nevertheless represent a disproportionate cost to smaller operators. Testing provides a viable alternative in these situations. It provides real information from the marketplace within a realistic environment, since potential customers are presented with a real offer or opportunity to which they must respond (or ignore). And, of course, it is relatively simple to implement. A change to the copy or layout of a direct mail piece is simple to produce and involves limited additional cost, yet may reward the investment with considerable additional revenue.

As with conventional market research, the process of testing offers a number of important advantages:

- *It reduces risk* – the investment in a test programme is comparatively small. Provided that the test sample is realistic and representative of the planned target population, a great deal of information can be derived from it. Most importantly, the costs of failure are small and the danger of losing large sums of money is avoided as a result of implementing a programme of activity without predetermining the likely outcomes.
- *It avoids the risk of alienating the customer base.* Since only a small number of customers will be exposed to the proposition, the dangers

of alienating them all with an inappropriate offer are removed.
- *It provides a means of maximizing levels of response*, since the test programme should evidence the most successful approach which, when fully implemented, is likely to generate the greatest potential revenue.
- *It may assist in the reduction of costs*, since different approaches can be tested. If these are based on less expensive formats, e.g. smaller mail pieces, less costly incentives, etc., the impact on the overall programme can be considerable.

Potential areas for testing

Direct marketing affords wide scope for the testing of products, audiences, offerings and other initiatives. The most important areas for test consideration are discussed below.

The product or service

Although, in many cases, the product or service will have been previously identified, it often remains possible to make small modifications which will enhance its attractiveness to the potential audience.

The target audience

Using different mailing lists or different media in a test environment, it may be possible to identify those potential consumers who are more likely to respond to a particular offer.

The offer

The price, terms of purchase or other incentive offered to the prospect is likely to have a major impact on the level of response. Testing affords the opportunity to check out different combinations in order to determine the one most likely to achieve the desired level of take-up.

The timing

In some cases, the seasonality of a product is immediately apparent from its nature. However, others may not be so obvious. Testing can determine the appropriate time at which an offer should be made to the target audience to elicit the maximum level of response.

The format

The nature of the mailer or advertisement may, again, have a direct bearing on the levels of response, and the opportunity to test different formats allows the user to identify the most effective route prior to the campaign commencing. Sometimes it may also be possible to determine areas of potential cost saving which will have an impact on the overall costs of the campaign.

The creative content

The nature of the proposition expressed in terms of headline and copy, layout and visual treatment, chosen typefaces and so on can, similarly, be evaluated before their full-scale implementation.

Testing techniques

As well as using conventional market research techniques (see Chapter 2), there are a variety of devices which are more specific to the field of direct marketing.

- *Grid testing.* A sample of each list is tested and the results compared.

- *List sampling.* Using every nth name on a new list, an accurate cross-sample of the entire list is obtained.
- *New magazine testing.* Many titles offer split run facilities in which it is possible to insert advertising into a small proportion of the total run.
- *Split run testing*, in which different executions are inserted in different parts of the magazine run.
- *Multiple split run* uses both of the above approaches.
- *Supplying preprints.* Many different versions of an advertisement can be preprinted and delivered to the magazine or newspaper for insertion into their regular editions.
- *Format tests* – includes colour versus black and white; large space versus small; positioning; vertical versus horizontal ads.

The application of direct marketing

According to Ogilvy and Mather (in *Marketing Director International*, Spring 1993), the application of direct marketing breaks down as shown in Table 11.5.

Table 11.5

Consumer market (% of total)	Type	Business market (% of total)
25	Lead generation	40
25	One-stage sell	10
5	Prospect follow-up	15
10	Database building	20
5	New customers welcome	–
5	Customer loyalty programme	5
25	Cross-selling	10

Financial services and mail order companies tend to be more self-sufficient in developing their own databases, which represent a source of significant competitive advantage. 'If we buy in both data and skills, we are buying what's available to everyone else. That might not be the way to get the competitive edge. Our current concern is what to do with the internally generated information' (Callingham, 1995).

Analysing direct marketing results

Response rates to any direct marketing campaign will depend on a variety of different factors: the list, the product, the offer, the creative content and the timing. However, there are a variety of 'standard' bases on which to assess the performance of any direct marketing campaign. The most important of these are:

- Cost per enquiry;
- Response values;
- Conversion values;
- Cost per order;
- Average order values;
- Test results by cell;
- Repeat order values;
- Renewal ratios;
- Returns.

The Direct Marketing Information Service recently conducted a survey of direct marketing users which provides the basis of effectiveness comparisons across a variety of direct media outlets (Table 11.6).

The same research also provides information on the response rates by action requested (Table 11.7).

Table 11.6   Response rates by sector and medium

Medium	Number of campaigns	Response rate	Cost per item (pence)	Cost per response (£)	Average campaign size (000's)
Consumer campaigns					
Direct mail	613	7	43	6	184
Door drops	36	2	12	6	888
Press	22	0.2	2	10	1260
Inserts	27	0.8	6	8	552
Business campaigns					
Direct mail	628	4	64	16	215
Door drops	4	0.05	4	80	343
Press	30	0.25	20	80	128
Inserts	30	1	8	8	62

Source: DMIS

Table 11.7 Response rates by action requested

Action	Consumer			Business		
	Response rate (%)	Cost per item (pence)	No. of campaigns	Response rate (%)	Cost per item (pence)	No. of campaigns
Give coupon to retailer	24	68	22	0.86	30	5
Free event	18	55	5	6	157	16
Questionnaire	15	81	11	12	66	14
Free trial	14	181	9	9	58	9
Visit store	9	42	22	9	153	2
Order without payment	7	50	54	3	50	149
Donation	6	36	69	0.1	80	1
Order with payment	5	39	283	1.5	34	112
Request further information	5	29	136	5	67	363
Prize draw	4	38	77	8	167	

Source: DMIS

Business-to-business activity

Although direct marketing techniques are increasingly being applied to consumer goods and services, they are especially relevant to the business-to-business area. Indeed, to a far greater degree, business-to-business marketing relies on the underlying mechanics of direct marketing as a key platform for marketing communications. There are a number of reasons which serve to explain this situation.

Identification of contacts

In many instances, the sales universe for business products is comparatively small. Often, we are talking about thousands of potential customers (or even hundreds) against multiple millions for most consumer goods. It is thus relatively easy to identify – by name and title, in many cases – the individual targets for a business-to-business proposition.

Sales force size

Few business-to-business organizations maintain large sales forces. In some cases, the number of representatives is in low single figures. Accordingly, some mechanism is required to maximize their effective strike rate. Maintaining conventional contact with potential purchasers would otherwise be extremely hit and miss, or over a very extended time frame.

The need to create/reinforce awareness

The interval between purchases may be extremely long, and relationships with alternative suppliers may be quite strong. In this context, organizations need to ensure cost-effective contact with potential purchasers over an extended time period to maintain an awareness of their company and its products at a reasonable level.

The decision-making unit

In many company purchasing decisions, it is unusual that a single person will have the necessary authority to arrange the purchase. Often there will be several people, fulfilling different functions within the organization, who will all contribute to the decision-making unit. Each of them will need to be exposed to the product or service proposition, and it is quite likely that they will require different aspects of the offering to be detailed. Some, for example, will be interested in the performance of the product itself; others in the financial aspects of the proposition; yet others in the technical aspects of integration with existing machinery or materials; and so on.

For many organizations, direct marketing represents the most cost-effective solution to their marketing communications requirements. In this context, direct marketing can ensure:

1 Cost-effective lead generation, by maintaining regular contact with potential purchasers and prospects.
2 Corporate and product awareness, by targeting specific messages which are 'tailored' to the needs of named individuals or job functions.
3 A more effective sales visit, by ensuring that prospects have pre-awareness of the proposition – and may be motivated to request a sales call.

Non-profit organizations

Direct marketing can offer similar benefits to non-profit organizations, where the cost per response may be the key to their long-term financial survival. With the exception of the very largest charitable bodies, non-profit organizations have extremely limited budgets to support their communications activities. Moreover, the nature of their message may have a highly specific appeal to comparatively small numbers who comprise their target audience.

Here again, the ability to reach small sectors of the population, or individuals who possess certain characteristics, may be the critical factor in effective communications campaigns. Existing databases may be interrogated to ensure consistency against the defined criteria to maximize the response rate. Often, the message itself requires detailed communication, which would otherwise not be possible within the bounds of conventional media.

Finally, direct marketing, and particularly direct mail, can be more readily controlled within limited financial constraints. Even where a large list of potential contacts exists, a non-profit organization may not have the funds to finance the mailing to them all. A small proportion can, thus, be mailed in the first instance, and the revenue generated by the mailing used, in part, to fund subsequent activity.

Relationship marketing

Over the past few years, marketers in many sectors of the economy have been talking about the merits of relationship marketing. Uncles (1995) suggests that 'firstly, it is about knowing your customers (your intermediaries or distribution channels) and consumers (your end users); secondly, it is about forming a partnership with these customers and consumers, with constant backwards and forwards information flows'. In the short term, the task is to get to know the customers, with the longer-term aim of delivering customer satisfaction and securing loyalty. However, many manufacturers continue to have a trade focus rather than an integrated trade and consumer focus built around category management.

There are several questions to be asked. To what extent is extra loyalty secured by investing in relationships? Are the needs of all of the customers being met, or just those of a privileged few? Would customers rather buy on price and basic delivery?

Relationship marketing embraces database and direct marketing on the consumer side and partnership management on the trade side. It concerns the attraction of customers, and the development and retention of customer relationships.

One aspect of relationship marketing that seems to be agreed upon is that it has continuity as a characteristic. Gronroos (1991) described marketing as taking place along a time continuum; therefore, focus should not be placed on individual, discrete transactions but on the continual development of a relationship over time. Noordewier, *et al.* (1990) also believe that there should be expectations of a continuity of a relationship which proposes that there will be a possibility of future interactions between two companies or individuals.

The relationships that are established should have definite aspects of co-operative communications and, therefore, try to establish closeness between firms and the achievement of relationship-specific goals. Rather than buyers and sellers conducting a series of transactions over a period of time, there should be long-term orientations, with the likelihood of future exchanges (Ganesan, 1994).

The position is effectively summarized by Keith Holloway, the Commercial Director of Grand Metropolitan:

'The notion of the consumer as an active participant in the brand rather than a passive recipient is, in my opinion, no longer a future hypothesis but a present day fact. The implications for everyone concerned with brand marketing are far reaching.'

Integrating direct marketing

The fundamental need, as we have already seen, is to ensure the total and complete integration of all marketing communications activities.

The potential consumer cares little about the source of the message, only its content. And, even then, he or she will give only scant attention to what the company has to say about its products or services. The imperative must be to achieve the most cost-effective communication of the message to the target audience using the appropriate vehicles for its communication.

'It follows that when all your advertising – both in direct and mass media – works to the same strategy, you gain greater consistency of tone and design. What's more, when direct and general advertising work together, both sales and awareness increase.'
(Ogilvy and Mather)

In this sense, therefore, the selection of the techniques of marketing communications must be based entirely on their appropriateness for the task and their ability to deliver against the defined objectives. There is a need for integration of direct marketing techniques with other marketing activities. If a mailshot is to be used in a support role, it must integrate the brand and the message into a creative piece that reflects the advertising.

The underlying stimulus for the growth of relationship marketing has been an increasing recognition of the benefits it can deliver. Buttle (1996) suggests that these are two-fold. Firstly, there is the need to recognize that it is more expensive to win a new customer than to retain an existing one. Secondly, the longer the relationship between the company and the customer, the more profitable is the relationship for the firm. Relationship marketing places an emphasis on calculating the 'lifetime values' of a customer, rather than simply considering individual transactions.

'Integrated Direct Marketing seeks to maintain contact with the customer at multiple points during the sales cycle and throughout the long-term relationship to ensure on-going effective communications including:

1 pre-sale contact to determine the needs, interests and preferences of prospects and customers
2 precise integrated communications during the sales process that are designed for ever increasing focus on customers' requirements, and

3 on-going communications to maintain the customer relationship – as customers' needs change – whether a sale has been closed or not.'
(Roman, 1995)

International direct marketing activity

Direct marketing has a unique ability to achieve cross-border communications, especially through the use of targeted direct mail and the use of the telephone. As Europe heads towards greater commercial and political union, integrated markets play an increasingly important role. Direct marketing is well established as an advertising medium in many European countries, and its use continues to grow.

Table 11.8 European receipt of direct mail per head of population, 1995/1996

Switzerland	108
Germany	103
Belgium*	87
The Netherlands*	75
Sweden	67
France*	64
Norway*	56
Finland	50
United Kingdom	50
Denmark*	40
Ireland	22
Spain**	21
Portugal	14
Poland	1
European average	57

*1995 data
**1994 data
Source: Postal Direct Marketing Service

Variations in the receipt of direct mail between countries is understandable (Table 11.8). For many years, some European countries have not had the options available to them. Legal restrictions on the use of personal data also vary from country to country and have influenced the development of the European direct marketing market.

Clearly, large variations exist between countries in terms of their response levels to direct marketing. Moreover, for the most part, direct marketing activity continues to operate on a national rather than on an international level. Nevertheless, it is clear that a major opportunity exists for the expansion of direct marketing techniques as the processes themselves achieve better understanding and as knowledge grows as to the response to these techniques within different markets. Already, the availability of satellite channels, which are beamed consistently throughout Europe, or separately throughout Asia, have brought with them the opportunity to achieve direct response messaging throughout several countries simultaneously.

As elsewhere, however, the vital need is to ensure an adequate understanding of the consumer in these diverse markets. Only in this way can we isolate those areas which are held in common in order to ensure the effective communication of a constant message which will be received in different countries and cultures.

References

Bickert, J., Database Marketing – An Overview, in *The Direct Marketing Handbook*, Nash, E. L. (editor in chief), 2nd edition, McGraw-Hill, 1992

Bird, D., *Commonsense Direct Marketing*, 3rd edition, Kogan Page, 1993

Brown, H. E. and Bruskirk, B., *Readings and Cases in Direct Marketing*, NTC Business Books, 1989

Buttle, F. (ed.), *Relationship Marketing: Theory and Practice*, Paul Chapman Publishing, 1996

Callingham, M., 'Tight Focus for a Close Up View', *Marketing*, 13 July 1995

Forshaw, T., Testing – The Direct Route to Continuous Improvement, in *The Handbook of Direct Marketing*, IDM, 1995

Ganesan, S., 'Determinants of Long Term Orientation in Buyer/Seller Relationships', *Journal of Marketing*, April 1994

Gronroos, C., *The Marketing Strategy Continuum: Towards a Marketing Concept for the 1990s*, Management Decision, 29(1), 1991

Lewis, H. G., *Direct Marketing Strategies and Tactics*, Dartnell Corporation, 1992

McCorkell, G., 'Direct Marketing – A New Industry or a New Idea', *The Practitioners' Guide to Direct Marketing*, The Institute of Direct Marketing, 1995

Mouncey, P., Using MR for Better Direct Marketing, in *The Direct Marketing Handbook*, IDM, 1995

Nash, E.L., *The Direct Marketing Handbook*, 2nd edition, McGraw-Hill, 1992

Noordewier, T. G., George, J., Nevin, J. R., 'Performance Outcomes of Purchasing Arrangements in Industrial Buyer/Vendor Relationships', *Journal of Marketing*, October 1990

Ogilvy and Mather, *Never Sell to a Stranger*, · DM Information Pack

Roman, E., *Integrated Direct Marketing*, NTC Business Books, 1995

Shaver, D., in *The Direct Marketing Handbook*, Nash, E. L. (editor in chief), 2nd edition, McGraw-Hill, 1992

Uncles, M., 'Branding – the Marketing Advantage', *Journal of Brand Management*, August 1995

Additional reading

Bird, Drayton, *Commonsense Direct Marketing*, 3rd edition, 1993, Kogan Page

The Practitioner's Guide to Direct Marketing, 1995, The Institute of Direct Marketing

Brown, H. E. and Bruskirk, B., *Readings and Cases in Direct Marketing*, 1989, NTC Business Books

Nash, Edward L. (ed.), *The Direct Marketing Handbook*, 2nd edition, 1992, McGraw-Hill

Roman, E., *Integrated Direct Marketing*, 1995, NTC Business Books

Fairlie, Robin, *Database Marketing and Direct Mail*, 1990, Exley

Christopher, Martin, Payne, Adrian and Ballantyne, David, *Relationship Marketing*, 1991, Butterworth-Heinemann

McKenna, Regis, *Relationship Marketing*, 1991, Century Business

Buttle, Francis (ed.), *Relationship Marketing: Theory and Practice*, 1996, Paul Chapman Publishing

Public relations

- To provide definitions of public relations;
- To distinguish between public relations and advertising;
- To consider the advantages of public relations;
- To examine the strategic dimensions of public relations;
- To gain an insight into the functions of public relations;
- To identify the audiences for public relations;
- To demonstrate an understanding of the management of public relations;
- To learn about using public relations consultancies;
- To become familiar with public relations campaign development;
- To explore the evaluation of public relations;
- To investigate the tools of public relations.

Public relations represents an important part of the overall marketing communications mix. Its functions are both wide and varied and, to some degree, there is an inevitable overlap with other parts of the mix. Many public relations executions take on a sales promotion format, for example. A newspaper-based competition designed to create awareness of a new product might originate from either a sales promotion agency or a public relations consultancy.

Whilst this may seem like a semantic distinction, it is important from the perspective of the management of the overall communications programme. Irrespective of the source of the idea, who should be responsible for its implementation and evaluation? These issues, together with the overall functions of public relations and the contribution that it can make towards achieving an effective communications programme, will be explored within this chapter.

Public relations is the dimension of communications which is specifically concerned with establishing and enhancing goodwill between an organization and the various publics with which it seeks to communicate. Although sometimes used independently, more often PR is integrated with other aspects of the promotional mix, for example, advertising, sales promotion or personal selling.

The Institute of Public Relations (IPR) defines public relations as:

'the deliberate, planned and sustained effort to establish and maintain mutual understanding between an organisation and its publics.'

The Public Relations Society of America adopts a broader-based definition and, more importantly, identifies a series of specific functions relating to public relations:

1 Anticipating, analysing and interpreting public opinion, attitudes and issues which might

impact, for good or ill, on the operations and plans of the organization.

2 Counselling management at all levels with regard to policy decisions, courses of action and communication.

3 Researching, conducting and evaluating, on a continuing basis, programmes of action and communication to achieve informed public understanding necessary for the success of the organization's aims.

4 Planning and implementing the organization's efforts to influence or change public policy.

5 Managing the resources needed to perform the functions of public relations.

It is important to make a distinction between public relations and *publicity*. In simple terms, publicity may be any form of information from an outside source used by the news media. It is largely uncontrollable, since the source of the news item will have little control over how and when the story will be used and, most importantly, on how it will be interpreted. Although much of public relations is concerned with the gaining of publicity, not all publicity derives from public relations. The responsibility of public relations is to create and influence publicity in such a way as to have a positive impact on the company for which the activity is undertaken.

A comparison between public relations and advertising

The goals of advertising and PR are somewhat different. The primary goal of advertising, as we have already seen, is to inform and persuade consumers in relation to a specific product offering. The primary goal of PR is to establish goodwill, and to develop favourable attitudes and an understanding of the organization and its products or services.

A major distinction between advertising and PR is the credibility of the alternative routes to message delivery. PR messages are included in media vehicles as news stories and are, as a result, somewhat more credible than advertising. Advertising is inherently based upon the self-interest of the organization placing it and paying for the exposure. The consequence is that it is approached with a greater degree of scrutiny and is often discounted by the reader or viewer. PR messages, on the other hand, are not immediately apparent as such. They appear as editorial content within a newspaper, magazine or television segment and are often seen as 'independent' of the company which originated them. The consequence is that PR stories are less likely to be viewed cynically and are likely to be more acceptable to the intended public.

In the 'soap wars' – the battle between Procter & Gamble and Lever Bros. over the efficacy of Persil Power and the alleged damage it did to clothing – PR was a major component of the communications activity. An aggressive campaign was mounted by P&G, securing coverage in all major media outlets. The impact on the sales of the Lever product was dramatic and, ultimately, the product was withdrawn at massive cost to the company.

In many respects, the story carries the apparent endorsement of the media vehicle which carries it and, hence, is viewed with greater credibility. Moreover, the nature of the media vehicle can actually enhance the value of a public relations message. If the vehicle inherently has a high degree of credibility, then the messages it conveys will tend to be viewed in a similar light. If, for example, a charitable activity is featured prominently within a national television news programme, that activity effectively receives the 'endorsement' of the television station.

A further issue is the relative cost of using advertising as opposed to public relations. The former is paid for on an insertion-by-insertion basis – and often, as we have seen, the associated costs of media space or airtime, together with production costs, are high. In general, public relations stories appear without a direct media cost to the company which originated them. However, this should not be taken to imply that PR is free. Far from it. The public relations company will charge fees for the services which it provides to its clients, and there will be associated costs, often at a high level.

Against these obvious advantages, there are also a number of shortcomings associated with the public relations route. Unlike advertising, where the nature and content of the message (subject to obvious legal and regulatory constraints) is entirely within the control of the initiating company, a public relations message is uncontrollable. Once the message has been conveyed to the media, it is the latter who will determine whether the message will appear at all and, if so, in what form. There is certainly no guarantee that the message will appear in its original form. Often, the medium will modify the story even to the point of changing the intention of the message, and this is entirely outside the control of the company.

In February 1997, British Airways orchestrated a massive PR campaign to celebrate the anniversary of Concorde with a 'giveaway' of flights at a cost of £10. The company established a dedicated phone number in conjunction with BT and, initially at least, both widespread and positive publicity was created. Undeniably, the campaign received significant impact, with the number of calls to the line estimated to be in excess of 30 million. Subsequently, however, the promotion attracted adverse publicity when it was discovered that two BT staff members, who were working on the installation of the dedicated line, had managed to connect with the number ahead of the millions of other callers (the chances of which were estimated at over 25 million to one!). Questions were raised by MPs in the House of Commons, and the BBC devoted a segment of one of its consumer programmes to the activity.

Again, unlike advertising, which seeks to communicate directly with the desired target audience, PR must appeal simultaneously to at least two audiences. In order for the story to receive any form of exposure, it must first motivate the recipient within the media organization in which it is hoped that the message will appear. Only if it achieves this goal will a message in any form actually be seen.

Other benefits of public relations

PR is comparatively inexpensive since, as noted above, there is no direct media cost. By the same token, associated production costs are often extremely low, consisting in many instances of a press release and an accompanying photograph. In many instances, a public relations campaign can achieve substantial effect for relatively little cost.

IBM achieved a significant world-wide impact with a PR campaign to 'prove' that they can produce a computer capable of beating the world's best at chess. The latest contest between Gary Kasparov and IBM's 'Deep Blue' cost an estimated $5 million in publicity, prizes and the cost of putting the computer and its program together. It has been estimated that the campaign received over $100 million worth of media exposure.

PR has a greater degree of credibility.

PR can often cut through the surrounding 'noise'. Whilst a consumer may choose to ignore a paid-for message initiated by a company, he or she may actively seek information which derives from a public relations source. Major periodicals often run feature articles on new products, recipes and restaurants which will be read by a wide variety of potential consumers. The recent launch of *Stuff* magazine provides an ideal vehicle for the exposure of any new high-tech product, whilst most newspapers and magazines carry regular recipe columns which feature branded items as an integral part of their message.

Virgin mounted an extensive PR campaign to launch the creation of its equity fund. The coverage received created both a high level of awareness and demand for its financial services.

Public relations can address issues outside conventional marketing. In many instances, public relations can communicate directly with audiences with messages which would be less effective in an advertising environment. For example, it might seek to communicate specific company values to interest or activist groups in order to ensure their understanding of the company role; it might seek to persuade potential investors or analysts of the current and future prospects of the organization; it might seek to involve local communities and influential groups such as local government with the aims and ambitions of the company, and so on.

Recently, Tesco embarked on a charity funding operation designed to reinforce its green credentials. The company funded a £100,000 campaign by the RSPB to save the skylark. Its outlets were involved at a local level and the Tesco Club Card was used to promote the charitable association to its 7 million members. Importantly, the scheme received the backing of both the Department of the Environment and the Agriculture Ministry.

PR may be the only cost-effective means of reaching some audiences. Most organizations will need to communicate with a wide variety of different audiences on many different levels. The cost of mounting an advertising campaign, for example, in all of the appropriate media required to reach these groups might be totally unaffordable. PR can be used to reach small, discrete audiences both effectively and cost-efficiently. Small retail outlets can often gain coverage in local newspapers for a new opening or some other activity which is likely to arouse local interest.

PR can be used to publicize a company's name and reputation. This is clearly seen at times of awards, e.g. the Queen's Award to Industry. The recipients of these and other awards engage in a dialogue with the media at both national and local level to create additional awareness of the receipt of the award, with the objective of enhancing the company reputation.

PR agencies will often be engaged to produce a wide variety of printed material both for internal and external use. These will include such items as brochures and booklets, specific reports on topics of wider interest, together with in-house periodicals focusing on issues of relevance to the company and its publics. Similarly, the PR agency or consultancy will often be used to edit employee publications, newsletters and similar items. Specialist publications, which often have great significance for the interpretation of a company's performance, such as annual reports and other management communications, will often be prepared in conjunction with external specialist PR advice.

At a somewhat lower level, although no less important in the context of communicating information about the company, will be the preparation of press releases, reports, booklets, articles for placement in specialist trade or more general magazine titles, the preparation of film sequences for inclusion in other programmes, the development of radio and television copy, together with a wide range of technical material which can be disseminated on behalf of the company.

Often, public relations involves the creation of special events, either to provide a vehicle for direct communication to others, or through those third parties to wider audiences. Such events would include press gatherings, open houses, fashion shows, etc. The Mercury Music Awards generates substantial publicity directed towards the target audience as a result of the extensive TV and other media coverage of the event. Similarly, Sony's involvement in the music industry is underpinned by its own awards ceremony.

An increasingly important role is the identification of stories which might attract interest, and the development of speeches for others to communicate those issues relevant to the organization. And, importantly, the PR function involves the development of continuous and consistent programmes of activity involving some or all of the above areas.

Public relations can deliver against a wide variety of objectives:

- Increase awareness of the company;
- Increase awareness of the brands or services provided by the organization;
- Reinforce the business objectives of the organization;
- Identify and explain company policy;
- Provide a focus of attention on those issues which are important to the company;
- Encourage external debate on those issues;
- Help to change opinions to those which are favourable to the organization;
- Assist the process of changing attitudes towards the organization and its operations;
- Create positive attitudes towards the company's products and services;
- Help in the building of the reputation of an organization;
- Motivate staff and enhance the recruitment process;
- Help restore the credibility of a company, particularly after some specific crisis;
- Reinforce the marketing and sales efforts;
- Build upon or change purchasing behaviour.

Speaking at the 1994 conference on 'Building Brands Through PR', Peter Gummer, the Chairman of Shandwick PR, suggested three areas in which public relations can make a contribution to brand strategy:

1 *Topicality* – linking the product with news events as they occur. For example, a survivor on a recent attempt to climb Mount Everest stated that he owed his survival to a Mars Bar. A PR campaign ensured that this fact received widespread publicity in many of the most important media outlets.
2 *Credibility* – PR offers the implied endorsement of a third party commentator.
3 *Involvement* – creating interactive opportunities.

The functions of public relations

PR may, at different times, fulfil a variety of different functions. The following section identifies some of the most important aspects of public relations but, undoubtedly, there will be a number of other activities which might be added.

Opinion forming

An increasing thrust of contemporary society is the development of opinions concerning governmental policies, the activities of companies and organizations, and other aspects beyond the nature of the products and services which those companies produce. To the extent that companies operate within the bounds of public attitudes, it is likely that the products they manufacture will be well received (or at least favourably considered). The converse, however, is equally true.

Organizations must increasingly recognize that they cannot sit idly by ignoring the underlying attitudinal changes which are taking place within society. In fact, it is increasingly important that they take a proactive approach to shape and form those opinions. Whilst few would doubt that positive moves to protect various aspects of the environment will improve society in general, the desire for rapid change (beyond, say, the state of technological knowledge) may impact unfavourably on an organization's performance. A prime example of public opinion being shaped by PR activities in this context is the work of The Body Shop. Not only has the reputation, standing and, ultimately, the profitability of the organization been shaped by favourable PR, it has also fundamentally affected consumer attitudes towards the product category in general.

To counter the possible dangers, companies must continuously seek to demonstrate, for example, how they are responding to these environmental pressures, but, at the same time, ensure that the various publics are made aware of the possible consequences of the abandonment of current technology.

Counselling senior management

More and more companies are recognizing that all aspects of their internal and external actions are likely to have an impact on the public perceptions of their organizations. Senior management must be continuously aware that they need to frame their activities in a way that makes them, as far as possible, both socially and politically acceptable. Public relations counselling can make an important contribution not only in the way that companies behave, but in the way that they communicate their activities.

The recent adverse publicity which has surrounded the departure of a number of senior managers with multi-million-pound pay-offs has, for example, resulted in a number of organizations giving careful consideration to the remuneration packages paid to management.

Liaison with public officials

Many decisions which affect the company require either the positive decision of local and national officials or, at least, their tacit acceptance. Maintaining close and realistic relationships with local and central government officials and other regulatory bodies is a key dimension of positive public relations.

Communications policies

As we will see in Chapter 14, dealing with corporate communications, it is not just the specifics of communication which must be addressed, but also the framework in which such communications activity takes place. Public relations, therefore, is a key management function which, potentially, can influ-

ence all aspects of the organization's internal and external communications. The image and identity of an organization is increasingly recognized as a vital dimension of its commercial well-being.

Years of carefully planned public relations activities for Shell, designed to foster an image that the company adopted a socially responsible policy, were undermined by its poor communications policy towards the destruction of its Brent Spar oil rig in the North Sea. The consequence was a consumer boycott in Germany and shareholder disenchantment in the UK. The very nature of Shell's social policies has been further challenged by shareholder moves to make the company respond to their demands for an external social audit.

Community relations

No organization exists in isolation of the various communities within which it exists. Like other aspects of its operations, these are multi-dimensional. On one level, the company operates within a localized environment. It is simultaneously an employer, and the source of local income and wealth; it is the user of a variety of resources, which may affect community life. The siting of a manufacturing plant may, for example, result in heavy lorries having to travel down narrow country lanes – possibly to the detriment of local residents.

It may be the source of a variety of community benefits, which enhance its reputation in the immediate area – the traditional provision of clubs and other facilities enhanced the early reputation of companies such as Cadbury's and others. However, the recent decision of Renault to move part of its production from Belgium to Spain resulted in protest and bad press throughout Europe.

It will often possess membership of trade and similar organizations, which will respond variously to the activities of the company in relation to other members. And, in an international context, the company may serve as the 'representative' of the national identity in the countries in which it operates.

In-house activities

Most companies recognize the need to maintain positive relationships with all members of staff. Rather than distancing management, the role of public relations will be to explain and secure support for the variety of management decisions which will be taken. Often, the organ for such communications will be some form of in-house journal, designed to create a bond between the people who work within the organization.

Product or service publicity

The external perception of public relations is its involvement with the creation of publicity for the products and services which the company provides. Whilst this is, undeniably, an important aspect of public relations, it is only one dimension of PR activity. Nevertheless, the area of product placement, which will be dealt with more fully in the next chapter, has expanded rapidly, recognizing the importance of the broader context in which products are seen by potential consumers.

Financial activity

To varying degrees, companies are dependent on the interpretation of their activities – positive or negative – by financial analysts, to secure additional funding, or to maintain the value of their shares. Public relations can seek to maintain and improve these relationships and ensure that the financial sector is provided with relevant and appropriate information upon which to base their judgements.

The dramatic growth in the number of public flotations and management buyouts has been paralleled by the growth in the development of specialist agencies to handle the financial aspects of public relations. Many of these consultancies also play an active part during hostile take-overs, when the development of the attitudes of fund managers may play a significant part in the company's ability to defend its ownership.

Media relations

The appearance of positive publicity for a company or organization does not happen by chance. Invariably, it is the result of carefully nurtured relationships between the various media and the company over a long period of time. Journalists, like others, are people with opinions. How they interpret a press release, for example, will be affected by the underlying views of the organization responsible for creating the release. Even positive news may be interpreted negatively, if the opinions held towards the company are unfavourable.

Event management

An increasingly important aspect of public relations activity is the management of events, either on a local or national basis. Most often, such events are used to create positive relationships between the company and one or more of its target audiences, often of an informal nature. The company may, for example, invite staff, key suppliers, retailers or others to some 'entertainment' event during which social relationships can be established to reinforce the day-to-day business relationships which exist.

Business sponsorship

A similarly important area of activity is that of creating business sponsorships which serve to associate the company with some specific activity, designed to enhance the image associations of the organization. Inevitably, there is some degree of overlap between this and the previously mentioned area, although they may well be separate and distinct.

The 'publics' of public relations

It is clear that public relations programmes relate to a variety of different audiences, each of which may represent a different role in terms of the effectiveness of the overall campaign. It should be remembered that not all publics will be important at the same time, and part of the public relations process must be to identify and prioritize the specific audiences for a particular campaign message. In the planning of a public relations campaign, any or all of the following may be targeted as recipients of the desired message.

Employees and potential employees

The success of any organization depends, to a substantial degree, on the contribution of its current employees and the extent to which it can attract potential recruits to fill vacancies which may arise. If the former group are to be effectively motivated, they must be made aware of the broad direction that the company is seeking to take and, importantly, the success it achieves. Bearing in mind that all employees communicate both internally and externally, it is vitally important that the company ensures that what they say accurately reflects the stance of the organization in the broader environment. There is little doubt that properly motivated employees at all levels contribute more effectively to the company than those who are disenchanted.

Any organization has a variety of tools at its disposal to communicate internally. Many organizations, for example, maintain a regular 'house' magazine, which provides a suitable communication vehicle for the dissemination of information on a wide variety of issues. This is particularly important as organizations grow in size and the employees become more dispersed, either around the country or the world. Articles might include successes achieved by the company, personnel changes, information on the products and services which the company produces, indeed, anything which serves to enhance knowledge about the company and to foster a strong

sense of involvement and a community spirit. At times of change, when, for example, the company is involved in restructuring or merger discussions, such a publication provides a means for senior management to communicate their views and to assist in the maintenance of morale. Other companies use periodic newsletters for the same purpose, together with information posted on internal notice boards.

Similarly, the broader-based reputation of the company will assist it in its task of attracting suitably qualified candidates for recruitment at all levels. Once again, the availability of published information about the organization in the form of news releases, press cuttings, even on the Internet, will ensure that the candidate has adequate knowledge regarding the company which seeks to employ him or her.

Shareholders and investors

A large number of companies rely on the publication of the annual report and the publicity it receives as the primary communications device between themselves and their shareholders or investors. However, this knowledge can be enhanced substantially by maintaining more regular contact to ensure the development of an appropriate relationship. Many companies communicate through newsletters and other devices, and develop incentives to ensure the maintenance of loyalty. These may take the form of discounts, for example, off the company's products or services to establish a stronger bond and a greater feeling of involvement.

Large, publicly quoted companies will maintain regular contact with important City and institutional investors, informing them of their plans for the future and designed to encourage their active support.

Suppliers to the company

The maintenance of good relationships with suppliers is equally important. Often, suppliers are the source of important new product ideas, packaging innovations and the like, and they will tend to favour those organizations with which they have close associations. Moreover, at times of change, suppliers will tend to be more loyal to those companies which have treated them well in the past.

Distributors of the company's products and services

As with suppliers, the development of positive relationships is vitally important to the smooth running of the company's functions. Although basically motivated by commercial factors, distributors will often remain loyal to companies through difficult times if they have worked well together in the past.

Equally important in this context is the fact that distributors are often the external ambassadors for the organization (as much as the company's own sales force). What they say about the company and its products or services will have a bearing on its performance in the marketplace.

Buyers and consumers

It is often stated that people 'buy' companies, just as much as the products they produce. Establishing a positive reputation is vitally important for continued success. Danone reinforces the positioning of its brands in France with a nutritional underpinning. The Institut Danone conducts nutritional research and provides a freephone customer line which gives advice on food and nutrition. In addition, the company has a customer magazine with a print run of 2 million.

The local community

The community at large needs to be made aware of the positive contribution that the organization makes towards its well-being. This may be in terms of investment within the community, the provision of employment and similar factors. In general, companies which work well as part of the community in which they exist tend to receive a greater level of support, for example, when seeking to expand premises, achieve local investment and so on.

The national community

The same principles apply to operating on a national level. In many instances, companies need to secure governmental support for the enactment of legislation which will favour the company, or to achieve tax changes which will enhance its commercial prospects.

Opinion formers

Relationships with pressure groups and other influencers can serve to enhance or restrict a company's performance. The provision of information about the way in which the company conducts its business, or its stance on societal and environmental issues, for example, may well be used to reinforce or improve the relationships.

The media – local, national and international

The establishment of positive relationships with media channels is a vital part of the overall public relations function, since they represent the means by which the organization may be able to communicate with its other publics. Many companies create a regular dialogue, even when there is no major news story to tell, to ensure that they have access to the media when the need arises. The nature of the audiences will, similarly, depend on the nature of the organization's activities. A large commercial company will, at different times, seek to communicate with some or all of those listed above. A smaller company may have a narrower base against which to target its message. A charity, similarly, will generally seek to influence a somewhat more limited group of publics. As with a commercial organization, these will include those who work for the body; the general public (although focused on those who are currently – or in the future may be – likely to be interested in the aims of the charity); opinion formers who might impact on the latter group; and the media in general.

A key issue will be the identification of the primary audience for a particular public relations campaign. Although, in many instances, these will be those people likely to be affected by the activities (or lack of action) undertaken by an organization, often they may be a different group which, by virtue of its standing or reputation, may be able to influence the opinions and attitudes of others. For example, a company wishing to secure a land site to extend its business operations will recognize that its audience will embrace all of those likely to be affected. However, the primary audience is likely to be those decision makers (possibly in local or national government) who will determine whether the expansion can be permitted or not.

In a survey conducted by the *IPR Journal* (November 1994), the dominant public serviced by PR was the media (52.9 per cent); corporate (38.3 per cent); employees (34.3 per cent); consumers (33.2 per cent); the community (26.9 per cent); government (20.9 per cent); and special interest groups (16.3 per cent).

The management of public relations

To a much greater degree than in other areas of the marketing communications process, the management of public relations remains, for many, the preserve of the senior management team. As we will see below, in the area of financial public relations this is not surprising.

There is little doubt that, to achieve the benefits of integration, public relations activities must command the full attention and support of the management of the company. However, other than in the smallest companies, the task of public relations demands a higher volume of input than can be provided by senior management. To meet these demands, varying structures have been established within organizations although, in the majority of instances, the senior management remains involved – at least with the strategic direction of activities.

Many large companies maintain a *public relations department*, which is responsible for all aspects of communications with its internal and external publics. In effect, they act as the interface between senior management and the various publics although, for the most part, this can be taken to mean the media. They are often responsible for co-ordinating the in-house publications; developing appropriate press releases to draw attention to company news stories; preparing the annual financial report; and, sometimes, having the responsibility for the implementation of the company identity programme. This is a clear recognition of the fact that public relations is an integral part of the organization's functions.

According to the 1994 Institute of Public Relations survey, 38.2 per cent of their members indicated that they reported directly to the chairman, managing director or chief executive, evidencing the importance which is attached to the PR function within many organizations.

Necessarily, the in-house individual or department will be expected to have a thorough understanding of company policies, its goals and objectives. Ideally, it should function as a part of the overall management team to ensure that there is speedy communication of decisions, and provide a rapid response to enquiries from third parties.

It is important to establish recognized lines of communication within the organization, which is somewhat easier to facilitate because of the development of interpersonal relationships. However, the internal team often suffer from the constraint that they may not see a sufficient range of alternatives. Over time, they become familiar with the particular practices adopted by the organization, rather than being exposed to the wider variety of options which would be the case if they were handling a broader range of requirements. Moreover, the status of the public relations function will, substantially, be dependent on the standing of the particular individuals within the organizational structure.

An alternative approach is the appointment of a *specialist public relations consultancy*. This will be appointed either to fulfil a specific programme of activity which has been developed against a company brief, or to assume the day-to-day responsibilities which would otherwise be carried out by the internal PR department. However, it should be recognized that such input is not without cost. The fees charged by the larger consultancies will often run into several hundreds of thousands of pounds – to which must be added the physical costs of the materials produced (press releases, photography, travel, etc.).

The advantage of the consultancy approach is that they can bring a wide range of skills to complement those which exist within the company. Importantly, they offer a degree of independence and represent a source of fresh ideas which are less likely to be inhibited by the organizational culture. They can bring a wide range of different experiences to the organization, often gained from exposure to other clients which they service.

A compromise approach is most commonly adopted, in which the in-house operation deals with the day-to-day public relations requirements, and a consultancy is appointed to have responsibility for the more strategic issues which require to be addressed.

Using PR consultancies

The scale and importance of the public relations function is witnessed by the growth both in the number and size of the specialist consultancies within the field. The *Marketing* magazine PR League Tables for

Table 12.1 Public relations agencies ranked by 1996 turnover

Rank	Company	Turnover (£ million)
1	Shandwick UK	39.17
2	Hill & Knowlton (UK)	31.2
3	Countrywide Porter Novelli	23.74
4	Burson-Marsteller	22.2
5	Dewe Rogerson	14.64
6	Citygate Communications Group	13.01
7	Biss Lancaster Group	11.47
8	Financial Dynamics	10.19
9	GCI Group London	9.67
10	The Grayling Group	8.42

Source: *Marketing*, 29 May 1997

1997 (*Marketing* magazine, 29 May 1997) covers the top 135 agencies, with a combined turnover of over £439 million. Importantly, the survey identified that almost a third of the businesses grew by more than 30 per cent over the previous year.

As an indication of their scale, Table 12.1 depicts the top ten PR consultancies based on their turnover for the year.

The survey also reveals other interesting information about the consultancies' areas of specialization. As within other areas of marketing communications, the field is fragmented by companies which seek to practise in specific areas of the profession. Some examples serve to illustrate this trend:

- Dewe Rogerson has over 80 per cent of its turnover in the field of financial services and investor relations;
- 56 per cent of Countrywide Porter Novelli involves business-to-business activities;
- Burson-Marsteller has a substantial volume of medical business, representing almost 40 per cent of its turnover.

Whilst the principles of selecting a PR consultancy with which to work are similar to those which apply in other areas of marketing communications, it is equally important to identify the appropriate match of specialist skills to those which the company seeks. The prior experience and current clients of a consultancy will indicate its range of abilities and the extent to which it will be able to operate efficiently within a market sector.

standing of company policies, its goals and objectives. Ideally, it should function as part of the management team to ensure that there is speedy communication of decisions, and provide a rapid response to enquiries from third parties.

There should be recognized lines of communication within the organization, which is much easier to facilitate because of the development of interpersonal relationships. However, the internal team often suffer from the constraint that they become so deeply immersed in the company approach that they may not see a sufficient range of alternatives. Moreover, the status of the PR function will be substantially dependent on the standing of the individuals within the organizational structure.

The external consultancy can provide a wide range of skills to complement those which exist within the company. Importantly, they offer a degree of independence and represent a source of fresh ideas which are less likely to be inhibited by the organizational culture. Inevitably, they can only function properly after they have undergone a deep immersion in the business of the company. They bring a range of different experiences to the organization, often gained from exposure to other clients which they service.

However, in both cases, there is a cost to be paid. For the in-house team, there will be a range of salaries and associated costs. For the external consultancy, there will be fees to be paid.

In-house versus consultancy

Many large companies retain substantial parts of the public relations function in-house. Clearly, this is a recognition that public relations is an integral part of the organization's functions. The individual or department will be expected to have a thorough under-

PR campaign development

The development of effective public relations campaigns, like that of all other aspects of marketing communications, is dependent on the adoption of a systematic approach towards the PR process. As such, it consists of four sequential stages (Figure 12.1).

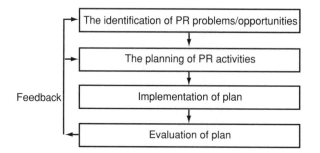

Figure 12.1

The identification of public relations problems and opportunities

Effective public relations is a continuous process, reliant on an ongoing examination of the relationships which an organization maintains between itself and its various publics. As with other areas, it is important to ensure that feedback mechanisms are used to ensure that the company is aware – at the earliest possible opportunity – of any concerns which might exist in relation to the organization, or of opportunities which may exist for it to enhance its reputation. It has to be said that, to a somewhat lesser degree than in other areas of marketing communications, the techniques of market research are used to provide this feedback.

To quote Cutlip *et al.* (1985):

'Historically, few practitioners have studied research methods. Moreover, many employers and clients view research as unnecessary ... For years, executives and practitioners alike bought the popular myth that public relations deals with intangibles that cannot be measured.'

This perspective is supported by the views of Raymond Wilson (quoted in Kavanagh, 1996), Communications Director of Norwich Union, who handles both corporate advertising and PR for the company. He believes that it is because of the relative cheapness of PR

that it is a poorly researched marketing discipline:

'When advertising, we do plenty of research. If you are looking at areas where the ad budget can be £10 million, you would expect that. But if you are looking at PR, where there may be a budget of £100,000 at risk, the pressure to research on the media relations side may not be so strong.'

In all practical terms, the application of market research to identify problems and opportunities and to evaluate programmes of activity is as important here as in other areas of marketing communications.

The starting point for any PR campaign activity must be the appropriate use of research to identify possible causes of concern with the organization or its operations among the various publics with which it deals. Until the organization is aware of the nature of the concerns, and can identify the specific identity of the publics who are affected, then appropriate campaign activity cannot be planned. By the same token, the use of similar research approaches will identify particular areas of opportunity which might present the company with the means of enhancing or changing its reputation.

PR can be used either defensively or proactively. Defensive or reactive public relations occurs when an organization responds to outside pressures or publicity which might have a negative influence on the fortunes of the organization. Sometimes these pressures result from negative publicity which is outside the organization's control, e.g. Shell's response to adverse reactions from environmental pressure groups regarding its proposed destruction of its Brent Spar oil rig; response to 'Watchdog' features, etc. Other causes might be competitive actions (recently, for example, Virgin Airlines mounted a campaign to draw attention to the implications of the planned merger between British Airways and American Airlines); changes in consumer attitudes; government policies, actual or planned.

Proactive public relations is a direct function of the organization's marketing objectives. In this context, it is seen as a valuable part of the overall task of communicating specific information to one or more target audiences. It is designed to augment other communications tools, such as advertising, sales promotion, direct marketing, etc., to generate additional publicity for a company or its products. In this context, PR has the facility to create newsworthiness and credibility to assist a conventional communications campaign. Its usage reflects the essential credibility which is associated with many forms of public relations activities. Unlike, for example, advertising, which is recognized as being placed by the organization with the specific intention of achieving particular goals, consumers are less likely to question a message which appears to be part of the editorial content of the medium in which it appears.

Programme planning

The development of a cohesive and effective PR plan is dependent, as we have seen, on a thorough understanding of the audiences for the campaign message. Here, as elsewhere, the adoption of an orderly approach will greatly assist both in the determination of the specific campaign objectives and in the monitoring of the extent to which they are achieved (Figure 12.2).

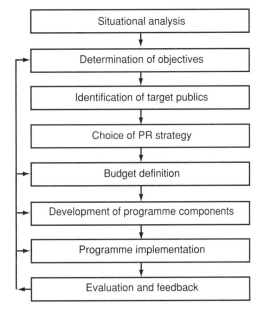

Figure 12.2

The situational analysis, both of the internal and external aspects of the operations, will identify any areas of shortfall between the desired image and the actual image. Only then will it be possible to begin the process of identifying campaign objectives and, with them, the target audiences for campaign activity. The latter may be, as we have already seen, those people who are directly affected by the activities of the organization although, in some instances, it may be preferable to target some group of opinion formers who, in turn, will impact upon that group.

The selection of the strategy will be dependent on a series of key dimensions: firstly, the specific nature of the objectives; secondly, the skills required – will the company implement the programme using only its internal resources, or will it employ an external PR consultancy?; and thirdly, the scale of the budget.

Once these factors have been considered and resolved, the identification of specific campaign components can commence. It will be important to remember that the campaign elements, although desirably cohesive in terms of the message, may well need to be varied to reflect the different values of the groups to whom the message is targeted. Using the example of a company wishing to expand its local operational base, the message to the local community (and local government decision makers) may revolve around the benefits of increasing local employment opportunities; whereas to the financial community – from whom the funding may be sourced – the nature of the message may be the profitability which will result from expansion, and so on.

Once the selected programme has been determined and implemented, it will be important to monitor the effectiveness of the campaign activity. In the short term, it may be necessary to refine specific elements to ensure the achievement of the campaign objectives. In the longer term, it is important to assess whether the overall objectives were met, how each of the campaign elements performed, and the cost-effectiveness of the campaign.

However, it is relevant to note here that many PR agencies use a variety of somewhat crude devices to assess the success of their campaigns. In many instances, these are both inconsistent and misleading. A common practice is to simply aggregate the audience or readership figures of clips or cuttings in which PR-initiated items appear. Unfortunately, this provides no real indication of how successfully the target audience has been exposed to the PR message. An alternative approach, equally unreliable, is the generation of an advertising value equivalence (AVE) which attempts to match the value of the column inches or airtime received to the value of the PR exposure.

Evaluation of public relations

Assuming that the objectives are clearly defined and quantified, the results should be capable of measurement. However, it is important to recognize the fact that PR rarely exists in isolation of other marketing communications activities and it is sometimes difficult to discriminate between the effects of a PR campaign and the effects of other activities.

Possible areas for measurement are as follows:

- Shifts in awareness;
- Shifts in attitudes towards the company or organization;
- Growth in enquiries;
- Reduction in level of complaints;
- Improvement in share price;
- Volume of coverage in target media.

Historically, the measurement of the column inches of press cuttings, or mentions on electronic media, were seen as simple evaluation techniques. At best, this provides only a crude indication of the effectiveness (or otherwise) of a PR campaign. In this, as in other areas of marketing communications, the establishment of precise objectives at the outset of the programme is a prerequisite for later evaluation (White, 1990).

James Swinehart (1979) suggests that in order to evaluate the achievements of a PR programme, five areas of questioning should be applied to the objectives:

- What is the content of the objective?
- What is the target population?
- When should the intended change occur?
- Are the intended changes unitary or multiple?
- How much effect is desired?

Tom Watson (1992), writing in *Admap*, suggests that there are a number of barriers to the efficient evaluation of public relations. He suggests, for example, the low level of training among practitioners, client ignorance, and the lack of budget for evaluation.

The tools of public relations

Public relations achieves its goals through the use of a variety of different tools and approaches. Since the individual aspects of the instruments of public relations are, largely, self-explanatory, it is not proposed to do more than to list them here. However, those students interested in gaining a greater in-depth knowledge of the development and application of these devices may wish to consult a specialist text in the area, such as *Public Relations Techniques* by Todd Hunt and James E. Grunig, Harcourt Brace, 1994.

- The press release;
- The exclusive story;
- Interviews;
- Press conferences;
- By-lined article;
- Speeches;
- Writing new releases, reports, booklets, speeches, trade and general magazine articles, film sequences, radio and television copy, production information and technical material;
- Editing employee publications, newsletters, annual reports and other management communications for internal and external audiences;
- Placing client or employer news and features with media editors and others responsible for selecting copy and preparing programmes;
- Promoting through special events, such as press parties, open houses, anniversaries, award programmes and institutional films;
- Speaking and preparing speeches for others;
- Producing brochures, booklets, special reports and house periodicals;
- Developing overall PR programmes;
- Publicizing a company's name and reputation.

Two additional tools of public relations, however, deserve special mention.

Advertorials

An advertorial is a combination of advertisement and editorial, paid for by the advertiser and appearing to look like editorial from the newspaper. Such activities must be flagged with the word 'advertisement'.

A survey conducted by National Magazines – 'Advertorials – The Reader's Perspective', among readers of eight of its titles in 1993/4 (research conducted by Research Business) showed that readers enjoy advertorials as a form of communication; appreciate that they usually provide more information than conventional advertising; and that they represent added value advertising. The survey suggested that advertorials can change the reader's perceptions of a product, involve the reader, and achieve product sampling.

Their success depends on:

- the relevance of the product to the reader;
- the fit with the motivations for magazine purchase;
- the product category relevance;
- the fit with the editorial style, content and image of the magazine;
- the balance between information and selling;
- the visual appeal.

Infomercials

These extend the premise of the advertorial into the television medium. They first started in the USA on cable and local TV. Similarly, in the UK, cable and satellite were the first to introduce infomercials. The growth of commercial television, and the advent of the vast numbers of digital channels in the near future, are likely to extend the potential application of the technique as brand manufacturers appreciate the benefits of the approach. By apparently presenting a television programme, the consumer may be deluded into thinking that the message is independent of the manufacturer who funds it.

Corporate public relations objectives

Establishing dialogue with target audiences

PR can work in both directions. Just as much as providing a vehicle for outgoing messages, so too the PR function can gather information from interested parties and groups. It is important that this information is conveyed to the senior managements of companies, in order that they can understand the attitudes and needs of these groups.

Ensuring consistency between company activities and external attitudes

The external environment for any organization represents one of continuous changes. In the same way that marketers must continuously monitor the marketplace to ensure that their products and services remain consistent with changing consumer needs and wants, so too the organization must ensure that its activities reflect changing values. Increasingly, consumers purchase products from companies whose images they respect. Public relations can play an important role in conveying the organization's response to these changes. For example, there is an increasing focus on broader issues such as environmental friendliness and respect for societal values. Equally, there may be a need to change, or at least to update, public perceptions of an organization. As companies develop images over time, it is likely that, without frequent re-examination, external attitudes may reflect a previously held belief. It is important that companies continue to update their various publics on their activities, attitudes and the values they hold.

Adding to brand values

Consumers buy company reputation as much as they purchase the individual products which those companies produce. A combined survey in the USA by DDB Needham and Porter Novelli concluded that consumers were more influenced by corporate values than ever before. Bob Drukenmiller, President of Porter Novelli, said, 'Companies should broaden their dialogues with consumers.

Most of the conversations companies have with their customers are related to their products and services. Now it is clear that some consumers also want to hear about how companies operate and what values guide their business decisions'.

The study identified five factors which had a major influence on consumers:

- 96 per cent rated product quality;
- 85 per cent the company's method of handling complaints;
- 73 per cent the way in which a company handles a crisis in which it is at fault;
- 60 per cent the handling of a challenge by a government agency about the safety of its products;
- 59 per cent an accusation of illegal or unethical trading practices.

Responding to crisis situations

A key role of public relations is the management of the relationship between an organization and its publics at times of crisis. This aspect will be dealt with in greater depth in Chapter 14.

Promoting goods and services

In this context, PR can achieve many things which, for example, serve to highlight public awareness of specific products and services or to extend their usage by consumers. This is commonplace within the market for food products, where recipes based on the company's products are placed in relevant magazines.

Financial public relations

Over recent years, financial public relations has emerged as a specialist function within the broader field of public relations. This is a direct consequence of the greater importance of the financial institutions and the financial press to the well-being of companies. Associated with this has been the recent spate of flotations by large public institutions – such as water companies, British Telecom, and others – the scale of which has demanded specialized attention to achieve the desired objectives. The recent highly contested bid for the Co-op provided ample evidence of the use of financial PR, as both sides sought to gain an advantage. According to Jonathan Clare, Deputy Managing Director of Citigate Communications (reported in *Marketing* magazine, 29 May 1997): 'No company would consider mounting a contested take-over or floating on the stock exchange without having a big name financial consultancy on the board beside the merchant bank, brokers, accountants and solicitors.'

As we have seen elsewhere, the trend towards financial services within the economy as a whole has led to the development of specialist advisers who use a variety of communications tools, and especially public relations, to assist these companies to achieve their objectives.

The responsibility for this aspect of PR is largely assumed by the key members of the management team – the chairman, the managing director, the financial director and the corporate affairs director. Since they are regarded as the primary determinants of company policy, they are often assumed to personify the strategic direction of the organization. Mostly, however, the primary focus rests with the chief executive. Sir Colin Southgate at Thorn EMI, Lord Young at Cable and Wireless, and Lord Hanson of the Hanson Trust, are all examples of this.

Financial public relations deals specifically with four identified publics – the City, the shareholders, staff and employees, and, of course, the financial journalists. The *City* remains the focal point for all activity, since it represents the means whereby the company can communicate effectively with its main audiences. Among these are the financial analysts and stockbroking houses whose advice is key to the desired outcome. Ensur-

ing that they are provided with important financial information on a frequent basis is the key to the maintenance of the company's financial reputation. Their advice and action will, in turn, impact on two further areas: firstly, the volume of *institutional investors* who maintain the majority shareholdings in most publicly quoted companies; and secondly, the *private investors* whose actions, for the most part, rely on the advice of City specialists. Equally important are the financial *journalists*. In many cases, these are non-specialist writers who rely for much of their information on the reports and comments of the City analysts, whose advice is considered as independent and credible.

Financial public relations remains a key strategic issue for many organizations. Its purpose is to promote the reputation and financial stability of the company and, inherently, it needs to take on long-term dimensions.

Charity PR

Charitable organizations and other non-profit organizations are prime users of public relations activities. Although, with the recent relaxation of advertising regulations, these bodies are now able to access the media through conventional advertising routes, the costs are often prohibitive. Public relations (together with direct marketing activities) represents a more cost-effective route to their communications needs.

A primary requirement for charitable bodies is the need to raise funds to finance their main activities. At the same time, however, it is important for such organizations to ensure the continued participation of their supporters to enable their aims to be fulfilled. Since the majority of charities depend both on voluntary contributions and voluntary participation, activity is needed which will maintain interest in the areas of concern. Clearly, in this context, publicity must be generated which will expose the work of the charity to a wider audience to enable a fuller understanding of the operation. Not only will this be designed to secure wider approval of the charity's actions, it will also aim to secure continued funding and participation.

In some instances, special events will be staged to provide exposure for these activities. Sometimes these will take the form of 'static' displays featuring some of their achievements. The Council for the Protection of Rural England (CPRE) mounted a series of photographic exhibitions, both to highlight its work and to focus attention on areas of the country which are under threat. Other charitable bodies have staged more participatory activities – such as 'fun runs', charity walks and similar events – to achieve fund-raising objectives.

In all cases, the use of public relations must relate to the strategic aims of the organization. It is important that any such events are designed to fulfil specific objectives which relate to the overall goals.

Integration of PR activities

It is extremely unusual for companies to use the tools of public relations in isolation from other forms of marketing communications. To achieve the maximum benefit from the activities, it is important that they are carefully planned to ensure a thorough integration. This, inevitably, demands that all parties to the communications process work together to ensure that the objectives are mutually understood and realized.

Echoing the comment regarding the 'blurring of the distinction' between the various tools of marketing communications, a new trend is emerging, in which specialist agencies – in the fields of public relations, sales promotion and advertising – are competing against each other for a share of the promotional budget. In many instances, the winning agency is responsible for the total imple-

mentation of the communications requirements. It follows that, even within specialist areas, practitioners are having to gain a greater understanding of the broader issues of marketing and marketing communications.

Undeniably, public relations activities can make a major contribution to the overall effectiveness of communications campaigns. Often, they can achieve a level of credibility for the activity which does not derive from other forms of marketing communications. However, to achieve this effect, common strategic goals must be determined and the same principles of research and evaluation applied to the tool of public relations as to other areas of the communications mix.

International aspects of public relations

As marketing activity increasingly takes on global dimensions, so too public relations must be considered as a vital ingredient in the global marketing communications mix.

Public relations activities can be used to target important areas of influence and decision making in a cost-effective manner, often in advance of the product's launch into a foreign market. As such, it can provide a foundation against which other marketing and marketing communications activities can function effectively. Public relations may provide the vehicle for adapting a global message to achieve local impact, assisting the process of ensuring the acceptance of a global brand in markets in which cultural and other factors may inhibit the potential for growth.

References

Cutlip, S. M., Centre, A. H. and Broom G. M., *Effective Public Relations*, Prentice Hall, 1985

Kavanagh, M., 'Audience Counts', *Marketing Business*, October 1996

Swinehart, J. W., 'Evaluating Public Relations', *Public Relations Journal*, July 1979

Watson, T., 'Evaluating PR Effects', *Admap*, June 1992

White, *Evaluation in PR Practice*, Cranfield/PRCA, 1990

Additional reading

Hart, Norman A., *Strategic Public Relations*, 1995, Macmillan Business

Haywood, Roger, *All About Public Relations*, 2nd edition, 1990, McGraw-Hill

L'Etang, Jacquie and Pieczka, Magda, *Critical Perspectives in Public Relations*, 1996, Thomson Business Press

Goldman, Jordan, *Public Relations in the Marketing Mix*, 1992, NTC Business Books

Stone, Norman, *The Management and Practice of Public Relations*, 1995, Macmillan Business

CHAPTER 13

Sponsorship and product placement

Aims and objectives

- To gain an insight into event management and business sponsorship;
- To provide definitions of sponsorship;
- To consider the growth of sponsorship activities;
- To discuss the evaluation of sponsorship;
- To examine the role of guerrilla marketing;
- To grasp the importance of product placement.

Event management & business sponsorship

Event management and business sponsorship are two important areas which are attracting increased attention in the field of marketing communications. Although initially part of the public relations armoury, these activities have grown to such an extent that they have become separated from that function. Specialist agencies in all of these related fields have emerged to provide a range of dedicated services to client companies.

At the lowest level, *event management* is the creation, implementation and administration of short-term activities designed to promote the organization. In some instances, these will be specially created to provide a vehicle for 'hospitality' which can be extended to clients and customers of the organization. In others, they will take the form of participation in conferences and exhibitions whose themes are relevant to the functions of the company. Such activities may have different aims and objectives, and it is important that the company should understand, in advance, the reasons for its participation.

Hospitality events provide the opportunity for the organization to express its gratitude to those people who have assisted it to achieve its aims in the past or who, it is hoped, will provide assistance in the future. Often, these will take the form of sporting or other 'entertainments' in which the company can participate by purchasing admission tickets and inviting its own guests (several companies, for example, purchase block tickets for events such as Wimbledon or the British motor racing Grand Prix). In some instances, they will be specially organized events which are only available to invited guests of the company.

Many commercial organizations mount periodic events at major venues which have a special appeal to a discrete audience. *Exhibitions* and *conferences* staged at such venues as Earl's Court, Olympia or the NEC in Birmingham may be used either simply to gain exposure for the products and services of the company, or to mount activities similar to those described above. Exhibitions fulfil a variety of different functions to the consumer and trade audience alike.

Most exhibitions offer a themed experience, in which manufacturers of related products and services are brought together within a single venue. In the consumer context, they provide the opportunity for companies to achieve a direct interface with potential consumers. In many respects, they provide an extension of the role of personal selling, in which the company can demonstrate their products and services, respond directly to customer enquiries and answer detailed questions. For the consumer, they provide an ideal opportunity to compare and contrast competing products and to sample product propositions prior to making a decision about the purchase. For the trade, they offer similar advantages. At one moment in time specialist retailers can meet with a wide range of manufacturers and suppliers to determine which of the variety of product offerings most reflect their retail requirements.

Sponsorship is a more embracing activity and often involves the organization in substantial levels of expenditure. It is the association of the company or organization with some third party activity, designed to achieve a series of separate, but mutually agreed objectives. Inevitably, sponsorship may take a wide variety of forms. It may, for example, be the re-naming of an established event to feature the name of the company or organization which, in return for an annual or other payment, takes 'ownership' of the event. Recent examples are the Carling sponsorship of the Premier football league, TSB's involvement in athletics, Budweiser's sponsorship of American football and the Skoda snooker Grand Prix. The sponsor seeks to achieve either name recognition or image association by their involvement with some particular sporting or other event. Such sponsorship may take on global proportions, as with the recent involvement of McDonald's and Coca Cola in the football World Cup.

Sponsorship

Commercial sponsorship may be defined as:

'An investment in cash or in kind, in an activity, in return for access to the exploitable commercial potential associated with that activity.' (Meenaghan, 1991)

'Sponsorship is a business relationship between a provider of funds, resources or services and an individual, event or organisation which offers in return some rights and association that may be used for commercial advantage.' (Sleight, 1989)

To Sleight, the key words in the definition are 'business relationship' and 'commercial advantage'. Rarely does sponsorship have anything to do with charity or patronage. That is not to say that these are not important, but they must be viewed differently from commercial sponsorship, which must be strategically sound to be valid in the context of marketing communications. Sponsorship is often associated with concessions and merchandising (Coca Cola and Euro 96), and endorsements (but these latter are often negotiated separately). The scale of cost can be seen from the recent decision of American Express to sign Tiger Woods to a five-year endorsement deal. He received an advance payment of $5 million as part of an overall $13 million package.

Sponsorship has come a long way, and the attitudes of the participants have changed significantly. In many early instances, the activity was seen as a necessary evil by the organizers of major activities who, sometimes begrudgingly, allowed the sponsor access to the event. Contrast this with the organizers of Euro 96, who ran a specific commercial featuring all of the major sponsors' logos as a way of saying 'thank you' for their participation.

Although the phenomenal growth of sponsorship activity has been a comparatively recent occurrence, sponsorship itself is not a new activity. Many companies have held a long-standing involvement with sponsorship. Coca Cola have a seventy-year association with such activities. Their first Olympic sponsorship came in 1928 and has continued through all subsequent events (Prendergast, 1993). Their involvement in the 1996 Atlanta Olympic Games was extensive, and will continue with the 2000 Games. Gillette, another global brand, commenced their involvement with sporting sponsorship with baseball in 1910.

Sponsorship targets its audience through their interests and lifestyle activities. It allows a particular audience to be targeted with an appropriate set of messages. Once a company has identified the profiles of an audience for its goods or services, it can then conduct research into their AIO to ascertain what leisure interests they may share.

A comparatively new form of sponsorship is in the sponsoring of music festivals, particularly important in the context of reaching the more elusive younger target consumers. Virgin's V98, Tennent's T in the Park and Carlsberg's Wembley event are all examples of current events designed to integrate these brands with the youth culture. Pepsi, for example, has reached its target audience through the sponsorship of a number of pop concerts and by featuring personalities such as Michael Jackson. This theme has been continued with Tina Turner, Madonna, Pamela Anderson and Cindy Crawford, and the company is currently using the Spice Girls to demonstrate the contemporary relevance of the brand to its target consumers.

Sponsorship can be used against a wide range of objectives:

- Name and brand awareness;
- Image reinforcement;
- Media exposure;
- Hospitality;
- Sales promotion, especially product sampling (but there are important integration opportunities with other on-pack offers);
- Staff motivation;
- Community relations.

An attempt was made to quantify the reasons why companies embarked on sponsorship activities with a survey among leading sports sponsors, with the following results:

Why do companies sponsor sport?

	%
Improve image of company	78
Build customer loyalty	74
Build brand awareness	78
Generate sales	57
Attract new customers	44
Support trade infrastructure	39
Generate leads or enquiries	30
Internal staff motivation	30
Greater cost efficiency	30

It is important to remember that sponsorship cannot work effectively in isolation from other forms of marketing communications. Many companies assume, somewhat naively, that having paid £x million to have their name and logo emblazoned above the title of the specific event, that is all that they need to do. The reality is that to forge proper links between the event and the company or brand, at least as much money again needs to be spent on exploiting the sponsorship involvement. A recent example is that of Green Flag. The company, which provides a national breakdown service in the UK, became the exclusive sponsor of the England football team in Euro 96. However, their advertising of this association was at a very low level. The result was that few people were able to identify the nature of the company. A survey conducted by students at the University of Greenwich showed a reasonable level of recall of the Green Flag name among those who followed the event, but a minimal ability to identify what the company did.

Texaco has recently established a three-year deal with ITV to sponsor the coverage of the Formula 1 Grand Prix series. An essential part of their activity is the development of marketing communications beyond the direct link with the programme – they have produced a full range of point-of-sale material for forecourt use, for example. Integration of activity is the recognized key to achieving success.

The identification of an appropriate sponsorship must be set against the strategic requirements of marketing communications. It should be capable of achieving significant exposure for the brand. Sub-sponsorship generally delivers little exposure, e.g. the mini logos on the sides of Formula 1 cars. Even the most devoted follower of the sport may be unaware of a particular brand's involvement.

It is important that sponsorship activities be considered in the longer-term context. The association between a sponsor and an event may take some time to register in the minds of a particular target audience, especially where the event has previously been sponsored by some other company. It is clear that a long-term association between a brand and an event can be used to create a natural association for the brand. After many years of sponsorship, the pre- Wimbledon tennis event is now uniquely referred to by the name of the sponsor, Stella Artois. To achieve such affinity takes time!

To maximize the benefits of sponsorship activities requires a dedicated implementation team – sometimes wholly within the company, but often using the facilities and resources of external agencies. It is essential to equate the desired image with a specific event in order to achieve an appropriate match. The intention is to transfer the image associated with the event to enhance that of the sponsor. It is key, therefore, to identify the image objectives prior to embarking on the sponsorship route. It is equally important to examine the credibility of the link between the sponsor and the event. Clearly, it is easier for an audience of an event to relate to the brand sponsor if there is a natural synergy. C&A has developed a licensing deal with the Cartoon Network to launch a range of merchandise featuring the Flintstones characters. Not only was the activity promoted at point of purchase, but an on-air promotion featured the link.

Consider also the scale of the event. Some events have an inherent status which will ensure widespread publicity. It is much easier to generate publicity for the brand in this instance. Minor events, which receive little exposure, can rarely deliver much to a brand except with a major effort on the part of the sponsor. Against this, however, is the fact that local events designed to achieve local exposure may be very precisely targeted. Although they may not generate significant levels of publicity – except locally – they may have a particular relevance and prestige within the local audience. This is especially important in terms of community relations, or where there is a need to develop an association between the company and its field force on a local level (e.g. country events sponsored by farm produce manufacturers). Such events are best left to the local management both to identify and organize, as they will have a far better understanding of their role within the target community.

Since different activities appeal to different groups of people, it follows that different forms of sponsorship will appeal to widely differing audiences. And the range is immense. Football alone offers everything from global/international events (the World Cup); European exposure (Euro 96); national coverage (the Premiership); to local sponsorships with individual teams.

A new form of sponsorship activity has emerged recently with the decision to allow companies to sponsor television and radio programmes. Here, the objective is to derive benefit from the association of the company name and a programme which has relevance to a desired target audience. The consequence has been a rapidly increasing level of activity with programme sponsorship. Hewlett Packard, for example, has forged a close link with the X- Files – 'The Solution is Out There'. The Texaco involvement with ITV mentioned above is but one example of a growing trend. Cadbury's have recently renewed their £10 million association with Coronation Street; Going Places, the retail travel agency, has linked with Blind Date; and Tizer with the Chart Show. Wella, which sponsors Friends on Channel 4, have reflected this involvement by using Jennifer Aniston in the TV commercials which support the Experience shampoo range.

The move into programme sponsorship has affected other media in the same way. On radio, for example, the previous Virgin Breakfast Show hosted by 'Russ and Jono' was sponsored by Kellogg's. When the hosts were replaced by Chris Evans, the show sponsor changed to Beamish Red, whilst in films a sponsorship deal was recently reported between Pepsi and Star Wars.

Company involvement with charitable bodies is another important form of sponsorship activity. In these instances, the organization promotes the aims of the charity with the objective of raising funds, for example. The objective is similar to other forms of sponsorship activity in which the sponsor seeks to achieve image benefits as a result of its association with the aims and objectives of the charity with which it participates. Examples are the involvement of Tesco with Save The Children, Texaco and the Royal Society for the Prevention of Accidents, and so on.

Sometimes sponsorship involvement is specifically designed to gain media exposure which might not otherwise be possible. Sporting and cultural events gain considerable levels of coverage in the media. The featuring of the sponsor's name alongside the event may generate a level of mentions worth hundreds of thousands of pounds. In some cases, such activity will be undertaken by products whose media activities are otherwise circumscribed – cigarette brands, for example, gain exposure on television from which they are banned from an advertising standpoint.

Other forms of sponsorship may include professional awards, educational awards, books and publications (the *Shell Egon Ronay Guide, The Guinness Book of Records*), and a wide variety of local events. As with other forms of marketing communications activity, such involvement must be planned against a

series of clearly identified objectives and monitored to ensure that these objectives are fulfilled cost-effectively.

The growth of sponsorship

Estimates of the total value of sponsorship activity are somewhat difficult to obtain. An assessment carried out by Mintel (Mintel Special Report on Sponsorship, 1995) depicted the growth of the activity over the period 1990–94 (Table 13.1).

Since the 1970s, the growth in arts sponsorship has been phenomenal. In 1975 it accounted for less than £0.5 million. Today it is worth in excess of £50 million. According to research conducted by MORI and reported in *Research Plus*, June 1997, arts venues are significant in attracting important opinion formers to their audiences, an otherwise difficult category of people to influence. The research revealed that 68 per cent of the captains of industry visited the Royal Opera House, 51 per cent the Tate Gallery, 43 per cent the English National Opera and 39 per cent the Royal Academy. Among MPs, attendance for the same venues was 16 per cent, 29 per cent, 3 per cent and 4 per cent respectively.

Table 13.1   Estimated value of UK sponsorship activities

	1990		1994	
	(£m)	(%)	(£m)	(%)
Sports	223	79	265	64
Broadcast	7	3	70	17
Arts	35	12	49	12
Other	16	6	31	7
Total	281	100	415	100

Source: Mintel Special Report on Sponsorship, 1995

For some product categories, especially where restrictions limit conventional use of marketing communication, sponsorship may play a greater role. It has been estimated that sports sponsorship accounts for around 16 per cent of all tobacco expenditure on promotion. This figure is capped, by agreement, at the 1985 level, allowing for year on year inflation. The impact on sport of a ban on tobacco sponsorship will be considerable, especially on minority activities which find it more difficult to attract sponsorship funding (*Times* Letter, Clive Turner, 13 May 1997).

With the desire to attract world-wide audiences, sponsorship activities have achieved even greater significance. Often, they have the ability to transcend national and cultural differences and achieve brand registration and identification across multinational boundaries.

The thirty-one matches featured in Euro 96 were watched in more than 190 countries around the world, by a global cumulative television audience of 6.7 billion. The final was watched by some 445 million people. The eleven official sponsors were featured together in a single commercial screened in British cinemas, on ITV and Eurosport. The impact of the event on the UK economy was no less significant. About half of the £80 million spent on official merchandise was spent in Britain. Supermarket lager sales, which had been growing at an annual rate of around 3 per cent in the last week of May, jumped by 55 per cent in the second week of June. On the day of the England v. Germany semi-final, Domino's Pizza reported an increase of 88 per cent on pizza deliveries compared with the same day in the previous week. The research indicated positive image shifts for companies involved with the event and, albeit at a low level, brand shifts to participating brands. Five per cent of the sample switched from their usual brand to one sponsoring the event (research conducted by Pegram Walters International, reported in *Research Plus*, June 1997).

The World Cup is close to overtaking the Olympic Games as the biggest global marketing event. It is estimated that, within five years, the sponsorship costs of the World Cup will be greater than those for the Games. Industry sources (according to *Marketing*, 6 March 1997) expect prices to double between the 1998 and the 2002 events, taking the top price to around $60 (£37) million for each of the eleven main sponsors. This compares with the $45 million (£28 million) for the 2000 Olympics charged to each of ten main sponsors. The 1998 World Cup in France is expected to generate around $700 million (£432 million) in revenue from its top sponsors. The football event generates three times the cumulative audience of the Olympics. The World Cup operates a system in which sponsors receive first refusal for subsequent events. So important is the event that Anheuser Busch (the owners of Budweiser) are keen to sign despite the fact that they may not be able to feature during the French event because of the Loi Evin. They are campaigning for a change to the French laws and appealing to the European Union.

Sponsorship issues

Sponsorship has grown beyond the point of the managing director wishing to seek involvement with a particular event or activity. To fulfil its rightful place in the marketing communications armoury, several key questions need to be answered before investing the often considerable funds:

1 Is there a fit between the activity and the brand or corporate positioning?
2 Is the sponsorship sufficiently distinctive?
3 Are there other sponsors associated with the event?
4 Does the activity have an existing identity, or does one need to be created?
5 Can the sponsorship be undermined by competitors, for example, by buying perimeter boards, signage or other activities such as hospitality to associate themselves with the event?

Table 13.2 Sponsorship league table

Team/Sponsor	Length of deal	Cost
Arsenal – JVC	3 years	£8 m
Aston Villa – AST	6 years	£6 m
Chelsea – Coors	3 years	£3 m
Derby County – Puma	1 year	£300,000
Leeds – Packard Bell	4 years	£4 m
Leicester City – Walkers	2 years	£200,000
Liverpool – Carlsberg	4 years	£4 m
Manchester United – Sharp	16 years	£24 m
Newcastle – Newcastle Brown Ale	3 years	£2 m
Spurs – Hewlett Packard	4 years	£4 m
West Ham – Dagenham Motors	4 years	£4 m

Source: RSL Sportscan reported in *Marketing Week*, 14 February 1997

6 Who are the audience for the event – both live and in terms of the expected media coverage?

7 What exploitation opportunities exist?

8 Is there synergy with the current advertising platform or other marketing communications activity?

'Advertising works in a direct way: creating its own values and context for the product, and stimulating the desired consumer response from the way they perceive the brand. Sponsorship, by contrast, works in a more indirect way. It borrows the values of the sponsored event or programme, making them part of the brand in the mind of the viewer. The creativity in advertising comes in defining the nature of the brand, while creativity in sponsorship comes in determining the nature of the fit between the required brand personality and the donated associations.' (Byles and Walford, 1991)

Sponsorship activity carries considerable risks. The Philip Morris £1.2 million sponsored OneAustralia, an entrant in the Americas Cup which sank off the coast of San Diego, cancelled out their opportunity to gain ongoing publicity from the event. Pepsi's involvement with Michael Jackson was rapidly curtailed when the adverse publicity surrounding his personal life emerged.

As a general rule, sponsorship costs significantly more than spot advertising. One exception is PowerGen's sponsorship of the national weather forecasts. For an investment of £2.4 million, the company receives exposure equivalent to an estimated £12 million if bought on a spot-by-spot basis.

Sponsorship activity designed to appeal to a world-wide audience is costly. At the start of 1997, Nike signed a deal worth £250 million over ten years with the Brazilian football team. Pepsi has reached a similar deal with the Argentinian national side (Baird, 1997).

Even on a national scale, sponsorship involvement requires considerable investment. RSL, a company involved in the field, recently calculated the cost to the sponsors of their direct involvement with leading football teams. These costs exclude the sponsors' promotion of the association (Table 13.2).

The evaluation of sponsorship activity

The increasing importance of sponsorship activities, and the corresponding requirement to ensure the appropriate evaluation of the techniques, has resulted in the creation of dedicated effectiveness measurements.

Millward Brown have developed a sponsorship tracking study which measures not only brand recall and awareness, but also brand image dimensions for companies involved in sponsorship activity. RSGB have developed a specific tracking study named ROAR to enable the targeting of the youth age group with greater precision. Findings reported in *Marketing* ('The Youth is Out There', 5 June 1997) suggest that as much as 48 per cent of the market feels that companies associate themselves with inappropriate events. Their study of earlier events suggests that V96 worked, whilst Lilt's association with the Notting Hill Carnival did not. Tennents was successfully associated with its event, but Carlsberg was seen to be cashing in on established events. The same study, in the sporting arena, indicated that Coca Cola's Cup found support among football fans, whilst the Gillette Cup did not.

Opinions derived from the ROAR study cast an interesting light on this form of sponsorship activity (Table 13.3). The study also reveals other interesting aspects regarding brand sponsorship. It is clear that the activity cannot do the entire job of re-positioning a brand, particularly when strong associations exist in the consumer's mind. The study identified that Del Monte's sponsorship of

'The Gladiators' failed because the company had not achieved a breakthrough in terms of creating an image for the brand as an energy drink. The latent association remains the man in the white suit, and there was thus no correspondence with the TV programme.

Other studies demonstrate the cost–value relationship of sponsorship involvement, and the difficulties of achieving consumer recognition. The eleven sponsors of the Euro 96 football tournament, the biggest UK sporting event for thirty years, spent a combined £38.5 million backing the event. However, according to research conducted by RSL and reported in *Marketing Week* (28 February 1997), only one of them – Coca Cola – made it into the top ten of sponsorship recalled during the year, and then only in tenth place. Major brands, each paying around £3.5 million, including McDonald's, Canon and Fujifilm, did not even rate a mention among the 19 000 people interviewed.

The brand with the highest recall was Robinson's Fruit Juices. It has enjoyed a presence at the Wimbledon tennis championship for many years, despite not being a sponsor! In second place was the association between Cadbury's and Coronation Street. The survey indicated that long-term sponsorships tend to lead to stronger awareness, with Carlsberg's association with Liverpool making it the third most recalled deal.

Table 13.3   ROAR panel opinions

Response	Agree	Disagree	Neither
I find sponsorship intrusive	21	31	46
Sponsorship complements advertising	16	7	32
I feel better about a company if they sponsor something I am interested in	50	15	35
Companies sponsor inappropriate events	48	16	34
Sponsorship is a good way to increase awareness of a brand	82	3	13

Source: RSGB ROAR Study

Research conducted by Millward Brown and presented at the 1997 MRS conference (Gamon and Millman, 1997) suggests that broadcast sponsorship can deliver specific benefits:

- It can raise TV presence for a brand;
- It can deliver extra presence for a brand;
- It can shape beliefs about a brand;
- It can do these things in a way which is complementary to spot advertising;
- It differs in the extent to which it does these things.

In 1996, Britannia Music sponsored three events, 'The Making of the Brits', 'The Brit Awards' and 'The Brits Uncut'. Following this activity, 31 per cent of respondents identified a presence for Britannia on TV (despite their not using any other form of TV than sponsorship). Among viewers of the programmes, this figure rose to 50 per cent. The same research also demonstrates that Cadbury (the sponsor of Coronation Street) has seen significant improvements in image, especially in terms of perceived product quality, following the sponsorship.

Guerrilla marketing

A new tactic, closely associated with sponsorship, is known as guerrilla marketing (sometimes called ambush marketing). Essentially, a company which is not an official sponsor of the event achieves close identification with the event through the use of traditional media devices close to the activity.

At a recent conference on sponsorship, delegates were shown awareness figures for Euro 96 immediately after the event had taken place. Each of the sponsors had paid £3.5 million to be involved with the event and, in return, received category exclusivity. Importantly, each of the companies had spent between twice and four times the amount on supporting their sponsorship.

When the league table was published – headed by Coca Cola – Nike were in seventh place, ahead of Fuji, Mastercard, Canon and

Philips. The company was not an official sponsor of the tournament but had spent about £2 million on press and posters around the event, convincing people that it was. Additionally, it distributed bags of give-aways to fans in the same way as the official sponsors. By handing out these bags and 'Just Do It' flags from vans parked outside the stadium premises, Nike were immune from prosecution. Whilst Umbro, the official sponsor in the category, scored a higher awareness figure from the event, it was only slightly higher than that achieved by Nike. During the London Marathon, Acsis had paid to be the official footwear sponsor, but again it was Nike who ambushed the event by mounting a bus shelter poster campaign along the route of the marathon.

Product placement

In the same way that recent years have seen the rapid growth and development of sponsorship activities, so too the placement of products into films, television programmes and other activities has grown significantly, both in practice and in significance. Product placement is somewhat ambiguous, with different definitions.

Frank Jefkins (1994), in *Public Relations Techniques*, suggests that it is 'the supply of products for use in films, television and plays'.

The Independent Television Commission (ITC), which regulates and licenses independent television, specifically includes the topic in its code of sponsorship (ITC Code of Sponsorship, 1994):

14a Product placement is defined as the inclusion of, or reference to, a product or service within the programme in return for payment or other valuable consideration to the programme maker or ITC licensees (or any representative of either). This is prohibited.

14b When a product or service is an essential element within a programme, the programme maker may, in those exceptional circumstances, acquire that product at no or less than full cost. This is not product placement. It is acceptable providing that no undue prominence is given to the product or service in question.

Creative placement involves finding methods of insinuating the brand into film and TV production. This can mean taking advantage of outdoor advertising sites, in street scenes, the wearing of branded clothing, or the use of real TV commercials in scenes requiring a TV set (Oliver, 1996). In some respects, the activity has parallels with the guerrilla marketing tactics described earlier, in the sense that the product demands attention through its association with some other form of activity. As such, there appears to be no overt promotion of the product. Rather, it is its appearance within a particular context that gives it a relevance and significance to everyday life. The product can achieve popular status through its association with some form of media activity, its apparent usage by a film character, or simply its presence, which makes it acceptable for subsequent use.

Ann Nicholls (1994) states that product placement can provide an active and independent demonstration of how the brand fits into people's lives.

Assessing the value of product placement remains an imprecise science. Although there has been no formal research conducted to evaluate the process, there is considerable empirical evidence that product placement can benefit the brand enormously. Reeces Pieces candy featured prominently in the ET movie. The company claims that this 'increased sales by 70% in June from May, and the candy was added to the concession of 800 movie theatres, where they had not previously been sold'.

According to Belch and Belch (1993) when Tom Cruise, in the film 'Risky Business', appeared in a pair of Ray-Ban sunglasses, the sales of the product immediately increased from around 18 000 to over 360 000 units. The company has continued to use product placement as an integral part of its overall communications strategy. Don Johnson wore the product in 'Miami Vice' from its launch in 1994, the consequence of which was to again double sales to around 720 000 units. In 1985 sales increased to around 826 000 when Bruce Willis wore them in the TV series 'Moonlighting'. In 1986 Tom Cruise again wore them, this time in his role in 'Top Gun', contributing to the sales growth to 1.5 million units (Leinster, 1987).

The Red Stripe beer placement in the film 'The Firm' cost the company around $5000. The sales of the product increased by around 50 per cent after its release in 1993 (Jacobson and Mazur).

Several brands featured with varying degrees of prominence in the recent James Bond film 'Goldeneye'. Among these were a BMW Z3 Roadster, the Omega Seamaster watch, Smirnoff Black Label vodka, Bollinger champagne, Church's shoes, Perrier Water and the IBM Thinkpad computer. Some of these products were promoted beyond the movie. Smirnoff, for example, extended the activity to encompass their Red Label brand of vodka, with the film featuring strongly on posters and table cards, in competitions to win merchandise, and prize draws with the opportunity to win tickets to the film. Pierce Brosnan, the star of the movie, featured heavily in the BMW activity, unveiling the car in Central Park, New York and in several other locations, featuring in a video produced for the dealerships and the offering of a variety of trade incentives to private screenings. Similarly, Omega integrated the activity with PR, cinema poster and print activity linked to Goldeneye with competitions in the press and quality magazines to win the watch (Marsh, 1995).

The James Bond film, 'Tomorrow Never Dies', secured product placement deals with five companies, several of which are continuing their association from the previous Bond movie. The companies are BMW, Omega, Bollinger, Smirnoff and Gateway. BMW alone paid a reported £17 million to ensure that their car appeared in the new film, outbidding several other car manufacturers, including Jaguar, in the process.

The potential benefits (and the risks) which product placement can deliver to a brand are witnessed by a pending lawsuit in the USA between Reebok and the makers of the Tom Cruise blockbuster 'Jerry Maguire'. The film features Cruise as a sports agent with a grudge against Reebok for denying him a sponsorship deal. As part of a $1.5 million product placement deal, Reebok paid for a scene in the film's finale in which it recognizes the athlete's gifts and includes him in a TV commercial which ends with the words, 'We ignored him for years. We were wrong. We're sorry'. Unfortunately, that particular scene was left on the cutting room floor. Reebok are suing TriStar and its parent, Sony Pictures Entertainment, for up to $10 million per complaint received. The lawsuit has again brought the area of product placement into focus.

Other examples include Michael J. Fox's consistent choice of Pepsi Cola in 'Back to the Future II', a Stone Age McDonald's dominating the screen in 'The Flintstones' and the multiple placement of child-related products in Walt Disney's 'Toy Story'.

Increasingly, however, companies are recognizing that, as with sponsorship activities, it is important to go beyond the simple placement of the product. To achieve maximum impact, the promotional activity of the brand needs to go beyond its presence in the film. Nokia mobile telephones were featured in the recent movie 'The Saint'. They subsequently showed a TV commercial based on the film and demonstrating the specific attributes and features of the Nokia equipment. Similarly, Mars spent £2 million in the UK to reinforce its product placement deal in the Rowan Atkinson 'Mr Bean' film. An on-pack promotion together with a (pan-European) 30-second ad were created to sell M&Ms and other Mars brands to the target group (12–24 years).

Product placement remains an emergent area of marketing communications, although only with proper research evaluation will its relevance and impact be fully understood. Thus far, product placement remains very much a hit and miss business, as Sharon Hanley of Lynn Franks PR admits: 'We got the Diet Coke man onto the Richard and Judy show and they insisted on calling him the star of the diet soft drink commercial. On the Selina Scott show on NBC Super Channel, they not only called him the Diet Coke man, but showed the whole commercial as well' (reported in *Marketing*, 28 November 1996).

References

Baird, R., 'Sponsors Look at Sporting Chances', *Marketing Week*, 10 April 1997

Belch and Belch (1993) *Introduction to Advertising and Promotion – An Integrated Marketing Communications Perspective*, 2nd edition, Irwin, 1993

Byles, D. and Walford, N., 'Advertising's Brother', *Admap*, May 1991

Gamon, J. and Millman, I., Can Broadcast Sponsorship Help to Build Brands, MRS Conference Paper, March 1997

Jacobson, M. and Mazur, L., Marketing Madness: A survival guide for a consumer society, Internet web site

Jefkins, F., *Public Relations Techniques*, 2nd edition, Butterworth-Heinemann, 1994

Leinster, C., 'A Tale of Mice and Lens', *Fortune*, 28 September 1987

Marsh, H., 'Bond Product Deals a Licence to Sell', *Marketing*, 16 November 1995

Meenaghan, T., 'The Role of Sponsorship in the Marketing Communications Mix', *International Journal of Advertising*, 10, 1991

Nicholls, A., 'Terms of Endorsement', *Media and Marketing Europe*, September 1994

Oliver, B., 'The Latest Screen Stars', *Marketing*, 13 March 1996

Prendergrast, M., *For God, Country and Coca Cola*, Orion Books, 1993

Sleight, S., *Sponsorship: What It Is and How To Use It*, McGraw-Hill, 1989

Winski, J., 'Hershey Befriends Extra Terrestrial', *Advertising Age*, 19 July 1982

Additional reading

Sleight, Steve, *Sponsorship: What It Is and How To Use It*, 1989, McGraw-Hill

Corporate communications

- To consider the growth of corporate activity;
- To appreciate the importance of corporate identity and image;
- To examine the objectives of corporate communications;
- To provide an insight into the management of corporate communications;
- To identify the audiences for corporate communications;
- To gain insight into the process of establishing a corporate identity;
- To consider the measurement of corporate communications;
- To learn about the nature of crisis management;
- To understand the key dimensions of crisis management;
- To appreciate the importance of handling a crisis.

The growth of corporate activity

Recent years have seen an increasing role for corporate advertising, and a recognition of the importance of developing a corporate identity.

When this area is carried out effectively and efficiently, it is the epitome of good integrated marketing communications. The process is an important one, and has significant strategic implications. Above all, it is the means by which an organization communicates the very nature of itself to its various publics. Importantly, it is more than just a change of logo, the typeface used on the company letterheads, or the external colour of the corporate headquarters. The task is, primarily, to ensure the consistency of communication across all media of a common message to a variety of audiences. There are sound commercial and communications reasons for this increased level of interest.

Historically, companies have suffered from the decentralization of the various communications activities. Today, major companies must increasingly consider that the way in which they operate, and what they have to say about their company's relationships with the community at large, affects the way that people think about them.

There has been an increasing recognition that consumers choose between the various products and services available to them for a wide variety of reasons. Significantly, not all of these are derived exclusively from the product or service itself. In many purchase situations, company recognition and image are important factors in the decision-making process. Moreover, as the cost of marketing communications increases, the ability of a company to provide support for all of the products within its portfolio becomes more remote. The market segment, whilst profitable, may be too limited to justify media expenditure, or the share of market might be too small to fund a marketing communications campaign.

Those brands which are embraced by an identifiable and positive corporate identity will tend to be chosen by consumers in a purchasing environment over those which have no identity or which stand alone. This may be exemplified in the purchase of a medicinal product. Whether it is taken to alleviate the symptoms of the common cold or to relieve a headache, the nature of consumption attaches considerable importance to the purchase decision. Familiarity with the corporate name of SmithKline Beecham or Fisons will help overcome the relative unfamiliarity of names such as Veno's Cough Mixture, Ralgex or Opticrom.

A further impetus to the process has come from the expanding rate of globalization. Mergers and acquisitions, together with organic growth, have resulted in many corporate operations opening up in different parts of the world. Their operations expand and become more dispersed, with the inherent danger that each operating unit, by retaining responsibility for its own communications programme, produces materials which are inconsistent with other parts of the operation.

The growing importance of corporate communications

Many organizations simply assume that they need only communicate when they want to. However, it is inevitable that deliberate and unintended messages get through to audiences all the time. Failure to control all aspects

of the communications process may result in the offsetting of those aspects of communications which are more within the company's control, such as advertising and public relations, and resulting in a confused image.

The recent adverse publicity associated with Shell following its decision to abandon the Brent Spar oil rig in the North Sea, and the problems associated with the company's apparent support of the Nigerian government, have overturned years of prior activity. Shell has been consistent, both in its advertising and in its other activities, in identifying itself with environmental issues and concerns. The result has been the creation of a very favourable and positive image of an environmentally friendly and caring organization. However, that image has been severely dented by these and other recent events. Shell's attitudes towards its social responsibilities have been challenged by shareholders, resulting in considerable negative publicity for the company.

Remember Gerald Ratner, the visible head of his jewellery chain, Ratners? After a very public joke about the poor quality of his products, he was not only forced to leave the company he had founded, but it erased all traces of him by renaming itself 'Signet'. The company has taken several years to recover from these off the cuff remarks.

Companies are increasingly coming to recognize the damage to their reputations which can occur from a failure to manage their corporate communications effectively. Camelot was a recent victim, when it failed to recognize that an increase in directors' salaries at a time when donations to charitable causes were falling was likely to result in a public relations disaster.

It is important to remember that corporate identity and corporate strategy will be closely related to each other. The strategic direction of an organization will be influenced by its identity, whilst its identity will be affected by the nature of the strategy. A core strategic decision which an organization must take is its approach to the market.

Table 14.1 Dimensions of corporate identity across Europe

	Britain	France	Germany	Spain
The external projection of company image	51	50	38	55
The visual presentation of the organization	44	10	33	20
The expression of the company culture, values and philosophy	4	20	40	15
The internal projection of the organization	7	13	38	5
Advertising and marketing communications	2	5	5	5
Product and brand support	5	8	5	0

Corporate image and identity

Corporate image is the picture of an organization as perceived by the various target groups, whilst *corporate identity* is associated with the way in which a company presents itself to those target groups.

As well as there being many different definitions of the meaning of these terms, it would appear that there is considerable diversity in terms of the practical implementation. This can be seen from some of the results of a telephone study conducted by MORI in 1993 to study the concept in several different European countries (Table 14.1). In total, some 160 interviews were conducted with people responsible for the implementation of corporate identity. Only four countries have been used to illustrate the divergence of attitudes.

Nicholas Ind (1990) suggests that it is important to consider the corporate identity in the context of the corporate mission. In his view, the corporate view and the identity created for the organization are inseparable: 'A company that has a clear generic strategy is likely to perform well. A company that does not pursue a clear strategy will tend to be stuck in the middle and thus perform poorly.'

The objectives of corporate communications

Aberg (1990) suggests that communication has four distinct functions within the organization, which must be fully integrated if the desired goals are to be achieved:

1 Supporting internal and external core operations.
2 Organization- and product-oriented profiling.
3 Informing internal and external audiences.
4 Socializing individuals into good organizational citizens.

He depicts these as the total communications circle, which shows the interrelationship between these roles and the functional activities of the organization (Figure 14.1).

The process of developing a consistent corporate communications strategy delivers many opportunities and advantages to the organization, which extend the premise developed by Aberg. The following is a listing of the key objectives which may be met.

The creation of a strong internal identity

Many organizations suffer from being dispersed, both nationally and internationally.

Figure 14.1

The provision of a strong and consistent identity for all parts of the operation will serve to unify the attitudes, goals and motivations of the employees, and ensure that they feel part of an overall structure. Cable and Wireless, resulting from the merger of Mercury, Bell Cablemedia, NYNEX Cablecomms and Videotron, undertook a major campaign to communicate the benefits of the new operation to staff and the external audience.

To enhance the external awareness of the organization and an understanding of its businesses

As has already been seen, the diffuse and diverse nature of communications may be inconsistent with the desire to present the company as a cohesive whole. A single organization will appear to be stronger if its component parts are unified in their representation to external audiences.

The new Cable and Wireless company has committed a reported £30 million on a corporate campaign to identify the benefits of the organization to the public. In the shorter term, immediately following the establishment of the new structure, full-page advertisements appeared in the national press with the headline: 'They Work Better Together'. The 'Yellow' campaign commenced with a dominant presence in all of the important national newspapers, in which every available colour space was purchased for the campaign. This was accompanied by television commercials which followed the same 'yellow' motif.

To provide the flexibility for expansion

This is especially important in a global context. The limitations imposed by, for example, a national name may inhibit the opportunities for expansion in overseas markets. The perceptions of British Petroleum are narrower than those of BP, and BT has become a global player. Would the same opportunities be open to British Telecom or the Royal Mail?

The British Airways redesign is intended to position the company as a 'citizen of the world'. Rather than the Union Flag, they feature art from all over the world, reflecting the fact that over 60 per cent of their passengers are from overseas.

The same principle is equally applicable to companies which may discover that their sphere of activities is restricted by their operating name. The change of the parent identity from Woolworth's to Kingfisher served to embrace a variety of acquisitions, including Comet, Superdrug and B&Q alongside the original Woolworth's company, whilst removing the focus of attention from the latter, whose fortunes were less positive.

To integrate operations following merger or acquisition

A singular corporate identity presents the opportunity to fuse acquisitions with existing operations and ensure a single, consistent identity for the new company. This approach was adopted by a new company, Novartis, following the merger of Ciba and Sandoz.

To enhance the share price or other financial aspects of the company in order to secure investment

This issue is one which enjoys sharp focus at times of take-over bids or defences. In order to maximize the perceptions of corporate strength, the corporate identity will be a vehicle for raising awareness of different aspects of the operation.

To withstand or launch a take-over or merger

Although the specific target audience – that is, those with the power to influence the final outcome – may be small, the sphere of influence is much wider. Increasingly, take-overs are being fought out in public, with each of the participants seeking to communicate its virtues and strengths.

To communicate new strategies

The recent demerger of ICI and the establishment of a separate operation, Zeneca, is a demonstration of the new corporate direction which the company proposes to take.

To advocate change

Organizations may use corporate communication to encourage change – social, political, attitudinal – which may be useful to the organization or its publics. This area is particularly, although not exclusively, associated with charitable bodies. The recent campaigns conducted by the RSPCA, designed to bring about the introduction of dog registration or the ending of live animal transportation, are both examples; or advertising conducted at times of industrial unrest, to explain an organization's position in a dispute.

To resolve organizational structures

The acquisition by Philip Morris of a number of companies within the food industry has been addressed by the change of identity to present a consistent approach to the various audiences. After operating as separate companies, Kraft was merged with General Foods to become KGF; the subsequent restructuring following the acquisition of Jacobs and Suchard has been resolved by naming the new company Kraft Jacobs Suchard.

To define the positioning of the organization

Corporate identity programmes enable the company to address what is, arguably, the single most important issue – that of their overall positioning in order to present a unique identity.

To aid the process of recruitment and staff retention

An organization which is seen to be well established, or one which has a reputation for graduate recruitment and training, will enhance its prospects of securing the best of each year's crop. Employees will be more likely to remain with a company which has a positive reputation in terms of its dealings with them.

To demonstrate the company's achievements or contributions to the economy

Companies will use corporate communications to bring industry or national awards – e.g. the Queen's Award to Industry – to the attention of a wider public. By the same token, a particular policy to export more, for example, or recycle its waste, may be used as the basis for image enhancement. Thames Water has embarked on a corporate radio campaign in which the company seeks to present the positive moves that it has taken in a variety of areas. These include the discovery of a new underground reservoir, the creation of a wildlife habitat and special techniques to avoid water loss through leakage.

To overcome poor attitudes towards a company

This may be the result of previous poor performance in a particular area, of some form of crisis, or simply its failure to communicate effectively in the past. The Co-op Bank introduced an ethical banking policy in 1992 which guaranteed that it would not lend money to companies that did not meet its criteria for ethical business practice. Undoubtedly, this move has strengthened its relationship with its customers and expanded its business base.

The communication of company image

The development of a cohesive corporate identity programme has the twin benefits of avoiding inconsistencies, and of binding the diverse parts of the operation together. The alternative is the lack of a shared identity, with the risk that the operations move apart and the benefits of globalization are lost. Inherent in this statement, however, is the recognition of the need for corporate identity programmes to work across national divides, and with different languages and cultures. Not only words, but symbols and colours may communicate a different impression from the one intended and desired. In addition, there is the need to ensure that companies in competing industries identify a means of differentiating themselves from each other. However, it must be remembered that image and identity change are no panacea for other ills.

A simple audit of the present identity will establish whether images among the target audiences are positive or negative. In the latter instance, work needs to be done to enhance the image. However, if the reality falls short of the image – actual or desired – then it is clear that there is a fundamental problem within the organization which needs to be addressed.

The corporate identity can supply the focus for the organization and provide a unique position in the marketplace. In many respects, the corporate identity reflects the personalities and values which are associated with a company.

In various research exercises, Virgin is seen as an outstanding company that people can trust because of the reputation of its founder, Richard Branson. Anita Roddick and the emotional values she projects have become synonymous with the corporate identity of The Body Shop, the company she founded. A similar view could be expressed about the revival of Asda's fortunes under Sir Archie Norman, an equally charismatic figure.

It is obvious that companies communicate, whether they do so deliberately or by default. The issue to be addressed is how companies go about the process of communicating to their various publics. Comparatively few companies have a corporate communications strategy, although the number is growing along with the recognition of the importance of the area. The result is that the image and identity they portray is one that 'happens' rather than one which is deliberately fostered for the overall benefit of the company.

Several years ago, the then Chief Executive of GrandMet saw a refuse disposal lorry bearing the corporate name. As part of its then diversification, the company had entered a number of service areas which contributed to the overall income. However, it was the recognition of the fact that the lorry would be seen by, among others, people in the City or in the media, and that the image conveyed would be contrary to that desired. It didn't take long before a directive was issued to remove the GrandMet name not only from the rubbish van, but from all other operating companies without express permission. Although this is a long way short of developing a proper corporate identity programme, it was the first step in the appreciation of the fact that all means of communication impact on the various publics who are exposed to them.

Companies which don't communicate – internally or externally – do a great disservice to themselves. Non-communications may often be interpreted as negative communications, implying that the organization has something to hide. If a company says nothing about an issue, its publics will infer a response. Increasingly, the public is becoming more concerned with how a company relates to it, and the beliefs that it holds or the actions that it takes, than simply with the nature and quality of the products or services it provides.

David Ogilvy (1995), in his excellent book *Ogilvy on Advertising*, says:

'Big corporations are increasingly under attack – from consumer groups, from environmentalists, from government, from antitrust legislators – who try their cases in the media. If a big corporation does not take the initiative in cultivating its reputation, its case goes by default.'

Bob Worcester, of MORI, who for many years have conducted specific studies into aspects of corporate image and identity, suggests three elements of corporate advertising:

- This is who we are.
- This is what we can do for you.
- This is what we think.

The management of corporate communications

The responsibility for communications within companies embraces all levels of the organization, although ultimately the direction of that communication must derive from the chief executive.

Work carried out by Pincus et al. (1991) suggests four such roles:

1 Developing a shared vision of the company within the organization.

2 Establishing and maintaining trust in the leadership of the organization.
3 Initiating and managing the process of change.
4 Empowering and motivating employees.

According to a study conducted by Kathryn Troy (1993), the role of communications managers has become somewhat more significant. Whereas, in the past, they were the facilitators of information flowing to senior management, their present role has become much more that of strategic advisers.

Corporate advertising is only one of the means by which a company communicates with its various publics. Bernstein (1989) identifies nine distinct media which serve to communicate and convey a company image:

1 *The products the company produces.* Every company offers a range of products or services to its customers, the perceived quality of which, and the way that they are presented, underpin or diminish the identity of the parent company. Particularly if a consumer has a poor experience or image of a product or service which is closely identified with its provider, his or her perceptions of that company will be diminished.
2 *Its correspondence.* The materials used for correspondence – the letterheads, envelopes, etc. – as well as the style and content will impact on the image of the company.
3 *Public relations.* The image of an organization will be substantially influenced by the relationships which it has with its various publics. A company which has a good, open and honest reputation is likely to be regarded as producing good products; the opposite is equally true.
4 *Personal presentation.* Many companies are, quite rightly, concerned with the way that people who represent the company present themselves. Shoddy dress, poor use of language (written and verbal), poor manners, and so on will reflect adversely on the company they personify. Increasingly, for example, retailers insist not only on an

appropriate dress code for their employees, they actually provide 'uniforms' which present a consistent image to the public they serve.
5 *Impersonal presentation.* The same principles apply equally to the intangible aspects of a company's presentation. The style of its buildings, company vehicles, offices, will all depict the stature of the organization to others. The Eddie Stobart organization, a leader in the field of transportation, insists that all of its vehicles are presented in the best possible light. Lorries must be cleaned regularly, and it is extremely rare to see a vehicle that has been damaged in a traffic accident.
6 *Literature.* All companies produce great quantities of printed material, from brochures and annual reports to leaflets and handouts. The care and attention which goes into those items will reflect favourably or unfavourably on the way that the company is perceived. Quality materials tend to evoke a positive response. Items produced 'on the cheap' are likely to undermine the image.
7 *Point of sale material.* Point of sale material designed to support a product or service at the point of purchase will have the same impact as other items of literature. Shoddily produced items – even though cheap to create – can do a great deal of harm to both the brand and the company's identity in the minds of those who see it.
8 *Permanent media.* Permanent media consists of signage, showcases and other items which are on continuous display. Sometimes, although not always, old-fashioned typefaces and logo styles will present the company as possessing a similar identity. Care must be taken not to confuse heritage and history with an old-fashioned image, although even here, attention to detail is important and a 'quality heritage' may need to be modernized from time to time.
9 *Advertising.* Advertising is the focal point of communication for many organizations. The style and tone will say as much about the nature of the company as the content of the message.

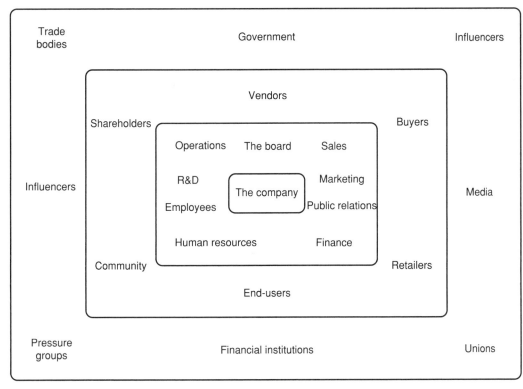

Figure 14.2   The audiences for corporate communications

Audiences for corporate communications

The extent to which the company needs to communicate can be seen in Figure 14.2, which depicts most of the major groups with which it needs to maintain a dialogue.

In the same book, Bernstein (1989) identifies nine different audiences for corporate communications:

1 *Internal.* Many companies tend to forget that their staff and workforces all represent potential ambassadors for the organization. If they have a positive relationship with their employer, they will tend to communicate a favourable impression. To engender such feelings, it is vitally important that the

employees feel involved with the company and, wherever possible, are exposed to the company's thinking at regular intervals. This can be achieved by periodic meetings at local, regional or national level in which staff are exposed to the views of the management team. In the same way, regular newsletters or company magazines are often used to disseminate views and to cement relationships between the organization and the people it employs.

2 *Local.* Companies need to develop positive relationships with the community in which they exist. If, for example, the company is seen to be a contributor to the local economy, it will tend to receive more support for such things as planning applications and the like. British Nuclear Fuels has for many years maintained a close dialogue with the local community in which

it operates to communicate the impact that it has on the level of local employment.

3 *Influential groups.* Whether on a local or a national basis, there will be a variety of external bodies which will have an impact on the company's activities. These may consist, among others, of pressure groups and public officials. Their relationships and perceptions of the organization will have an impact on the way that they respond to the company's activities. Shell, for example, have cultivated a positive relationship over many years with environmental groups who, in turn, have been more supportive than might otherwise have been the case. Unfortunately, this has been somewhat undermined by the recent actions of the company, mentioned above.

4 *The 'trade'.* Most companies are dependent on wholesalers, retailers and others who act as intermediaries between them and their ultimate customers. The cultivation of good relationships and a positive image will be an important contribution to their support.

5 *Government.* The actions of central government will have a marked impact on company performance. The introduction of unfavourable legislation may well diminish a company's profitability. The support of government agencies who represent them in overseas markets, for example, may be pivotal in gaining major foreign contracts.

6 *The media.* The media, in general, are the recipients of a variety of messages concerning the company. Some derive from positive public relations activities; others from impressions received from other sources. The interpretation they place on stories about the company will have a substantial impact on the way that those messages communicate.

7 *Financial.* The financial community will require a great deal of information about a company, its past performance and its prospects for the future. In order to secure a continued flow of investment, these relationships will need to be developed to ensure a positive response to company actions.

8 *Customers.* We have already seen that, to an increasing degree, customers are concerned as much about the nature of the company, the actions it takes on important issues and its general beliefs as with the quality of the products and services it produces. Because of the recent focus on environmental issues, companies have been able to secure positive images (and negative ones) from the actions which they have taken in this area – and, in turn, this is likely to impact on the sales volume they achieve. Remember, there are always alternatives available, and a company which is poorly received may well find that its customers turn to others to supply products and services.

9 *The general public.* The image of the company to the general public is of similar importance. Ultimately, for many companies, the general public are their consumers. How they think of a company will often determine whether they purchase from that company or another. Periodic research, such as that carried out by MORI, repeatedly demonstrates that companies with a positive image are expected to produce 'better quality' products.

The process of establishing a corporate identity

Dowling (1986) suggests a model for the development of corporate image in which a number of factors are important (Figure 14.3).

Having decided upon the corporate identity, the company must determine the best means of communicating it and its corporate strategy to its various audiences. The starting point is to consider all aspects of printed or visual communications in order to assess the consistency of the approach. It is inevitable that the larger the company, the more dispersed will be the responsibility for commissioning and producing these materials – with the consequent loss of consistency

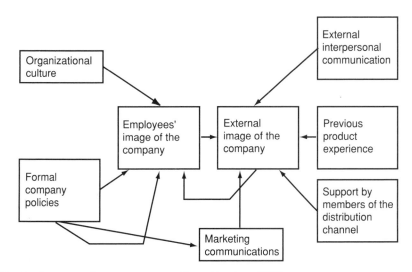

Figure 14.3 The development of corporate image (From Dowling, 1986)

and the danger of delivering a confused message.

The organizational structure and the naming policies for the subsidiary operations need to be examined in the light of the corporate strategy. Here again, it is important to ensure consistency. Many organizations have responded to this need by the creation of a corporate identity manual which embodies the look and style of the parent company and its subsidiaries. Not only does this provide the focus for internal examination, it also ensures the consistent application of the principles in all forms of communication.

At the same time, it will be possible to ensure that there is a logic and consistency in the graphical representation of the organization. The question to be asked is whether all parts of the company look similar, or whether they can be seen as independent operations. As well as ensuring that typography, colours and other aspects of printed communication are consistent in their representation of the corporate image, it is also important to question the tone of voice which is used in these materials. Does it convey a sympathetic feeling, or does it stand in sharp contrast to other aspects of the image?

Types of corporate identity

Olins (1989) divides corporate identities into three distinct categories.

Monolithic

This is the structure in which the organization uses a single name and visual style throughout all of its operations, where items of communication that the company uses serve to reinforce the identity of the parent company. Examples would be IBM, BMW, Shell and Prudential.

Endorsed

In this case, the organization maintains a separation between its subsidiary companies and the activities it pursues, but endorses those activities by the addition of the group name and identity alongside that of the operation company. Here, examples would be BAT and P&O. The former has diverse interests in the fields of tobacco, insurance, etc. and uses its corporate name to add stature and credibility. The latter, similarly, owns companies in areas such as house building (Bovis), exhibition halls (Earl's Court and Olympia) and others, alongside its more familiar cruise liners and cross-channel ferries. It is only in the last two operations that the P&O name is used directly. Elsewhere, the P&O logo and identity are used alongside the operating name.

Branded

Here, the company operates through a series of brands which may be unrelated to each other. Procter & Gamble owns operating companies in diverse markets such as soap powders, toiletries, perfumes, etc., with brands such as 'Oil of Ulay', 'Vidal Sassoon', 'Pantene' and others. In some cases, the identities are deliberately kept distinct to enable products to compete in the same market. Unilever has adopted a similar stance.

Kammerer (1995) (quoted in Van Riel, 1995) suggests that these identity structures are related to the goals of the parent company:

1 *Financial orientation.* In this instance, subsidiary companies are viewed purely as financial participants. Each subsidiary maintains its own identity, and the management of the parent company refrains from interference in the day-to-day running of the subsidiary, or in the determination of its strategy.
2 *Organisation-oriented corporate identity.* Here, the parent company assumes one or more of the management functions of the separate divisions. The parent influences the culture of the subsidiaries, and such differentiation of identity as exists within the subsidiary is purely internal. It is not communicated to the outside world.
3 *Communication-oriented corporate identity.* The identity of the parent company is clearly identified in advertising and other forms of marketing communications. Ultimately, the objective is to communicate the overall scale

of the operation. In turn, this can inspire confidence in the subsidiaries, especially where their individual identity is less well established. It also ensures that the goodwill of one subsidiary can be exploited by others.
4 *Single company identity.* All actions and communications are designed to speak as one.

Corporate communications

In order to communicate with all of an organization's audiences – internal and external – the process of communication must be addressed systematically. Although the process of design may be the initial focus of activity, it embraces far more than simply the change of name or logo. Various models have been described for the management of corporate communications, such as that by Ray (1982). His suggested procedure is as follows:

1 Conduct a situational analysis to establish the relative areas of strength and weakness for the organization and identify overall objectives.
2 Determine the marketing objectives.
3 Establish the total communications budget for the organization.
4 Allocate resources to the various communications activities embraced by the campaign.
5 etc.

Ray proposes that there are a series of questions which need to be answered in the context of a corporate message:

- Is the message consistent with the corporate strategy?
- Is it relevant to the identified target segment?
- Is it appropriate in the context of the communications mix?
- Does the concept offer 'leverage', that is, will it have a multiplier effect?

- Is the concept simple and uncomplicated?
- Is the concept specific to the organization, or can it be readily copied?
- Is it applicable to the wide variety of mass communication devices?
- Is it resistant to counter-attack from competitors?
- Does it offer longevity?

However, it is important to recognize that this process will result in a visual statement which identifies what the company stands for and presents a consistent message to diverse audiences, including consumers, customers, suppliers, the financial sector and other external audiences, together with management and employees within the company.

Measuring corporate communications

As with other aspects of marketing communications, the application of scientific rigour is an important part of the process. Without proper measurement, few organizations can hold a true picture of the ways in which they are perceived by others. Indeed, research will assist in the identification of the key dimensions which are important to the various audiences, and which will provide the subsequent basis for defining the corporate communications programme.

Research will need to be undertaken among all possible audiences for the corporate message (see list above). The key dimensions of image can then be plotted against a multiattribute scale, as shown in Figure 14.4.

The next stage will be that of plotting the company's results on these image dimensions against the established scale. Only then will it be possible to undertake the process of improving the perception of the organization in those areas which are seen to be weak. The process should be ongoing. Not only do image

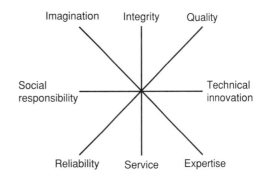

Figure 14.4

values change as a result of both internal and external factors, but the scales themselves may differ over time.

Not that long ago, few companies would have been concerned about the environmental issues relating to their operations. Today, the changed importance which is attached to this area has forced companies to address this issue as a matter of urgency. As a demonstration of its environmental concern, Alcan has mounted an advertising campaign to encourage users to recycle its aluminium cans. The advertising provides a freephone telephone number from which callers can identify their local recycling point, with the added benefit that the proceeds will generate income for charitable causes. The company claims that the campaign has raised £13 million for good causes in a single year.

Remember also that the strong and positive image attributes need to be maintained. The publics will have short memories, and past strengths can soon be forgotten. Corporate identity programmes should not be considered as the unique province of major manufacturers, or those involved within the fields of fmcg. The process is equally applicable to both profit and non-profit organizations. One only has to look at work carried out by government departments (such as the Department of Trade and Industry), charitable bodies (Barnardo's, Worldwide Fund for Nature), trade unions (The National Union of Teachers) and other organizations (British

Rail, British Telecom) to recognize that their respective identities have all been re-examined and redesigned in order to convey the appropriate desired images to their target audiences.

Key aspects of corporate communications

1 *The need for a long-term perspective.* In a dynamic and changing environment, corporate communications activities must focus on the longer-term aspirations of the organization. They must not inhibit change or potential movement into other operational areas.
2 *Clear statement of objectives.* Effective corporate communications, like all other aspects of marketing communications, must be based on a series of clearly stated and quantifiable objectives.
3 *Commitment of management.* Corporate communications are the embodiment of the corporate philosophy. The involvement of senior management in the process is imperative if the activities are to achieve the desired objectives.
4 *Involvement of employees.* Steps must be taken to ensure the active and positive involvement of staff at all levels. People within the organization must feel a pride of ownership if the activity is to secure their support.
5 *Consistency is paramount.* All aspects of the organization and its operations must be examined to ensure that the communications process provides a single unified view, and all aspects of the communications process must be integrated to provide the consistency desired.
6 *People and systems must be in place.* Corporate communications demand constant attention. They do not happen on their own. It is important that a process is established to ensure the consistency of approach and application in all areas of the company's operations.

7 *Evaluation.* No marketing communications campaign is perfect, and that is no less true of corporate activities. A proper programme of research and assessment must be an integral part of the corporate communications plan. Feedback and revision will be essential components of successful implementation.
8 *Only make changes for good reasons.* The oft quoted adage – 'If it ain't broke, don't try to fix it' applies here. Changes to the strategy should only be made for sound reasons. Change for its own sake will often result in more problems being caused than resolved.

Crisis management: an important dimension of corporate communications

Crisis management is a further area of corporate communications which is increasingly becoming recognized as a major aspect of the management of corporate identity and image. Perrier in the UK, Tylenol in the USA and others have all faced varying degrees of 'crisis' which they have had to deal with.

Two definitions help explain crisis in this context:

'The process of dealing with a pressurised situation in a way which plans, organises, directs and controls a number of inter-related operations and guides the decision making process of those in charge to a rapid but unhurried resolution of the acute problem faced by the organisation.' (Armstrong, 1990)

'A situation faced by an individual, group or organisation which they are unable to cope with by the use of normal routine procedures and where stress is created by sudden change.' (Booth, 1993)

There has been a considerable increase in the recognition of the role of crisis management. Significantly, companies have recognized that, in general, this does not represent major financial expenditure on the part of the company until a crisis actually occurs. The nature of their respective responses to their individual problems illustrates the importance of having a positive approach to crisis management. The company that is seen to fail in its response to a disaster, or whose response is deemed to be inadequate, has only itself to blame for the subsequent decline in its perceived persona.

'All media and communications are global and instant; the risks of things getting out of control are much greater. This is a major factor in the timing of response.' (Seymour, 1994)

'One in three companies which experience a major crisis never recover to pre-incident trading levels and some simply never survive.' (Fox, 1995)

Companies need to be prepared in advance to deal with a crisis – even though it is unlikely that they will know its precise nature – and have an established system and process to deal with and respond to the issues as they are raised. The process of anticipation is key. A crisis management programme ensures that the company can act quickly in the face of a crisis. By pre-planning, the procedures are in place to ensure that the company can respond speedily to the situation as it develops.

'Everyone in a position of authority should view and plan for the inevitability of a crisis in much the same way one views and plans for the inevitability of death and taxes; not out of weakness or fear, but out of the strength that comes from knowing you are prepared to play the hand that fate deals you.' (Fink, 1986)

It is important that there are clearly established and identifiable pathways of responsibility within the organization. Ideally, nominated individuals will be in place to deal with enquiries and become the focus for company statements, both internally and externally. Too many people acting on behalf of the company results in the danger of confused or contradictory responses, or responses based on poor information or knowledge of the situation.

Ideally, a company should have some form of plan in place which will be used to identify all areas of potential risk and, importantly, how to deal with them. This will enable a speedy response. As we have seen earlier, the lack of a direct response may itself be inferred as intentional on the part of some members of the audience. In any organization, it is possible to ensure that some 'crises' are identified in advance, although not prevented or eliminated. It may be inherent in the nature of the business that some problems will occur, e.g. deaths in hospitals, layoffs of staff during a downturn in the economy, and so on. Others cannot be so readily foreseen, but the need for a speedy and informed response will be the same.

Walkers Crisps avoided serious damage to the reputation of its brand after it was discovered that glass fragments from a broken lens on the production line had contaminated some packets. The company operated a crisis management team drawn from several different disciplines which met twice a year to rehearse crisis situations over a 48-hour period. When the crisis occurred, the company was ready to deal with it. Despite the fact that few packets were affected, the company withdrew the entire line, totalling 9 million packs. Press statements were drafted and issued, and within 24 hours it had a dedicated consumer helpline operating. The brand emerged from the crisis with its reputation untarnished (reported in *Marketing Week*, 19 April, 1997).

Chris Fill (1995) provides an organizational matrix (Figure 14.5).

Pearson and Mitroff, quoted in Booth (1993), attempted to identify the factors which result in companies becoming crisis-prone:

1 Organizational strategies – the plans and procedures for dealing with a crisis.
2 Organizational structure – related to whether or not the enterprise has structures to deal with the crisis.
3 Organizational culture – concerned with whether the organizational beliefs and rationalizations are crisis prone.

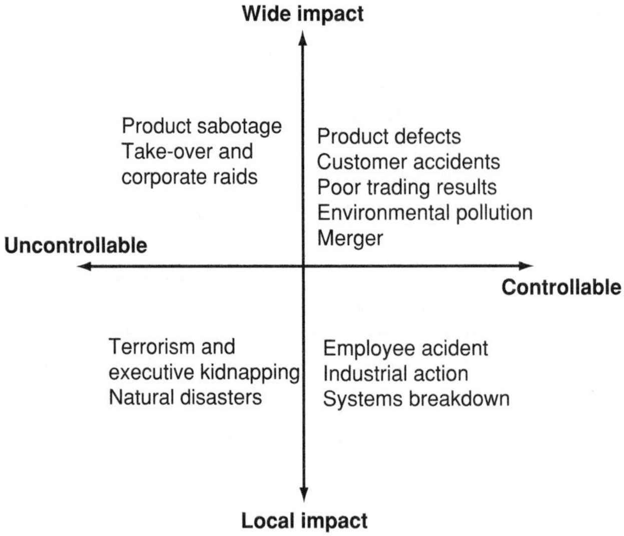

Wide impact

```
                          Product sabotage  │ Product defects
                          Take-over and     │ Customer accidents
                          corporate raids   │ Poor trading results
                                            │ Environmental pollution
                                            │ Merger
   Uncontrollable ◄───────────────────────────────────────────► Controllable
                          Terrorism and     │ Employee acident
                          executive kidnapping│ Industrial action
                          Natural disasters │ Systems breakdown
```

Local impact

Figure 14.5   Organizational matrix for crisis management (From Fill, 1995)

4 Characteristics of individuals working for organizations – the ability to handle increased levels of pressure and stress caused by a crisis.

Additionally, they have identified six fundamental forms of crisis:

1 Mega damage – environmental accidents.
2 External economic attacks – extortion, bribery, boycotts, hostile take-overs.
3 External information attacks – breach of copyright, information loss, counterfeiting.
4 Breaks – recalls, product defects, plant defects, computer breakdowns, poor security.
5 Perceptual – damage to reputation.
6 Psychological – terrorism, executive kidnappings, sexual harassment, rumours.
(Pearson and Mitroff, 1993)

Phases that crises go through

1 *Signal detection.* With very few exceptions, crises leave a trail of early warning signals. In some cases, organizations not only ignore these signals, but may make a conscious effort to avoid them.
2 *Preparation and prevention.* Every organization should do as much as possible to avoid the possibility of the crisis event occurring in the

first place and to effectively manage those which occur. Organizations should systematically search for potential problems before they become too large to resolve, and prepare for crises.
3 *Containment.* Despite the best preparation, some crises will inevitably occur. The objective must be to ensure a limitation on the damage which will be done to an organization as a result of the crisis.
4 *Recovery.* Companies must have appropriate plans to enable both their short-term and long-term recovery from a crisis event.
5 *Learning.* It is important that companies learn from a crisis event in order that they can develop adequate plans and procedures for the future. According to the study carried out by Pearson and Mitroff (1993), many companies avoided this stage because they felt that 'it would only serve to open old wounds'.

Mallozzi (1994) describes four basic phases to crisis communications:

1 Crisis preparedness.
2 The initial response.
3 Taking corrective actions.
4 Evaluation and follow-up.

Key dimensions of crisis management

The integration of any crisis management plan is achieved 'through planning, organising, leading and controlling a firm's activities and assets immediately before, during and after such an occurrence to preserve the resources the firm needs for the fullest feasible long-term recovery' (Hoban, 1995).

Developing a risk assessment and an appropriate operational audit enables a company to establish proper crisis management programmes. The plan must be reviewed and updated regularly. The key components of effective crisis management are:

• *Speed* – companies are evaluated in terms of the rapidity with which they respond to the crisis situation.
• *Accuracy* – information provided must be based on fact rather than speculation.
• *Credibility* – little undermines the interpretation of quality of response more than subsequent retractions of information previously delivered as 'fact'. Moreover, the chosen spokesperson must deliver the news in a form which is acceptable and believable.
• *Consistency* – positions adopted must be adhered to, and differing views or explanations avoided.

Preparedness for dealing with a crisis 'involves changing an organisation to reduce the extent to which shock events are novel and unanticipated and to improve the speed with which they are effectively managed' (Richardson and Richardson, 1992):

1 Develop a specific programme to deal with crisis management.
2 Identify specific personnel at a senior level whose responsibility it will be to deal with events as they occur.
3 Identify potential crisis areas in advance – and obviously devise programmes to avoid their occurrence.

4 Formulate specific strategies to deal with crisis events.
5 Devise effective communications channels.
6 Formalize the plan and ensure that it is communicated throughout the organization.

Handling a crisis

Mike Seymore (1991), Executive Director of Issues and Crisis Management at Burson Marsteller, says, 'Past training on crisis management had generally been concerned with senior management focusing on how to cope with the media. But now many experts feel that everyone within an organisation has to have an awareness'.

Several dimensions can be readily identified which will assist in the process of handling and dealing with a crisis:

1 Take the initiative by maintaining close contact with the media.
2 Provide accessibility by designating named individuals who should be contacted.
3 Do not offer speculation or guesses. Only established facts should be released.
4 Defer questions until facts are available.
5 Ensure that internal communications are good.
6 Anticipate the questions and keep the responses simple.
7 Think in terms of people implications.
8 Monitor all media coverage.
9 Follow up.

'Crisis planners should pay particular attention to the communication process and the decision making authority and coordination issues which arise during a crisis.' (Quarantelli, in Richardson and Richardson, 1992)

According to Wisenblit (1989), a crisis management plan should include the following components:

• A mechanism for determining potential crises;
• Identification of the audience(s) that would be affected;

- Procedures to follow during a crisis;
- Contingency plans to continue doing business during the crisis;
- Appointment and training of a crisis management team;
- Development of a crisis communication plan.

British Airways, who make extensive preparations to cope with any sudden crisis, have an emergency procedures information centre (EPIC) at Heathrow. It is operated by BA but is available to approximately forty subscribing airline operators in the UK. The centre has played a key role in a number of incidents; for example, it was involved with the Lockerbie disaster. This has served to increase its credibility and the trust of the company among its publics and even its competitors.

References

Aberg, L., 'Theoretical Model and Praxis of Total Communications', *International Public Relations Review*, 1990

Armstrong, M., *How To Be An Even Better Manager*, 3rd edition, Kogan Page, 1990

Bernstein, D., *Corporate Image and Reality*, Cassell, 1989

Booth, S., *Crisis Management Strategy*, Routledge, 1993

Dowling, G. R. 'Managing Your Corporate Image', *Industrial Marketing Management*, 15, 1986

Fill, C., *Marketing Communications, Frameworks, Theories and Applications*, Prentice Hall, 1995

Fink, S., *Crisis Management* 1986, Management Books 2000

Fox, P. MD, Grayling Group, 'Emergency Services', *Marketing*, October 1995

Hoban, D., 'Crisis Management', *Certified Accountant*, July 1995

Ind, N., *The Corporate Image: Strategies for Effective Identity Programmes*, 1990. Kogan Page

Mallozzi, C., 'Facing the Danger Zone in Crisis Communications', *Risk Management*, January 1994

Ogilvy, D., *Ogilvy on Advertising*, 1995, Prion

Olins, W., *Corporate Identity*, Thames & Hudson, 1989

Pearson, C. and Mitroff, I., *A Framework for Crisis Management*, Academy of Management Executive, 1993

Pincus, J. D., Robert, A. P. R., Rayfield, A. and DeBonis, J. N., 'Transforming CEOs into Chief Communications Officers', *Public Relations Journal*, 1991

Ray, M. L., *Advertising and Communications Management*, Prentice Hall, 1982

Richardson, W. and Richardson, R., *Business Planning – An Approach to Strategic Management*, 2nd edition, 1992, Pitman

Seymore, M., 'Planning for Crisis', *European Management Journal*, March 1991

Seymour, M., Burson Marsteller, *Marketing*, 28 July 1994

Troy, K., Managing Corporate Communications in a Competitive Climate, Conference Board, 1993

Van Riel, C., *Principles of Corporate Communications*, Prentice Hall, 1995

Wisenblit, J., 'Crisis Management Planning Among US Corporations', *SAM Advanced Management Journal*, Spring 1989

Additional reading

Gregory, James R. and Wiechmann, Jack, *Marketing Corporate Image*, 1991, NTC Business Books

Van Riel, Cees, *Principles of Corporate Communication*, 1995, Prentice Hall

Ind, Nicholas, *The Corporate Image*, 1989, Kogan Page

Bernstein, David, *Corporate Image and Reality*, 1989, Cassell

Booth, Sarah, *Crisis Management Strategy*, 1993, Routledge

CHAPTER 15

International marketing communications

Aims and objectives

- To consider the growth of international marketing;
- To examine the development of global brands and their management;
- To discuss international branding considerations;
- To grasp the importance of understanding the international consumer;
- To learn about the legal and regulatory requirements;
- To gain insight into issues of media availability and usage;
- To develop an awareness of the international competitive environment;
- To become familiar with the move towards global marketing communications;
- To understand the control issues of international marketing communications;
- To consider the use of marketing communications agencies in an international framework;
- To become familiar with international marketing communications strategies and the development of international marketing communications activities;
- To appreciate the importance of international market research.

The growth of international marketing

The years since the Second World War have seen an increasing tendency towards the internationalization of brands. Indeed, the term used to describe the process – 'globalization' – is itself comparatively recent. Increasingly, companies are recognizing that their competitiveness, even in domestic markets, is a reflection of their ability to develop their brands on a global basis. Their focus, progressively, must be to develop products and services which satisfy a wider range of consumer needs. With this growth comes increased expertise, successive product improvements, and economies of scale. As domestic markets have reached positions of virtual saturation, manufacturers have turned to new and often distant markets to ensure a continuation of their growth potential.

Multinational versus global marketing

We can make an important distinction between these two approaches to foreign markets – which have significant implications for the determination of marketing communications strategies.

The *multinational* company readily perceives the fundamental differences between the various markets it serves. In general, it believes that its success is dependent on the development of individual marketing and marketing communications programmes for each of its territories. As a result, it tends to operate through a number of subsidiaries which, for the most part, act independently of each other. Products are adapted or developed independently, to meet the needs of the individual markets and the consumers within them. By the same token, the other elements of the marketing mix are, similarly, developed on a local basis. Although there may be some cross-fertilization of ideas through some form of central function, the primary aim is to satisfy the needs of individual country markets, rather than the specific identification of common elements which might allow for the standardization of activities.

The *global* organization strives towards the provision of commonality, both in terms of its products and services, and the propositions which support them. As far as possible, it attempts to standardize its activities on a world-wide basis although, even within this concept, there is some recognition of the need for local adaptation to respond to local pressures. The fundamental objective is the identification of groups of buyers within the global market with similar needs, and the development of marketing and marketing communications plans that are standardized as far as possible within cultural and operational constraints.

The impetus for a more detailed examination of the implications of international marketing was provided by a seminal article by Theodore Levitt in the *Harvard Business Review* in 1983. The thrust of his argument in 'The Globalization of Markets' is that a variety of common forces, the most important of which is shared technology, are driving the world towards a 'converging commonality'. The

result, he argues, is 'the emergence of global markets for standardized consumer products on a previously unimagined scale'. Levitt suggests that 'companies must learn to operate as if the world were one large market, ignoring superficial regional and national differences'. However, this is far from being an accepted view. Philip Kotler, among others, considers globalization as a step backwards to the so-called production era of business, when organizations were more concerned about producing as many standardized products as possible, rather than worrying about satisfying individual consumer needs and wants (Kotler, 1994).

From a personal standpoint, I would argue that it is the convergence of communications which has, and will continue to have, a far greater impact and will assist those companies which are seeking to develop both standard products and standard marketing communications approaches. We have already seen that consumer motivations towards the purchasing of products and services are the result of the influence of a wide range of factors. One central factor which impacts upon many, if not all, of them is the mass media. As the peoples of the world are exposed to the same messages via television, film and other media, it is inevitable that their attitudes towards the products and services depicted will move towards a common central point.

Irrespective of our location, it is likely that most of us will listen to the same music (the bands that top the charts in one country often enjoy similar levels of success in others); the same films (which country has not yet been exposed to 'Jurassic Park: The Lost World', 'Independence Day' or the various 'Batman' movies, to name but a few); the same television programmes; the same computer programs (just consider the world-wide launch of the Microsoft operating system Windows '95); and even the same articles in the media.

Whilst it is undeniable that cultural differences will continue to prevail, at least for some considerable time into the foreseeable future, so too we are witnessing the coming together of many attitudes and beliefs, which enhance the potential for products and services which respond to those common and shared values.

The development of global brands

It is inevitable that the progressive standardization of products results in significant economies of manufacture which, potentially, leads to lower prices and a more competitive positioning for the brand. The high investment in product development will be rapidly amortized if the market for the resulting product is global and enormous rather than domestic and limited. Such developments, however, will not obviate the need in many instances to adapt the product to meet 'special' local needs, however these are occasioned.

Some manufacturers perceive the world of the future to be one in which global brands dominate. The perceived benefits of a single world-wide brand identification outweigh those of country-specific products with separate brand identities. However, it is important to remember that, even here, it is not essential that the product delivered in each market is identical – only that the branding and the imagery associated with it are the same.

Each year, Fortune publishes a list of the top 500 companies. Several interesting dimensions emerge from an examination of the current listing (*Fortune* magazine, 4 August, 1997). The USA and Japan are the bases of the most significant global companies. Of the top twenty, eight companies are American in origin, whilst ten are centred on Japan. Only the Royal Dutch Shell Group (Anglo/Dutch) and Mercedes Benz (Germany) manage to make the top twenty. Five of the world's largest companies are involved in the manufacture of cars, and a further three produce petroleum products. Although ranked outside the top twenty, several other familiar names figure prominently. Ranked at 21 is the highest placed UK company, British Petroleum, whilst VW and Daewoo occupy 23rd and 24th places respectively. The world's largest food company is Unilever at 31, followed by Nestlé at 36.

The last-named organization has adopted essentially the same packaging and style for its leading brand of instant coffee across most international markets. However, the specific product may well be different in many of those markets to reflect local taste characteristics.

Even where it is necessary to subjugate the current brand identity in favour of a single consistent world-wide brand mark, major manufacturers have determined that the long-term benefits are likely to outweigh the short-term losses. Despite enjoying considerable consumer acceptance in the UK with their Marathon brand, Mars opted for a standardization of the brand under the name of Snickers across all markets. The same policy is now being applied to Opal Fruits, renamed Starburst.

Global branding

As globalization is increasing, the scope and rationale for local differentiation is being reduced. In practice, the number of truly standardized global brands is limited – Burger King, BMW, Mazda, Coke and Pepsi. Many brands, like Kit Kat and Colgate, are global in name but have shown significant differences in positioning, branding and packaging from country to country. The reality of globalization is that usually some decisions are standardized, whilst others are tailored to local needs (Club Med attempts to standardize its villages, quality and advertising themes, but not its promotional activities and budgets). Very often, global brands coexist with local brands.

The world's leading brands are familiar to people in virtually every country in the world. The 1996 Interbrand survey assesses some 350 brands against a series of criteria:

- Brand weight – the extent of the dominance of a brand over its market;
- Brand length – the extent of brand extension outside its original category;
- Brand breadth – the strength of the brand across age, gender, nationality and religion;
- Brand depth – a measurement of consumer commitment to the brand.

Based on these dimensions, the top ten global brands in 1996 were as shown in Table 15.1.

Table 15.1 Top ten global brands, 1996

1 McDonald's
2 Coca Cola
3 Disney
4 Kodak
5 Sony
6 Gillette
7 Mercedes Benz
8 Levi's
9 Microsoft
10 Marlboro

Source: 'The World's Greatest Brands', Interbrand, reported in *Marketing Week*, 15 November 1996

The Interbrand study illustrates the changing fortunes of global brands. Not only have there been a series of changes in the positions occupied, but several have dropped out of the top ten since 1990. At that time, Coca Cola was the largest brand, now down to second position. However, the list also included IBM, American Express and Nescafé, all of which have declined over the period.

The management of global brands

Companies adopt varying approaches to the management of global brands. Research conducted by Focus (Aitchison, 1995) indicated that, among the companies surveyed in their study representing a cross-section of major international brands, there was a general consensus that there should be conformity of product or service delivery. The varied attitudes and approaches to international branding issues can be seen from the following company statements:

'In our business, globally consistent product performance and packaging, coupled with visual consistency, is a prerequisite.' (Shell)

'We are committed to standard product performance with a consistent presentation across all markets.' (Kellogg's)

However, a key factor was the ability to recognize and respond to consumer needs:

'A global brand has an appeal that can transcend political, ethnic, social or cultural boundaries.' (IBM)

'We create and satisfy the same need, using the same values in each country.' (Coca Cola)

The research suggests that successful global brands satisfy at least one of three categories of consumer needs: physiological, personal utility or self-worth. In each instance, however, the satisfaction of those needs also requires the endorsement of brand values and positionings which themselves have universal relevance. Without such endorsement, the brand remains open to competition from locally produced brands, either 'me-too' or those of an innovative nature.

A major benefit of globalization is efficiency and economies of scale:

'A global brand gives us significant economies of scale right across the board – in media and production costs, sponsorship, manufacturing and management costs.' (International food and drinks manufacturer)

'Global branding gives us major cost efficiencies in marketing and production as well as a powerful tool to control our brand through joint ventures and third party distributors.' (Global brewer)

'We ended up with too many centres of manufacturing across Europe, with too many products and with too many brand names; we have been rationalizing on all fronts.' (Pedigree Petfoods)

'Our consistent brand image and wide availability is very important to our customers – they themselves are very international in outlook.' (Bacardi)

Differing attitudes and approaches are evidenced towards the development of international marketing communications campaigns:

'We impose strong control from HQ, with clearly defined brand and advertising strategy being passed down to the local offices. All advertising is approved at HQ and local freedom is largely limited to local promotion and distribution activity.' (Bacardi)

'The development of the British Airways brand and its sub-brands (such as Club World) is managed from Head Office. A partnership process between Head Office and the regions jointly agrees a three-year plan.' (British Airways)

'The HQ marketing function underpins our national marketing decisions. We put forward our plans and budgets with an overall brand framework.' (Moulinex)

International branding

Even the use of the word 'brand' has to be reinterpreted in the international context. According to Mary Goodyear (1996), Western marketers tend to focus on the product as a brand; in Japan and Korea, 'brand' tends to refer to the corporate entity. The consequence is that it tends to be evaluated over a much longer time scale. Individual 'brands' can come and go, but the total corporate share becomes the centre of long-term planning. Mitsubishi and Daewoo are good examples of this, with both companies maintaining diverse interests in a wide variety of sometimes unrelated markets.

It is important to recognize that, in developing countries, brands play a significantly smaller role in terms of the regular shopping process. Many products which have become brands in Western society (bread, biscuits, milk, sugar) remain as commodities which continue to be purchased loose.

International branding considerations

In the development of companies, many find themselves forced to seek further opportunities to continue the process of brand expansion. In many cases, these opportunities exist by expanding into new countries. The benefits which can be derived from the economies of production, and the apparent similarity of the markets in other countries, have attracted some brands to expand beyond their original marketplaces. The process of developing *international* brands is very similar to that adopted for *national* brands although, inevitably, it is both more complex and time-consuming – especially if the underlying desire is to achieve parity of brand image in all of the markets in which the product is sold.

A series of fundamental questions must first be asked about how products in the category are expected to perform in different markets. The functional areas of a product may be different from country to country. The fact that many consumers in different countries all drink instant coffee, for example, should not suggest that their expectations of product performance are the same. Almost all of the Latin countries, for example, tend to drink their coffee much stronger than, say, in the UK. Offering the same blend to all markets might lead to acceptance in some, but would find rejection in others. The evaluation of the performance of washing powders might be the same in most markets – how clean do they get my clothes – but factors such as the way in which the product is used may have an important bearing. Is the penetration of automatic washing machines similar, or do many consumers in some markets still wash by hand?

Understanding the brand personality is, arguably, even more important in the inter-national context. We have seen that the dimensions of brand personality are largely perceptual. They relate to the images which have been created over time by the various aspects of marketing communications. Equally important, however, they relate to elements of consumer behaviour in the dif-ferent markets. In some markets, the use or possession of a particular product may have no meaning beyond its functional purposes. In others, it may be regarded as a symbol of success or affluence. Setting what, for some, is an aspirational product in a mundane environment – but a wholly appropriate set-ting for others – for advertising purposes is likely to undermine the values associated with the brand. It is important to ensure that there is an adequate 'fit' between the positioning of the brand and the perceptions of the consumers in all of the markets in which it is to be sold.

Ultimately, of course, it may be possible to alter the underlying perceptions and reach a point at which all markets share a common view of the brand. Until that time is reached, however, it is important that the brand con-tinues to deliver against the expectations of the consumers who purchase it.

There are several important international dimensions to aspects of branding:

1 Certain products have strong associations with particular countries – pasta with Italy, perfume with France, for example. This has an impact on the brand name decision even if the product does not originate from the particular country. Japan has long been associated with high-quality products in the field of high technology. Many electrical products have adopted Japanese-sounding brand names even though they are manufactured elsewhere. Both Germany and Japan enjoy strong reputations for the production of high-quality cars.

Recently, Cadbury's were ordered to withdraw a chocolate bar sold under the name of 'Swiss Chalet' because it implied that the product was Swiss.

This notion of 'country of origin' has been suggested by a number of writers to have a 'halo effect' on the purchasing decision, particularly in those circumstances where the consumer is unfamiliar with the particular brand (Johansson et al., 1985; Min Han, 1990).

2 The image of imported products as opposed to products produced in the home country. This ethnocentricity has an important bearing, which may be either positive or negative. France has long had a reputation for biasing consumption to domestically produced products. Its car market enjoys a significantly higher penetration of domestically produced cars compared with most other countries.

The opposite impact of the country of origin can be seen from an example provided in a paper by Bilkey and Nes (1982) in which they cite a Puerto Rican shoe manufacturer which exported its entire production to New York and then re-imported them in order that it could advertise the shoes as being from New York. The manufacturer felt that the shoes would be better received as being made in New York than in its own country.

3 The national image of the manufacturing company, e.g. Waterford Glass is seen as being an Irish product, although part of its production is sourced from Poland.

David Head (1998), writing in the *Inter-national Journal of Advertising*, suggests that there are three distinct categories of 'made in' appeals:

1 Appeals to national pride and the patriotism of consumers.
2 Appeals that highlight stereotypical attributes of a country and associate those attributes with a specific brand.
3 Appeals that suggest a particular expertise which is associated with a country. Switzerland is associated with manufacturing expertise in the field of watches, for example.

The majority of international brands were originally conceived on a national level and developed to achieve a recognition within their original markets. Brand names were more often selected because of the impact in their own national context. This can lead to particular problems when the product is exported to other markets.

A major brand of lemonade in France is sold under the name of Pschitt, whilst Zit is a soft drink in Greece; one of the leading brands of toilet tissue in Scandinavia is retailed under the name of Krapp; Fanny is a canned tuna product, Skum a Swedish confectionery, whilst Colon is a Spanish brand of washing detergent. Each of these products might encounter difficulties in other markets!

International brands share a number of consistent characteristics:

1 The products all share a long-term orientation. The majority of recognized international brands have established long-term consumer awareness and recognition which, in turn, achieves brand goodwill. Coca Cola was first introduced in 1886. Ivory Soap is over 100 years old. Kellogg's first produced Corn Flakes in the 1880s. Avon was adopted as the name for the company previously trading as the California Perfume Company. Today, it has an estimated 1.6 million representatives in over 100 countries. Cadbury started manufacturing drinking chocolate in 1831 and eating chocolate in the early 1870s (the use of the name Bourneville was a reflection of the then prestige of French chocolate). Production of the safety razor by King Camp Gillette commenced in 1903. George Eastman produced the first Kodak camera in June 1888, and has been associated with photographic products since that time. Lego, synonymous with children's toys, is a derivative of the Swedish words *leg godt* (play well). The company first introduced its product in the 1930s and today produces 97 per cent of its products for export, to over 106 countries.

2 International brands are mostly those products which have established a consumer reputation based on considerable and cumulative advertising expenditure. The advertising budget for Kellogg's was as high as $1 million in 1911. Heinz adopted the slogan '57 Varieties' in the late 1880s, even though the company manufactured more than 60 even then. The copy line has remained unchanged since that time.

3 According to Shalofsky (1987), many of these international brands have a basic credibility which relates to their national image. Marlboro cigarettes and Coca Cola share an American heritage. Buitoni (now owned by Nestlé) is synonymous with Italy, the home of good pasta.

Understanding the international consumer

If marketing communications demands a thorough understanding of consumers and the environmental factors which surround them, this is even more true of marketing communications in an international context. Where we can reasonably expect to understand important facets of consumer behaviour in a domestic context, this is far less likely to be the case in different and separate markets where culture, tradition and other factors may result in vastly different meanings being attached to the communications message.

Market research will play an important part in identifying those areas of similarity in order to allow for the development of a single consistent message, if that be the objective. It should be clear that, in order to develop an effective multinational or global communications strategy, a number of 'new' dimensions will have to be considered, beyond those which would be appropriate for a single market communications strategy.

The model of communications, discussed earlier in Chapter 1, needs some re-examination in the international context (Figure 15.1).

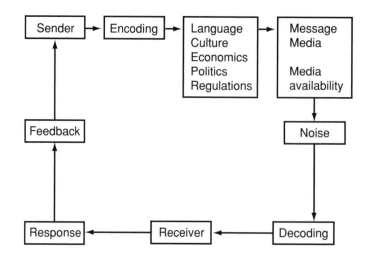

Figure 15.1

Language

Language is an obvious discriminating factor in the international context. It has been suggested that there are over 3000 different languages in current use. Some are indigenous to a single country or region, others are commonly spoken in several different countries. Many countries are multi-lingual. Canadian law requires that all product packaging be produced in both English and French. In Belgium, potential consumers may speak French or Flemish. India has over 200 distinct languages or dialects.

Although English is increasingly the lingua franca of many major international businesses (many companies are American-owned and insist that business is conducted in their own tongue), it was Winston Churchill who suggested that the USA and Britain were two nations separated by a common language. Recently, an American advertiser described his product in a domestic campaign as 'a little bugger'. The word has a somewhat different meaning in the UK. Brand names may suggest different connotations in different markets. The brand name Durex is the leading brand of contraceptives in the UK, whilst in Australia it is a major brand of adhesive tape!

Increasingly, international advertising campaigns feature words in English, although their appearance is scheduled for countries where English is not the mother tongue. While on the surface this might not appear to pose a problem, it may have negative consequences if the words used can be incorrectly translated. The Vauxhall Nova, for example, was introduced to Spain, where the word literally means 'doesn't go'. A previous Pepsi campaign slogan – 'Come Alive, You're in the Pepsi Generation' – was translated into German. Unfortunately, the German slogan meant 'Come alive out of the grave'!

Multinational communications campaigns often fail because the message is simply *translated* rather than *reinterpreted*. This is not simply merely a semantic difference. Not only is it true that specific words often will not have a correspondence in another language, sometimes the true translation will have a negative impact on the target audience. Colgate Palmolive launched its Cue toothpaste in France without first establishing the meaning of its brand name. To its surprise, it subsequently discovered that the word is a pornographic expression. Schweppes discovered that its leading tonic water product translated into Italian meant bathroom water.

Culture and tradition

A critical dimension of international marketing communications is the divergent nature of the cultures in which the activity will be seen. Culture, as discussed earlier, is that complex whole which includes knowledge, beliefs, art, morals, customs and the various other capabilities and habits which are acquired as a member of a particular society.

Arguably, this is one of the most difficult areas of multinational communications. Perceptions which are based on tradition and culture are extremely difficult to overcome. Fundamental areas, such as pack colours or symbols, may have totally different meanings resulting from cultural interpretation.

Culture is learned behaviour, passed on from one generation to another. Often it is a difficult barrier for the outsider to cross, substantially because we tend to observe other people in the context of our own cultural values. In many cases, the differences between societies are quite subtle and may not be immediately apparent. They may influence, for example, the ways in which people relate to each other; the roles of men and women within society; eating habits; relationships with authority; and dress habits, both within the working environment and in informal situations. Any of these elements may be a component of a marketing communications campaign which, in order to communicate effectively, must be considered within the context of the cultural values of the society in which the campaign is to be run.

When Disney introduced its theme park to Paris, it adopted the same style of operation as had been successful elsewhere. As in the USA and Japan, alcoholic drinks were banned. Subsequently, however, the organization was forced to change its policy when it recognized the French tradition of drinking wine with meals.

At a superficial level, cultural values can be modified over time, resulting in the creation of a form of 'global culture'. Sometimes this is the result of people working within multi-national companies, which may seek to impose constant values in all the countries in which they operate. Equally, some of the imagery created by brands may become accepted within many otherwise diverse cultures.

Work conducted by the Henley Centre for Forecasting has suggested that there are important factors of consumer convergence throughout Europe and elsewhere. The increasing domination of Anglo-American culture in terms of music, films and so on carries with it a variety of cultural and brand values. Films, particularly those of American origin, gain almost immediate world-wide distribution. This is less true in reverse. Music and film material developed elsewhere gains, at best, limited distribution, and often only in exclusive 'arts' theatres.

Most significantly, the cultural values, sometimes derived from religious views, result in markedly different attitudes towards products and services. Several examples will illustrate. It would be an anathema to show pork or shellfish ingredients in a product intended for a predominantly Jewish market; the same would apply to beef in Hindu communities or alcohol for Muslims.

Recently, McDonald's suffered from a failure to understand the cultural dimensions of one of its markets. Orthodox Jews in Israel campaigned for the removal of McDonald's advertising from television. The advertising standards committee at Israel's Channel 2 network put their weight behind the proposed ban, since they recognized that the campaign offended religious observers.

Nike has been forced to withdraw a line of training shoes because the logo, intended to look like flames, resembled the word 'Allah' in Arabic and has offended Muslims. In 1995, the company was forced to remove a poster which showed a basketball player with the headline 'They called him Allah'.

Whilst the specific advertising message might avoid such obvious errors, it is important to remember that the surroundings in which the message is set (a home, a retail outlet, etc.) may, similarly, contradict existing cultural beliefs. In some markets, for example, it would be inappropriate to depict a woman wearing Western clothes; in others, a commonly used motif of a man stroking a woman's skin to connote smoothness would be regarded as taboo.

Even large brands sometimes fail to appreciate the significance of local cultural factors. Retail audits suggest that Pepsi controls up to 80 per cent of the Saudi Arabian market. Several years after entering the market, Coca Cola has been unable to gain a significant share. Much of Coke's advertising has featured images of everyday people – predominantly Western – with which the Saudi people find it difficult to associate. Pepsi has tended to take an impersonal approach, featuring just the brand logo itself, without the use of people. If people are used, they will be Middle Eastern. By these means, Pepsi has identified itself as part of the Saudi Arabian society.

Equally, the nature of the individual purchase decision may vary as a result of cultural influences. The role of the family may, in certain circumstances, be more important in the final determination of which products and services to purchase. This is particularly true in parts of Asia. For example, discretion over the use of income is heavily influenced by the expected contribution to the family. The tradition of deference to parental wishes affects patterns of buying in clothing, leisure expenditure, etc. (Redding, 1982).

Perception

The perception of shapes, colours and symbols varies across cultures. White is the colour of birth, and in the West it is usually associated with weddings; whereas in China, Japan and India the colour symbolizes mourning. Green, a colour normally associated with freshness and good health in the West, is sometimes associated with disease elsewhere. The colour is favoured in Arab countries but forbidden in Indonesia. Black is often seen as the universal colour of mourning; however, in many Asian countries it is white, in Brazil it is purple, in Mexico yellow, and in parts of Africa dark red. Red suggests good fortune in China, but death in Turkey.

In India, the owl is a symbol of bad luck, the equivalent of the black cat, while the stork, which in the West is associated with birth, symbolizes maternal death in Singapore, (Copeland and Griggs, 1986).

International marketers must gain a cultural understanding of the meaning of both colours and symbols in order to ensure that their packaging and product design and even advertising messages communicate the appropriate and desired values. As Jacobs *et al.* (1991) comment, 'Marketers in a particular nation often take colour for granted, having experienced certain colour associations all their lives, and do not even question whether other associations may exist in different societies'.

Motivation

It is important to consider the motivations to own, to buy, to spend, to consume, against the background of the intended market. Usenier (1996) suggests that Maslow's Hierarchy of Needs should be readdressed in the international context. Importantly, whilst Maslow argues that needs must be satisfied at each level before the higher-order needs appear, this is contradicted within specific societies. To some extent, the level of economic development exerts an influence. Clearly, in third world countries where the economies are somewhat less developed, the population in general tend to have more basic survival needs. In contrast, however, some of those same cultures encourage self-actualization in a manner which does not imply material consumption.

Learning and memory

The level of literacy is shaped by the education system. Prior experiences of product categories will have an important bearing upon the acceptance (or otherwise) of a new product launched into a foreign market.

Meaning

Edward Hall (1976) has provided a concept to explain the cultural framework of meaning. He distinguishes between low and high context, where the former place an emphasis on words whilst the latter are more reliant on contextual cues. In low-context societies, such as Germany and much of Scandinavia, advertising tends to be more logical, scientific and provides evidence to substantiate the product claims being made. In high-context countries, such as Japan and China, advertising tends to be more intuitive and appeals to the consumer's emotions. Advertising formats which are extensively used in many European campaigns – which provide a focus on the merits of a particular product, often making comparative claims, for example – fail to have any real impact in high-context marketplaces.

Age

Consider the respective valuation of younger and older people within society. Also, how purchasing power is distributed across generations.

Self-concept

How do people consider their roles and, importantly, how do particular products and services relate to these roles? Ownership of a car may have purely functional values in some markets; elsewhere, the car is an extreme symbol of status within society. Following the breakdown of the barriers between Eastern and Western Europe, many car marques are sold in the former Eastern bloc because of the status values associated with their names.

Group influence

To what extent are individuals influenced in their attitudes and buying behaviour by their group? How does consumer behaviour reflect the need to self-actualize individual identity or to manifest group belonging?

Social class

Are social classes important locally? Is social class demonstrated through consumption? What types of products or services do social status-minded consumers buy? Are there exclusive shops?

Sex roles

Who makes the decisions? In Japan, the housewife makes the majority of major purchases. More significantly, she receives her husband's pay cheque and allocates a sum of money for him to spend on personal requirements, including his lunch. In this context, targeting the housewife is a priority for major Japanese advertisers. Who shops – he, she or both?

Decision making

Family models (nuclear versus extended family) differ markedly between countries. In some, particularly where the extended family is paramount, the family 'elder' may exert a disproportionate influence on the nature of the products and services purchased; elsewhere, it is important to consider the influence of children on the decision-making process.

Purchase

The patterns of purchasing frequency differ markedly between countries, sometimes resulting from differences in income levels, on other occasions the results of patterns of usage. In some parts of the East, for example, fresh produce is bought on a daily basis, whereas elsewhere shopping, even for fresh ingredients, may be carried out weekly and the resultant purchases stored in the fridge or freezer.

Motivational factors and aspirations

These are also different from one country to another, leading to difficulties in communicating aspirational 'norms' where such values either do not exist or have different parameters.

Loyalty/purchasing environment

In most Western countries, consumers expect their 'favourite' brands to be available on a regular basis in the outlets they frequent. Elsewhere, factors of distribution may have an important influence on availability. In some instances, consumers become accustomed to purchasing from the product category, rather than expecting to be able to purchase any given brand. Similarly, the influence of sales-persons may have greater or lesser importance in different markets.

Post-purchase

Here again, a distinction can be drawn between Western and developed markets and those of the underdeveloped nations. Expectations of product quality will inevitably differ between them. Similarly, there may be different 'cultures' which relate to the nature of consumer complaints.

Standards of living

Products which are consumed on a daily basis in some countries may be considered as luxuries in others – particularly if the relative cost is high. Cigarettes, for many purchased in packets of 20, are sold singly in some African markets, with the resultant difficulties of the lack of packaging to communicate brand values. Elsewhere, the incidence of fridges may preclude the sale of some packaged convenience foods, and so on.

Legal and regulatory requirements

There are few common standards for marketing communications across all markets – although there are progressive moves towards harmonization in some areas, such as the EC. Yet tobacco advertising, for example, is still commonplace in many parts of Europe, while being limited or totally prohibited in others. Most countries now see condom advertising as part of the global campaign to control AIDS. However, in certain countries with strong religious beliefs, such advertising would be unthinkable. Sales promotion techniques which are commonly accepted and widely used in some markets are not allowed in others.

There are increasingly complex differences when marketing across borders. Either morally or from the standpoint of regulations, the situation differs from market to market. In the UK, for example, there is no problem with advertising confectionery. In Finland, however, there are not only restrictions of the advertising of confectionery products, but also sugar taxes designed to directly cut consumption. In Sweden there is a complete ban on advertising directed at children under the age of 12. In Germany comparative and price advertising are heavily restricted. Rules on prizes and promotional draws are also constrained. It is also against the law, in Germany, to cold-call or mail-shot a prospect even if you have the person's card (Haigh, 1996).

The controls imposed on such activities as advertising and sales promotion will vary significantly between countries. What is considered perfectly acceptable in one country may be regarded as offensive in another:

1 *Restrictions on product types.* Many countries impose bans or other forms of limitation on the specific types of products and services which may be advertised freely. Many countries, for example, have complete prohibitions on the advertising of cigarettes; others control the promotion of alcohol. Tougher restrictions on advertising to children currently exist in Greece, Sweden, Norway and parts of Belgium, where bans on toy advertising are in place. In France the use of children in food ads is banned, and Sweden has outlined plans to propose a Europe-wide TV ban on advertising to children under 13. In Canada and Sweden, advertising to children during children's programmes is banned.

2 *Comparative advertising.* Comparative advertising is almost commonplace in the USA. Elsewhere, as in Germany, comparative claims can only be made following fairly rigorous tests of the statements. In the UK, comparisons have tended to be less direct, e.g. 'Brand X'. In Japan, such comparisons tend not to be made more for cultural than for legislative reasons.

3 *Taxation on advertising.* Some countries impose comparatively high levels of taxation on advertising expenditure. This adds significantly to the raw media costs and, for some smaller companies, may preclude access to mainstream media-based activity.

4 *Locally produced advertising.* Several countries restrict the use of advertising which is produced outside that country. For example, Australia requires that commercials must be produced with local crews in attendance.

Media availability and usage

A primary consideration, especially in the context of global campaigns, is the need to access constant media outlets. After all, if a major aim of standardization is to eliminate costly production, then the same media must be available in all markets. However, not only are certain media not available to the marketer in some areas – certain countries, for example, have only limited television penetration, whilst others do not allow advertising – the patterns of usage may also differ. In some countries, spot advertising throughout the day is commonplace. In others, all advertising is grouped together and broadcast at set times of the day.

Other aspects of media are equally important. In different markets, different media have a different status, such that advertising placed in them has greater or lesser credibility. This is particularly the case in those markets where media have a distinct religious or political orientation.

The competitive environment

Just as consumers differ between markets, so do the brands available to them. Identifying the aspirational values for a brand, in order to define a unique positioning, becomes more difficult as the number of markets increases and the competitors differ in their stances. Often, a desired positioning is already occupied by another brand in a particular market. And, as we have seen, the relative position of a brand – leader or follower – will have important implications for communications strategy determination. It is extremely unlikely that all but a very few brands occupy the same position in all of the markets in which they are available.

It is clear from the above that the task of developing a singular marketing communications strategy, whilst not insuperable, is an extremely difficult one. Many companies have accepted that, in order to achieve their communications objectives, they must adopt a somewhat different stance. Indeed, such consensus as exists suggests that the policy towards multinational marketing communications campaigns should be based on the statement 'Think globally, act locally'. Inherent in this statement is the acceptance of the fact that common communications strategies can be developed across all markets, but that their implementation must be effected on a local basis, in order to reflect the multitude of differences which – despite convergence – continue to exist.

The move to global marketing communications

In the same way that we have seen the progressive move towards the standardization of brands, so too there has been the movement towards the development of standardized marketing communications programmes. The rapidly accelerating costs of producing separate campaigns for individual markets, the difficulties of co-ordinating separate campaigns in physically close markets, together with the desire for the establishment of a single world-wide identity for its brands, have induced many companies to explore the potential of single campaign development across many, if not all, markets. Inevitably, there are polarized views on the merits of such moves. At one extreme, as a response to the pressures indicated above, some companies have developed central campaigns which provide the core of all of their marketing communications activity in all markets.

For a number of years, Coca Cola have run essentially similar campaigns in many markets, with all or most of the elements being constantly applied in all of the territories in which they operate. Their sponsorship of the 1994 World Cup, for example, was featured prominently on cans sold as far apart as Thailand and Malaysia and the UK. In the past, identical advertising, save only for the language of the voiceover, has been run by the brand across all territories.

At the other end of the spectrum are a wide range of international brands which continue to develop 'local' advertising propositions which, in their view, enable them to more readily reflect the needs and desires of the individual markets in which they operate.

Between these two positionings are those brands which adopt a common communications strategy, but allow for the local development of specific executions. In these instances, there is a cohesion in the underlying message of the brand in all of its markets, but room for the development of tightly focused and tailored propositions which reflect the subtleties and nuances of the local marketplace.

Some manufacturers have developed this approach to the position where they develop 'pattern book' communications campaigns. An overall stance for the brand will be taken centrally, with semi-finished examples of advertising and sales promotional approaches laid down by the centre. These, however,

provide the 'shell' of activity, and the local operations have the flexibility to adjust the specific content to meet their local requirements.

It is this latter area which has witnessed the greatest growth over recent years. Indeed, even the ubiquitous Coca Cola have recognized the need to develop specific messages for individual markets to respond to pressures on the brand's position. The company has always prepared a pool of commercials for international use. In April 1997 it unveiled sixteen new commercials in the 'Always Coca Cola' campaign. However, the regional companies are no longer forced to use them. In the UK, for example, only one commercial adapted from the pool has run in the past six months. Here, the work which was originally developed for Euro 96 – 'Eat Football, Sleep Football, Drink Coca Cola' – has continued to dominate the communications programme. The head office continues to generate brand strategy but, subject to their approval, the local markets can develop creative work more in tune with the local environment. The company claims that 'our marketing structure translates global into local'.

The evolution of the full service multinational agency is seen by many to be the obvious response to two of the most fundamental issues of the 1990s – the integration of marketing communications, and the globalization of brands.

The scale of expenditures of the world's global marketers can be seen in Table 15.2. (extracted from *Advertising Age's* top 50 global marketers outside the USA, November 1996).

Central or local control of marketing communications

A company operating on an international basis must pursue 'one of three alternative approaches:

Table 15.2 Top ten global marketers, 1995, ranked by world-wide advertising expenditure

Rank	Advertiser	World-wide Ad. spend ($ million)	USA Ad. spend ($ million)	Ad. spend outside USA ($ million)
1	Procter & Gamble	5337	2777	2560
2	Philip Morris	3413	2577	836
3	Unilever	3268	858	2410
4	General Motors	2860	2047	813
5	Nestlé	1903	487	1416
6	Ford	1875	1149	726
7	Toyota	1815	733	1082
8	PepsiCo	1576	1197	379
9	Johnson & Johnson	1484	1173	311
10	McDonald's	1353	880	473

1 Centralize all marketing communications activities.
2 Decentralize all decisions to local markets.
3 Adopt a combination approach.

Centralization

This approach emphasizes a high level of central control over all forms of marketing communications. All aspects of the marketing communications planning process are determined centrally. It obviously provides a high degree of control over promotional activity and affords the opportunity for complete integration. It eliminates many of the problems associated with diffuse campaigns in separate markets and eases the tasks of co-ordination. For the most part, the same campaign is used in all markets in which the company operates.

There are a number of problems associated with the centralized approach. The company may lack the ability to deal speedily with changes as they occur in individual markets; may not be able to deal with competitive challenges; and may inhibit managerial and entrepreneurial initiative in individual markets.

Decentralization

All, or at least most, of the important decisions relating to advertising and other forms of marketing communications are taken at a local level. This enables campaigns to be planned within the context of the particular local requirements and to reflect the needs of local consumers. Much more focus can be achieved, particularly in the context of dealing with such issues as culture, tradition, political and legal factors. As might be expected, local managers tend to be more supportive of this approach, as it provides them with a greater level of flexibility to develop their own communications campaigns. Importantly, local efficiency can often be improved and the company can respond more speedily to competitive and other pressures.

Combination

Here, the decision-making process in relation to marketing communications is shared between the head office and local managers. For example, the broad strategy may be determined centrally, with individual implementation left to local managers. There are many variations on this theme. In some cases, policy decisions may be centralized, but the specific details of implementation may be planned at a local level. Often this results in a significant duplication of effort, with each country developing individual and separate responses to the communications requirements. Photo shoots and the preparation of campaign materials will often be replicated, with significant cost implications. To overcome this disadvantage, some companies go somewhat further in the planning process. Here, not only is the strategy determined centrally, but the main thrust of advertising may be developed there also. The preparation of materials will be planned and co-ordinated to avoid duplication, but local managers will be provided with a range of materials in order that they can 'personalize' or tailor the execution to meet their individual requirements.

For many years, the Outboard Marine Corporation adopted this approach to its European activities. After consultation with area managers (responsible for one or more European countries), a consistent look was adopted for the brand advertising, with separate campaigns being developed for Evinrude and Johnson powerboat engines. Photographic shoots were planned to ensure that all regional requirements were catered for (to take account of such factors as boating styles, environmental and legal factors, and so on). Individual managers were then able to call off their specific advertising requirements within this central framework.

An adaptation of this approach, which is gaining support, is the grouping of markets which share common factors. These can then be handled out of a central location or a regional hub.

The merits and demerits of standardized communications

We have already seen that the proponents of standardized communications campaigns cite the cost savings to be accrued from the development of a single campaign, together with the comparative ease of co-ordination, as partial justifications for the move towards common global marketing communications activities. It cannot be denied that the cost savings may be enormous, with the average cost of production of a television commercial being of the order of £200,000–£300,000 and, very often, much more than that. British Airways are rumoured to have spent around £2 million on their 'World' commercial, whilst *Campaign* reported the production costs of the Vauxhall Nova launch campaign at around £3 million. Moreover, if several creative teams are working in different parts of the globe to resolve the communications needs, the time involved and the associated costs will be considerable. And if, as we have seen, there is an underlying commonality of requirements, much of that time will be spent covering the same ground as others in the search for the communications message.

Not only does a standardized process eliminate the problems of conflict arising from dissimilar messages being communicated in adjacent territories, it also saves a considerable amount of management time involved in resolving such difficulties. Similarly, management would otherwise need to be involved – within each market – in the briefing and approval of creative work, the development of separate sales promotion campaigns, PR activity, and even packaging changes. Equally, agencies can develop an ever increasing pool of knowledge which they can bring to bear on their clients' requirements. According to Tom Sutton of JWT, 'The interaction of different types of talent in different countries started to contribute everywhere. The cross-fertilisation of ideas, the exchange of people, the exposure to new situations, all helped to bring a stronger whole'.

As well as saving time by dealing with one agency, the multinational client can derive savings in several important areas. Importantly, one consistent creative strategy can be developed to cover the entirety of the territories in which the company operates. The 'through the bottle' campaign for Smirnoff developed by Lowe Howard-Spink ran almost unchanged in some forty-three countries, with some sections being cut to ensure local relevance and application. For example, several different end shots were developed to cater for the different vodka mixers that were used in different markets. IBM's 'subtitles' campaign was made for only a reported £150,000 and ran in twenty-six different countries. Similarly, BBH's campaigns for Levi's run virtually unchanged all over the world.

Ultimately, the key benefit results in the creation of a single consistent image for the brand across all markets. The management and monitoring of the campaign can be more consistent, and the implementation process simplified.

Against these benefits, however, it can be argued that there are a number of significant disadvantages. Inevitably, if the brand is at a different stage in its development, it may be less responsive to a marketing communications campaign developed for all markets than to one specifically designed to deal with its own particular needs. We have already seen that different objectives, such as creating awareness, stimulating repeat purchase, and so on, will require different motivations and, hence, different messages. Similarly, in order to ensure universal appeal and comprehension, the resultant execution may be bland and boring and satisfy none of the individual requirements satisfactorily. This may, in turn, inhibit the opportunity to generate sales volume and result in management frustration.

Indeed, the problem is often one of motivation for staff, both within the company and the agencies it uses. Since they may be uninvolved with the development of the marketing communications programme, they may perceive it as being irrelevant to their needs, and they will often feel no commitment to its successful implementation. Often, since multinational campaigns take a long time to create and produce, this reduces the ability, on a local level, to respond rapidly to local pressures.

Sometimes the attempt to globalize the image results in costly blunders. When Elida Gibbs paid $3 million to entice Steffi Graf to appear in its Sure commercials, it discovered belatedly that she was only well known in her home country (Germany), the UK and the USA. Elsewhere, her endorsement of the product held little significance.

International campaigns are often criticized as appealing to the 'lowest common denominator'. If the campaign is to work at its most effective level, there must be a concentration on identifying the highest denominator, both strategically and executionally. It is important to concentrate on issues such as common life stage, common youth culture, common aspirations of cultural associations, and similar common values.

The development of multinational communications agencies

Globalization (or at least internationalization) has been the driving force behind many of the changes in the advertising scene. The multinational agencies followed their clients into the marketing into which they were expanding. BBH announced (in April 1996) that it would be expanding the agency into Asia, specifically to service its existing client base. 'We're there for brands who want a consistent image across various countries', according to Nigel Bogle, chairman of BBH (Yates, 1996).

In some cases, agencies expand into international markets because they see them as being strategically significant, for example, in the emerging economies of Eastern Europe. More often, agencies become multinational by being pulled along by their multinational clients and then picking up local business later. Other agencies have had to become international to avoid the risk of losing business. In 1986, Backer and Spielvogel became part of Saatchi and Saatchi – merged with Bates – after they were excluded from several new account pitches because they did not have access to an international network.

The 1980s and 1990s have seen rapid and dramatic consolidations of agencies into mega networks. By acquiring agencies specializing in complementary services such as sales promotion, media buying and research in various countries, agencies can get closer to offering their clients a consistent 'one-shop' facility on a global basis. WPP now owns J Walter Thompson, Ogilvy & Mather – both of which are leading advertising agencies; Hill & Knowlton – specializing in public relations; Millward Brown – a market research agency; together with several other specialist communications companies.

In the same way that companies have become international, so too have advertising agencies, PR and sales promotion consultancies and others. Two important and parallel trends have occurred.

There has been the progressive 'internationalization' of the service companies to the point where few do not have representation in all of the key markets. As a result of mergers, acquisitions and alignments, the major practitioners in the field of marketing communications have subsidiaries or associates in all the major countries of the world. Increasingly, global clients are appointing global agencies to handle and co-ordinate their marketing communications business across all of their territories. The recent appointment, in May 1994, of Ogilvy & Mather to handle the IBM account typifies these movements. The company turned its back on the forty-plus advertising agencies around the world that it has previously used, consolidating its annual £250-million account into a single agency. The

intention, according to Abby Kohnstamm, Vice President of IBM, was 'for an overall international campaign, modified as necessary for each country. Beneath that there will be more localized advertising for specific products'. Subsequently, the agency was awarded the account to handle the worldwide advertising for the Lotus Software company following its acquisition by IBM.

Indeed, the key requirement to inclusion on the shortlist for many such accounts is the extent to which the companies have the ability to service the business on a multinational basis. Dulux have moved their entire global advertising business, worth an estimated $50 million, into BBDO (*Campaign*, 5 January 1996). Often, companies will maintain a roster of agencies to handle their business, particularly where they have multiple brands. In most cases, the same agency will be used across the brand in all markets. Examples of this practice may be seen with Procter & Gamble, Mars and others.

This trend towards the large agency network appears to be gathering pace. Homepride Sauces recently appointed Y&R to its £6 million business, an agency which had only recently joined its world-wide roster. CPC International is reducing its roster of agencies from twenty-three to four, all of which are global. Nestlé similarly cut its agency list from 100 to five, all of which are represented throughout the world. Other clients which have followed the same philosophy are Colgate Palmolive, Bayer and Reckitt and Colman.

A significant factor is the easier process of exporting successful advertising campaigns into different markets. Bass, for example, has extended its successful Caffrey's Ale commercial into Scandinavia, whilst Unilever brought its ice-cream brand, Ranieri, into the UK. Both of these companies used the same agency network. At the same time, it saves costs.

Other companies adopt a different stance. The global advertising campaign for Windows '95 was created in the USA by Wieden and Kennedy. Individual countries were required to create localized advertising through the available media. In the UK, for example, the launch was handled by Euro RSCG Wnek Gosper. Microsoft's Director of Marketing Services, Shaun Orpen, stated, 'It isn't necessary to have one agency worldwide to enforce a global model. You need to take the best of what's local too'.

Multinational agencies

As noted above, the trend has been for the large agencies either to acquire or establish branches in all those markets in which they might reasonably expect to generate international client opportunities. Indeed, some of this process has been client-inspired, in the sense that the agency is encouraged to establish an office in a country in which the client is intending to operate.

Over the past two decades, led originally by agencies of American origin, but more recently by British and Japanese agencies, groupings have been assembled to respond to client needs. WPP is now the largest agency grouping in the world. In Europe, however, JWT ranks ninth and Ogilvy & Mather tenth. By contrast, Euro RSCG claims top European spot, but is only fifth in the UK. Interpublic comprises McCann, Lowe Howard-Spink, Lintas and a variety of other agencies specializing in PR, direct marketing and sales promotion (Table 15.3).

Such has been the growth of this process that the lists of the top ten agencies in most countries are broadly similar in content – although not in order – to each other. Table 15.4, taken from *Advertising Age*, shows the top ten advertising agencies in five countries, with many of the same agencies present in all lists.

Independent networks

To offset the competitive threat posed by the multinationals, networks and confederations have been formed to provide the global coverage demanded by some client companies. CDP Europe, Alliance International and ELAN (European Local Advertising Network) are three examples of such groups.

Table 15.3 World's top advertising organizations, 1996

Rank	Agency group	Billing ($ million)
1	WPP Group	24 740
2	Omnicon Group	23 385
3	Interpublic Group	20 045
4	Dentsu	14 048
5	Young & Rubicam	11 981
6	Cordiant	9 740
7	Havas	7 295
8	True North Communications (FCB)	7 041
9	McManus Group	6 830
10	Hakuhodo Inc	6 677

Source: Advertising Statistics Yearbook, The Advertising Association, NTC Publications, 1997

Table 15.4   Top ten agencies in selected countries, 1996

USA	UK	Germany	Italy	France
BBDO	Abbott Mead Vickers BBDO	BBDO	Young & Rubicam	Euro RSCG
Young & Rubicam	J. Walter Thompson	Ogilvy & Mather	Armando Testa	Publicis Conseil
Foote Cone Belding	Ogilvy & Mather	Grey Gruppe	J. Walter Thompson	DDB
Leo Burnett	BMP DDB	Young & Rubicam	McCann Erickson	BDDP
J. Walter Thompson	Saatchi & Saatchi	Publicis FCB	Saatchi & Saatchi	Young & Rubicam
McCann Erickson	D'arcy Masius Benton & Bowles	Ammarati Puris Lintas	BGS/DMB&B	Ogilvy & Mather
DDB Needham	Publicis	J. Walter Thompson	Milano & Grey	CLM/BBDO
Grey	M&C Saatchi	McCann Erickson	Ogilvy & Mather	McCann Erickson
Saatchi & Saatchi	Lowe Howard-Spink	Springer & Jacoby	Pirella Goettsche Lowe	DMB&B
Ogilvy & Mather	Bates Dorland	DMB&B	Publicis	Ammirati Puris Lintas

Source: *Advertising Age*, 21 April 1997

From the agency perspective, these associations meet the clients' needs to operate on a global basis, while preserving their own independence. Usually, these groupings are based on 'like-minded' philosophies, with agencies who have similar views of the marketing communications process coming together (creative style, media prowess, the role of planning, and so on).

Local independents

In many countries, newly emergent agencies remain bitterly jealous of their independence and, at least in the short term, are prepared to forgo some international accounts. Indeed, many such agencies remain independent in the longer term as a means of offering their own unique positioning in a crowded market.

The selection of an agency for international business

The principles underlying the selection of an agency to handle business across a number of markets are, essentially, the same as those involved in the appointment to handle an account within a single market, detailed in Chapter 6. Obviously, the decision as to agency selection will, to a large degree, be governed by the strategic direction of the company. As such, there are a number of separate options to be considered:

1 The appointment of a single multinational agency.
2 The appointment of an international agency network.
3 The appointment of a series of local agencies.

Before deciding on its agency, any client must consider a set of important criteria in the international context:

1 *To what extent is it planned to implement a single communications strategy in all markets?* For those companies wishing to pursue a global communications strategy, it is sensible to consider only the first and second options. The benefits of already established links will ensure the speedy transfer of knowledge and understanding which, in turn, should facilitate the process of implementation in the variety of countries in which the campaign will run.

2 *To what extent will the intended agency be precluded from operating in other market areas?* Some companies adopt a strict policy whereby the incumbent agency is not only precluded from handling directly competitive business, but also from those other areas in which the client company has an interest. This, it has to be said, is becoming an increasingly untenable situation. As multinational companies expand their businesses, both horizontally and vertically, they embrace ever more diverse market segments.

Acquisitions of companies and brands result in their taking an interest in markets far beyond their original businesses. P&G have interests in diverse fields, including hair care preparations, sanitary protection, cough and cold remedies, soap powders and toothpaste, to name just a few. Apart from their coffee interests, Nestlé operate in the following markets: confectionery, bottled waters, cereals, tinned soups and yoghurts and mousses. Here again, the list is only partial.

Clearly, to function profitably, the multinational agencies have to think carefully about client conflicts, current and for the future, before taking on a new account. Though the short-term increase in billings might be attractive, their tenure of a particular client might inhibit their growth potential in the future. In turn, therefore, some agencies with otherwise desirable credentials may be precluded from consideration.

3 *Do the multinational or network agencies possess all the appropriate skills in all markets?* Often, a multinational agency may have relatively weak representation in one or more of the markets considered important to the company. The same is equally true of agency networks, where not all of the participants may have the same reputation and skills.

4 *Are there specific local skills which need to be accessed?* In some instances, a local independent agency may have a far greater in-depth knowledge or understanding of the market, the consumers or the general environment, which it may be important to access. Indeed, the independent local agency may have greater prowess, for example, in media planning or creativity. It should not be assumed that simply because an agency is part of a wider international grouping it will possess all of the skills required.

Where co-ordination is not a requirement, some companies have taken the decision to locate the creative development with one agency – usually referred to as the 'lead' agency – and to appoint several local agencies to handle the implementation. In other instances, they have chosen to appoint the 'best' agency in each market, to ensure access to the necessary skills in all areas.

5 *How will the company cope with co-ordinating the campaign globally?* Deploying company personnel to the co-ordinating task may be one solution to the requirement. An alternative, particularly where a multinational agency is appointed, is to devolve that responsibility to the agency. Usually, a senior member of the agency structure is appointed to the specific role of ensuring consistency, both of creative work and implementation, throughout all markets. It will be his or her role to ensure cohesion between all aspects of the campaign in all markets although, ultimately, it will be the client's responsibility to determine whether the role has been fulfilled adequately.

This internal agency role is often of considerable importance to other aspects of the smooth running of the campaign. The task involves overcoming the 'not invented here' syndrome, whereby the local brand management team responsible for the implementation of the activity may feel detached from it, since it was created elsewhere. Similarly, the international co-ordinator may have the responsibility for allocating funds between branches to ensure that such tasks as market research are carried out adequately. In many cases, although the work is an important aspect of the understanding of the communications task in the market, the branch office may not generate sufficient income to afford their contribution.

International marketing and marketing communications strategy

The development of the international marketing plan covers the same dimensions as those of the domestic planning process, with any or all of the following areas being subject to review for potential changes:

*   *Brand name and logo.* Some companies seek to impose a consistency of brand identity across all markets in which they operate – as we have seen, Mars have committed substantial expenditure to re-identifying the 'Marathon' brand as 'Snickers'. Others, like Unilever, accept the inconsistencies. One of their cleaning products is Jif in the UK, Vif in Switzerland, Viss in Germany, and CIF in France.
*   *Product specification.* Nestlé adopts the same identification for a number of its products across all markets, but allows for variances in the nature of the product itself.
*   Packaging; Product positioning and strategy; Pricing; Advertising strategy; Advertising execution; Media strategy; Sales promotion; Public relations activities; Direct marketing.

The development of international advertising

The effectiveness of advertising is substantially dependent on the cultural and linguistic attitudes of the target population. Advertising often uses colloquial language which may have limited understanding across national boundaries and is seldom capable of being translated effectively.

Marieke de Mooij (1994) argues that 'Advertising, to be effective, must derive from and be part of a culture sharing the language and values of the target audiences'. However, global brands such as Coke and Pepsi have worked their way around this problem by developing 'universal' themes based on common imagery, lifestyle concepts and heroes.

Consumers in developing markets will need to be told about the functional nature of the product, whilst the sophisticated, advertising-literate consumer will expect more. He will want advertising that entertains, makes him laugh, and gives him a sense of being in touch with what's going on (Goodyear, 1994).

We need to be aware that the comprehension of an advertising message is substantially dependent on the level of advertising literacy. In most Western developed nations, consumers grow up surrounded by advertising. In effect, they grow up speaking two 'languages' – their mother tongue and the 'language' of advertising. The consequence is that they rapidly become aware of the nature of the advertising process and comprehend a variety of shorthand devices and metaphors to 'explain' the relevance of brands. Elsewhere, advertising is a comparatively new phenomenon. Potential consumers need to be reminded of the functional benefits of the brand, since the emotional context (so familiar in Western advertising) will have little or no relevance to them.

Mary Goodyear (1996) differentiates the components of advertising literacy in Table

Table 15.5 Advertising literacy

Low consumerization	High consumerization
Product attributes	Product benefits
Focus on product	Focus on usage
Rational	Emotional
Realistic	Symbolic
Fact	Metaphor
Maker's language	Brand language
Salesman	Consumer
Pack shot	Consumption
Left brain	Right brain
Selling	Buying

15.5. The importance of developing an understanding of advertising literacy, according to Goodyear, is the need to anticipate the audience for the company's products and services, and to produce creative work which is familiar enough to be recognized, and new enough to have saliency.

There are alternative approaches to the development of advertising for international deployment, as we have seen above. These have been effectively summarized in Table 15.6, taken from the work of Klippel and Boedwadt (1974).

The advertising proposition must be approached from a multilingual perspective from the outset. Good international advertising seeks to avoid subtleties of language, nuances, puns and idiomatic expressions. These are rarely capable of translation into different languages. Moreover, some languages require more physical space in which to express the same meaning. An ad translated directly from English to German, for example, will require approximately 25 per cent more space. It is equally important to understand that humour doesn't travel easily.

The tone of voice must be clearly established and verified in the context of local requirements. In some countries, what appears as an authoritative statement elsewhere may be misconstrued as a directive – and possibly rejected. Translated words may have different meanings. One way to overcome this is by using a method known as 'back translation'. The original piece is translated into the language in which it is intended to appear. A second translator converts the translation back into the original language and the two versions are compared for inconsistencies.

Table 15.6

Standardized approach (advertising extension)	Modular approach	Localized approach (advertising adjustment)
Fundamental similarities across countries	Consumer expectations	Differences among customers in different countries
Universal selling appeals		Individual selling appeal
Homogeneous product offerings	Encoding and decoding	Heterogeneous product offerings
Mass marketing		Target marketing
Uniform consumer expectations	Silent language	Varying consumer expectations

Klippel, R. E. and Boedwadt, R. J., 'Attitude Measurement as a Strategy Determinant for Standardisation of Multinational Advertising Formats', *Journal of International Business*, Spring 1974

Avoid using translators who have been away from their home country for a long period of time. Language changes over time, and someone who is separated from the current version of the language may not be aware of subtle changes. Equally, check out each language version in the country in which the material is to appear. The Spanish used in Spain is significantly different from, say, that used in Mexico. Equally, Canadian French is different to the language used in France.

It is important to consider the dimensions of media availability and relevance, since these may play an important part in determining whether a consistent campaign can be implemented across all markets. The table on page 170 in Chapter 9 shows some of the changes which have taken place in terms of the availability of media across Europe. On a wider basis, and looking at only one media outlet – television – it can be seen that access to the medium differs markedly in different parts of the world (Table 15.7).

Even where the medium is widely available, its role in the overall communications mix differs markedly. According to the European Marketing Data and Statistics, *Euromonitor*, 1994, TV accounts for only 1.4 per cent of total advertising expenditure in Sweden, 4.0 per cent in Israel, 4.9 per cent in

Norway and 6.8 per cent in Switzerland. This compares with 30.9 per cent in the UK and 35.3 per cent in the USA. At the other end of the spectrum, TV accounts for as much as 75 per cent of expenditure in Mexico, 66.2 per cent in Ecuador and 65.1 per cent in Venezuela.

Similar principles apply to the consideration of other media opportunities. Newspaper coverage, for example, is a function of the levels of literacy in different markets. To illustrate the point, over 50 per cent of the inhabitants of India and 27 per cent of those of China are functionally illiterate. This would impose severe limitations on a press-based campaign mounted in either of those two countries.

Even if a particular medium is available, the quality may be significantly different from what is normally associated with that channel. Newsprint quality in some countries is so poor that quality reproduction will be unobtainable. Similarly, whilst television may be available, colour may not be. This will affect the interpretation of advertising which uses colour as a major component of the message. Further, where there is a limited availability of media, or where shortages of time or space are common, the rates charged for advertising will tend to be considerably higher.

Table 15.7 People per TV in selected countries

USA	1.2
UK	2.3
Germany	2.6
Hong Kong	3.6
Turkey	5.7
Indonesia	16.7
India	31.3
Kenya	111.1
Laos	143.0
Nepal	500.0

The development of international sales promotion

The development of international sales promotion activity has been hampered by two important factors: firstly, convention and usage; and, secondly, the framework of legislation in which sales promotions operate.

Convention and usage

Whilst the broad-scale application of sales promotional activity covered in Chapter 10 is commonplace in the UK and some other parts of Western Europe, different practices in each of the countries means that the promotional tools will have greater or lesser significance. The offering of bonus packs with free product, often a standard format, is considered wasteful in countries like Japan. Similarly, free gifts tend to have less appeal in that country.

The legal framework

The single most important limitation on the development of global, or even pan-European, sales promotion campaigns remains the diverse nature of the legislative framework in which such activity must operate. Several examples serve to illustrate the difficulties which confront the sales promotion planner.

In Italy, promoters are required to pay 55 per cent tax, in advance, on any prizes they intend to award in a competition; French products rarely offer extra product for free because the amount of free fill is restricted to 7 per cent; in Germany, there are no banded offers, such as three for two, as these are banned; similarly, cash discounts to the consumer are limited to 3 per cent in that country. The Grand Prix award-winning promotion for Cadbury in this year's Sales Promotion awards offered an instant win facility, but could not be run in Ireland, where the interpretation of what constitutes a lottery rather than a competition is different from that in the UK.

The international sales promotion agency IMP, part of the McManus Group, have developed a guide to the legal restrictions on sales promotion activity, which is reproduced below in Table 15.8 with their permission.

The development of international public relations

The internationalization of marketing communications applies equally to the field of public relations and, in some respects, to a greater degree. Issues that arise in one market are no longer compartmentalized there. The nature of world-wide communications means that if, for example, a company experiences a 'crisis' in a single market, that information will be transferred to all of the other markets in which it operates within hours – and, of course, it will be called upon to respond to questions and queries in each of those markets.

Governmental bodies often transcend national boundaries, and the same principles which apply to public relations in the domestic environment need to be applied here also. For example, legislation affecting a company may be contemplated in a trading bloc such as the European Community. The company will need to influence the legislators in several countries simultaneously to ensure that their views can, wherever possible, be made to correspond with the company's interests.

The development of international direct marketing

Recent years have seen as dramatic an increase in the international application of direct marketing techniques as has been experienced within individual markets. The globalization of brands, on the one hand, and the availability of appropriate media for direct marketing, on the other, have spurred that growth.

The growth of satellite channels enables the accurate targeting of potential consumers in several different markets simultaneously. Similarly, the increasing use of the Internet means that users can be communicated with, irrespective of where they are based and often without regard to time zone.

The same need for consistency in communication drives the desire among many

Table 15.8 The legality of sales promotion across Europe

	UK	Irish Republic	Spain	Germany	France	Denmark	Belgium	Netherlands	Portugal	Italy	Greece	Luxembourg	Austria	Finland	Norway	Sweden	Switzerland	Russia	Hungary	Czech Republic
On-pack price reductions	Y	Y	Y	Y	Y	Y	Y	Y	Y	Y	Y	Y	Y	Y	C	Y	Y	Y	Y	Y
Banded offers	Y	Y	Y	C	Y	C	N	Y	Y	Y	Y	N	C	C	C	C	N	Y	Y	Y
In-pack premiums	Y	Y	Y	C	C	C	Y	C	Y	Y	Y	N	C	Y	N	C	N	Y	Y	Y
Multiple purchase offers	Y	Y	Y	C	Y	C	C	Y	Y	Y	Y	N	C	C	Y	C	C	C	C	Y
Extra product	Y	Y	Y	C	Y	Y	C	C	Y	Y	Y	Y	C	Y	C	C	C	Y	Y	Y
Free product	Y	Y	Y	Y	Y	Y	C	Y	Y	Y	Y	Y	Y	Y	Y	Y	Y	Y	Y	Y
Re-usable pack	Y	Y	Y	N	Y	Y	Y	Y	Y	Y	Y	Y	C	Y	Y	Y	Y	Y	Y	Y
Free mail-ins	Y	Y	Y	C	Y	C	Y	Y	Y	Y	Y	C	N	Y	Y	N	N	Y	Y	Y
With-purchase premiums	Y	Y	Y	C	Y	C	C	C	Y	Y	Y	N	C	Y	C	C	N	Y	Y	Y
Cross-product offers	Y	Y	Y	C	Y	C	N	C	Y	Y	Y	N	C	C	N	C	N	Y	Y	Y
Collector devices	Y	Y	Y	C	C	C	C	C	Y	Y	Y	N	N	C	N	N	N	Y	Y	Y
Competitions	Y	Y	Y	C	C	C	Y	C	Y	Y	Y	C	C	Y	C	Y	Y	Y	Y	Y
Self-liquidating premiums	Y	Y	Y	Y	Y	Y	Y	C	Y	Y	Y	N	Y	Y	Y	Y	N	Y	Y	Y
Free draws	Y	Y	Y	N	Y	N	N	N	Y	Y	Y	N	N	Y	N	N	N	Y	C	Y
Shareouts	Y	Y	Y	N	C	N	N	N	Y	C	C	N	N	C	C	N	N	Y	C	Y
Sweepstake/Lottery	C	C	C	C	C	N	C	C	C	C	C	C	C	Y	N	C	N	Y	C	C
Money-off vouchers	Y	Y	Y	N	Y	C	Y	Y	Y	C	Y	C	C	C	N	C	N	Y	Y	Y
Money off next purchase	Y	Y	Y	N	Y	N	Y	Y	Y	C	Y	N	N	C	N	N	N	Y	Y	Y
Cashbacks	Y	Y	Y	C	Y	Y	Y	Y	Y	N	Y	N	C	C	C	Y	N	Y	Y	Y
In-store demos	Y	Y	Y	Y	Y	Y	Y	Y	Y	Y	Y	Y	Y	Y	Y	Y	Y	Y	C	Y

Y: Permitted; N: Not permitted; C: May be permitted with certain conditions companies to ensure cohesion in the marketing communications activities planned in all of those markets in which they operate. And there is corresponding pressure on agencies to ensure that they have the capacity to implement their proposals in all of those markets.

The development of other international communications activities

Of the other tools of marketing communications, one can be singled out as being especially suitable for international consideration – sponsorship. As we have seen in Chapter 13, the largest activities appropriate to sponsorship are inherently global in their nature – the World Cup, the Olympics and similar events receive simultaneous coverage in all parts of the world. Inevitably, the scale of costs associated with those events means that they can only be afforded by truly global marketing organizations. It is anticipated that the main sponsors of the year 2000 Olympic Games will each be called upon to pay around £28 million. By the year 2002, it is estimated that sponsors of the World Cup will be charged around £37 million each for the privilege.

Sponsorship of these events has the unique ability to transcend national boundaries and to enable the development of brand images and associations. Indeed, for companies operating in markets with legal and other restrictions, sponsorship may provide the means of bypassing these limitations. However, it is important to ensure that sponsorship works well on a local level. Simply because an event has an 'international' following should not be taken to imply that it enjoys wide support in individual markets.

International market research

A critical area of international marketing communications is the role of market research.

Given the complexities involved in developing creative work for implementation in separate markets – especially given the cultural and environmental factors mentioned earlier – market research must be used at all stages to ensure that the intended message communicates effectively. It can never be assumed that simply because a campaign works effectively in one or more markets, it will work equally well elsewhere. Specific research testing of the concepts and executions will be required in all markets in which it is intended to run.

However, the area is subject to a series of important considerations:

- Comparability of international data. Whilst it is often true that, certainly in developed nations, there is access to considerable amounts of secondary data, what is less certain is the compatibility of the information. Even if the data exists, the problem of definition may make the information of low comparative value.

  Several factors need to be examined.

- How was the data collected? The way in which the data was obtained will have an obvious impact on the potential for comparison. In some instances, data will be collected by government bodies; in others, it will be obtained by commercial companies. Some information will be available as 'hard' facts; other information will be based on estimates.

- When was the data collected? In most countries, data is collected on a periodic basis. However, the intervals between collection may vary considerably. The result is that the marketer will be confronted with significant time gaps in terms of the availability of information.

- What is the source of the data? As noted above, data will be collected by different bodies, some governmental, others commercial. Inevitably, some information will be more reliable than other, and it is important to verify the source before assuming that data is comparable.
- In the less developed nations, reliable data may not exist. Even such things as population statistics may be, at best, rough estimates.

If problems exist with secondary data, there are even greater problems with the collection of primary data:

1 *Cost.* The expense of collecting information in different countries will vary markedly.
2 *Attitudinal differences.* Much primary research will be designed to determine the attitudinal values of the intended target audience. But it is important to recognize that the values on which such attitudes are based may themselves be somewhat different.
3 *Semantic differences.* The meanings of words will have a bearing on the interpretation of the research findings.
4 *Availability of research skills.* In some countries, even basic research skills may not exist. Accordingly, it may be necessary to bring in specialists from elsewhere to carry out the work.
5 *Infrastructure.* In order to conduct some forms of research, reliable information and infrastructure must be available. For example, the researcher may wish to conduct a series of interviews by telephone. Not a problem where the use of telephones is widespread, but in many countries the penetration of telephones may be at a very low level. Transport may not be available in order to access people living in rural communities. Sampling may be made difficult by the lack of adequate street maps or house numbers.
6 *Literacy* will have an impact on the potential for collecting data from self-completion questionnaires.
7 *Willingness to participate.* In some countries, it may be impossible to collect data because of the lack of willingness to participate in research programmes. Certain topics may be taboo. Individuals may be reluctant to provide information to a stranger.

References

Aitchison, G., Global Branding, MRS Conference Paper, March 1995

Bilkey, W. J. and Nes, E., 'Country of Origin Effects on Product Evaluation', *Journal of International Business*, Spring/Summer, 1982

Copeland, L. and Griggs, L., *Going International*, Plume Books, 1986

De Mooij, M., *Advertising Worldwide*, 2nd edition, Prentice Hall, 1994

Goodyear, M., 'Keeping Up With The Jones', *Admap*, September 1994

Goodyear, M., Divided by a Common Language, MRS Conference Papers, 1996

Haigh, D., 'Accountability', *Marketing Business*, October 1996

Hall, E., *Beyond Culture*, Anchor Books, 1976

Head, D., 'Ad Slogans and the Made in Concept', *International Journal of Advertising*, 7, 1998

Jacobs, L., Keown, C. and Ghymn, K., 'Cross-Cultural Colour Comparisons: Global Marketers Beware', *International Marketing Review*, 1991

Johansson, J., Douglas, S. P. and Nonanka, I. 'Assessing the Impact of Country of Origin on Product Evaluations', *Journal of Marketing Research*, 1985

Kotler, P., *Marketing Management: Analysis, Planning, Implementation and Control*, 7th edition, Prentice Hall, 1994.

Min Han, C., 'Country Image: Halo or Summary Construct', *Journal of Marketing Research*, 1990

Redding, S. G., 'Cultural effects on the Marketing Process in Southeast Asia', *Journal of the Market Research Society*, 1982

Shalofsky, I., 'Research for Global Brands', *European Research*, May, 1987

Usenier, J.-C., *Marketing Across Cultures*, 2nd edition, Prentice Hall, 1996

Yates, K., 'Why BBH Has Decided to Head East instead of West', *Campaign*, 26 April 1996

Additional reading

de Mooij, Marieke, *Advertising Worldwide*, 2nd edition, 1994, Prentice Hall

Usenier, J.-C., *Marketing Across Cultures*, 2nd edition, 1996, Prentice Hall

Mueller, Barbara, *International Advertising: Communicating Across Cultures*, 1995, Wadsworth–Thomson Publishing

Vardar, Nukhet, *Global Advertising: Rhyme or Reason*, 1992, Paul Chapman Publishing

CHAPTER 16

Future developments in marketing communications

Aims and objectives

- To consider the impact of environmental changes;
- To explore possible changes in consumer and consumer behavioural patterns;
- To become aware of future media issues;
- To examine the likely impact of changes on the marketing function;
- To learn about the changing face of the communications industry.

The process of future-gazing is fraught with difficulties. The only certainty that we can have about the future is that there will be significant differences. Some, based on current understanding of the important facets of the industry and the new technologies which are impacting on the way that business is conducted, can be predicted with a reasonable level of certainty, at least in the short term. Other changes, however, will be unforeseen. What follows, therefore, is a consideration of the important issues which face the communications industry. Wherever possible, these are based on an estimate of current trends.

Changes in the broad environment

There are a series of areas which will, inevitably, have a fundamental impact both on the nature of marketing and on marketing communications. Several of these are already undergoing visible changes, and similar changes can reasonably be predicted for the others. By the same token, there is a considerable overlap and interaction between these separate dimensions, as changes to one bring about responsive changes elsewhere.

Consumer dimensions

We are already witnessing fundamental changes in the underlying social and demographic framework. These issues have been covered in some detail in Chapter 2, but it is worth repeating some of the more important changes which have taken and will continue to take place:

- the continuing shift of women from the home into the workplace and, with that, changes in family roles;

- the reduction in job security and expectations of annual salary increases and bonuses;
- changes in personal values;
- reduction in the number of young people and a corresponding increase in the importance of the 'grey' market. Importantly, the 'new greys' are the youth of the 1960s and carry with them many of the social values developed during that period – a far cry from their parents' generation;
- By the year 2010, those over 70 will represent around 12 per cent of the population.

All of these factors will have an important impact on the very nature of the products and services that consumers demand, the way in which they wish to make their purchases, and the dialogue that they wish to establish with manufacturers and retailers.

Changing consumer behaviour patterns

The nature of the buying process and, importantly, the relationships established between retailers and their customers will undergo significant changes, some of which can already be observed. The pressure on retailers to respond to customer needs has already resulted in dramatically extended opening hours, and these are set to increase even further. The distinction between separate retailers, which has become increasingly blurred over recent years, similarly will develop apace, with consumers relying on a preferred retailer for most of their retail purchases. At the same time, however, we are also witnessing two contrasting trends. Firstly, there has been a growth in the truly specialist retailers, evidenced by the expansion of outlets such as Tie Rack and Accessorize. At the same time, there has been a growth among 'craft' outlets, offering consumers handmade products.

The Internet and other interactive media, still in their infancy, represent the potential for massive changes in the way in which consumers make their purchases. Experiments

with virtual retail outlets are already under way, and many consumers are willing to pay the premium in exchange for the ability to make their purchase selections in the comfort of their own homes and at the times which are most convenient to them.

This same trend is also seen in the growth of mail order, which has undergone a considerable transition over recent years. Where it was once the province of the lower social classes, with the most important benefit often being the ability to spread the cost of purchase over several months, mail order has become an increasingly upmarket provision.

Relationships with the trade and retailers

The new technology potentially places significant power in the hands of consumers. Already people are shopping without ever visiting a retail outlet. Retailers may literally be worlds apart from the customers they serve. Indeed, they may not even exist in a physical sense. For some, the Internet is the means to shop around the world and make their purchases using an existing charging platform, such as a credit card. A generation will grow up with those facilities at their disposal and, importantly, will interact with each other to convey information about product purchases, product failures and similar information from diverse parts of the globe.

Product development and evolution

The role of new product development takes on new dimensions in today's increasingly competitive environment. On the one hand, the task of developing innovative new consumer offerings is simplified, to some degree, by the pace of technological improvement. On the other, manufacturers must accept that many of their competitors have the technological capacity to respond to those improvements within months, or even weeks. Where once even small innovations were sufficient to discriminate between competing brands, today these developments no longer offer significant competitive advantage. Establishing emotional 'bonds' between brands and their consumers becomes an increasingly important dimension of establishing loyalty.

Environmental factors

Environmental issues are becoming increasingly important to consumers, although responding to these pressures alone is not sufficient to ensure clear discrimination between competing brands. Ultimately, the product must deliver its underlying proposition if it is to succeed in the marketplace. Nevertheless, a new generation of consumers is emerging who place their environmental concerns at the top of their personal agendas. Increasingly, it becomes imperative that manufacturers respond to these concerns if they are to retain their respective positions.

IT and communications development

Increasingly innovative technological approaches allow for a greater degree of interactivity between companies and their staff, consumers and retailers, retailers and their suppliers and so on. Although the acceptance of such technology is moving at a comparatively slow pace, it is inevitable that there will be increasing pressure to ensure both increased efficiency and cost saving through the widespread use of ISDN, conference phones, video links, etc.

'Flatter organisations, less hierarchy, virtual offices, "hot desks", video conferencing, ISDN transfer, time based competition, etc., will all play a part in the development of the advertising agency future.'
(Gatfield, 1995)

The impact of information technology on the future development of marketing and, in particular, on marketing communications is undeniable. Munro and Huff (1985) have adapted Porter's Five Forces to specifically demonstrate the influences that IT has on the business environment:

Force	IT potential
Buyers	Reduce buyer power by increasing switching costs to buyers, e.g. link technology systems with home banking, computer-to-computer ordering, locking in buyers.
Suppliers	Supply chain management by retailers and Just in Time (JIT) manufacturing systems demand much more from suppliers and transfer costs. Suppliers of information, as with EPOS systems controlled by retailers, gain power.
Substitutes	IT creates substitutes for many products and services, as with electronic mail and hard copy letters and communications. IT can be used to shorten NPD processes, to duplicate or replace products and, by adding benefits, can create unique packages.
New entrants	Existing entry barriers are often neglected and new ones created, by the requirements for investment in computers and telecommunications networks.
Rivals	IT changes rivalry, as in IT-based consortia using shared databases and ordering facilities. New rivals are created.

Media issues

Satellite deployment and the increase in technology will create new media options for global advertisers. Technological improvements such as high-definition television, computer interfacing, the Internet, electronic mail, etc., will provide new creative challenges. The recent announcement of literally hundreds of new digital television channels will further fragment media audiences and place increasing emphasis on the media planner's need to understand the underlying behavioural patterns of the potential consumers he wishes to reach. More media implies more skill in selection, use and evaluation.

Several events have changed the relationships established between the individual and his or her television. The appearance of the video cassette recorder (VCR) in the early 1980s provided consumers with their first opportunity of physically affecting the flow of television. This, together with remote control devices, afforded consumers an opportunity to avoid advertising. Over recent years, the growth of multi-channel TV and the remote control have contributed to the refinement of the viewer's relationship with television and, in particular, with advertising messages.

A further factor which will become increasingly important is the ending of the dependency relationship between the media and advertising. For many years, media owners have derived a substantial part of their income from paid-for advertising. Increasingly, this is no longer the case.

The expansion of the European and world market

Competition in all forms will increase as businesses in Europe, the Pacific Rim and Latin America generate new, attractive products and services. Some of the largest nations, e.g. China and India, are slowly increasing the buying power of their population and providing a viable market for foreign products. In New Europe, the progressive elimination of trade barriers will heighten forms of competition.

The impact on the marketing function

In order to reflect and respond to these changes, companies themselves will have to undergo major reconstruction if they are to be able to respond to the challenges which face them in the years ahead. The need to be market-driven will impact substantially on the way that organizations conduct their businesses. Many writers argue that we are witnessing the end of the large marketing department which reviews and approves all activities relating to the company's offering to customers. In many respects, the large marketing department is the antithesis of a market-driven company, especially if it is part of a hierarchical, bureaucratic structure dominated by rules, policies and procedures (Webster, 1995).

Webster argues that marketing's job under the new concept is to ensure the provision of information to assist the decision-making process throughout the organization. He establishes a series of important facets of the new market-driven company:

- The essential requirement for a customer focus throughout the organization;
- The need to identify and nurture an organization's distinctive competence;
- The importance of recognizing marketing as the provision of market intelligence;
- The requirement to target customers precisely;
- The imperative of measuring and managing customer expectations;
- The requirement to ensure the development of customer relationships and loyalty;
- A commitment to continuous improvement and innovation.

Webster summarizes the new marketing role as follows:

'Every business should redefine itself as a service business committed to continuous improvement and innovation, managing culture along with strategy to create customer focus throughout the organisation. The customer is the ultimate arbiter of value, but marketers can manage satisfaction by targeting the customers most likely to appreciate the company's distinctive competence.'

The changing face of the communications industry

There is little doubt that, as we approach the new millennium, the face of the communications industry will undergo a number of significant changes. Coming out of a recession which saw a drop of some 30 per cent in advertising agency staff numbers, the agency scene is already undergoing significant changes both in terms of structure and purpose.

Writing in *Admap* in July/August 1994, David Haigh, Managing Director of Publicis Dialogue, suggests five important areas in which agency changes need to take place.

Industry structure

Within agencies, the structures of the past often fail to reflect the needs of their clients. The classic pyramid of agency skills represents a hierarchy which is more about traditional values than a response to the changing requirements of the client base. Progressively, agencies will need to provide their clients with servicing structures which are capable of providing them with the specialized inputs which their businesses demand. In some cases, this is happening already. In those agencies with specialist clients, in areas of retail, finance, high-tech, pharmaceutical business and so on, teams have been constructed to provide the range of inputs which more accurately reflect the particular needs of those clients.

In the business as a whole, the progressive partitioning into specialist agencies, from advertising to sales promotion, public relations to direct marketing, has made the task of integration more difficult. In some respects, we are witnessing a return to the 1960s concept of the 'full service' agency in order to provide seamless integration of all of the marketing communications activities, with the consequent reduction in the duplication of overheads.

Some clients demand and receive totally integrated services. Increasingly, through-the-line activity has become the norm rather than the exception. Many agencies have already restructured to provide everything from strategic input to marketing and marketing communications planning, the development of advertising, sales promotion, public relations and direct marketing campaigns, even to the development of point-of-sale materials, the preparation of sales literature, the planning of event marketing and the securing of sponsorship and product placement deals.

Yet, at the same time, there is a trend towards an à la carte solution. Some clients continue to select specialized agencies – or even skilled individuals – who can participate in each stage of the development of the communications process. Recently, the RAC created a 'superteam' of individuals rather than appoint a single agency to handle the development of its creative platform.

Communications strategy

Recent years have seen the continued fragmentation of the media. There is an ever increasing number of conventional media outlets – more television stations (both terrestrial and satellite-based), more newspapers, magazines and radio stations – as well as the emergence of a variety of new media, especially within the electronic superhighway. These provide the advertiser with the ability to more precisely target individual consumers and establish a dialogue with them. Tomorrow's agencies will need to adapt and respond to these new opportunities.

Not only does this demand a greater understanding of the roles that these new media can play within the overall marketing communications mix, it also demands the development of a more objective communications planning process which recognizes the contribution that can be made from other areas of marketing communications.

Integration

The integration of marketing communications – the buzz words of the 1990s – requires a greater degree of consistency and coherence in conveying messages to the consumer. Whether executions are prepared within a single group of companies, one integrated agency or a series of independent agencies, the integration of activities provides the opportunity to increase the impact on the target audience and to avoid the waste of resources.

The need to understand the importance of interlinking marketing communications techniques will be an increasing requirement of the recognition that no single discipline is capable of delivering a comprehensive response to the communications brief. This is already being seen in the agency moves towards a multi-disciplinary approach in dealing with marketing communications.

At the same time, however, there is no reason to doubt that the present fragmentation of the industry will continue to increase. Where once agencies were able to provide the totality of the communications input and execution, we have witnessed the progressive change to specialist functions and the emergence of companies which operate in a single field of communications. In turn, however, these too are fragmenting – specialists, for example, in the field of direct marketing concentrate on list development and brokerage; others on fulfilment. In the area of public relations, specialists have emerged to deal with specific parts of the function, concentrating, for example, on financial, industrial or other parts of the PR industry. The sponsorship function has seen the growth of several specialist companies, dealing with the areas of sport, the arts and so on. Companies have emerged which, uniquely, deal with issues related to product placement.

The task of achieving integration becomes ever more difficult, with the need to coordinate the many different specialist functions, each of which can make a relevant contribution to the overall achievement of the marketing communications plan. And, at the centre of the debate, is the need to preserve the integrity of the brand. With so many avenues with which to provide exposure, someone within or outside the organization has to undertake the responsibilities of being the custodian of the essential brand values – ensuring that the myriad communications tools deployed are in sympathy, rather than conflicting with the desired brand image.

Information technology

A wealth of new technologies is now available to enhance the communications process. Whether this takes the form of videoconferencing to avoid the time and effort taken to travel to business meetings; the introduction of facilities which enable the work to proceed from electronic brief to digital media output; virtual offices which enable staff to operate from dispersed locations; or any of the other technological changes which are yet to occur, agencies of the future will need to embrace them and reassess their own operating procedures.

Much progress has been made within many agencies, especially those which operate within the field of retail advertising, where the inherent speed of response has demanded such change.

Agency remuneration

There is little doubt that the future will see an increasing pressure on agencies to change their basis of remuneration from a commission-based system to one derived from the costs and time required to develop a marketing communications campaign. This is an inevitable consequence of the increasing move towards integrated marketing communications, as an expanding volume of the agency's output will not be in the form of commissionable media activity.

Moreover, many have argued that it is the underlying suspicion of the commission basis of remuneration which continues to act as a barrier to closer relationships between clients and their agencies. It is likely that there will be a progressive move towards more objective and transparent bases of agency remuneration. These will include a greater number of fee-based packages, reflecting the time and resources devoted to clients' businesses. Some agencies, such as Rainey, Campbell, Roalfe, have already moved towards remuneration systems which reward the agency for the scale of the idea, rather than reflecting the media or other budget required for its implementation.

Some clients will have sufficiently large budgets and complex demands to want their agencies to specialize in 'advertising' in the narrow sense of that word; others will be looking for a broader-based communications package, covering advertising, direct marketing, sponsorship, public relations, sales promotion and other services within the field of marketing communications.

To these five significant factors outlined above can be added a number of other important factors which will change the demands placed upon the communications agencies of the future.

Global marketing

An ever increasing number of clients are developing their strategies on a global, or at least multinational, basis. The structure of the major international agencies will need to adapt to reflect and respond to this demand. An inevitable consequence is that many advertising professionals will do more business away from their home countries as they build confidence and expertise in global advertising. In turn, advertisers, agencies and the media will put a premium on people who have international experience and multiple language skills.

Accountability

In the increasingly competitive environment of the late 1990s, clients are demanding that their agencies be more accountable for their contribution to the marketing communications process. It is increasingly less about winning awards than achieving the specific objectives of the marketing communications plan.

Education and training

Tomorrow's marketing communications staff are likely to be more multi-disciplined than ever before. In order to make a sound input to the strategic planning requirements of their companies or clients, staff will need to have a greater understanding of the contribution of the various components of marketing communications.

This will not replace the need for the possession of specialist skills of the individual facets of communications. Specialisms will abound. But the process of integration can only proceed if the individuals responsible for the process – both at the agency and the client end of the spectrum – possess a comprehensive understanding of the contribution of the individual specialist areas.

The business itself is already taking an initiative in the field of integration. Recently, the IPA, along with the SPCA and the PRCA (Public Relations Consultants Association), established the Integrated Marketing Communications Initiative in order to provide cross-disciplinary education and training to people within the business.

For the agencies of the future to respond fully to the needs of their clients, they will have to undergo a process of reassessment of their core competences. Unless they can truly provide the desired inputs, they will be unlikely to survive. With this will come a reassessment of the traditional skills hierarchy, in which particular disciplines have been presumed to be superior to others. For years, traditional advertising occupied the higher ground, with the other disciplines playing a somewhat subservient role. The agency of the future will pride itself on providing a comprehensive solution to its clients' communications requirements. What will matter will be the effectiveness of the communications planning process, integrating the whole range of activities.

That the future represents change is inevitable. The real issue is to determine the nature of those changes. Undeniably, advertising will continue to be an important part of the process of marketing communications, but the other tools will gain an increasingly important role as companies seek to ensure that their position in the marketplace is seen to be distinctive from that of their competitors.

References

Gatfield, S., 'Brand Building and the Agency', *Admap*, January 1995

Munro, M. and Huff, S., 'Information Technology and Corporate Strategy', *Business Quarterly*, 1985

Webster, F. E., 'Executing the New Marketing Concept', *Marketing Management*, 3 January 1995

Additional reading

At best, soothsaying is a difficult business. To keep pace with developments in marketing communications, students should regularly read the trade press – *Campaign, Marketing* and *Marketing Week*, together with *Admap*.

Glossary of terms

Above the line Any paid form of advertising (television, press, radio, cinema, posters) on which commission is paid by the media to the agency

Account executive The person within the advertising agency responsible for the administration of a client's business

Account planner The advertising function which seeks to develop an understanding of the consumer's relationship with the brand in order to brief creative development

ACORN An acronym for A Classification of Residential Neighbourhoods, which enables consumers to be classified on the basis of the area of residence

Adoption process The mental and behavioural stages through which an individual passes before making a purchasing decision

Advertising Any form of paid-for media used by the marketer to communicate with his target audience

Advertising agency A company that develops and implements advertising activity

Advertising appeal The particular approach, based on rational or emotional arguments, which seeks to develop a direct link between the product or service and the consumer's needs or wants

Advertising campaign The development of a series of advertisements placed in one or more media in order to communicate a proposition to a designated target audience

Advertising objectives The specific tasks which advertising is designed to fulfil

Advertising manager The person within a company or organization who is responsible for the development and co-ordination of advertising activities

Advertising plans The establishment of a sequence of events relating to the intended activity

Advertising strategy A statement of the broad goals which the advertising is designed to achieve

Advertorial A style of advertising which seeks to depict the message as editorial

Advocacy advertising Campaigns designed to disseminate ideas, often of public importance, in a way that promotes the interests of the advertiser

Affordability method The apportionment of a communications budget after deduction of the desired level of profit and all other costs

AIDA model A model of personal selling subsequently used to explain the process of advertising

Attention The process of arousing the interest of an individual in some activity

Appropriation The sum of money allocated to a campaign

Attitude Knowledge and feelings – both positive and negative – towards a subject

Attributes The physical or emotional qualities which a product or service possesses

Audience The number of individuals reached by an advertising medium

Awareness The stimulation of knowledge about a person or object

Beliefs A conviction regarding the existence or characteristics of something

Below the line Marketing communications activities which are not subject to commission being paid to the advertising agency

Benefit segmentation A grouping of consumers based on the specific benefits they desire from a product

Billings The agency's revenue derived from direct advertising expenditure

Black box model A simple model of the communications process relating level of expenditure to sales effect

Bonus packs Packaging which offers the purchaser additional volume at no extra cost

Brand A name, term, design, symbol or any other feature that identifies one seller's goods or services from those of other sellers

Brand equity The assignment of a capital value to a brand. Sometimes used to describe the intangible benefits associated with the use of a brand

Brand image The total impression created in the consumer's mind by a brand and all its associations, functional and non-functional

Brand loyalty A measurement of the extent to which consumers are committed to a particular brand

Brand switchers Consumers who alternate purchases between different manufacturers' products

Broadcasting Media designed to reach the mass market

Burst A pattern of media expenditure in which activity is concentrated into a comparatively short period

Business-to-business The promotion of its products or services by one company to another

Case rate method A method of budget calculation in which expenditure is calculated as a percentage of the sales value of a case of product

Category management The responsibility for co-ordinating the activities of all the company's brands within a particular market sector

Circulation The number of issues of a media title that are sold

Cognitive response The interpretation of stimuli and the organization of thoughts and ideas

Commission The method of remunerating advertising agencies by means of a payment directly from the media – traditionally set at 15 per cent of the advertising expenditure

Communication The process of dissemination of information to establish shared meaning between the sender and the receiver

Comparative advertising The contrasting of one manufacturer's products or services with those of another, either by naming the competitor or inferring its identity

Competitions A sales promotion technique in which the consumer is offered prizes in return for solving some form of puzzle

Complex problem solving Purchasing decisions in which the consumer will require additional information on which to base an evaluation of alternatives. Most often occurs where the capital outlay is great or the risk is high

Comprehension The creation of an understanding about a product, service, object or person

Concept testing A research procedure in which outline ideas are exposed to current and potential consumers to learn about their response

Consumer behaviour The activities in which people engage in order to satisfy needs, wants and desires

Contingency A sum of money held in reserve to respond to unforeseen circumstances

Continuous advertising A campaign of advertising over an extended period (usually at a low level of impact)

Co-operative advertising A programme in which the manufacturer pays an agreed percentage of the retailer's advertising costs in return for the featuring of the manufacturer's brand

Copy testing The process of using market research to gain an understanding of consumer response towards an advertising proposition

Core values The central values associated with a product or service

Corporate advertising Campaigns created to promote awareness and understanding of a company

Corporate identity The programme of communication and change that a company undertakes in order to communicate its values

Corporate image The way in which a company is perceived, based on its history, beliefs and philosophy

Corporate strategy The determination and definition of the long-term goals of an organization

Cost per thousand A calculation of the cost of exposing an advertising message to 1000 members of a designated target audience

Coupon A sales promotion technique in which the consumer receives a voucher enabling a reduced price to be paid for an identified product

Coverage A calculation of the size of the audience that will be exposed to an advertising message using a particular media vehicle

Creative strategy The identification of the specific goals which advertising is designed to fulfil

Crisis management The establishment of procedures for anticipating and dealing with communications problems

Culture The shared values, beliefs and behaviours of a society

DAGMAR A model of the advertising process developed by Russell Colley. Incorporates a precise method for the selection and quantification of communications tasks

Database A computer-based listing of the names, addresses and other details of current and potential customers, which can be used for purposes of direct marketing

Database management The process of maintaining and refining accurate customer information

Decision-making unit Those individuals who participate in the purchasing decision process, usually in the context of company purchases

Decision stage That part of the process of consumer buying behaviour which results in an evaluative judgement about the alternatives

Decoding The means by which the recipient of a message transforms and interprets it

Demographics Groupings of individuals based on characteristics such as age, sex, race and income

Diffusion The spread of a new idea throughout a group of individuals

Direct mail The use of postal and other delivery techniques to communicate with a defined target audience

Direct marketing An interactive system of marketing which uses one or more advertising media to effect a measurable response and/or transaction at any location

Direct response A method whereby the advertiser provides the consumer with a means of communicating directly with the organization

Direct selling The process of achieving the sales of products or services without the use of intermediary sales channels, such as wholesalers and retailers

Display allowance A sum of money paid to a retailer in return for the featuring of a manufacturer's products prominently at the point of purchase

Drip A pattern of media expenditure in which the budget is deployed at a comparatively low level over an extended period

Emotional responses Those non-rational reactions to a proposition which are based on intangible benefits or associations which a product or service can induce

Emotional strategy The identification of non-rational stimuli as the basis for an advertising campaign

Encoding The process of putting information into a symbolic form of words, pictures or images

Endorsement The recommendation of a product or service by someone other than the advertiser

Ethics The principles that guide an individual's or organization's conduct in its relations with others, and the values it wishes to communicate

Evaluation of alternatives The consumer's consideration of the various options available to resolve an identified need or want

Event sponsorship The association of a company or brand name with a public activity

Every day low prices (EDLP) A pricing policy adopted by some companies in which short-term promotional pricing is either reduced or eliminated and replaced by a consistent level of lower prices

Exposure The consequence of presenting an advertising campaign to target audiences

External databases Computer-based records compiled from external sources which can be used for the purposes of direct marketing

Family life cycle A sequence of stages through which the individual passes over time

Feedback The process of ensuring an understanding of the recipient's comprehension of a message by the sender

Flighting A pattern of media scheduling in which periods of advertising are alternated with periods of inactivity

Free mail-ins Incentives offered to the purchaser of a product in which the purchaser sends proofs of purchase to a handling house in exchange for a free gift

Frequency A calculation of the number of times a target audience is exposed to an advertising message during a given period

Full service agencies Those agencies which offer a comprehensive creative, account handling, planning and media service to their clients

Generic branding A policy by which products or services are sold using their category name

Geodemographic segmentation A method of segmenting the market using a combination of psychographic and geographic data

Geographic segmentation The identification of market or audience segments based solely on geographic factors

Global marketing The adoption of a common marketing strategy and implementation plan for all countries in which a manufacturer markets his goods

Gross margin The calculation of net sales value minus the cost of goods over a defined period

Halo effect The creation of an aura or beneficial image which is transferred from one category to another

Hierarchy of effects The identification of a sequence of stages to explain the working of advertising

Image The creation of an identity for a product or service by its association with other values

Impulse purchase Products or services bought without prior consideration, usually in response to some stimulus at the point of purchase

In-pack premiums Free gifts offered to the consumer which are contained within the brand's packaging

Integration The process by which the tools of marketing communications are used in combination to reinforce each other

Internal databases Computer-based records compiled from internal records such as sales registrations, warranty cards and other sources for the purpose of direct marketing

JND or **Just Noticeable Difference** The amount by which a product or service needs to be changed to ensure that the change is observed by the consumer

Learning The process of change to an individual's behaviour resulting from experience

Lifestyle The way in which a person lives, identified by his activities, interests and opinions

List broker An organization which provides mailing lists to companies

Logical appeals Advertising approaches based on the performance, features or attributes of a product or service

Look-alikes Products which adopt the visual cues of another brand in order to facilitate the inclusion of the product within the category of choice

Loyalists Consumers who exhibit a consistent purchasing preference for a particular brand

Manufacturer branding The use of a manufacturer's name or logo to identify the products or services produced by the company

Market research The gathering and assessment of data and other information

Market segmentation The means by which the characteristics of homogeneous groups of consumers can be determined

Market structure The ways in which a market for any product or service can bedefined or segmented

Marketing The management process responsible for identifying, anticipating and satisfying consumers profitably

Marketing communications The process by which a marketer develops and presents stimuli to a defined target audience with the purpose of eliciting a desired set of responses

Marketing concept The process by which the marketer responds to the needs and wants of the consumer

Marketing mix The combination of the elements of the marketing programme, including product, price, place and promotion

Marketing objectives The determination of specific and measurable goals to be achieved by the marketing programme

Marketing plan The formal document containing the information designed to guide the development and implementation of the marketing strategy

Marketing strategy Specific plans of action for the achievement of designated marketing objectives

Mass marketing An approach in which the advertiser attempts to appeal to the entire market using a single marketing mix

Mature market The stage at which a market for a product or service ceases to expand

Media The vehicles of communication by which a message is transmitted to its audience

Media mix The combination of two or more different media to be used to fulfil a media plan

Media plan The document embodying the specific media objectives, strategy and tactics designed to support a brand

Media planning The process of determining the means by which an advertising message will be communicated to a defined audience

Media schedule A graphic representation of the dates, times and media sources in which advertising is to be placed

Merge and purge The process of eliminating the duplication of names and addresses contained within two or more mailing lists

Money-off promotions Sales promotion techniques in which the potential consumer is offered the product or service at a reduced price

Motive An aroused need that directs behaviour towards a specific goal

Multi-branding A strategy adopted by some manufacturers in which the parent name is subservient to those of the individual brands which they produce

Multinational advertising The process of developing advertising campaigns to run in several different countries based on the identification of common values and needs

Multinational agencies Those agencies which operate a network in many different countries and offer clients a common approach to the resolution of advertising requirements

Narrow casting The fragmentation of media audiences resulting from the increase in the number of media channels

Needs The gap between a consumer's current state and the desired state

Noise The external stimulus factors in the environment which surround the communications message and inhibit its effective transmission

Non-verbal communications The process of ensuring the transmission of a message without the use of words or language

Objective and task method The nature of the task is determined and the cost of achieving the specific objectives is calculated and a budget allocated accordingly

Objectives The specific goals to be achieved during the timescale of a plan

Opinion leader An individual who reinforces an advertising message and to whom others look for guidance

Outcomes The results and consequences of any activity

Percentage of sales method A budgeting procedure by which the expenditure is calculated as a finite percentage of the sales value

Perception The process by which an individual receives, organizes and interprets information

Perceptual mapping A technique of market research in which the key attributes of a product or service are identified and competing products rated according to their ability to satisfy the desired ratings

Personal selling The process by which a salesperson communicates with one or more prospective purchasers for the purpose of making sales

PEST + C An acronym standing for the political, economic, social, technological and consumer factors used in the analysis of a marketing environment. Sometimes written as PESTI + C, the 'I' standing for international

Planning The process of anticipating the future, establishing goals and objectives

Point of purchase Promotional items designed to attract the attention of the consumer in those places where the products are purchased, sometimes referred to as point of sale

Positioning Identifying the place in the market or the mind of the consumer which the company or product wishes to occupy

Post-purchase dissatisfaction A response to a purchasing decision in which the consumer feels that the product or service has failed to deliver the expected performance on some dimension

Post-purchase satisfaction A response to a purchasing decision in which the consumer's direct experience of the product or service matches or exceeds its expected performance

Premium The offer of a free gift to encourage the purchase of a specified product or service

Problem identification The recognition of an unfulfilled want or need

Problem solving The process by which the consumer resolves an identified need

Product life cycle A management technique in which a product is depicted as passing through a series of progressive stages

Product placement The inclusion or mention of products or services in films, television programmes or elsewhere, usually in exchange for a fee

Promotion That element of the marketing mix which includes all forms of marketing communications

Promotion management The process of determining and co-ordinating the elements of the promotional mix

Promotional mix The use in any combination of advertising, sales promotion, public relations, direct marketing and personal selling to achieve specific objectives

Psychographics The understanding of the psychological profiling of prospective consumers

Public relations All forms of planned communications between any organization and its publics with the purpose of establishing mutual understanding

Publicity Any communication concerning a company, product or service which is not paid for or sponsored

Pull strategy A promotional strategy in which the manufacturer or supplier promotes a product or service to the end-consumer with the aim of stimulating demand

Pulsing A media scheduling approach in which short, heavy bursts of advertising are followed by extended periods of low-level expenditure

Push strategy A promotional strategy in which the manufacturer or supplier promotes a product or service through a series of marketing intermediaries with the aim of pushing the product through the channels of distribution

Qualitative research Techniques used among relatively small groups in order to identify and evaluate subjective opinions

Quantitative research The collection of data from samples of the target population to enable quantification and analysis

Rate card cost The published costs of advertising in a specific media outlet

Rating point A measurement of a media audience – usually television – in which the size of the audience is calculated and expressed as a percentage. One rating point is equivalent to 1 per cent of the total viewing potential

Rational decisions Decisions based on the qualitative assessment of the performance of a product or service which relate to specific features, attributes and benefits

Reach The percentage of a total audience which will be exposed to a message during a defined period of time

Readership The calculation of the number of individuals who read a single copy of a media title

Rebate A sales promotion technique whereby a purchaser is given back part of the purchase price. Most commonly, this is associated with retailers achieving a previously agreed sales target

Receiver The target audience for whom a communications message is intended

Reduced price offers Sales promotion technique which offers a price reduction to the consumer as an incentive to purchase

Reference groups Those groups within society with which the consumer identifies and to which he or she would wish to belong

Refund A sum of money given back to the consumer following purchase of a product or service, usually in exchange for some form of proof of purchase

Relationship marketing The process of getting closer to the customer by means of customer service and quality delivery

Remuneration The income received in return for the provision of services

Road blocking A media approach in which the same advertisement appears simultaneously on several different channels

Routine problem solving Situations in which the consumer possesses sufficient prior knowledge to take a purchasing decision without seeking additional information

Sales promotion The use of short-term, often tactical, techniques to achieve short-term sales objectives

Sales quota A quantitative expression of a target to be achieved by a salesperson or team during a given period of time

Sales territory The area or region for which a salesperson or team is responsible

Sampling The process of encouraging the consumer to try a specified product or service

Segmentation The process of dividing a market into smaller groupings based on an understanding of consumer needs and wants

Selective attention The process by which receivers only notice some of the messages to which they are exposed

Selective distortion The process by which receivers modify or change received information to fit in with existing attitudes and beliefs

Self-liquidating premium A gift or incentive in which the consumer pays for the cost of the gift, usually at the time of purchasing the primary product

Self-regulation The process by which manufacturers agree to abide by codes of practice without the force of law

Semiotics The study of the nature of meaning

Sender The person or organization transmitting a communications message

Share of voice A calculation of the share of category media expenditure

Social class An open grouping of people with similar social ranking

Source The sender of a message

Sponsorship The connection of a company or product with a public event in which the manufacturer contributes towards part or all of the costs in return for the benefit of association

Strategy The determination of the longer-term goals and targets

Sweepstakes A sales promotion technique in which the consumer is offered a chance to win a prize. To satisfy legal requirements, such promotions are rarely based on a purchase requirement

SWOT An acronym standing for strengths, weaknesses, opportunities and threats used in the analysis of a company or brand's competitive position

Symbolic representation Words, pictures or images used to convey a message

Tactics Specific actions designed to implement strategies

Target audience The identification of a group of potential consumers who have specific characteristics in common

Target marketing The selection of specific market segments at which to aim marketing or marketing communications

Telemarketing A form of personal selling in which the communications process is conducted via the telephone

Tracking study A market research technique which analyses consumer response and buying behaviour over an extended period of time

Trade allowances Sums of money negotiated by manufacturers with distribution channels in return for the carrying out of certain functions or activities

Unique selling proposition An advertising approach developed by Rosser Reeves which is designed to make the product the focus of the advertising message by identifying a unique aspect, attribute or benefit

Want conception The process of activating latent needs or wants

Want development The identification of new uses for an existing product

Want focus The identification of a consumer need or want in order to establish a relevance with the product or service being promoted

Want satisfaction The provision of reassurance to the consumer to confirm the purchasing decision

Word of mouth Information about products and services conveyed from one individual to another

Zapping The use of a remote control device to change channels during commercials

Zipping The avoidance of television commercials that have been pre-recorded on videotape

Index

Above the line, 337
A.C. Nielsen MEAL, 180, 211–12
Account executive, 337
Account planner, 37
Accountability, 334
ACORN, 239, 337
Adoption process, 337
Advertising, 4–6, 119–42, 144–66, 337
  advantages and limitations of, 122–3
  advertising appeals, 150–3, 337
    appeals to ego or self-esteem, 152–3
    emotional appeals, 151, 340
    rational appeals, 150–1
  advertising manager, 337
  advertising plan, 139–41, 337
  advocacy advertising, 337
  brand personality and, 161
  brand positioning, 132–3
  business-to-business advertising, 142
  campaign evaluation, 161–6
    competitor information, 163
    consumer research, 163
    monitoring research, 163–6
    strategy development, 163
  comparison with public relations, 251–2
  consistency in, 56
  corporate advertising, 288, 339
  creative brief, 144–9
  creativity, 158–60
    evaluation of, 161
  disillusionment with, 73
  diverse nature of, 119–20
  expenditure, 4–6
  functions of, 120–2
  international advertising, 320–2, 342
  leading advertisers, 59
  music in, 157–8

  objectives, 138–9, 140–1, 337
    awareness, 140–1
    changing attitudes, perceptions and beliefs, 141
    communications objective, 144
    image, 141
    product line building, 141
    reinforcing attitudes, 141
    relating product to consumer needs, 141
    reminder, 141
  process of, 124–30
    understanding of, 126–30
  strategies, 130–2, 134–8, 337
    determination of creative platform, 149–50
    product life cycle and, 135–8
    strategy development, 163
  styles of, 153–6
  types of, 123–4
    comparative advertising, 124, 151, 338
    competitive advertising, 124
    pioneer advertising, 123–4
  see also Media
Advertising agencies, *see* Agencies
Advertising avoidance, 149
Advertising/sales (A/S) ratio, 89
Advertorials, 265, 337
Advocacy advertising, 337
Affordability method, 92, 337
Ageing population, 19–20, 71
Agencies, 86–7, 97–115, 337
  advertising agencies, 99–106
    account management, 101
    agency management team, 100
    creative department, 103–4
    media department, 104–5
    planning, 102–3
    production, 105–6

Agencies – *continued*
    agency structures, 98–107
    agency/client relationship, 109
    criteria for agency selection, 113–15
    disillusionment with, 73
    finance, 106
    full service agencies, 340
    information department, 106
    multinational agencies, 315–20, 342
        independent networks, 317–18
        local independents, 318
        selection of, 318–20
    personnel, 106
    regional agencies, 107
    remuneration, 110–13
        changing face of, 333–4
        commission, 110, 338
        cost-based remuneration, 111
        fee-based remuneration, 111
        negotiated commission, 110–11
        performance-based remuneration, 111–12
        production costs, 112
        time-based remuneration, 111
    sales promotion, 216–18
    specialized agencies, 107–9
        a la carte, 108
        creative boutiques, 108
        media specialists, 108
    UK agency scene, 97–8
AIDA model, 126–7, 337
Ambush marketing, 278
Andrex, 77
Animation advertising, 156
Appropriation, 337
Asda, 61
Association of Independent Radio Contractors
    (AIRC), 181
Assorted media mix, 182
Attention, 25, 337
Attitudes, 30, 337
Attributes, 337
Audience, 338
    corporate communications, 289–90
    target audiences, 147, 181, 344
Audit Bureau of Circulation (ABC), 180
Awareness, 140–1, 338

Banded packs, 202
Beliefs, 141, 338
Below the line, 338
Benefit segmentation, 338
Benetton, 156

Billings, 338
Bisto, 78–9
Black box model, 338
Blind taste tests, 38
Boddington's, 133, 148
Bonus packs, 201–2, 338
Brand heritage and history advertising, 155
Brand managers, 84
Branded corporate identity, 292
Branding:
    definitions, 37–8
    dimensions of, 39–44
    global branding, 301–2
    international branding, 303–5
    marketing communications roles in, 55–8
    strategy, 39, 44–6, 47
        generic branding, 46, 340
        manufacturer branding, 44–5, 341
        mixed branding, 45–6
        multi-branding, 45, 341
        multi-product branding, 44–5
        private branding, 46
Brands, 36–7, 338
    brand equity, 43–4, 338
    brand extensions, 53–5
    brand franchise, 206–7
    brand leadership, 48–9
    brand loyalty, 205–6, 338
    brand name, 40–1
    brand positioning and image, 32–3, 50, 135, 338
        advertising and, 132–3, 161
        altering brand imagery, 51–3
    brand promise, 33
    brand relationships, 58
    brand values, 49–51, 266
    budgeting, 93
    challenges facing brands, 58–64
        brand look-alikes, 61–3, 341
        brand response, 63–4
        changes in retailing, 58–9
        consequence of manufacturer failure, 60–1
        growth of private labels, 59–60
        weakening brands, 58
    consumer perceptions and, 46–9
    global brands, 301–3
        development of, 301
        management of, 302–3
    importance of, 36–7, 38–9
    market research, 32–3
    objectives, 93
    proliferation of, 7
    protection of, 42

service brands, 64–5
valuation of, 42–3
see also Branding
British Airways, 252, 298
British Code of Sales Promotion Practice, 215
British Rate and Data (BRAD), 179
Broadcast Audience Research Board (BARB), 29, 181
Broadcasting, 339
Budgeting, 87–93, 147
  competitive expenditure, 91
  DAGMAR approach, 91–2
  desired share of voice, 91
  experimentation, 92
  for integrated marketing communications, 93–6
    allocating the promotional budget, 94–5
    budget contingency, 94
    consumer continuum, 95–6
  integration and, 81
  marginal analysis, 88–9
  media inflation, 91
  new products, 93
  percentage of anticipated turnover, 90
  percentage of product gross margin, 90
  percentage of sales, 89–90, 342
  residue of previous year's surplus, 90
  sales promotion, 197
  Unit–Case–Sales ratio method, 90–1
  'what we can afford' approach, 92, 337
BUPA, 54–5
Burst, 338
Business-to-business activity, 338
  advertising, 142
  direct marketing, 245–6
Butterfield diamond framework for strategic analysis, 131
Buying behaviour, *see* Consumers; Organizational buying behaviour

Cable and Wireless, 284
Case rate method, 338
Category managers, 85–6, 338
Celebrities, use in advertising, 152–3, 156–7
Centralization, 313
Charity public relations, 267–8
Cinema advertising, 174
Cinema and Video Industry Audience Research (CAVIAR), 181
Circulation, 338
Co-operative advertising, 339
Coca Cola, 38, 55, 132, 205, 271–2, 308, 312
Cognitive response, 338

Commission, 110, 338
  negotiated commission, 110–11
Committee of Advertising Practice (CAP), 215
Communications, 338
  communication channels, 13
  future developments, 330
  integration, 14
  noise/interference, 13, 342
  non-verbal communication, 72, 155, 158, 342
  process of, 12–14
  public relations role, 255
  see also Advertising; Corporate communications; Marketing communications
Communications industry, changing face of, 332–5
  accountability, 334
  agency remuneration, 333–4
  communications strategy, 332–3
  education and training, 334–5
  global marketing, 334
  industry structure, 332
  information technology, 333
  integration, 333
Community relations, 255
Company structure, 83–4
Comparative advertising, 124, 151, 338
Competitions, 204–5, 338
Competitive advertising, 124
Competitive strategy, 33, 135
Complex problem solving, 338
Comprehension, 338
Concentrated marketing, 20
Concentrated media mix, 181–2
Concept testing, 338
Consortia, 79
Consultancies:
  direct marketing, 237–8
  public relations, 260–1
Consumer market, 16–19
  future developments, 331
  market segmentation, 17–19, 340, 341, 344
  market structure, 341
  market targeting, 20, 344
  mature market, 341
  understanding the market, 29–32
  see also Market research
Consumers:
  buying behaviour, 16, 21–5, 206, 338
    attention, 25, 337
    changing patterns, 328–9
    decision-making process, 22–3, 134–5
    factors influencing buying behaviour, 23–5

Consumers – *continued*
  buying behaviour – *continued*
    perceptual selection, 25, 70–1
    problem solving, 23, 134, 338
    promotional activity and, 200
    purchasing patterns, 185, 206
  characteristics of, 19–20
  consumer continuum, 95–6
  consumer loyalty:
    brand loyalty, 338
    direct marketing and, 232–5
    loyalty programmes, 74, 232, 234–5
  discerning consumers, 70, 73
  interactivity with, 225
  international consumers, 305–10
    culture and tradition, 307–10, 339
    language, 316
    standards of living, 310
  targeting of, 20–1
    identification of target audiences, 147, 181
    testing, 242
  transactional information, 225
Contests, 204–5, 338
Contingency, 338
  budget contingency, 94
Continuing character advertising, 155
Copy testing, 339
Core values, 338
Corporate cohesion, 76
Corporate communications, 281–98
  advertising, 288, 339
  audiences for, 289–90
  communication of company image, 286–7
  corporate advertising, 339
  evaluation of, 293–4
  growth of, 281–2
  key aspects of, 294
  management of, 287–8, 292–3
  objectives, 283–6
  public relations, 265–6, 288
  see also Corporate identity; Crisis management
Corporate identity, 283, 339
  establishment of, 286, 290–1
  types of, 291–2
Corporate image, 283, 339
  communication of, 286–7
Corporate strategy, 339
Corporations with autonomous units, 79
Cost per thousand, 339
Coupons, 201, 339
Coverage, 182, 339
Creative boutiques, 108

Creative brief, 144–9
Creative strategy, 339
Creativity, in advertising, 158–60
Credit facilities, 8
Crisis management, 266, 294–8, 339
  dealing with crisis, 297–8
  key dimensions of, 297
  phases of crises, 296
Culture, international consumers, 307–10, 339
Custom marketing, 20
Customers, *see* Consumers

DAGMAR approach, 91–2, 127–8, 139, 339
Daily Mirror, 213
Databases, 225, 227–31, 339
  external databases, 228, 340
    use of, 228–9
  internal databases, 227–8, 340
  management applications, 231
  marketing applications, 230
  profiling, 229–30
  sources of relevant information, 228–9
Decentralization, 313
Decision-making process, 22–3, 134–5, 309, 339
Decision-making unit (DMU), 26, 246, 339
Decoding, 339
Defensive strategy, 33–4
Demographic factors, 17, 19–20, 339
DHL, 154
Diesel Jeans, 189
Differentiated marketing, 20
Diffusion, 339
Direct marketing, 220–48, 339
  advantages of, 224–6
  application of, 243–4
  business-to-business activity, 245–6
  consultancies, 237–8
  costs of, 226
  direct mail, 5, 239, 339
  evaluation of, 226, 244
  growth of, 220–2
    contributing factors, 222–4
  impact of, 222
  integration of, 247–8
  international activity, 248, 323–5
  limitations of, 226–7
  management of, 235
  market research use, 239–42
  media use, 238–9, 240
  non-profit organizations, 246
  objectives, 231–3
  planning process, 235–7

relationship marketing, 233–5, 246–8
   strategic approach, 231
   telephone marketing, 239, 344
   testing, 226, 242–3
   see also Databases
Direct response, 339
Direct response television, 239
Direct selling, 339
Display allowance, 339
Distribution, 7
   direct marketing, 232
   distributor relations, 258
Drip, 339
Dyson, 121, 146, 151

Education, 334–5
Ehrenberg model, 129–30
Emotional strategy, 340
Encoding, 340
Endorsed corporate identity, 291–2
Endorsement, 340
   in advertising, 154
Environmental issues, 71, 73, 330
Ethics, 340
Eurostar, 124
Event management, 256, 270
Event sponsorship, 340
Every day low prices (EDLP), 340
Exhibitions, 270–1
Exposure, 340

Family composition, changes in, 71
Family life cycle, 340
Fantasy advertising, 156
Feedback, 225, 340
Financial Services Act (1986), 215
Flighting, 340
Free gifts, 202–3
Free mail-ins, 203–4, 340
Full service agencies, 340

Generic strategy, 135
   generic branding, 46, 340
Geodemographic segmentation, 340
Geographic segmentation, 340
George and Michael model, 129
Global marketing, 72, 299–301, 340
   changing face of, 334
   global brands, 301–3
      management of, 302–3
   global marketing communications, 311–12
   see also International marketing

Gold Blend campaign, 155
Goldeneye, 279
Granada, 41
Grand Metropolitan, 287
Green Flag, 272
Green imperative, 71
Gross margin, 90, 340
Guerrilla marketing, 278

Häagen Dazs, 33, 132, 147, 148, 188
Halo effect, 33, 340
Hard sell advertising, 150
Heightened Appreciation model, 129, 130
Heinz, 61, 135
Hierarchy of effects, 340
Hoover, 213
Hospitality, 270
Households, 20, 71
Howard-Sheth model, 22
Human resources, 84

IBM, 252, 315, 316
Impulse purchase, 340
In-pack free gifts, 202
In-pack premiums, 340
In-store sampling, 205
Infomercials, 156, 265
Information access, 72–3
Information overload, 69–70
Information technology, 330, 333
Institute of Sales Promotion (ISP), 215
Integrated marketing communications (IMC), 14,
   333, 340
   barriers to integration, 80–1
   benefits of, 75–6
   budgeting for, 93–6
      allocating the promotional budget, 94–5
      budget contingency, 94
      consumer continuum, 95–6
   competitive environment, 311
   definition, 68–9
   direct marketing integration, 247–8
   driving forces behind, 73
   impact of, 74
   organizational approaches to integration,
      79–80
   process of achieving integration, 76–9
   see also Marketing communications
Integrated organization, 79–80
Interaction, 76
Interference, 13

International marketing, 299–326
  central versus local control of communications, 312–14
    centralization, 313
    combination, 314
    decentralization, 313
  direct marketing, 248, 323–5
  growth of, 299
  international advertising, 320–2, 342
  international branding, 303–5
  legal and regulatory requirements, 310–11, 323
  market research, 305, 325–6
  media availability and usage, 311
  multinational agencies, 315–20, 342
    independent networks, 317–18
    local independents, 318
    selection of, 318–20
  multinational versus global marketing, 299–301
  public relations, 268, 323
  sales promotion, 218, 322–3
  standardized communications, 314–15
  strategy, 320
  understanding international consumers, 305–10
    culture and tradition, 307–10, 339
    language, 306
    standards of living, 310
  see also Global marketing
Investor relations, 257

Joint Industry Committee for Regional Press Research (JICREG), 181
Just Noticeable Difference (JND), 341

Language, 306
Lavidge and Steiner model, 127
Lever Bros., 251
Levi's, 50, 51, 54, 135, 148, 157, 189
Living standards, improvements in, 8
Local Trading Standards Officers, 215, 216
Look-alike brands, 61–3, 341
Loyalty:
  brand loyalty, 205–6, 338
  direct marketing and, 232–5
  loyalty programmes, 74, 232, 234–5

McDonald's, 307
Magazine advertising, 4, 172
Mailing lists, *see* Databases; Direct marketing
Manufacturer branding, 44–5, 341
Manufacturing services, growth of, 6
Marginal analysis, 88–9

Market research, 8, 27–34, 341
  brand positioning and personality, 32–3
  brand promise, 33
  contribution to strategic direction, 33–4
  direct marketing and, 239–42
  effective reach of target consumers, 33
  external sources, 29
  internal sources, 29
  international marketing, 305, 325–6
  market planning, 28–9
  process of, 28
  public relations and, 262
  stages of, 28
  understanding the market, 29–32
Market segmentation, 17–19, 340, 341, 344
Marketing communications, 341
  background to, 4–6
  changing nature and role of, 3, 107
  discipline overlap, 8–9
  global marketing communications, 311–12
  growth of, 6–8
    specialist companies in, 8
    understanding of use of, 8
  historical perspective, 3–4
  impact of external factors, 69–73
    ageing population, 71
    changes in family composition, 71
    discerning consumers, 70
    green imperative, 71
    growth of global marketing, 72
    growth of narrow casting, 71
    information overload, 69–70
    non verbal communications, 72, 155, 158, 342
    perceptual values, 70–1
    speed of information access, 72–3
  relationship marketing, 74–5, 76
  research, 32
  roles in branding, 55–8
  standardized communications, 314–15
  strategic marketing communications, 11
  see also Communications; Corporate communications; Integrated marketing communications (IMC)
Marketing communications mix:
  expanded marketing communications mix, 11–12
  integration within, 14
  see also Integrated marketing communications (IMC)
Marketing concept, 341
Marketing function, 311–32
Marketing mix, 341
  see also Marketing communications mix

Marketing objectives, 341
Marketing plan, 341
Marketing strategy, 341
Markets, *see* Consumer market
Mars, 42, 121, 280
Mass marketing, 341
Matrix organization, 79
Media, 4–6, 147, 168–91, 341
    changing face of, 169–71, 190–1
    characteristics of, 171–4, 175
        cinema, 174
        posters, 174
        press, 172
        radio, 172–4
        television, 171–2
    direct marketing and, 238–9, 240
    future developments, 330–1
    information sources, 179–81
    international marketing, 311
    media mix, 341
    media relations, 256, 258–9
    media specialist agencies, 108
    new media, 174–6
    planning, 176–8, 341
        contingency planning, 189
        evaluation of media plan, 189–90
        implementation of media plan, 187–8
        role of, 168–9
    scheduling issues, 182–7, 341
        competitive environment, 183
        creative factors, 186
        intrusive nature of message, 182–3
        marketing factors, 185–6
        media factors, 186–7
        message length, 183
        nature of message, 183
        number of exposures, 183–4
        purchasing patterns, 185
        seasonality factors, 185
        status of brand, 185
    strategy, 178–9, 181–2
    wider reach of, 8
Merge and purge, 341
Mini-drama advertising, 155
Mixed branding, 45–6
Money-off promotions, 200–1, 341
Monolithic corporate identity, 291
Motivation, 76, 308, 309
    direct marketing and, 225
Multi-branding, 45, 341
Multinational marketing, 299–300
    see also Global marketing; International marketing

Murdoch, Rupert, 42
Music, in advertising, 147–58

Narrow casting, 71, 342
National Readership Survey (NRS), 181 ·
Nescafé, Gold Blend campaign, 155
New products:
    direct marketing applications, 232
    future developments, 329–30
    marketing communications budget, 93
    sales promotion, 198
    see also Products
Newspaper advertising, 4, 172
Nike, 57, 188–9, 307–8
Noise, 13, 342
Nokia, 280
Non-profit organizations, 246–7
Non-verbal communication, 72, 155, 158, 342

Objective and task method, 342
On-pack free gifts, 202
Opinion forming, 254–5, 258
Opinion leader, 342
Opportunistic advertising, 155
Organizational buying behaviour, 25–7
    buying centre, 26
    derived demand, 27
    purchasing process, 26–7
Organizational structure, 83–4, 285–6
    agency structures, 98–107
    communications industry structure, 332
    integrated organizations, 79–80
OSCAR, 181
Outboard Marine Corporation, 314

Packaging, brand image and, 57–8
Participation, 76
Pastiche advertising, 155
People like me advertising, 155
Pepsi, 38, 213, 272, 280
Perceptions, 141, 342
    brands and, 46–9
Perceptual map, 50, 342
Perceptual selection, 25, 70–1
Perrier, 42, 121, 146
Personal selling, 342
    decline in, 7
PEST + C, 342
PG Tips, 146
Pioneer advertising, 123–4
Pioneer strategy, 33

Planning, 341, 342
  advertising plan, 139–41, 337
    advertising agencies, 102–3
  direct marketing, 235–7
  market planning, 28–9
  media planning, 176–8, 341
    contingency planning, 189
    evaluation of media plan, 189–90
    implementation of media plan, 187–8
    role of, 168–9
  public relations, 263–4
Point of purchase communications, 207, 288, 342
Polychronic Time Use, 190
Positioning, 21, 342
  brand positioning, 32–3
Post-purchase dissatisfaction, 342
Post-purchase satisfaction, 342
POSTAR II, 181
Poster advertising, 174
  direct marketing and, 239
Premium, 342
  self-liquidating premium, 344
Press advertising, 4, 172
Pretty Polly, 188
Price discrimination strategy, 199–200
Print media, 4, 172
  direct marketing and, 239
Private label brands, 46, 59–60
Problem solving, 23, 134, 342, 343
  complex problem solving, 338
Problem–solution advertising, 153
Procter & Gamble, 45, 85, 86, 251
Product as hero advertising, 153
Product placement, 278–80, 342
Products:
  demonstration of, 153
  life cycle, 342
    advertising strategy and, 135–8
    management and, 36–7
  sales promotion objectives, 197–8
  testing, 242
  see also New products
Projective techniques, 50
Promotion, 342
  management of, 343
  promotional mix, 343
  see also Sales promotion
Prudential Corporation, 77–8
Psychographic factors, 17, 343
Public relations, 250–68, 343
  benefits of, 251–4
  brand image and, 57

campaign development, 261–2
charity PR, 267–8
comparison with advertising, 251–2
corporate public relations, 265–6, 288
direct marketing and, 239
evaluation of, 264
financial public relations, 266–7
functions of, 254–6
identification of problems and opportunities,
    262–3
integration of, 268
international aspects of, 268, 323
management of, 259–60
planning, 263–4
PR consultancies, 260–1
  in-house versus consultancy, 261
publics of, 256–9
  buyers and consumers, 258
  distributors, 258
  employees, 257
  local community, 258
  media, 258–9
  national community, 258
  opinion formers, 258
  shareholders and investors, 257
  suppliers, 257–8
tools of, 264–5
see also Relationship marketing
Pull strategy, 343
Pulsing, 343
Purchasing behaviour, see Consumers;
    Organizational buying behaviour
Push strategy, 343

Qualitative research, 241, 343
Quantitative research, 239–41, 343

Radio:
  advertising, 4, 172–4
    costs of, 173
    direct marketing and, 238
    programme sponsorship, 172, 273–4
Radio Joint Audience Research (RAJAR), 181
Rating point, 343
Ratners, 282
Reach, 8, 33, 182, 343
Rebate, 343
Reduced price offers, 200–2, 343
Reebok, 280
Reference groups, 343
Refund, 343

Regional agencies, 107
Relationship marketing, 74–5, 76, 343
  direct marketing and, 225, 233–5, 246–7
  see also Public relations
Renault, 155
Retailers, power shift towards, 73
Road blocking, 343

Safeway, 46
Sainsbury's, 62, 64
Sale of Goods Act, 215
Sales promotion, 192–218, 343
  agencies, 216–18
  benefits of, 194–5
  brand franchise, 206–7
  brand image and, 56
  budgeting, 197
  evaluation of, 196, 210–12
  growing role of, 192–4
  integration of activities, 218
  international activity, 218, 322–3
  joint promotions, 209–11
  legal framework, 215–16, 323
  limitations of, 195–6
  objectives, 196–9
    consumer objectives, 197–8
    determination of, 196–7
    trade objectives, 198–9
  point of purchase communications, 207, 342
  promoting to consumers, 205–6
  research into, 213–14
    desk research, 213–14
    monitoring research, 214
    pre-testing, 214
    qualitative research, 214
    quantitative research, 214
  strategies, 199–200, 207–9
    consumer behaviour, 200
    price discrimination, 199–200
  techniques, 200–5
    contests and competitions, 204–5, 338
    free gifts, 202–3
    free mail-ins, 203–4
    in-store sampling, 205
    reduced price offers, 200–2, 343
    self-liquidating offers, 204, 344
Sales Promotion Consultants Association (SPCA)
  awards, 214
Sampling, 205, 344
Scheduling issues, *see* Media
Seasonality factors, 185
Segmentation, *see* Market segmentation

Self-liquidating offers, 204, 344
Services:
  management over life cycle, 36–7
  service brands, 64–5
Share prices, 256, 285
Shareholder relations, 257
Shell, 255, 263, 282
Shock advertising, 156
Slice of life advertising, 154
Snickers, 175
Soft sell advertising, 150
Spokespersons, 57, 154
Sponsorship, 56–7, 256, 270–8, 340, 344
  evaluation of, 276–8
  growth of, 274–5
  guerrilla marketing, 278
  international aspects, 325
  issues, 275–6
  radio programmes, 173, 273–4
  television programmes, 172, 273–4
Standards of living, international consumers, 310
Stella Artois, 38
Strategies, 341
  advertising strategies, 130–2, 134–8, 337
    creative strategy, 339
    determination of creative platform, 149–50
    product life cycle and, 135–8
    strategy development, 163
  challenges, 9–11
  communications strategy, changing face of,
    332–3
  competitive strategy, 33, 135
  corporate strategy, 339
  defensive strategy, 33–4
  direct marketing, 231
  emotional strategy, 340
  generic strategy, 135
  international marketing, 320
  market research contribution to, 33–4
  media strategy, 178–9, 181–2
  pioneer strategy, 33
  pull strategy, 343
  push strategy, 343
  sales promotion strategies, 199–200, 207–9
    consumer behaviour strategy, 200
    price discrimination strategy, 199–200
  strategic brand building, 39
Subaru, 132
Sunlight Soap, 37
Supplier relations, 257–8
Sweepstakes, 344
SWOT analysis, 344

Tango, 51, 58, 160
Target Group Index (TGI), 29, 181
Targeting, 20–1
    direct marketing and, 224, 232
        testing, 242
    of consumers, 20–1
        identification of target audiences, 147, 181
    of markets, 20, 344
    see also Positioning
Teaser advertising, 156
Technology, growth in, 7
Telephone marketing, 239, 344
Television:
    advertising, 4, 171–2
        costs of, 171–2
        direct marketing and, 238
        direct response TV, 239
        expenditure, 4–5
    programme sponsorship, 172, 273–4
Tesco, 46, 48, 253
Testimonial advertising, 154
Testing, 226, 242–3, 338
    copy testing, 339
Tetley Tea, 218
Texaco, 272–3

Thames Water, 286
The Body Shop, 254, 287
Tracking study, 344
Trade allowances, 344
Tradition, international consumers, 307–10
Training, 334–5
Transportation, improvements in, 7
Tylenol, 42

Undifferentiated marketing, 20
Unique Selling Proposition, 344
Unit–Case–Sales ratio method, 90–1
Usage, 30
Usage and Attitude (U&A) Studies, 29–30

Value for money, 73
Values and lifestyles (VALS2) model, 17–19
Virgin, 55, 253, 263, 287
Visual communication, 72

Walkers Crisps, 295
Weights and Measures (Miscellaneous Foods)
    Order (1997), 216
With-pack free gifts, 202
Wonderbra, 147